the esoteric origins of the
American Renaissance

Arthur Versluis

OXFORD
UNIVERSITY PRESS

2001

OXFORD
UNIVERSITY PRESS

Oxford　New York

Athens　Auckland　Bangkok　Bogotá　Buenos Aires　Calcutta
Cape Town　Chennai　Dar es Salaam　Delhi　Florence　Hong Kong　Istanbul
Karachi　Kuala Lumpur　Madrid　Melbourne　Mexico City　Mumbai
Nairobi　Paris　São Paulo　Shanghai　Singapore　Taipei　Tokyo　Toronto　Warsaw

and associated companies in
Berlin　Ibadan

Copyright © 2001 by Arthur Versluis

Published by Oxford University Press, Inc.
198 Madison Avenue, New York, New York 10016

Oxford is a registered trademark of Oxford University Press.

Library of Congress Cataloging-in-Publication Data
Versluis, Arthur, 1959–
The esoteric origins of the American Renaissance / Arthur Versluis.
p.　cm.
Includes bibliographical references and index.
ISBN 0-19-513887-2
1. American literature—19th century—History and criticism.　2. Occultism—
United States—History—19th century.　3. United States—Intellectual life—
19th century.　4. American literature—European influences.　5. Transcendentalism
(New England)　6. Occultism in literature.　I. Title.
PS217.O33 V47 2000
810.9'37—dc21　　　00-026124

1 3 5 7 9 8 6 4 2

Printed in the United States of America
on acid-free paper

C.1

Contents

The Esoteric Origins of the American Renaissance

Introduction

In *American Transcendentalism and Asian Religions*, I detailed the immense impact that the Euro-American discovery of Asian religions had not only on European Romanticism, but above all, on American Transcendentalism. There I argued that the Transcendentalists' discovery of the Bhagavad Gita, the Vedas, the Upanishads, and other world scriptures was critical in the entire movement, pivotal not only for the well-known figures like Emerson and Thoreau, but also for lesser known later figures like Samuel Johnson and William Rounseville Alger. That Transcendentalism emerged out of this new knowledge of the world's religious traditions I have no doubt. But there were also pre-existing traditions in western Europe that contributed a great deal to the emergence, not only of Transcendentalism, but also of what has come to be known as the American Renaissance, that extraordinary period during the mid-nineteenth century when so much of American literature came into being. Primary among these European traditions was Western esotericism.

Until relatively recently, there was not much reliable scholarship on Western esotericism, and indeed, it remains the most important new field of religious and interdisciplinary scholarship. The central figure of contemporary scholarship on Western esoteric traditions is Antoine Faivre, who holds a chair in the Sorbonne on precisely this subject. Faivre's numerous books and articles unquestionably make him the leading scholar in the field, but his scholarship goes beyond articles and books that focus on primary figures and movements in esotericism. Faivre also has sketched the primary characteristics of Western esotericism more generally, and these will form a useful starting point from which to launch into an extensive investigation of how Western esoteric currents provided the ambience for and informed the American Renaissance. It should be remarked that this is the first such investigation of its kind: there is no other book on this subject.

There have been, however, a few books that have begun to reveal the extent to which nineteenth-century America was influenced and, one might even say, permeated by Western esoteric traditions. Chief among these is John L. Brooke's excellent *The Refiner's Fire: The Making of Mormon Cosmology, 1644–1844*; another such work is Michael Quinn's *Early Mormonism and the Magic World View*.[1] These historians, in seeking out the hidden history of Mormonism, have also helped in revealing the extent to which esoteric views and traditions helped shape the American intellectual landscape in the eighteenth and nineteenth centuries. The application of these discoveries to literature has many ramifications, not least of which is a re-evaluation of many major literary figures—both American and European—in light of their interests in Western esotericism.

The term Western esotericism refers to a wide range of esoteric spiritual currents including alchemy, Hermeticism, Kabbala, Rosicrucianism, and Christian theosophy, to name only those that will figure most prominently in this study. There are also what might be called practical forms of esotericism, and these include the various "mancies," (chiefly forms of divination) like cartomancy, geomancy, or necromancy; as well as alchemy, astrology, herbalism, and magic. All of these varied forms of esotericism were known in Western Europe during the seventeenth and eighteenth centuries, so it is not surprising that they would all be carried over to North America by colonists or settlers. Such practices as divination or various kinds of folk magic become much more comprehensible when we consider how uncertain the future must have been to someone who left behind friends, culture, homeland, and sometimes family for the new world. Those who practiced some form of esotericism in Europe were entirely likely to continue it in the New World.

In a companion to this book, entitled *Western Esotericism, Literature, and Consciousness*, I discuss the primary currents of Western esotericism and develop a view of literature and language that emerges from an understanding of the Western esoteric traditions as uniquely literary in nature. Here the words *literary* or *literature* are used broadly to refer not only to modern forms of literature like fiction, essays, or poetry, but also to specifically esoteric literature like alchemical treatises, visionary accounts, metaphysical and cosmological surveys, and indeed to the full range of esoteric writings. In Western esotericism we find underlying all the various forms the traditions take, an underlying recognition that literature is not merely a means to communicate data, but also a vehicle to transmit means of spiritual understanding. Inherent in this recognition is the view that the entire cosmos emerges out of the combination of divine letters, that there is a divine writing or "book of life," an archetypal realm that nature and humanity reflect. One way to understand Western esoteric literature is to see it as allowing us to read one or another aspect of this transcendent, multivalent divine writing that is reflected in the cosmos: astrology is reading the stars and planets; herbalism is reading plants, and so forth.

Given how central literature is in Western esotericism, we should not be surprised to discover that there is a long history of interrelationships between literary figures and esotericists. Poets, dramatists, novelists, essayists—all have gone to esoteric currents for inspiration, perhaps because there is such a natural correspondence between esoteric metaphors and literary metaphors, between esoteric ways of "reading the world," and literary ways of seeing. This correspondence became especially pronounced during the romantic era: one finds esotericism woven throughout the lives and works of such figures as Goethe and Novalis, not to mention Blake, Coleridge, and Shelley. It seems likely that these poets and authors came to esotericism because they saw in its various currents alternatives to the emerging secular materialist worldview that so impoverishes and disenfranchises poetry. Poetry, as Yeats pointed out, needs to draw on ancient springs of religious inspiration or it becomes dry and uninteresting, and esotericism is one major way to find such inspiration without necessarily entering into a particular religious tradition.

The Western esoteric traditions, after all, often exist on the margin or border of religion, and this too may account for their attractiveness to authors in the modern era, when institutionalized religion often seems constricting or oppressive to them. On the whole, Western esotericism entails individual spiritual work, and is only infrequently if at all institutional in nature. Hermeticism and Platonism, for instance, can be found in Christian, Jewish, and Islamic contexts, but themselves belong to none of these traditions. What is more, there is no sign of any institutional structure for either of these. They constitute currents of Western esotericism, and as such exist on the boundaries between religion and secularity, just as they exist on the margins of academic disciplines.

One major reason that Western esoteric traditions did not receive much academic attention until the end of the twentieth century, and the beginning of the twenty-first, is that these traditions are inherently transdisciplinary. "Transdisciplinary" refers to a sphere of knowledge that not only cuts across a wide range of disciplines, but also ramifies beyond any particular discipline. So, for instance, the study of alchemical treatises includes the histories of science, literature, religion, and art, but belongs to none of these alone, and has ramifications beyond any one category. This transdisciplinarity makes Western esotericism difficult to place in an academic environment concerned primarily with disciplinary turf. Only recently has academia begun to venture into the realms beyond particular disciplines, where Western esotericism is to be found, and only recently have previously eclipsed spheres of knowledge come into view, chief among which are the Western esoteric currents.

But exactly this same transdisciplinarity made the various esoteric currents attractive to poets and authors from the romantic era onward, even if these currents have remained largely invisible to academia. Writers found in esoteric currents alternatives to what they often perceived as the deadening nature of both modern secular materialism and conventional religion. Modern society has tended to reward specialization; but for the author with an inquiring mind, specialization in a limited field like vertebrate biology or organic chemistry seems constricted; the poet or author wants a comprehensive way of understanding, and for this it is often esotericism that offers an integration of the various realms of life. Such a wide-ranging integration is precisely what Goethe, for instance, intended to create with his scientific work late in life, informed as it was by a lifetime studying alchemy and other esoteric subjects. For the poet, the artificial opposition of religion to science, and of both of these to the humanities, is often intolerable. Thus the poet or author turns to the study of one or another form of esotericism.

This is precisely what we find behind what has come to be known as the American Renaissance: the efflorescence of brilliant authors in New England, nearly all of whom were heir to and inspired by Western esoteric currents. As we will see, each of our authors took from different esoteric traditions—Alcott and Emerson from Hermeticism, Christian theosophy, and Neoplatonism; Fuller from alchemy and Rosicrucianism; Hawthorne from alchemy; Melville and Poe from Gnosticism. In this indebtedness, these authors followed very much in the tradition of the earlier European Renaissance, which was also largely inspired by the esoteric interests of Ficino, Pico della Mirandola, and others. Initially, I had doubts about using the term *American Renaissance*, but as I have come to see the extent of the parallels between the two renaissances, chiefly in their indebtedness to Western esotericism and their universalist aims of uniting the sciences, the humanities, and spirituality, I have come to see the accuracy of such a term.

Yet despite the countless volumes of literary criticism devoted to these authors of the American Renaissance, their indebtedness to Western esoteric traditions has remained almost totally ignored. There are a number of reasons why this is so. One reason, of course, is that esotericism has been frequently excluded from the purview of academia as a whole for the past several centuries, often relegated to a dusty bin in the back room marked "superstition." But another reason has to do with the efforts of such influential twentieth-century literary critics as F. O. Matthiessen to demonstrate that nineteenth-century American literature belongs to "high culture" on a par with Shakespeare. Such "high culture" was assumed to have nothing to do with topics like alchemy or magic. Of course, there is a striking irony in such assumptions, since in fact Shakespeare's own works are replete with references to magic and to all manner of esoteric traditions. But this, too, is a subject only infrequently examined.

One clear implication of this book is that many preconceptions about Western esoteric traditions must be re-examined, particularly those that label alchemy, magic, and Hermeticism as "low" or "vulgar," in contradistinction to an imagined "high literature" free from them. The truth is, such esoteric interests in fact cut across socio-economic classes, from the farmer with his astrological almanac to the New England governor with his alchemical laboratory, and are to be found among virtually all of the major American authors of the nineteenth century, as well as among American Protestant clergy of the eighteenth century. One cannot say that such Western esoteric traditions belong to a category "beneath the American Renaissance," to cite the title of David Reynold's book—such esoteric traditions are intimately woven throughout the

American Renaissance, and were much more widespread in America before this period than many scholars have cared to acknowledge.

Indeed, even the presence of Western esotericism in the New World—let alone its influences on major American authors—has been thoroughly neglected, so much so that this book is among the very first to venture into this new territory. Included here is a great deal of previously unexplored material that certainly calls for far more investigation. In this book we survey the primary materials available and point those interested in the direction of further enquiry in the hope that there will be subsequent and deeper forays into what might well be termed a veritable wilderness of primary and hitherto unexamined sources. The history of Western esotericism in the New World has yet to be written in full, but this book represents a significant step in that direction.

two

European Esoteric Currents

Although it is not feasible to offer a complete survey of Western esotericism here, it is necessary to introduce the main currents that will be central to this particular study of the American Renaissance. There are already some very good introductions, some in English, to various European esoteric currents, and there is an excellent overview of the field by the leading scholar, Antoine Faivre, entitled *Access to Western Esotericism*.[1] However, there remains a great deal of work to be done in this field, particularly in terms of English and American forms of the various esoteric currents. Here I will sketch the primary European esoteric currents that in turn are important for the American Renaissance, but will begin with some more general remarks about European esotericism.

The term "esoteric," as Faivre has noted, is subject to many and perhaps too many meanings, but at heart refers to inner knowledge as opposed to the *exoteric*, or outward forms of various religious traditions. Esotericism refers in general to an individual spiritual path based in direct spiritual experience, and in this respect differs from exoteric religious practices that entail more dogmatic formulations and acquiescence en masse. In general, esotericism entails *gnosis*, a Greek word that means "knowledge," both rational and suprarational. We can see different kinds of gnosis in the various esoteric currents, some cosmological, as in the case of alchemy, others transcendent, as in the works of Meister Eckhart. Of course, even these remarks are somewhat problematic, inasmuch as esoteric traditions have themselves taken on numerous outward forms, some rather baroque, as in the cases of Rosicrucianism and Freemasonry.

Yet there remain some fundamental characteristics of European esotericism such that we can make some generalizations about esotericism in the abstract. Faivre offers the following four primary aspects of Western esoteric traditions:

1. Correspondences (between humanity, nature, and the divine).
2. Living Nature (not a dead cosmos consisting of discrete objects to be manipulated).
3. Imagination and Mediations (the imagination represents a means of human inner knowledge; "mediations" refers to the symbols or other means that offer or reveal this knowledge).
4. Experiences of Transmutation (as of lead into gold, or of essences into an elixir).

To these four, Faivre adds two more:

5. Praxis of the Concordance (an approach that unifies various currents of thought, that is willing to join various traditions and see them as one).
6. Transmission (meaning from a master to a disciple, in an initiatic chain).

These categories are extremely useful because they emphasize the various elements that in general characterize European esoteric cosmologies and traditions, including Hermeticism, alchemy, theosophy, and so forth.

But my close study of Christian theosophy (an esoteric tradition that begins in earnest with Jacob Böhme [1575–1624]) has suggested in this case a different set of four characteristics that reveal less cosmological focus than is found in some forms of esotericism, like Freemasonry for instance.[2] As I have elsewhere remarked, theosophy represents a paradigm with certain common elements that reappear even if various groups are wholly unaware of one another, including (1) the focus upon Wisdom, or Sophia, (2) an insistence upon direct spiritual experience, including visions, (3) reading nature as a spiritual book, and (4) a spiritual leader who guides his or her spiritual circle through books, letters, and oral advice. These four characteristics are found in the teachings or work of all the major theosophic groups and individuals, and show that, when we turn to a particular esoteric tradition, we may have to readjust categorizations.

It is important to remember that esotericism does not exist historically in the abstract, but in specific traditions and applications. These applications are often rather practical, and hence until the nineteenth century were not exotic but commonplace in many Europeans' lives. It is true that astrology or astromancy, for instance, emerge from and reflect a broader esoteric context, but in the lives of ordinary people were not seen necessarily in such a context, but simply as a useful discipline. If one were going to build a house or a church, it was considered in some circles entirely sensible for the surveyor to also be schooled in geomancy, a form of earth divination closely allied with astrology. Such a surveyor, by examining a particular site and determining its astrological/geomantic characteristics, could see where the most auspicious place might be for a building, and how that building might best be situated. Exactly this kind of practical discipline was exported to the American colonies.

Other forms of esotericism might not seem as practical to us, but were often seen in just such a light during the seventeenth or eighteenth centuries. Alchemy, for example, nowadays widely depicted as a kind of wild-goose chase, was at one time taught in the universities, both European and American, and often seen as eminently practical: the herbal alchemist, for instance, was a natural source for various plant medicines or elixirs. It is true that in America in the nineteenth century one finds a proliferation of spurious elixirs sold by con men, but this was a degraded form of what had existed earlier and in much better repute as herbal alchemy. On the American frontier, where doctors were in short supply, it was undoubtedly at the very least useful to know something of herbal folk remedies for various ailments, or to have in one's vicinity someone who was familiar with herbal alchemy, also known as spagyric medicine. As we shall see, these practical kinds of esotericism were exactly what colonists often took with them to America from the Old World.

In what follows, we will focus chiefly on the forms of European esotericism that were in fact brought to North America, and provide at least some background against which American esotericism can be understood.

Alchemy

The origins of European alchemy (the art and science of transmutation) in antiquity are not entirely clear, but are often associated with the figure of Hermes Trismegistus, or Thrice-Greatest Hermes, and in turn with ancient Egypt. Scholarship has confirmed that there is a connection between the *Corpus Hermeticum*, or body of Hermetic dialogues that date from the early Christian era, and prior Egyptian teachings, but it is not clear exactly what the connection is between ancient Egypt and alchemy.[3] In any case, there certainly are well-known Greek alchemical treatises compiled probably during the seventh century, some of which belong to the third and fourth centuries, among them the writings of Zosimos of Panopolis. Later one finds the writing of Morienus, dating probably to the early eighth century, but much of European alchemy was derived from or inspired by a series of translations of the Latinized works of Arabic authors such as Al-Rhazi (ca. 825–932), known as Rhazes, and Jabir ibn Hayyan, whose work became known in the West under the name of Geber. As we can see, in other words, the Hermetic art of alchemy traditionally is drawn from a very wide range of sources, and may well be spoken of as a "third stream" in addition to Judaism and Christianity.

In the thirteenth century one finds the first efflorescence of European alchemy in its own right: Roger Bacon (1214–94); Arnold of Villanova (1235–1312), with his *Rosarium philosophorum*; Ramon Lull (1235–1316), famous for his "Lullian art" of memory, but also known for a host of alchemical treatises, some of which were probably genuinely his; and Nicholas Flamel (1330–1417), whose *Book of the Hieroglyphic Figures* remains justly renowned. Paracelsus (Theophrastus Bombastus von Hohenheim, 1493–1541) remains enormously important.[4] But the height of alchemical publication came in the fifteenth through eighteenth centuries, with the advent of magnificent fusions of art, literature, and even music in order to illustrate the alchemical work. Flamel's work in some respects helped inaugurate this trend, which produced the flurry of such works as Michael Maier's (1568–1622) *Atalanta Fugiens*, a remarkable combination of music, lyrics, and images; treatises by Basilius Valentinus, George Ripley, Eirenaeus Philalethes, and Jean D'Espagnet; and numerous works, like *Mutus Liber*, that relied on images or the countless images that featured what we might call the adventures of the heart (a heart with a flask-like opening depicted being hit with a hammer, illuminated with a lamp, and so forth).

The alchemical works produced in Europe and England from the fifteenth through the eighteenth centuries were those that the American alchemists were to carry with them from the Old World and were to rely upon for their own guidance as they developed laboratories and furnaces of their own. Although alchemy is often depicted farcically as mere "puffery" and as the often vain effort to turn lead into gold, one would do well to recall C. S. Lewis's remark that, in Shakespeare's day, alchemy was something that one's neighbor down the street engaged in. What is more, alchemy's influence is found throughout the literature of the day, not only in the works of such poets as Henry Vaughan, whose brother Thomas was a well-known author of alchemical works, but also implicitly in the plays and poetry of Shakespeare, Milton, and countless other authors of the day. Alchemy represented an entire worldview, and was far from merely a technical enterprise.

In essence, the alchemical worldview that we see enunciated in works like the 1678 collection entitled *The Hermetic Museum* requires a fundamental change in our approach to the world if we are to understand it aright. Alchemy, both as laboratory alchemy and as spiritual alchemy, holds that the cosmos is alive and that we are not separate from it. Whereas scientific rationalism and the technology derived from it are founded in the separation of subject from object, so that the subject can manipulate the object, alchemy in its various forms is based in a profoundly different approach, representing a discipline in which subject and object are revealed to be in fact inseparable. Given this profoundly different view of subject and object, one can see how the various aims of alchemy flow from it, including the possibility of turning lead into gold, or of creating an elixir that can prolong physical life indefinitely or bring about immortality. These aims are brought about, from an alchemical viewpoint, by the union or transcendence of subject and object by way of various laboratory or spiritual "operations."

An example of a brief alchemical account can be found at the beginning of Basilius Valentinus's treatise on the "Great Stone of the Ancient Sages," found in the 1678 *Hermetic Museum* collection of alchemical writings. Valentinus tells the story of how in his monastery there was an ailing brother with a kidney disease that responded to no treatment. Valentinus determined to cure him and so experimented for six years with all manner of herbal medicines, to no avail. Thus, he wrote, at last

> I determined to devote myself to the study of the powers and virtues which God has laid into metals and minerals; and the more I searched the

more I found. One discovery led to another, and after God had permitted unto me many experiments, I understood clearly the nature and properties, and the secret potency, imparted by God to minerals and metals.

Among the mineral substances, I found one which exhibited many colours, and proved to be of the greatest efficacy in art. The spiritual essence of this substance I extracted, and therewith restored our brother, in a few days, to perfect health. . . . And his prayers, together with my own diligence, so prevailed with God, that there was revealed to me that great secret which God ever conceals from those who are wise in their own conceits.

Thus have I been wishing to reveal to you in this treatises, as far as may be lawful to me, the Stone of the Ancients, that you, too, might possess the knowledge of this highest of earthly treasures for your health and comfort in this valley of sorrow.[5]

This quotation from Valentinus reveals in its devotional language how alchemy could be seen as a natural part of Christian learning, as indeed it was regarded not only in some Catholic but also in some Protestant circles. Indeed, alchemy was one of the primary streams that fed into another esoteric tradition of great importance for colonial American history: Christian theosophy.

Theosophy

Christian theosophy—which long precedes and has nothing whatever to do with the Victorian society that Madame Blavatsky founded and that took its name—has been the subject of several of my prior books, including *Theosophia: Hidden Dimensions of Christianity* (1994), and *Wisdom's Children: A Christian Esoteric Tradition* (1999). Here I will offer a cursory sketch of the tradition and urge the reader to consult these other works for more detailed study. The word "theosophy" derives from the Greek word *theosophia*, meaning "divine wisdom," and is distinguished from "theology" by referring not to discursive or rational knowledge, but to direct experiential knowledge of the divine, sometimes termed "gnosis." In fact, as I have suggested in an article, "Christian Theosophy and Ancient Gnosticism," there are striking parallels between ancient Gnosticism and Christian theosophy.[6] But our subject here, Böhmean theosophy, is a distinctly modern tradition, which begins at the turn of the seventeenth century, and stretches into the twentieth century.

Theosophy began in earnest with the writings of Jacob Böhme, a shoemaker who was also a visionary and author of an amazing number of complex theosophic treatises that combine many currents of Western esotericism together into a unique synthesis. One finds traces in Böhme's writings of Paracelsian spagyric medicine, as well as Rhineland-Flemish gnosis on the order of Meister Eckhart and Johannes Tauler, and Sophianic, chivalric, alchemical, and Kabbalistic ideas and terminology. All of these currents are joined in Böhme, but take on a specifically Pietist or devotional tenor that made them immensely attractive not only to intellectuals and nobility, but also to ordinary people who recognized in Böhme's writings a voice insistent that outward show or learning is not as important as the state of one's heart, and that spiritual knowledge may well be more likely found among the poor than among the wealthy or powerful.

Böhmean theosophy is especially important because it represents, in a largely Protestant, albeit nonsectarian ambience, a peculiarly medieval synthesis of virtually all the major esoteric currents of Europe, transposed into a form that could be brought to North America. The theosophical groups that came to America, mostly in the early eighteenth century and mostly to Pennsylvania, established some of the longest lasting and interesting semimonastic communities in the history of North America, the most well known of which was Ephrata. These Protestant semimonastic communities contributed a great deal to the richness of early American colonial history, and as I have shown in my book *Wisdom's Children: A Christian Esoteric Tradition*, practiced a wide range of esoteric traditions under the aegis of theosophy that included alchemy, astrology, herbal medicine, and magic, as well as their own particular form of Christian Sophianic mysticism.

Theosophy in Europe reached its most active point around the turn of the eighteenth century, when many of the most influential German, Dutch, and English theosophic groups could be found. This was the era of such important figures as Johann Georg Gichtel (1638–1710), who founded the Angelic Brethren, a semimonastic group of men in Amsterdam who pledged themselves to Sophia, or Divine Wisdom. Gichtel dispensed spiritual advice to many correspondents, both men and women, as seen in his voluminous collected correspondence, *Theosophia Practica* (7 vols., 1721). Two other important figures were John Pordage (1608–81), who led a theosophic circle in England until the time of his death and wrote a number of books, including such titles as *Theologia Mystica* and *Sophia* (1683), that were published only after his death and in many cases only in German; and Jane Leade (1623–1704), who led Pordage's circle after his death, gave it the name "the Philadelphians," and left records of visions in numerous books published around the turn of the eighteenth century. Leade's titles include *The Revelation of Revelations* (1683), *The Laws of Paradise* (1695), and *A Fountain of Gardens*, (3 vols., 1696–1700). Naturally, I cannot here mention anywhere near the full number of such groups and individuals from this, the richest period of theosophic activity.

However, from this flurry of theosophic activity in Europe and England around the turn of the seventeenth century, we can well understand how it was that such activity should overflow from Europe and England to North America, which was widely seen in millennialist terms as the setting for a kind of New Jerusalem in the wilderness. Some theosophers, like Gichtel, scoffed at the idea that one must go to America in order to practice theosophy, but many others saw America as a place where they could practice without fear of persecution, and even claimed America was a kind of frontier paradise. Such wide-eyed immigrants were often disillusioned by the sheer difficulty of living conditions on the American frontier, but certainly there were also some who established lasting theosophic communities there, and continued to publish theosophic books both in German and English. Theosophy was, in brief, quite influential in European religious history, but also in colonial America, and it is therefore not too surprising that this same tradition should recur as an influence in the American Renaissance.

Secret Societies

If theosophy represents a synthesis of various esoteric currents, so, too, do subsequent European esoteric traditions, among the most influential of which was undoubtedly Rosicrucianism, or the Order of the Rosy Cross. It may be, as some scholars have speculated, that Böhme was himself familiar with the same movement that, ten years before his death, began to emerge under the name "Rosicrucian" with the publication of the *Fama Fraternitatis* (1614) and the *Confessio Fraternitatis* (1615). In any event, Böhme's writing and thought both paralleled and influenced that of the Brotherhood of the Rosy Cross, which first came to general public attention with the publication of the *Fama Fraternitatis*. This brief work, like its companion treatise, the *Confessio*, captured the imagination of the age with its tale of Christian Rosencreutz and his mysterious journeys through exotic lands and secret knowledge, as well as with its assertion of a secret order as keeper of profound and powerful knowledge.

Historian Frances Yates argued that the word "Rosicrucian" may better be seen as a word that describes a particular kind of approach to arcane knowledge than as a specific organized order, even if at times such orders did exist.[7] The Rosicrucians' goal, according to the *Fama*, was to follow Christ by renewing all arts to perfection, "so that finally man might thereby understand his own nobility and worth, and why he is called Microcosmos, and how far his knowledge extendeth into Nature."[8] Although Rosicrucianism was probably begun as a kind of insider's joke, it so quickly captured the imagination of Europe that these two treatises, and their complement—the incredibly complex and symbolic *Chemical Wedding of Christian Rosenkreutz*—in turn sparked a host of Rosicrucian publications, as well, eventually, as a host of secret orders of the Rosy Cross.

The Rosicrucian furor lasted only a few short years, disappearing around 1620, the time of political upheaval in Germany and the advent of the Thirty Years' War. By 1623, there was a great deal of anti-Rosicrucian sentiment, particularly in France, even a kind of nascent Rosicrucian witch-hunt. Such opposition was tied in with the emerging rationalist and materialist paradigm of the so-called Enlightenment—which was precisely opposed to the Rosicrucian Enlightenment. The Rosicrucian dream, which we see outlined in the *Fama* and *Confessio*, as well as in subsequent literature, was of a nonsectarian, peaceful, universal culture dedicated to the investigation of the language of nature, written in the microcosm and in the macrocosm; it was a culture founded on Kabbala and alchemy, that is, on a pansophic mysticism.

Here we must introduce the word "pansophy," or "pansophia." One finds this word frequently in Hermetic publications immediately following the Rosicrucian announcements, as in for instance Joseph Stellatus's *Pegasus Firmamenti sive Introductio brevis in veterum sapientiam* [*Pegasus of the Firmament, or a Brief Introduction to the Ancient Wisdom, Once Taught in the Magia of the Egyptians and Persians and Now Rightly Called the Pansophia of the Venerable Society of the Rosy Cross* (1618)]. The word "Pansophia" here separates this new form of esotericism from "Theosophia," which is specifically Christian gnosis.

Pansophy is universalist in its aims and in the sources upon which it draws; it emphasizes magic, alchemy, herbalism, healing, cabala, and inquiry into nature more generally, and draws eclecticly on much earlier "pagan" traditions like those attributed to Egypt and Persia. In many respects, pansophy resembles the aims and works of Giordano Bruno, who was central to the subsequent emergence of modern forms of esotericism. Stellatus cites Hermes Trismegistus, Ruechlin, Paracelsus, and Michael Maier, and thus places himself squarely in the mainstream of the primary Western esoteric currents. Pansophy is a universalist Western esotericism willing to draw on all previous esoteric movements—Christian or not—magical, alchemical, cabalistic, and gnostic, in order to form the basis for a new, universal culture like that imaged in Bacon's New Atlantis or other utopias of the time.

The word "pansophy" itself largely disappears from the European vocabulary after the seventeenth century, but what the word signifies certainly does not disappear. The emergence of a pansophic approach to esotericism seems very much a counterbalance to the emergent extreme rationalism and materialism that also gave birth to scientism, mechanism, and technologism. The latter are all based in an objectivization of the cosmos or of humanity as objects of study, hence on our separation from and manipulation of them. It is true that chemistry, for instance, derived from alchemy, but one might well see chemistry as a diminution of alchemy—for alchemy requires humility and selflessness, whereas purely chemical experimentation requires nothing of oneself except to be a firmly rationalist observer. The pansophic view, an esoteric universalism that includes alchemy, certainly was temporarily vanquished by rationalist materialism, but the pansophic impulse nonetheless has continued to govern Western esotericism up to the present day.

From the seventeenth until the twentieth centuries, in other words, Western esotericism often aimed at universal knowledge, at a truly comprehensive metaphysics and cosmology. Such a universalist goal did not exclude the human, specifically, the social and political realm. It was in the socio-political realm that the Rosicrucian impulse had considerable impact, first with the consistent emphasis of Rosicrucian works on the transformation of society and the establishment of a utopia, and later in the development of modern Freemasonry. All of the Rosicrucian, theosophic, and pansophic movements we have discussed in turn fed into Freemasonry, which unlike these other more individualistic movements, maintained a definite organizational hierarchy and structure.

Freemasonry, of course, began in the medieval period as one of many craft guilds, each of which guarded its particular mysteries, those of masonry belonging to the arts of architecture and building, and associated with the vast cathedrals of medieval Europe. Masonry, not surprisingly, flourished in the vicinity of Jewish scholarship and Kabbalism, contact probably having its origins in the lengthy period of communication between Islamic, Jewish, and Christian circles in Spain and Provençe. It is true that there were other such guilds with their own rites and mysteries, but the Freemasons endured the longest, primarily because of Kabbalistic influence that allowed Freemasonry to transform itself completely from a society devoted to the arts of building, into a speculative, semireligious occult fraternity.

Although early-eighteenth-century Freemasonry, especially in England, had an exoteric, nonsectarian basis, it quickly began to develop an esoteric emphasis, especially in France. This esotericism came about largely through the efforts of Andrew Michael Ramsay (1686–1743), a Scotsman who early in his life was a member of the Philadelphian Society of Jane Leade and Francis Lee, a theosophic circle in London. From there he went on to stay with Pierre Poiret, who then sent him to Archbishop Fénelon, after which he became secretary to Madame Guyon, all of whom were known for their mysticism. Following Guyon's death, he became a tutor to various aristocratic families while publishing numerous books. During this time, Ramsay, who had been initiated into Masonry years before, became prominent in French Masonry, and in 1737 gave an oration in which he discussed the importance of chivalry and the Templars, thus stimulating a host of higher degrees.

In this oration, Ramsay called for a massive project of universal illumination:

> All the Grand Masters in Germany, England, Italy, and elsewhere exhort all the learned men and all the artisans of the Fraternity to unite to furnish materials for a Universal Dictionary of the liberal arts and useful sciences, excepting only theology and politics.
>
> The work has already been commenced in London, and by means of the union of our Brothers it may be carried to a conclusion in a few years. . . . By this means the lights of all nations will be united in a single work, which wil be a universal library of all that is beautiful, great, luminous, solid, and useful in all the sciences and in all the noble arts.[9]

Such a project reflects the Rosicrucian aims of a century before, but here they take on a distinctly rationalist flavor, and indeed, it is not surprising that this project, announced in Ramsay's oration, has subsequently been credited with at least some of the inspiration for the later French philosophes and their *Encyclopédie*.

Freemasonry had, as we shall see, a profound impact upon early American history and the founding of the United States, but this impact was not entirely due to the esoteric elements of Masonry.[10] Within Masonry itself, one finds a continuous struggle after at least the eighteenth century between adherents like

Jean-Baptiste Willermoz (1730–1824), one of the founders of the Rectified Scottish Rite and a powerful proponent of speculative or esoteric Masonry, and others who insisted on a much more exoteric, fraternal Freemasonry, consisting in three degrees of apprentice, fellow craftsman, and master mason. Both of these currents fed into American Masonry, which thus was another vehicle by which various currents of European esotericism, particularly the stream of universalism, fed into North American Anglo-European civilization.

Swedenborg

Without doubt, the most influential European esotericist for nineteenth-century America was Emanuel Swedenborg (1688–1772). Swedenborg's name and influence are to be found virtually everywhere, even where it seems unlikely, and will recur as we examine the background of the American Renaissance. One finds his work central for Emerson, and visible in the works of authors that range from Poe to Henry James Sr., as well as in the works of countless popular writers and movements, including various communal experiments of nineteenth-century America. As we shall see, Swedenborg was uniquely suited to the nineteenth-century American mind. But who was this strange figure, the spirit-seer from Sweden who had such attraction for and impact on American literature, philosophy, and religion? And what relation does his work bear to the Western esoteric traditions?

Although Swedenborg was influential in nineteenth century America, he firmly belonged to eighteenth-century Europe. Swedenborg's father was Jesper Swedberg, a pious man, a professor of theology at the University of Uppsala, later dean, and finally Bishop of Skara. Swedberg's elevation to this position of bishop meant the family's elevation to the rank of noble, after which the family name changed to Swedenborg. Emanuel Swedenborg's mother, Sara Behm, died when he was eight years old. She came from a family prosperous through mining, and thus the two sides of Swedenborg's family line emphasized, on the one hand, pious religion and, on the other, science and practical technology. These two emphases were to shape Swedenborg's entire life, eventually in highly unexpected ways.

Something of a prodigy, after a peaceful childhood, Swedenborg at the age of eleven entered the University of Uppsala, where he took courses in philosophy, science, and mathematics, and learned Latin, Greek, Hebrew, English, Dutch, French, and Italian. He recalled of his childhood that he was in those days "constantly engaged in thought upon God, salvation, and the spiritual diseases of mankind."[11] At the university and thereafter, he exhibited great interest in physics, astronomy, and practical mechanics, particularly when, after he completed his studies in 1709, he traveled to England and then to Holland. His studies included watchmaking, cabinetry, engraving, and bookbinding, as well as physics, astronomy, mathematics, mineralogy, geology, economics, physiology, mining, and chemistry. When, in 1716, King Charles XII appointed

Swedenborg to the post of Extraordinary Assessor in the Royal College of Mines, he entered a position that he more or less retained until 1747 as a member of the Swedish Board of Mines, a post that made him responsible for inspecting and administering one of Sweden's most important industries of the time.

Swedenborg led a busy and unusual life. When his father was appointed bishop, Swedenborg himself entered nobility, and from 1719 until near the end of his life, he attended most sessions of the Swedish House of Nobles. He was not merely a titular member, but weighed in on many of the political controversies of his day. During this time he was also appointed engineering advisor to the king, mainly on the strength of his having edited *Daedalus*, a periodical devoted to the natural sciences. Thus he engaged in some inventive engineering, including designs for a new drydock, a canal, and a means of moving large warships overland. Swedenborg also engaged in research in metallurgy and physiology, in particular examining the functions of the brain and glands. At the same time, he published a number of large works, including the three-volume *Philosophical and Mineralogical Works* (1734), and the two-volume *The Economy of the Animal Kingdom* (1740−41).

In 1745, Swedenborg's life changed from an outward to an inward focus. In April 1745, when dining in a London inn, the room grew dark and an apparition spoke to him. When he returned to his room, the vision recurred and a spirit spoke to him, telling him that he could be the means for a divine revelation like those that had come to the Old Testament prophets. For the following several years, he engaged in an intense study of and commentary on the Bible, which, one may recall, he could read in Hebrew and Greek. In 1747, he began to publish his multivolume *Arcana Coelestia*, a study of Genesis and Exodus that included more than seven thousand pages. He wrote eight volumes on the book of Revelation and numerous other books on subjects like *Divine Love and Wisdom* and *Heaven and Hell*, the latter perhaps his most well-known book. In 1768, he published *The Delights of Wisdom Pertaining to Conjugial Love*, which elaborated his theory of sexuality and marriage. Much of what he published on spiritual matters until 1759 was anonymous, and much of his time he spent in relative seclusion, writing or experiencing visions.

There are several stories about Swedenborg's clairvoyance that are frequently told, and that should briefly be related here. One is that in July 1759 he was visiting William Castel in the city of Gothenburg, several hundred miles from his home in Stockholm. During his stay, Swedenborg became pale and withdrew from company; when he returned, he said that a fire had broken out in Stockholm not far from his house, and he feared that fire would destroy some of his manuscripts. At 8 P.M., he sighed and said "Thank God! The fire is extinguished three doors from my house." It was several days before a messenger arrived from Stockholm to confirm Swedenborg's vision. Another such story concerns Queen Lovisa Ulrika, who had by 1761 heard of Swedenborg's abilities. She asked if he would speak in the spirit world with her brother, who had died two years earlier. Some days later Swedenborg returned to the Queen, and then in a private audience told her a secret that, she said, only her brother would know.

These kinds of events brought Swedenborg public renown, but also made him notorious in some circles. Indeed, in 1766, no less a figure than Immanuel Kant wrote a book entitled *Dreams of a Spirit-Seer* that denigrated Swedenborg. In 1768, at the age of eighty, while Swedenborg was completing his two-volume *The True Christian Religion*, he was publicly attacked by the Lutheran consistory of Gothenburg as a heretic and menace to the population. This denunciation was carried over to a Royal Council, which in 1770 published a report that again denounced Swedenborg, totally condemning and rejecting his writings and doctrines. However, despite these denunciations, Swedenborg's works continued to circulate widely; if anything, the notoriety spurred their circulation. In the meantime, Swedenborg traveled to England, where he predicted his own death on 29 March 1772, the very day that he did indeed die.

The relationship of Swedenborg to previous esoteric traditions, in particular to the theosophy of Jacob Böhme, remains a vexed question. Certainly Swedenborg was well read in a vast number of fields, and it seems highly unlikely, given his predilection for theology from an early age, that he would have completely missed reading from so influential a tradition as Böhmean theosophy. Indeed, many have remarked upon "the startling likeness between many of Swedenborg's ideas and theirs [the theosophers]."[12] Swedenborg spent a great deal of time in libraries in Leipzig, Dresden, Amsterdam, and London, and must have encountered the works of theosophers like Gichtel there, as well. As Signe Toksvig wrote, the mystical speculations of Böhme "bear so much resemblance to Swedenborg's that later he was constantly being asked if he had read Böhme." This he denied, but as Toksvig goes on, "he could easily have found the same ideas in other books to which he had access. J. G. Gichtel, who lived forty years in Holland and who wrote a book whose doctrine of the Grand Man much resembles Swedenborg's, was a disciple of Böhme's, while others of the 'occult' fraternities entertained many of the ideas of the Beyond which Swedenborg seemed to regard as 'arcana' revealed to him alone."[13]

Indeed, Swedenborg corresponded with Friedrich Oetinger, himself a well-known theosopher who was interested in Swedenborg's visions of the spiritual realms.[14] That Swedenborg knew of theosophy is certain; how much he drew upon it to create his own doctrines is an open question. It is clear that his writings had great influence in esoteric circles in Europe, and in America, as well.

Although Swedenborg himself did not encourage the founding of any sect or church in his name, shortly after his death a London man named Robert Hindmarsh came across a copy of *Heaven and Hell*, and shortly thereafter organized a group of Swedenborgian followers to study Swedenborg's works. A member of Hindmarsh's group in England, James Glen, brought Swedenborg's works to Philadelphia in 1784, and from that time dates the history of what became known as the "New Church" in America. Glen placed the following advertisement in the *Pennsylvania Gazette*: "A Discourse on the extraordinary sci-

ENCE of Celestial and Terrestrial Connections and Correspondences, recently revived by the late honorable and learned Emanuel Swedenborg, will be delivered by Mr. James Glen, an humble Pupil and Follower of the said Swedenborg's at 8 o'clock on the evening of Saturday the 5th of June 1784, *at Bell's Book-Store*, near St. Paul's Church, in Third Street Philadelphia."[15] Among listeners Glen drew in during his various lectures—at least one of which occurred at the Masonic "Green Dragon" tavern, originating point of the Boston Tea Party and meeting place for the American Revolution—was Francis Bailey, who learned the art of printing from Peter Miller of Ephrata, the theosophic community we will discuss shortly. Bailey was a friend of Benjamin Franklin, printer for the state of Pennsylvania, and publisher of John Clowes' *A Summary View of the Heavenly Doctrines* (1787) and *The True Christian Religion* (1789).

Regardless of how much Swedenborg himself read or was influenced by previous European esoteric traditions, his work was itself highly influential and formed a means by which many people in late-eighteenth- and nineteenth-century America became familiar with commonplace esoteric ideas like the correspondence of microcosm and macrocosm, the possibility of seeing spirits and visiting spiritual realms, clairvoyance, and the Kabbalistic idea of the *macroprosopos*, or the cosmos as a great man. Swedenborg also represented the union of science and religion, as well as the possibility of what one may call religious science or scientific religion. However, most of all, he represented direct spiritual experience. In some respects, Swedenborg represented the most pragmatic of writers on spiritual topics; his inventory of the inhabitants of heaven or hell resembles his earlier inventories of minerals for the Swedish government. This peculiar combination of pragmatism and extravagance was precisely the kind of approach to appeal to Americans, not in the form of Swedenborgian churches, but rather in the wide diffusion of his writings and thought. We will encounter him again in what follows. But first we will turn to the process of how the various esoteric traditions made themselves at home in the New World.

three

Esotericism in Early America

Reading most histories of colonial America gives one little indication that there was any presence of Western esotericism in the New World at all. Historians have been chiefly concerned with the realm of events, of wars and famines, of treaties and exploration of the new continent, and have paid very little attention at all to whether or how the various currents of Western esotericism made their way into the colonies. Yet when we look more closely at the lives of colonists in North America, we discover that all manner of esoteric disciplines were brought over from Europe, and sometimes played major roles in people's lives. Generally speaking, the forms of esotericism brought from Europe to colonial America can be separated into two main categories: pragmatic esotericism and spiritual esotericism.

Astromancy and Folk Magic

One can certainly understand why colonists would be interested in pragmatic forms of esotericism like astrology, geomancy, and folk magic: these were ways that, in an unfamiliar and often hostile New World, one perhaps could foretell or even forestall some future tribulation. Astrology offers knowledge of possibile future patterns in life, and in the New World, any such knowledge was often welcomed, if sometimes surreptitiously. Astrological almanacs that showed the positions and dispositions of the planets were among the most popular publications in colonial America, and one finds them in profusion from the presses of America's earliest printers. Traditionally, European astrology was, of course, more than simply calculating the positions and relationships of the planets; such calculations represent the foundation of what must be interpreted. Thus, the popularity of astrological almanacs in colonial America suggests that during this period a great many people were capable of such interpretations.

Among the most prolific producers of colonial astrological almanacs was Daniel Leeds (1652–1720), who lived much of his life in Burlington, New Jersey, but whose almanac was printed by William Bradford (1663–1752), in Philadelphia. Leeds was prominent in West Jersey as the surveyor general, and in 1696 published the first map of "The Streets and Lots of Land Laid in the Town of Burlington." Surveying might seem a prosaic occupation and not connected with esotericism, but as we shall shortly see, this is not always the case. For there is an esoteric form of divination called "geomancy," which was sometimes practiced by surveyors in the colonial period, and which requires astrological knowledge. We cannot say whether Leeds practiced geomancy or not, but it is certain that he knew astrology, for in 1687 he began to publish his astrological almanac, "Particularly Respecting the Meridian and Latitude of Burlington, but May Indifferently Serve All Places Adjacent."

There exists no complete collection of Leeds's astrological almanacs, but they were published through 1713, when his son, Titan Leeds, took over calculations and publication in a new series that lasted from 1714 to 1746. Another of Leeds's sons, Felix (1687–1744), was also an astrologer who published an almanac for the years 1727–30. Titan Leeds is known as a victim of one of Benjamin Franklin's practical jokes—in his first almanac of 1733, "Poor Richard" predicted the death "on October 17, 1733, 3 hr. 29 m., P.M." of "his good friend and fellow-student, Mr. Titan Leeds," and the following year, Leeds's published protests notwithstanding, insisted that "there is the strongest probability that my dear friend is no more," because "Mr. Leeds was too well bred to use any man so indecently and scurrilously" as "Poor Richard" had been abused in Leeds's protest. This incident, while amusing, also reveals some of the context out of which Franklin's well-known almanac emerged, for as we shall see later, however skeptical he might have been toward it, Franklin lived in an ambience filled with various forms of European esotericism, and his almanac was largely a parody of the real thing, prominent among which were the almanacs of the Leeds family. The almanacs of the Leeds family are important for revealing the use of astrology for practical matters in colonial America, particularly for agricultural timing, traditionally linked to the lunar cycle.

However, Leeds is not known only as compiler of astrological almanacs; he was also a prolific religious controversialist. Leeds was earlier in life associated with the Quakers, but when his second almanac of 1688 was suppressed by the Society of Friends of Philadelphia, and all the copies of the printer Bradford were burned, Leeds went on the offensive and published a series of broadsides against the Quakers, including *News of a Trumpet Sounding in the Wilderness* (New York: 1697); *A Trumpet Sounded Out of the Wilderness of America* (1699); *The Rebuker Rebuked* (1703); and the direct attack on Quaker leader George Fox, *The Great Mistery of Fox-Craft Discovered* (1705). He was encouraged in his attacks on Quakers by his friend George Keith (ca.1638– 1716), who was widely known as a former Quaker become anti-Quaker preacher and activist, and who was also a surveyor general in New Jersey. Leeds's attacks on Quakerism, although comprehensible given the background of the controversy over the burning of his second almanac, become even more comprehensible when we consider Leeds's theosophic writing.

Leeds is perhaps most notable for having published through the press of William Bradford what is probably the very first Christian theosophic works in American history and the first book published in Philadelphia, *The Temple of Wisdom for the Little World; in Two Parts* (1688). The first part of this book consists of a compilation from the works of Jacob Böhme, and the second part, rather oddly, includes "Essayes and Religious Meditations of Sir Francis Bacon, Knight." Leeds describes the theosophic heart of his book as follows: "Now then as to the first part I say, that most of what the diligent Searcher and Enquirer shall find dispersed in the whole Works or Writings of Jacob Behme, he will here find collected, contracted, and comprised in a little room. . . . What is here immited to thy view is in his own words and sentences . . . as I found them dispersed."[1]

Temple of Wisdom begins with Böhme's challenge to "the Doctors and Schollars, and Readers of his Writings:" "Come on ye Doctors, if ye are in the right, then given an answer to the Spirit; What do you think stood in the place of this world before the time of the World? 2ndly, out of what do you think the Earth and Stars came to be?"[2] Such a challenge undoubtedly was congenial to the combative Leeds, who in what has come to be an American tradition, surely also identified more with the unlettered mystic shoemaker Böhme than with the "Doctors and Schollars."

The majority of *Temple of Wisdom* was taken more or less directly from the English translations of Böhme's works, which had begun to appear in England as early as the 1640s. Leeds included a discussion of characteristically Böhmean themes like the "Seven Forms or Properties of the Eternal Nature," as well as the "three Principles or Worlds." These "Seven Forms" are symbolized by the seven planets, which represent the forming principles of the cosmos. The three worlds are the wrath-world, the divine or paradisal light-world, and the physical realm of nature. However, Leeds also drew from the post-Böhmean theosophic tradition in which Böhme's complex writings were condensed into tabular or diagrammatic form, as in the following set of correspondences.

I. ♄☽ II. ☿♃ III. ♂♀ IV. ☉ V. ♀♂ VI. ♃☿ VII. ☽♄

I. Harsh, Desiring Will / II. Bitter, Stinging / III. Anguish / IV. Dark or Light Fire / V. Light, Love / VI. Sound, Mercury / VII. Substance, Nature[3]

Thus, we can see how astrological symbolism was encompassed within Böhmean theosophy: it is not that astrology was a practical form of esotericism totally separate from Christian theosophy, but rather that the various forms of esotericism here were complementary and mutually explanatory.

Leeds did not dwell on such astrologically based symbolism; he offered as much as possible of Böhme's complex gnostic writing in a relatively brief work. He included a discussion of the nature of the soul, for instance: "The Tincture is the true Body of the Soul, for the Soul is fire, and the Tincture ariseth from the Fire, and draweth it again into it self, and allayeth it self therewith, so that the wrathful Source is quenched and then the Tincture subsideth in meekness. . . . The soul only, beside the Spirit, is a Globe of Fire, with an Eye of Fire, and an Eye of Light, which turn themselves backward into one another, as the Wheel in Ezekiel."[4] One wonders what someone in colonial America would make of such observations as these, had they no context in which to understand them. This is in fact a characteristic theosophic passage from Böhme, and if seen in the larger context of theosophy, is not particularly difficult to understand: all its images and terms are found in both German and English theosophic traditions.[5] Leeds defines the word "Tincture" as meaning "the power and virtue of Fire and Light; and the stirring [up or putting forth like a Bud] of this virtue is called the holy and pure Element."[6] The symbolism of the eye and the globe was developed extensively in English theosophy, particularly in the work of Dr. John Pordage. The problem is that Leeds's work offers little exegesis of such a passage, which leads us to wonder whether Leeds published *Temple of Wisdom* for an audience largely already familiar with Böhmean theosophy, and appreciative of a brief compendium. As we shall see, this hypothesis is not so far-fetched as it might at first seem.

In any event, it becomes clear later in *Temple of Wisdom* that Leeds himself was drawn to theosophy because it offered a metaphysical or religious context for astrology. He confesses near the end of the book that "My first design here, was to be only particular of Astrology."[7] Leeds discusses the zodiacal houses and an astrology based in Böhme, noting at the same time that although he bears an "affection" for astrology, he "takes leave" of it after having studied Böhme, pointing us instead to "Those stars that should give Light unto my Mind."[8] He concludes by transposing outward astrology to its inner symbolism, writing that the "First is the House of Judgement," the "Second, Humility and Lowliness," and so on. Such a transposition is particularly interesting because Leeds continued to publish his astrological almanacs for many years thereafter, suggesting that theosophy offered him inner interpretations of astrology that were not necessarily in conflict with what we might call outward or predictive astrology.

Indeed, Leeds conjoined both major streams of esotericism, which we here will term pragmatic and spiritual, that Europeans brought to the New World. Pragmatic esotericism is represented, of course, by astrology; whereas spiritual esotericism is represented by Böhmean theosophy. What is more, there is no conflict between these two streams; rather, they reinforce one another. Both offer practical means to orient oneself in daily life, but theosophy has spiritual dimensions that extend well beyond the limits of astrology. Theosophy has to do with one's inner life; astrology has to do with one's worldly life. At the same time, one finds in theosophy a rather extensive tradition not only of drawing on astrological terms in order to explain theosophic cosmology, but also of marking theosophic events by their astrological timing or correspondences.[9]

How widespread was such esoteric knowledge in colonial America? This, of course, is not an easy question to answer. It is particularly hard to determine a satisfactory answer inasmuch as documentation is relatively spotty, and sometimes appears almost by happenstance. Pamphlets and broadsheets were not all preserved, and family papers sometimes were expunged of references to esotericism, particularly as the nineteenth century approached and materialist rationalism began to hold sway. However, during the seventeenth and into the eighteenth centuries in Europe, England, and America, interest in esoteric topics was widespread and not anathematized. Indeed, the early- and mid-seventeenth century in Europe and England saw an efflorescence of publishing about esoteric themes, including alchemy and Rosicrucianism: this was the heyday of publishing on these topics, unequalled since. It seems more than likely that many colonists carried over to America esoteric knowledge and practices, even if they did not leave much documentation to that effect.

Support for this hypothesis can be found in surprising and on first glance unlikely places. For instance, when we look at the surveying papers of Christian Lehman, who was responsible for mapping Germantown, now in Philadelphia, Pennsylvania, we find numerous maps and documents, none of which are particularly interesting.[10] However, atop all of those documents is one of very great interest indeed: it is a manuscript written in a neat hand, mostly in Latin but also with some German text, that includes a host of dot patterns next to various aphorisms. That this manuscript was kept on top of all the papers may be an accident, but one doubts it, because the papers in question are all surveying records, and this manuscript links them as a manual of geomancy.

Currently, geomancy is generally depicted as a system of divination, and so it is. The dots are arrived at by one method or another, and the future foretold from their patterns, rather like the *I Ching*. However, geomancy, as the name itself suggests, deals not only with divination from a system of dot patterns, but also with patterns in the earth itself, more or less on the order of the Chinese *feng shui*. *Feng shui*, which means "wind water," is an ancient tradition whereby one reads the patterns of the elements and landscape in order to determine the energy flows prevalent in a given site. Some sites are propitious for building; others are not at all. Although geomancy is a divination tradition, it is also a tradition of use to surveyors, and one can easily see why Lehman was interested in and used it to help people map land and situate new buildings. The origins of geomancy are not certain, but tradition holds that Christian monastics maintained it during the medieval period, and that esotericists rediscovered it during the late Renaissance.

One English author on esoteric subjects, widely read, was John Heydon, in whose book *Theomagia* (1663–64) we find a useful account of a wide range of esoteric practices, including astrological geomancy. In chapter 15 of *Theomagia*, entitled "How the Idea's are infused into The Sixteen Figures by the Seven Rulers, through the help of the Soul of the World," Heydon writes that

"Ideas" are "above Bodies, Souls, Minds," as "one simple, pure, immutable, indivisible, incorporeal and eternal," and are "stamped" in all things, which thereby participate in the "mind of God."[11] There are, Heydon continues, twelve Ideas, and these "have power over the face of the whole Earth."[12] They include

I. Malchidael
```
      *
      *          Puer
   *     *
      *
```

II. Hasmodel
```
      *
   *     *        Amissio
      *
   *     *
```

III. Hambriel
```
   *     *
   *     *        Albus
      *
      *  *
```

IV. Muriel
```
   *  *
   *  *           Populus
   *  *
   *  *
```

There are twelve of these Ideas, distributed over the face of the earth, but the descriptions are strictly from a European perspective; there is in *Theomagia* no reference to the New World. However, one can see how such a system could be applied to North America, for instance, since the Ideas are defined in terms of principles. Hence Muriel is defined as "watery, cold, moist, and feminine," corresponding to the "paps" and stomach, and to "Islands, Seas, marsh, and rivers," exemplary places being Holland, Tunis, Scotland, Venice, and Genoa.

How is this system connected to divination? Heydon tells us that "the *RosieCrucians* have . . . the projecting of this Art to be made with signs upon the paper. . . . [They] also Judge the hand of the projector or mover to be most powerfully moved and directed by the *Idea's* or *Genii* when they Ascend and Descend in their Regions."[13] Thus divination and cartography are not disconnected: the "projector" is in touch with the Ideas themselves that in turn inform and govern various places on the earth. The same relationship, he continues, is responsible also for the powers of "telesmatical" images or talismans. That is, the images bear the imprint and power of the Ideas or genii, and therefore embody them, channeling their energy into a particular place, for instance a temple. In this way, it is possible to change the reigning energy of a particular site. All of this would have been of considerable interest to someone engaged not only in mapping but also in advising clients on building, as Lehman was.

It is true that Heydon was often vilified as flagrant plagiarizer, but for our purposes, this vilification only increases the value of what he wrote because it was drawn from other works and thus reflects views that prevailed in esoteric circles of his day. I draw on Heydon's work here because it helps explain the general context in which the geomantic manuscript that accompanied Lehman's surveying documents can be understood. Examining a subject like geomancy cannot be done in isolation from its larger esoteric context, and indeed, means that we must enter into a much broader context of which astrology, magic, and divination are also a part. There is, in other words, a coherent theoretical framework within which geomancy is to be seen from the viewpoint of that era; and Lehman was engaged in applying this tradition to his own locale, chiefly the vicinity of Philadelphia, Pennsylvania.

Who was Lehman? From a German family, he immigrated to Germantown, Pennsylvania in 1730/31, and relatively quickly became a leading member of the community. He and his friend Christopher Witt were responsible for what became known as the Germantown Library, which consisted chiefly in Lehman and Witt's books. Witt was a truly Renaissance man: he was a botanist, a physician, a teacher, a clockmaker, a musician, a pipe organ maker, and an artist responsible for the earliest oil portrait in Pennsylvania (of theosopher Johannes Kelpius, of whom we shall say more shortly).[14] However, Lehman also had his hand in a range of activities and had a wide array of intellectual interests, including many of those of Witt. In the *Pennsylvania Chronicle* of 12 April 1768, Lehman advertised the sale of his house, which was "well-known for its elegant situation," and would suit "any W. Indian or other Gentleman for a pleasant, healthy, & commodious County Seat." His house included a collection of "curious plants, shrubs, & seeds of the growth of this climate." Thus we know that Lehman shared Witt's interest in botany.

However, there is more that we can tell from this description of Lehman's house. First, we should remark that the house's "elegant situation" supports what we know about his interest in geomancy: he undoubtedly used geomantic means to locate his own home. Second, he thought that the home would suit a "West Indian" gentleman. Why West Indian specifically? When one looks at what we might call common occultism of the day (i.e., palmistry and so forth), one finds that oftentimes the occult tradition in question is attributed to a "West Indian" source even it if clearly came from a European's hand. Such an attribution became much more common around and after Lehman's time, chiefly because the Western esoteric traditions were being more frequently denigrated in public.[15] As astrology or magic, for example, was increasingly regarded as suspect, they were projected onto "West Indian" or other sources as though they didn not have European origins at all. Thus the reference to a "West Indian" gentleman here carries a hidden message.

In Lehman's use of geomancy, we see a practical application of esotericism: what could be more useful in settling a new landscape than understanding its hidden energies? When we look closely at Lehman's manuscript, we find that indeed it corresponds very closely with the figures we saw in Heydon's

Theomagia. Lehman's manuscript includes useful notes pointing out which combinations of certain formations are fortunate or unfortunate, as well as a *Tabula Geomantica*. This table, and several others along with it, show the correspondences of the various dot patterns, including their planetary, elemental, directional, and other aspects. It is quite clear, from examining these tables and diagrams, that the term "astromancy" would be equally appropriate, for there is clearly a strong astrological component to the practice of geomancy. Indeed, there is a sample chart here, as well as a *Speculum Astronomicum*, and *Tabula Horarium Planetarium*, or planetary table of the day's and night's hours. These would be useful, for example, if one wanted to begin building at a particularly suitable day and hour in order to draw upon the most fortunate planetary energies for a given place.

Although this kind of astromancy might seem to be in conflict with at least some forms of New England Christianity, in fact astrology provided a means for ordering many aspects of daily life, and was supported even by many ministers. For instance, on 8 February 1656, the minister at Cambridge, Jonathan Mitchell, delivered a sermon on Genesis 1:14, that the stars and planets were "to be for Signes." Mitchell said in his sermon that the word "Signes" did not refer merely to the seasons or to the movement of time, but rather the stars indicated when to time the actions of "many Civill Actions and affairs," among which he included "plowing, sewing, planting, pruning, gathering, reaping," and "taking physick at fit times of the yeare."[16] Astrology for both farming and medicine was "a most worthy, excellent, and most commendable Science." And geomancy was undoubtedly also acceptable. Indeed, so popular were the astrological almanacs in seventeenth-century New England that they constituted 80 percent of all printed secular literature, and even Cotton Mather produced an almanac, remarking in it that the almanacs came into almost as many hands as the Bible.[17] The earliest almanacs (up to 1675) were compiled and published primarily by Harvard graduates, because Harvard College possessed the only printing press.[18]

But not all astrology was acceptable. In particular, astrological prognostication was forbidden, not because it did not work, but precisely because it often did. To tell an inquirer what was going to happen, or even what was likely to happen, from a New England Christian viewpoint was to interfere with God's will, to take upon oneself the work of Divine Providence, and probably to get in league with the devil or his minions. Thus Charles Morton, a minister in Charlestown, Massachusetts, held that in judicial or prognosticating astrology "the Divel . . . had a greater stroak therein than the Art." Through astrology, the devil led the unfortunate to become "perfect wizards, Atheists, [and] Pagans."[19] In fact, often those in the community who had practiced fortune-telling of one form or another eventually became the subject of witch-hunts. It was only a small step, evidently, from telling fortunes to influencing them. Thus, when in 1692 Dorcas Hoar was accused of witchcraft, it turned out that she had some twenty years earlier possessed a book of palmistry and was known for that practice, although she had at one point sworn it off.[20] Or, again,

Katherine Harrison, of Wethersfield, Connecticut, told her neighbors she had read a book by William Lilly, the famous English judicial astrologer, and in 1668 she was accused of witchcraft.[21]

The witchcraft trials in New England during the late-seventeenth century reveal the fundamental division in the way people of the time tended to view esoteric practices. Nearly everyone gave credence to the general idea that the planetary movements, particularly those of the moon, were intimately linked to human and especially agricultural life. What is more, practices based on this view were commonplace, and included numerous kinds of folk magic, most of which was carried over from Europe. What separated the witches were their malevolent intentions: they were willing to use those practices (in which most people believed) not for good, but for harm. Witchcraft was feared and detested because it interfered in peoples' lives; it was not the particular practices that the witches used, but the danger they were seen to pose for the community that brought them to trial.

It was, for example, fairly frequent for New Englanders afflicted by witchcraft to resort to magical countermeasures. Such countermagic included, according to one Puritan minister, "Burning the Afflicted persons hair; paring of nails, stopping up and boyling the Urine; [and] Their scratching the accused, or otherwise fetching Blood of them."[22] Yet those who specialized in the removal of witchcraft were in turn themselves often suspected of that very thing. At the same time, what we see in these common practices against witchcraft is the widespread acceptance of magic among ordinary people: so long as magic was used to help and not to injure, many people in New England saw nothing in particular wrong with it. Thus we can say that the vast majority of colonists, including those who sought to stamp out witchcraft, lived in an essentially magical cosmos.

Alchemy

To say that New England colonists lived in a magical cosmos is to say that their worldview was infused by what we are here broadly calling Western esotericism. However, there were numerous other esoteric currents in addition to magic and astrology that were also common in Europe, England, and the American colonies during the seventeenth century. Perhaps the most prominent of these was alchemy, that mysterious art and science of the transmutation chiefly of plants and metals. Alchemy is often depicted merely as the delusional searches for making gold or living forever that preceded and led to the modern sciences. Of course, there is some truth in this depiction, for it is the case that modern chemistry and physics, and even some industrial processes, have their origins in alchemy. But alchemy also represents a complete worldview of a fundamentally different nature than modern materialist rationalism; and the worldview it represents permeated the New England consciousness much more than has been generally recognized.

Alchemy was virtually omnipresent in England and Europe during the seventeenth century. Certainly this was true in most educated circles in Europe and England, so it is not surprising that one found alchemical work going on as well in the American colonies. The seventeenth and eighteenth centuries were the heyday of alchemy in western Europe; it was during this era that many of the most famous alchemical works were written, and the most intricate and beautiful of alchemical illustrations composed. The alchemical worldview had captured the imagination of the finest minds in Europe and England, as evidenced in such figures as John Dee (1527–1608), Robert Fludd (1574–1637), and Michael Maier, as well as Elias Ashmole (1617–92), to name only a few of those who composed alchemical works and undertook alchemical experiments.

What is the alchemical worldview? To answer such a question accurately is difficult, not least because alchemy has both outer and inner dimensions. It is true that alchemical work is undertaken in a laboratory, using complex glassware and other equipment, as well as numerous substances often indicated in manuscripts and books by a series of symbols that require decoding. This work, which may involve the creation of medicines from plant or mineral extracts (called spagyric), requires work with actual substances. However, this outward work is complemented by inner work; hence alchemical writings are often enigmatic, poetic, and mythological in nature, full of arcane and mysterious imagery. In essence, the aim of alchemy is restoration of paradise not only in oneself, but in nature, as well. Alchemy is therefore spiritual in nature, and this spiritual dimension separates it unequivocally from the modern sciences like chemistry or physics.

Although there has been some excellent research on alchemy in Europe and England during the seventeenth and eighteenth centuries, very little has been done on alchemy in the American colonies.[23] Consequently, literary and religious historians have almost totally neglected the extent to which alchemy was influential in informing early American life or perspectives. This neglect is understandable, because Puritanism was not exactly conducive to alchemical research itself. However, the Puritan desire to read God's signs in nature and events is a religious expression of an impulse similar to what we find in alchemy, which nonetheless, like Western esotericism generally, often occupies an uneasy position on the margin of—or even outside—organized religion. At the same time, alchemy was so prevalent during this era in Europe and England that one would certainly expect to find its representatives in New England, and in fact we do.

We should begin our survey of New England alchemists with some background from England and Europe, chiefly concerning the origins of the Royal Society in England. As we noted earlier, the early- and mid-seventeenth century in Europe and England were abuzz with rumors and publications concerning the Fraternity of the Rosy Cross, or the Rosicrucians. Although there may or may not have been an original group by this name, there is no question that the publications that announced the Rosicrucians' existence, the *Fama Fraternitatis* (1614) and the *Confessio Fraternitatis* (1615), created a terrific stir in Europe and England, and in their wake came a host of initiatory groups. As I suggest in my book *Western Esotericism, Literature, and Consciousness,* Rosicrucianism is best discerned not by claimed initiatory lineages, but by the degree to which a particular group or author espouses Rosicrucian aims, chiefly universalist tolerance, and enquiry into pansophic research, that is, into the spiritual transmutation of oneself and nature.

Out of the Rosicrucian melange came some very real groups and highly sincere individuals who set about seeking the transformation of Europe. Hugh Trevor-Roper remarks that, among them, Cromwell's movement in particular was impelled by "three philosophers . . . the real . . . and only philosophers of the English Revolution," Samuel Hartlib (1593–1670), John Dury (1596–1680), and John Comenius (1592–1690).[24] The first two men, who had left Germany for England after the failure of the Palatinate, were at the center of a movement of educational and societal reform called the "invisible college," an esoteric network of intelligentsia. All three men had been active in Rosicrucian circles, and now in England they worked at the immediate transformation of society into a peaceful, nonsectarian utopia where all the divisions of knowledge could be studied together.

Hartlib, who had published an exceptional range of works that ranged from theology to beekeeping and was intent on the application of science to human welfare in England, was the center of a circle that included numerous people important in his day. Robert Boyle, one of its members, called this group the "Invisible College." The forerunner to the Royal Society, its members included numerous other relatively well-known figures, including Kenelm Digby, Robert Child, John Dury, Johann Morian, and the Americans John Winthrop Jr. and George Starkey (1627–65). All of them were familiar with and interested in alchemy, and many practiced it. We know a good deal about Hartlib's circle due to his copious note taking and the preservation of his many papers and notebooks at Sheffield University, in England.[25]

Hartlib's papers reveal that those in his circle were profoundly interested in alchemical research, albeit of a particularly chemical and practical nature. Indeed, inventories of various laboratories, including that of Kenelm Digby and others, as well as various alchemical recipes, are found among the papers.[26] It is quite clear that Paracelsus, as well as van Helmont, influenced the Hartlib circle, and that it took for granted the possibility of transmutation, as well as the efficacy of spagyric medicines. Robert Boyle, the well-known scientist, was very much a part of this group, and early on engaged, he wrote in a letter of 1647, in "an epistle I have drawn up to persuade men to communicate all those successful recepts, that relate either to the preservation or the recovery of our health."[27] It is evident that this entire group, in England, was intent not only upon alchemical work, but also upon all manner of practical experiments, including means to sow clover and to harden the barrel of a gun.

Thus it is not surprising that one finds similar focus among American members of this circle, notably John Winthrop Jr. (1606–76), first governor of Connecticut and son of the founder of the Massachusets Bay Colony. Winthrop is a fascinating character, not only because of his life, but also because of his library. Winthrop's library was greater than that of virtually anyone of his day, not least because Winthrop had managed to purchase many alchemical books that belonged to the famous Dr. John Dee, arguably the most influential esotericist of the preceding generation, books that had Dee's own notations in the margins. Winthrop's amazing library had been partly accumulated in England before he had emigrated to America to be with his father in 1631, but he was also an assiduous collector of alchemical books thereafter. These alchemical books, which included works by virtually all the major alchemists in Europe and England, were accompanied by a very large collection of glassware for practical alchemical work and formed the basis for much of the alchemical work done subsequently in the early American colonies.[28]

Winthrop was the first—but by no means the only—citizen of colonial America to be celebrated as an alchemical adept. He was well known and much sought after as a spagyric physician, and Cotton Mather termed him after his death "Hermes Christianus." The poet Benjamin Tompson wrote of him in a funeral elegy:

> Projections various by fire he made
> Where Nature had her common Treasure laid,
> Some thought the tincture Philosophick lay
> Hatcht by the Mineral Sun in Winthrops way,
> And clear it shines to me he had a Stone
> Grav'd with his Name which he could read alone . . .
> His fruits of toyl Hermetically done
> Stream to the poor as light doth from the Sun.
> The lavish Garb of silks, Rich Plush and Rings,
> Physicians Livery, at his feet he flings.[29]

Winthrop, in other words, was famous as a spagyric physician, not least because he often dispensed his prescriptions for free to the less fortunate, very much in the alchemical tradition. He also became a charter member of the Royal Society in 1663, and was America's first astronomer, owner of one of America's first telescopes, and discoverer of the fifth moon of Jupiter. Thus we can see that his alchemical pursuits were not only in the mainstream of his day's science, winning him accolades from Cotton Mather and the most respected scientists of his day, but were part of a wide range of investigations into natural philosophy.

Winthrop was generous not only with his spagyric remedies for illness, but also with his alchemical books. It is remarkable to consider how he and his correspondents, in what were at the time tiny outposts in the vast North American wilderness, found it possible to experiment so extensively with delicate alchemical glassware and equipment. But so it was. Among those to whom Winthrop lent alchemical books and taught alchemical practices were George Starkey and Jonathan Brewster (ca. 1593–ca. 1659). Starkey has been identified as the author of the alchemical treatises attributed to Eirenaeus Philalethes that were widely influential in seventeenth- and eighteenth-century alchemy.[30] Starkey, the more flamboyant and a bit of a raconteur, is by far the more well known of the two because he traveled to England and made quite a sensation as an American alchemist among members of the Hartlib circle, but Brewster is in some ways more interesting.

Jonathan Brewster, a trader at the Plymouth Trading Post on the Connecticut River and an alchemist, was the oldest son of William Brewster, a founder of the Plymouth Colony. Jonathan Brewster lived in the frontier village of Moheken, Connecticut, where he carried on alchemical work of a sophisticated kind, not only spagyric work with plants, but also the more difficult work with metals. Brewster had borrowed a number of alchemical books from Winthrop over the years, including George Ripley's *Compound of Alchymy* (London, 1591), and Artephius's *Secret Booke* (London, 1624), bound with Nicholas Flamel's *Exposition of the Hieroglyphicall Figures* (London, 1624). By 1656, Brewster had written to Winthrop that he had attained the red elixir, and that his work was proceeding very well. He was worried that he would be unable to complete his alchemical work, due to the dangers of hostile Indians in the vicinity, who indeed subsequently killed the Brewster's female servant at "Mistres Brewster's feet, to her great affrightment."[31]

It may seem incredible, but it is indeed the case that Brewster worked away at his alchemical labor in the frontier, all the while deciphering rare alchemical symbols. About Artephius's *Secret Booke*, Brewster wrote to Winthrop that, "The many synes given in this booke I really fynd trew, from the beginning to this present; also some opperationes I see now, as formerly, which before I understode not, now I doe by Artephius' booke, as the head of the Crowe, vergines milke, &c., espetially the 2nd worke (which is most difficult) is now mad plaine. . . . I may say with Artephus, 200:page it is of a worke soe easy & short, fitter for women & yong children then sage & grave men."[32] Brewster wrote that he understood the work perfectly, but would like to see the book again in a year, for then he would undertake "the second working, which is most difficult, which will be some 3 . . . monthes before the perfect white, and afterwards, as Artephius sayth, I may burne my bokes."[33] Unquestionably, Brewster wrote Winthrop with an air of certainty; he deciphered Flamel's *Hieroglyphicall Figures* quite easily and offered to write more advice to others, "if, as I say befor, my name be not knowen to them."[34] Whether, as he anticipated, Brewster had attained the philosopher's stone while living in the wilderness, we do not know, but he died around 1659, just three years after the correspondence cited above.

If it were the case that Brewster and Winthrop were alone in such alchemical endeavors, that would be one thing, but in fact there were numerous alchemists among the first colonists in the New World, many rather highly placed in society. For instance, one of Winthrop's other alchemist correspondents was Gershom Bulkeley (1636/7–1713), the son-in-law of Harvard's president Charles Chauncy. Bulkeley, who graduated from Harvard with an M.A. in 1658, was a minister and a surgeon who kept an alchemical library on the Connecticut River and owned a library of hundreds of books, including ones by Paracelsus,

Sendivogius, and other classical alchemists. Bulkeley was chiefly interested in spagyric medicine, but of course spagyric medicine is simply a branch of traditional alchemy. In fact, President Chauncy's own son, Elnathan, who graduated from Harvard in 1661, was also very much interested in alchemical research, and was a physician.[35]

Then there was George Starkey and his circle of friends, which included John Allin, John Alcocke, and other fellow students at Harvard, all of whom were engaged in alchemical laboratory work in their late teens. It has generally been thought that Winthrop introduced Starkey to alchemy, but a note by Starkey himself reveals a different scenario:

> In the year 1644 I was first invited to this study by Mr. Palgrave, physician of New England, while I was living at Harvard College, under the tutorship and presidency of Henry Dunster. At the time I was between my sixteenth and seventeenth year. . . . I was then assiduously studying philosophy, and I began this pursuit at the end of that summer, but in the next year, namely 1645, I began to work on the true matter, with God's assistance, with a certain comrade, John Alcocke, who said goodbye to this pursuit after two years, being intimidated by its tediousness.[36]

This is an important account because it reveals how widespread alchemical research was in the American colonies: it was not, as we might previously have thought, merely the occupation of one or two eccentrics, but so commonplace that a sixteen-year old could be familiar with and begin the work!

Unlike his friend Alcocke, Starkey and another friend, Allin, continued their alchemical work, and subsequently Starkey became quite famous as an alchemist, publishing several books on the subject after he emigrated to England and joined the Hartlib circle. Starkey, who received an M.A. from Harvard around 1649, established a flourishing medical practice shortly thereafter and married a daughter of Israel Stoughton, thus becoming the brother-in-law of the future governor of Massachusetts, William Stoughton. In 1650, Starkey moved to England, primarily because in England there was the possibility of better furnaces and laboratory equipment than was to be had in the colonies. In an autobiographical note, Starkey wrote that in February 1651, in London, he began alchemical work again with a better furnace, and

> I continued thus with great labor up to the year 1654, at which time the Good God taught me the whole secret. This was the tenth year after my initial introduction to the art, which years I spent in incredible perseverance, with constancy of spirit, in highly erroneous labors.
>
> Around the end of the year 1654 the whole secret was revealed to me by divine grace. From that time up to this year of 1660, I was impeded by various obstructions from bringing the work to complete perfection. This is the sixteenth year from my first introduction to this pursuit, and the fifteenth from my labors.[37]

Starkey began to publish shortly after he had learned "the whole secret," his titles including *Natures Explication* (London: Thomas Alsop, 1657), and *Pyro-*

techny, as well as the posthumously published *Liquor Alcahest* (London: W. Cademan, 1675).

The topic of Starkey's publications on alchemy brings us to a vexed area of scholarship: the identity of Eirenaeus Philalethes, the mysterious adept from America. Philalethes became one of the most cited of seventeenth-century alchemists, particularly for his *The Marrow of Alchemy*, in two parts (London: E. Brewster, 1654/55), and *Ripley's Epistle* (London: G. Dawson, 1655), but also for *Secrets Reveal'd* (London, 1669) and *Ripley Reviv'd* (London: W. Cooper, 1678), among many other works. Starkey, when he entered the English circle of Samuel Hartlib, told the members that he had manuscripts from a New England adept, but was sworn to secrecy by him, and would publish the manuscripts unless prohibited by their author. It is curious that Starkey did not publish them all during his lifetime, but it may be that he got more mileage out of them by circulating them privately. In any event, Starkey's story of the mysterious American adept, regardless of whether he himself was in fact the author, certainly added to the mystique of the American colonial alchemists.

The American Philalethes' works shortly made their way back to North America after being published in England, as evidenced by an anonymous manuscript in the Historical Society of Pennsylvania collection, beginning "from ye Fraternaty of R. C., only cal'd ye rosy Cross." This manuscript almost certainly dates from the late-seventeenth century and consists of notes from *Secrets Reveal'd* and *The Marrow of Alchemy*, with the page numbers alongside the quotations or summaries from the various works. In it, we read for instance, that "this root of ye world, Salt, if you bring his parts together againe, then will he run from . . . from green to red, & from red to black, to a million of Collours & these miraculous alterations will not cease till he hath worked out his own resurrection."[38] Evidently these are an American alchemist's notes from various alchemical works, chiefly by Eirenaeus Philalethes, demonstrating how intertwined the English and American alchemists were: the mysterious American alchemist's works, published overseas, were now being read in America.

Our anonymous note taker was not alone, for alchemy continued to be practiced in New England even after it had waned in England and Europe. At Harvard, chemistry as taught into the eighteenth century insisted on the very real possibility of alchemical transmutation, as shown in Charles Morton's *Compendium Physicae*, a manuscript used to teach undergraduate chemistry. Morton refers to the "Artifice of Gold by Alchymy," and "the finding of the Phylosophers stone," alluding to those who have accomplished this as "Adepti," among whom are Lully, Paracelsus, and van Helmont. There is certainly no sense here that alchemy is spurious.[39] Indeed, the president of Yale from 1778 to 1795, the Rev. Ezra Stiles, was quite interested in alchemy, and recorded a number of contacts with various men engaged in alchemical pursuits, including one with Gosuinus Erkelens, whom Stiles thought a "Projector," and who had purchased a mountain near East Haddam, Connecticut known as "Governor's Ring," so named because it was "the Place to which Gov. Winthrop of N[ew] London used to resort with his Servant; and after spending three Weeks in the Woods of this Mountain in roast[in]g Ores & assaying Metals & casting gold Rings, he used to return home to N. Lond. with plenty of Gold. Hence this is called the Gov. Winthrop's Ring to this Day."[40] Here we see the clear progression of alchemy's place in early America from an actual pursuit to the stuff of legends. Of course, the legend of "Gov. Winthrop's Ring" includes nothing derogatory about alchemy—quite the reverse, in fact. But it is evident that alchemy seemed to be becoming a thing of the past; as chemistry became more and more materialist in its premises, in turn the alchemical worldview receded into the realm of legends about the earlier colonists.

At the same time, there were practicing alchemists during this same period of the eighteenth century, men like Samuel Danforth, who graduated from Harvard in 1715, and who in 1741 became a county court judge in Massachusetts. Danforth supported the Excise Bill of 1754, and was ridiculed as "Madam CHEMIA (a very philosophical Lady) who some Years since (as is well-known) discover'd that precious Stone, of which the Royal Society has been in quest a long Time, to no Purpose."[41] It is evident that Danforth's alchemical pursuits were well known; in 1773 he wrote Benjamin Franklin, offering him some of the stone, and Franklin responded by thanking him for including him "in the Benefits of that inestimable Stone, which, curing all Diseases (even old Age itself) will enable us to see the future glorious State of our America." Imagine, Franklin wrote, "the jolly Coversation we and twenty more of our Friends may have 100 Years hence on this subject, over that well replenish'd Bowl at Cambridge Commencement."[42] Only four years later, however, Danforth died at the home of his son, and Ezra Stiles noted in his diary "He was deeply studied in the Writings of the Adepts, believed the Philosophers Stone a Reality, and perhaps for Chemical knowledge might have passed among the chemists for an [Adept]."[43] The clear implication is that, although Danforth might have passed among the chemists for an adept, he was not one.

As a number of authors have shown, alchemy was certainly present in early American poetry. One finds allusions to alchemy in a poem by Nicholas Noyes that prefaced Cotton Mather's *Christianus per Ignum* (1702) and that reads in part

There is a Stone (as I am told)
That turns all Metals into Gold:
But I believe that there is none,
Save pious Meditation.[44]

Clearly, alchemical language was sufficiently commonplace to become an extended trope in a poem prefatory to a work by no less a Puritan luminary than Cotton Mather. Of course, the most well-known figure to draw extensively on alchemy in poetry during this era was Edward Taylor, whose poems envision the poet's body as the vessel for divine "Liquor" of grace from the "Golden Still" of God; or that God a cosmic "Chymist is," whose elixir heals all; or, in a frequent simile of the period, that just as Gold requires an alchemist's fire to be born, so too the spiritual man requires God's fire in order to be reborn. Randall Clack offers a good, if excessively Jungian analysis of alchemy in Taylor's work—especially as central to Taylor's Meditation I:8—but there are a number of short studies along these lines that demonstrate the prevalence of alchemical language in colonial North American literature.[45]

On the face of it, of course, it is startling to discover just how accepted alchemy was in the North American colonies. Naturally, it is not as though every other neighbor might be an alchemist, but certainly it is the case that the possibility of alchemical transmutation was widely accepted among the highly educated in the seventeenth and eighteenth centuries, and by the late-eighteenth century, even if it had largely disappeared in practice, alchemy had become integrated into American legend. This widespread acceptance of alchemy in the early colonies is important for us because, when seen in light of the prevalence of astrology and magic during that era, it becomes quite clear that early American colonial life was very much informed by Western esotericism. However, before we move on to the nineteenth century and explore how these various forms of esotericism re-emerged during the American Renaissance, we need to discuss two more primary esoteric currents in America: Böhmean Christian theosophy and secret or semisecret societies.

Theosophy

Although the life and works of Jacob Böhme, the "mystic shoemaker" of Görlitz, Germany, have been fairly extensively studied, those who followed in Böhme's path of Christian theosophy have received far less attention. Christian theosophy as a tradition, especially in the English-speaking world, has remained relatively little known, particularly in relation to early American history. I have already devoted a book, entitled *Wisdom's Children*, as well as several articles, to the history, cosmology, and metaphysics of theosophy in Europe, England, and America, so there is little point in repeating what is available already there. Here, however, we are looking at the impact of theosophy on early American life, where we find that theosophy represents the meeting point of all the esoteric currents discussed thus far, and was far more influential than one might at first think.

We have already seen, in the book of Daniel Leeds, *Temple of Wisdom*, that Böhmean theosophy was present in the English American colonies, and that Leeds's book in particular included some astrological ramifications undoubtedly of interest for Leeds as an almanac compiler. Given the translations of Böhme's works into English dating from the 1640s, we can be reasonably certain that some English publications of Böhme's writing had been brought from England to the colonies by the time of Leeds's publication, and it is likely that his book, the first published in Philadelphia, was brought out precisely because Leeds and Bradford, his printer, knew that there was already a public waiting for such a book. The earliest theosophic circle in England was in the

1620s, as I have shown in my discovery of Robert Ayshford's *Aurora Sapientiæ* (1629), and there was by 1680 in England a theosophic circle around Dr. John Pordage, later to be led by Jane Leade (1623–1704), a group known as the Philadelphians.

It is interesting to note the prominence of the word "Philadelphian" in the history of Christian theosophy. The first use of the word in English theosophy was in Ayshford's *Aurora Sapientiæ*, which was dedicated to the "sixt church att Philadelphia," an allusion to the Revelation of St. John, starting at chapter 3, verse 7, where St. John is told to write to the "angel of the church in Philadelphia," that "Because you have kept my commandment to endure trials, I will keep you safe in the time of trial which will come for the whole world, to test the people of the world. Soon I shall be with you." The later English theosophic circle around Pordage and then Leade came to be called the "Philadelphians," a name that was taken up by some theosophic circles on the continent as well, and the only time a theosophic circle took a specific name for itself. Thus it can more easily be understood why, when European or English theosophic emigrants traveled to North America, they should naturally make their way to Philadelphia, Pennsylvania.

There were numerous such emigrants from Europe and England who came to North America for religious freedom because they were practitioners of Böhmean theosophy or pansophy and had been driven from their homelands. Many of these emigrants made their way to Pennsylvania, and a characteristic account of their stories can be found in a rare work entitled *Anonimus' travels throu' Europe and America, and some visions of many heavenly mansions in the house of God.... How he conversed with the inhabitants of the other world, and found, that their respective works had actually followed them* (Ephrata: 1793). The author tells us that Anonimus, who was born in Altona, Germany, around 1700, had searched European Christianity, but found there only "Babel."[46] Eventually Anonimus found occasion to sit down by a large tree, whereupon he saw a man who said "arise and come along with me." Anonimus was led to a vision of paradise, including "many millions of men, old and young, virgins and children," "beautiful fruits without tilling the soil," "balsamick" "dew," and so forth.[47] He and some of his circle traveled to America in 1750, and settled in Leacock Township, Pennsylvania, where their poverty-stricken group became known as "Die Stillen im Lande."[48] Unfortunately, they were too otherworldly to engage in "grubbing" and clearing land, so they lived on their neighbors' charity until Anonimus died, and the followers returned to Germany.

This is, of course, not exactly a success story like those we will shortly examine, but it reveals quite clearly the expectations of some European immigrants to America who were filled with the millennialist fervor of the times. North America appeared, at least to some, as potentially the place where Christ would come again, and where paradise would again be established on earth. What more likely place for such a scenario than the vicinity of Philadelphia, the very name mentioned in the Revelation of St. John? With such expectations as "beautiful fruits without tilling the soil," one can well imagine that the tough work of grubbing would be less than enthusiastically received by new settlers, and certainly there were those who traveled back to Europe as soon as they realized what frontier life in America was actually like, and were able to muster the means of returning.

That Anonimus's millennialist expectations of America were not an exaggeration, one need only consult the diary of Johannes Kelpius (1670–1708), the leader of precisely such a group of Christian theosophic emigrants from Germany. Kelpius had become the young leader of the exodus to Pennsylvania when Johann Jacob Zimmermann, the former leader and an astrologer and geomancer, died just before the group was to sail in 1691. Kelpius's diary of the group's voyage from England—where they had met and stayed with members of the Philadelphian Society of Jane Leade—to Philadelphia, Pennsylvania, is filled with astrological notations.[49] Kelpius had brought along a telescope and kept it trained at the sky in order to see if there were signs of the approaching millennium accompanied by the return of Christ.

Kelpius, sometimes called "Magister Kelpius," is an interesting figure not least because he is said to have represented in himself virtually the whole range of esoteric currents we have discussed. Having studied with Johannes Fabricius in Helmstadt, Kelpius indeed was learned, and he does appear to have practiced a range of esoteric disciplines, including astrology, alchemy, and certainly Christian theosophy. He and his group of some forty pilgrims arrived in June 1694 in Philadelphia, where they purchased 175 acres of wilderness above the Wissahickon River near Philadelphia, land called "the Ridge." They celebrated St. John's day, or Johannestag, the time of their arrival, by building a fire on a hilltop, and then set about building their dwellings. This wild area above the Wissahickon can in fact still be visited to this day, and there remains a place known as "Hermit's Cave," which is supposed to be where Kelpius went to meditate and practice alchemy in the wilderness. There is no question that this cave, facing east, with natural springs and in a high place above a river, could be regarded as a sacred site due to its geomantic situation. Whether it is the actual site of Kelpius's cave is a matter of some dispute.[50]

There are other controversies around Kelpius and subsequent German religious communities in the area, including one that centers on the degree of their esoteric knowledge. Some believe that Kelpius and his circle were simply pious German religious refugees, and not connected much at all with European esoteric currents. Others hold that Kelpius was in fact a Rosicrucian and an alchemist, an initiate and a gnostic. The truth is most likely a combination of these two views, because it is easy to overlook the degree to which what we now call esotericism was in that time an accepted part of learning. We have already seen how widespread alchemical research was in the American colonies and how comparatively commonplace astrology and geomancy were. It is certain that Kelpius practiced these disciplines, and, what is more, that as a Böhmean theosopher he was intent on spiritual illumination.[51] Does this make him a Rosicrucian?

Frances Yates has argued, and it is now more or less accepted, that there was not one original organized group called the Rosicrucians, but rather that the term "Rosicrucian" represented a pansophic spirituality with which groups and individuals were more or less in agreement. Given this definition, it seems reasonable to think that regardless of whether Kelpius had been initiated into a specific Rosicrucian group, the actual lives of his group had much in common with the Rosicrucian vision of the perfect society. He and his group of settlers erected a forty-foot square log house in which they lived with all things in common, remaining celibate and taking new names, Daniel Falckner, for instance, becoming "Gaius" and Kelpius becoming "Philologus." They spent considerable time praying and fasting, but also worked at aiding others, not only fellow settlers, but also American Indians.[52] The group became known as the "Woman in the Wilderness," a reference to Revelation 12:5–6, and not a particularly Rosicrucian name, but many of their practices did correspond to those in the utopian visions of the Rosicrucians.[53]

In 1708, Kelpius died from consumption, evidently at least in part due to his ascetic practices in the cave on the Ridge, and subsequently the community on the Wissahickon more or less disbanded, although there remained a few hermits, including Matthai, Seelig, and Dr. de Witt.[54] It was during this time, when the original "angelic life" of the Wissahickon community had for the most part ended, many members having married and joined Pennsylvania society, that Conrad Beissel (1690–1768) arrived in 1720, having heard great things in Germany about the extraordinary spiritual experiment of Kelpius's community. Beissel visited at least some of the similar social and spiritual experimental communities in Pennsylvania after his arrival, of which there was a long history. There had been a socialist community founded by Peter Cornelius Plockhoy in 1662 at Hoorn Hill near Philadelphia; there was a Labadist community at the head of the Chesapeake River, now in Maryland; and there were numerous Anabaptist and other communities in the Pennsylvania frontier.

Beissel, along with Isaac van Bebber, a Dutchman whose father was a member of Kelpius's community, visited the Labadist Colony at Bohemia Manor, founded by Petrus Sluyter and Jasper Dankärts in 1684. The Labadist colony took its name and teachings from Jean de Labadie (1610–74), who had been a Jesuit priest but had left the church after becoming drawn to theosophy and deciding to found a spiritual community modeled after the earliest Christians. The Labadist community was celibate, and quite ascetic; the members, led by Sluyter as bishop, lived in unheated cells and with few possessions. It is highly probable that Beissel took at least some inspiration from the Labadist group for the later community he himself founded, Ephrata. As for the Labadists themselves, Sluyter died the following year and the community disbanded some time thereafter. Nevertheless, the Labadists are an example of the kinds of groups that were coming from Europe to settle in America, and of their religious fervor.

In fact, people in the American colonies often spoke derisively of "the Pennsylvania religion" because of the religious ferment of the time and, in particular, because the region became a haven for extreme forms of Protestant individualist revival. Exemplary of this tendency is Matthias Bauman, an uneducated laborer from the Rhineland, who had a vision of paradise during a serious illness. Filled with certainty of his spiritual awakening, Bauman traveled to Pennsylvania in 1719, where he taught that, with spiritual illumination, people were freed completely from sin and thereafter had no need of Bible or church or any social constraint, but would live in a state of Adamic paradise.[55] Bauman's group was called the "Newborns," and scarcely continued past his death in 1727, but it shows something of the ambience in which Beissel and the gathering members of Ephrata existed.

There is no question that we do not have space here to devote to the full history of Ephrata, the spiritual community founded by Conrad Beissel, Michael Wohlfarth, and others. Undoubtedly, this is a subject worthy of an entirely new treatment, recognizing the value of earlier authors like Sachse, Stoudt, Ernst, and Alderfer, but drawing directly on original materials like the *Chronicon Ephratense*, the records of the Ephrata community. At the same time, it is also important to acknowledge the unique position of Julius Sachse, to whom we owe the bulk of the original Ephrata records. Sachse not only compiled a vast collection of letters and documents, he also spoke extensively to people still alive during his lifetime and in a position to know, via oral transmission through the centuries, much that would have subsequently been lost without Sachse's accounts. I remark on this matter here because, in looking back at the history of Ephrata, it is all too easy to edit out or ignore the esoteric dimensions of this group and of their ambience and to try to make of them merely predecessors to more modern forms of Anabaptism. However, it is unquestionably the case that Ephrata represented a unique and long-lasting spiritual experiment among whose traditions were astrology, folk magic, and alchemy, as well as theosophic spiritual practices.

One should recognize that the forms of astrology, astromancy, magic, and alchemy found in a theosophic community like Ephrata differed from more secular forms of these esoteric traditions in that, from the viewpoint of Ephrata, they were sanctified by and part of a complete theosophic worldview. Thus, for instance, the dimensions of Ephrata's buildings and their directional orientation were determined by the spiritual significance of certain numbers and directions, in particular, the number forty and the direction east. Likewise, the astrology and magic one finds in Ephrata are spiritual in nature and meant to protect the members and structures of Ephrata itself. Hence we find fairly elaborate rituals done only on a certain day of the week, on a waning moon, in order to inscribe plates with specific magical verses from the Bible and magical symbols or words that, in turn, protect the buildings from fire.[56] Without commenting directly on the efficacy of such practices, we could note that most of the buildings at Ephrata stand to this day.

If astrology and magic were part of the theosophic worldview found at Ephrata, so too was alchemy. There are two primary kinds of alchemy we might discuss here. The first, of course, is spiritual alchemy—that is, using the terms of alchemy, like the "philosopher's stone," to describe spiritual transmutation. One finds spiritual alchemy prominent throughout the theosophic tradition, beginning with Böhme, but also in such later theosophic authors as Johann Georg Gichtel, whose *Theosophia Practica* is full of scornful references to physical alchemists. Thus one would expect spiritual alchemy to be fairly prominent at Ephrata, but one also finds, first in the Wissahickon community of Kelpius, and later at Ephrata, many rumors of the practice of physical alchemy and the production of the "elixir of life." Sachse even wrote that he possessed himself a vial of the very elixir of an original member of the Ephrata community![57] Given the prevalence of alchemy among some early American English colonists, it would hardly be surprising to find such practices among such mystically inclined German colonists as those drawn to the Wissahickon or Ephrata communities.

As I have outlined in my book *Wisdom's Children*, Ephrata included the practice of every major form of esotericism already discussed, including astrology, magic, alchemy, and theosophic contemplation. The presence of these esoteric practices at Ephrata and the consciousness of esoteric interpretations of daily life and practices (like the mystical significance of honoring the Sabbath) separate it from superficially similar communities like the Moravian community of Count Nicholas Zinzendorf (1700–60), who initially sought rapprochement with Ephrata, but whose rival Pennsylvania spiritual community eventually fell to disparaging Ephrata as the tool of Satan.[58] What fundamentally separates Ephrata from many other such communities with somewhat esoteric origins is Ephrata's explicit emphasis on mystical theosophic spirituality, which is documented by what emerged from Ephrata's printing press.

The spiritual origins of Ephrata lie in the Böhmean theosophic tradition, to which Beissel shortly began to contribute himself, with the aid first of the printer Andrew Bradford, and then of a young printer named Benjamin Franklin. The first of these publications was Beissel's *Das Büchlein von Sabbath* (Philadelphia: Bradford, 1728), shortly followed by the more interesting *Mysterion Anomias: The Mystery of Lawlessness or, Lawness AntiChrist Discover'd & Disclosed* (Philadelphia: Bradford, 1729), translated into English by Michael Wohlfarth [Welfare]. *Mysterion* is a somewhat peculiar admixture of Sabbatarianism and mysticism. Composed in the form of a dialogue, an excerpt reads as follows:

> *Son*
> Art thou fully perswaded, that the whole Restauration of all Things doth depend upon the Seventh Time, according to what I have observed in the Writings of Moses, wherein great & deep Mysteries are typified & prefigured, and especially that of the Seventh Year & afterwards of the Seven times Seven, whereupon follows that great Jubilee? So that I suppose, thou hintest thither with all the Testimonies of the Seventh-Day Sabbath.
> *Father*
> Thou hast not misunderstood it my Son, but we are not come so far yet in our discourse to treat about these things.[59]

Several aspects of this dialogue are interesting, not least the fact that it is a dialogue, a time honored form of revelation in Western esotericism, one going back at least to the *Corpus Hermeticum*.

Mysterion's emphasis on and explanation of the mystical interpretation of the Sabbath as having a transcendent significance suggests much about the origin and purpose of the Ephrata community. At one point in the dialogue, the Son realizes that the "Seventh-Day-Sabbath is a Type of the Eternal Sabbath," and later the Father says that by contrast the "Antichrist doth not belong in the Seventh Time or Number, but must be destroyed in the six working Days, and must go in the seventh in the Burning Lake until the Eighth Day."[60] What we see, in other words, is much more than a simple impulse to keep the Sabbath as a day of rest from weekly toil: rather, we see an extensive esoteric understanding of how the Sabbath symbolizes deep numerical and cosmological mysteries that deal with the end of time and the "Eternal Sabbath." Such interpretations of the sabbath reveal the central difference between Ephrata and many other spiritual communities in colonial America: Ephrata was informed much more clearly by esoteric millennialism.

Indeed, Ephrata was the origin of a great many printed books on a variety of themes. In addition to the mystical sayings of Beissel and hymnals, books published at Ephrata include the first American edition of Böhme's *Christosophia* (Ephrata, Pa.: Jacob Ruth, 1811–12); *Ein systematischer Auszug des . . . Theosophi J. Böhmens Sämmt. Schriften* (Ephrata, Pa.: Joseph Bauman, 1822); and numerous original works such as Eliseba Boehler's *Abgefordete Relation der Erscheinng eines entlebten Gests dem Publico zur Nachricht* [E. B.'s *Narrative of the visions she experienced in Virginia, her travel to Ephrata, and the following spiritual manifestations, with Beissel's concluding remarks*] (Ephrata: 1761); and Elimelech's [Emanuel Eckerling's] *Die aufgehende Lilie, ist ein Theosophischer Discurs und Unpartheyisches Zeugniss zur Behauptung der Bible und des Welt-Erloeser* [*The Emerging Lily; that is, a Theosophic Discourse and Impartial Testimony on the Precedence of the Bible and the World-Savior*] (Lancaster, Pa.: Hamilton, 1815).

This outpouring of theosophic spirituality from Lancaster County, Pennsylvania had an effect on the English-Americans as well. Exemplary of this is James Bolton's "Treatise of the Universal Restoration," in which English cleric Bolton makes the case for the doctrine held by some German and English theosophers that at the end of time God will restore all things. Bolton makes a logical case, remarking that "Two things that are diametrically opposite to each other, cannot exist to all eternity; if both are infinite; they will mutually destroy each other; if one be infinite, & the other finite, the finite must be destroyed. . . . [Thus] Christian experience proves the restoration of all things." Or, he asks, pugnaciously, "Have you more compassion on your fellow-creatures than the God that made them?"[61] Bolton continues, noting that "Those people that believe in the universal restoration live stricter: than those who don't, in general: The German Baptists all believe it, yet no people live stricter or more moral than they do, and many hundreds besides them."[62] The only reason the Calvinist-inclined English preachers oppose this doctrine of more compassionate Germans, Bolton asserts, is that it would eliminate hellfire and brimstone sermons from their preaching!

Indeed, one certainly can make the case that Ephrata represents an important hidden tributary into the development both of American religious currents and of American government itself. So far as American religious currents are concerned, Ephrata was quite influential around the time of the founding of the United States, not only because of the many books that it had published, but also because the spiritual leader who had succeeded Beissel, Peter Müller (1710–96), knew many of founding fathers, including Benjamin Franklin, George Washington, and others. James Ernst remarks that Beissel's influence was "second to no other religious leader in the Colon[ies] and he may perhaps yet emerge as the profoundest spirit in Colonial America."[63] Müller may not have been as powerful a character as Beissel, but he had great influence in the colonies around the time of the American Revolution, particularly as a spokesman for conscientious objectors and for the freedom of religion. In letters to a number of prominent figures in the American cause, Müller made the case that government should not punish those who are acting out of principle, and thereby helped bring about one of the unique characteristics of the United States: its guarantee of freedom of religion and the separation of church and state.

We might recall that Philadelphia, Pennsylvania, was the center of the founding of the United States, and that Ephrata and Germantown were nearby—not only literally, but also figuratively. When Washington's army was defeated at Brandywine on 11 September, 1777, Washington, who knew and trusted Müller, sent some five hundred wounded soldiers to Ephrata for convalescence. The sisters and brothers of the cloister cared for the soldiers without recompense throughout the long winter, and many, some from Ephrata and the surrounding region, died from typhus and scarlet fever. One of the soldiers cared for at Ephrata wrote that "I came among this people by accident, but I left them with regret. . . . Until I entered the walls of Ephrata, I had no idea of pure and practical Christianity. Not that I was ignorant of the forms, or even the doctrines of religion. I knew it in theory before; I saw it in practice then. . . . Many a poor fellow, who entered there profane, immoral, and without hope or God in the world, left it rejoicing in the Saviour."[64] Müller in particular, but Ephrata in general were highly regarded by many for their industriousness and charity.

Indeed, one wonders how much theosophy influenced Franklin's nonsectarianism. One of the distinguishing characteristics of the Böhmean theosophic current, whether in Germany, France, the Netherlands, England, or North America, was its adherents' deliberate policy of nonsectarianism. The only group of theosophers to take a name for themselves was the Philadelphian Society of Jane Leade in England, and the Philadelphians were roundly denounced for that very reason, other theosophers being convinced that the founding of a sect would inevitably lead to sectarianism and clinging to doctrines in place of direct spiritual praxis.[65] Franklin, for his part, after the famous passage in his autobiography in which he outlines his efforts to practice virtuous conduct in every aspect of his life, remarks that his view of religion was totally nonsectarian: "tho' my Scheme was not wholly without Religion, there was in it no Mark of any of the distinguishing Tenets of any particular Sect. I had purposely avoided them; for being fully persuaded of the Utility and Excellency of my Method, and that it might be serviceable to People in all Religions, and intending some time or other to publish it, I would not have any thing in it that should prejudice any one of any Sect against it."[66]

How came Franklin to this extreme nonsectarianism? Later in his autobiography, Franklin remarks on the "Dunkers" of Pennsylvania, and in particular on one Michael Welfare, or Wohlfahrt, whom we might recall as one of the members of the Beissel circle at Ephrata. Franklin writes that, according to Wohlfahrt, the theosophers were constantly being unjustly maligned by members of various sects, to which Franklin replied that they should write up a list of their doctrines. Wohlfahrt replied:

> When we were first drawn together as a Society . . . it had pleased God to inlighten our Minds so far, as to see that some Doctrines which we once esteemed Truths were Errors, and that others which we had esteemed Errors were real Truths. . . . Now we are not sure that we are arriv'd at the End of this Progression, and at the Perfection of Spiritual or Theological Knowledge; and we fear that if we should once print our Confession of Faith, we should feel ourselves as if bound and confin'd by it, and perhaps be unwilling to receive farther Improvement; and our Successors still more so.[67]

Franklin observes that such modesty is "perhaps a singular Instance in the History of Mankind, every other Sect supposing itself in Possession of all Truth."[68] However, this nonsectarianism was not rare in theosophic tradition, and undoubtedly helped to form the prevailing attitude of religious tolerance in the early United States.

What happened to Ephrata and its affiliated communities, like the later one at Snow Hill, Pennsylvania? Although they continued and even prospered into the middle of the nineteenth century, by the last half of the nineteenth century they languished and their last members died in the twentieth century. One has to suspect that the waning of these theosophic communities is directly linked to the progressive loss of their impelling esoteric dimensions. The communities that surrounded Kelpius and Beissel were certainly infused with the major currents of European esotericism, but by the mid-nineteenth century, these currents were waning in the face of modern materialism and rationalism. One sees this in the virtual disappearance of the astrological almanacs and alchemical practice in North America: the esotericism that had very much informed life in the early American colonies had been supplanted by modernism, at least to a great degree. Communities like Ephrata, once bound together by their esoteric spirituality, inevitably disbanded when mere modes of living began to replace that spirituality: the appearance remained of communal spiritual life, but the emphasis on inner awakening slowly disappeared, and so the communities dissolved.

Of course, Ephrata and its affiliated, largely Germanic communities were not the only sources of theosophic spirituality in North America: there was also an English theosophic strain that continued the line of Böhme in the works of John Pordage and William Law (1686–1761). Law's writing, in particular, was influential in North America's religious revivals, as evidenced for instance by Henry Alline (1748–84), who was largely responsible for what became known as the "Nova Scotia Awakening."[69] That Alline had read and drew much from Law, who in turn was profoundly indebted to Böhme, is certain. However, because Law's work is abstracted from Böhme, and Alline in turn abstracted his work from Law, one does not easily see at first glance the affiliations between Böhme and Alline. Yet as Alline's editor, George Rawlyk, remarks, "A careful examination of Alline's theological writing [in particular *Two Mites* (1781) and *The Anti-Traditionist* (1783)] underscores the fact that he was very dependent on the four English writers William Law, John Fletcher, Edward Young, and John Milton."[70] Of course, not everyone applauded Alline's indebtedness: John Wesley, for example, grumbled about his rival evangelist, "he has been dabbling in Mystical writers in matters which are too high for him, far above his comprehension. I dare not waste my time upon such miserable jargon."[71]

What we see emerging here is the kind of division one sees frequently from the time modern theosophy emerged with the work of Böhme: on one hand we find those drawn to theosophic mysticism, and on the other we find those who cannot abide it. Although theosophy was influential in New England at the time of the American Revolution, it remained often an underground or suppressed current, denigrated by those who insisted instead on the more social or outward dimensions of Christianity. Of course, theosophy did not disappear as a force in American religious life; not only did Ephrata continue to publish theosophic books into the nineteenth century, but periodically, theosophy unexpectedly re-emerged in American thought.[72]

An example of this re-emergence is certainly to be seen with the emigration from Germany to America of Johann Georg Rapp (1757–1847), a Böhmean theosopher who established several theosophic communities in America.[73] Rapp was born in Württemberg, Germany, and although he did not begin life as a promising spiritual reformer, by midlife in the 1790s, he had established a small group of followers and had been almost exiled from his homeland. Rapp's group believed in absolute chastity, which they derived from the teachings of Jacob Böhme regarding the primordial androgyny of humanity and the necessity for returning to such a paradisal state. Rapp's followers finally emigrated to Harmony, Pennsylvania, north of Pittsburgh, in 1804, after corresponding with Thomas Jefferson regarding the purchase of land in Ohio, and in 1814 developed another community at New Harmony, Indiana, which they in turn left to return to Pennsylvania in 1825, despite the fact that they had become extremely prosperous and widely known in Indiana.

That the Harmonists in general and Rapp in particular were deeply influenced by major esoteric currents is clear. First, their symbol—widely known because it was used on the goods they produced, which were renowned for their quality—was the golden rose, which derived in part from Luther's use of the same symbol but also undoubtedly from the Rosicrucian or Rose + Cross movement in Europe. Rosicrucian millennialist tendencies certainly influenced the Harmonists's expectations of the coming millennium or thousand years of peace and paradise prophesied in the Revelation of St. John. Second, Rapp himself, as we already noted, drew his teachings explicitly from Jacob Böhme and the theosophic current. Third, Rapp definitely practiced alchemy, for which purposes he had as a companion a beautiful young woman named Hildegard Mutschler.[74] He sought to find the philosopher's stone, the key not only to transmuting other metals into gold, but also to health and transcendent wisdom and knowledge, thus alienating many of his more conservative followers. What is more, when Bernhard Mueller arrived from Germany claiming that he was the Messiah, and was welcomed by the Harmonists as the "Lion of Judah," he came also claiming he had the true philosopher's stone.[75] When the Rapp community finally dissipated after Rapp's death in 1857, Rapp was found to have accumulated half a million dollars in gold, kept in a vault in his home, and probably chiefly from the joint property and businesses of the Harmonists.

All of this goes to show that all of the primary esoteric currents we have been discussing continued into nineteenth-century America. What is more, here we are only discussing the more well-known groups and individuals; there remain countless lesser-known people during this same period, including the numerous seceders from or spin-offs of the more famous Rosicrucian, theosophic, or alchemical practitioners, who lived in relative obscurity scattered across the United States. It is not necessary for us to delve into details on all of these, nor is it even possible here; instead, we must turn to the next phase of theosophic emergence in the nineteenth century, with the American Renaissance itself. However, we must first examine two final influential esoteric movements in colonial America.

Rosicrucianism and Freemasonry

One could hardly conclude a survey of major esoteric currents in early American colonial life without recognizing the importance of Rosicrucianism and Freemasonry. I have saved these for the end of this overview because these currents draw upon much of what we have already discussed and may be considered pansophic rather than theosophic because they are less specifically Christian than theosophy and more freely draw upon traditions like Hermeticism. Furthermore, they emphasize very much the cosmological over the metaphysical. We have already discussed the origins of these movements in Europe, chiefly during the early-seventeenth century; it remains to recapitulate briefly these origins and to sketch how they, in turn, were influential in the founding of the American republic.

We must begin by recalling the esoteric scene in Europe during the eighteenth century. During that era, although of course there were some who den-

igrated esotericism, the cultural landscape was filled with various esoteric secret or semisecret societies. By that time, Rosicrucianism had gone from a series of enigmatic treatises published at the beginning of the seventeenth century to a wide array of actual initiatory organizations. As Antoine Faivre
remarks, this was the era of initiatory groups, and to this era many current
groups trace their origins. Indeed, Faivre calls the eighteenth century "A
Century of Initiations" and maps the outlines of what is undoubtedly one of
the most complicated and confusing areas of esoteric history, filled as it is with
countless figures, currents, and competing claims.[76]

Regardless of whether there were actual Rosicrucians behind the treatises
that created a furor in Europe during the early-seventeenth century, by the late-
eighteenth century when the United States was being founded, there were numerous initiatory groups that took the Rosicrucian name, or a similar one, like
the Gold- und Rosenkreutz [Gold and Rosy-Cross] Order that emerged during the 1770s in Germany and in 1777 formally affiliated numerous lodges under the name "Golden Rosy-Cross of the Ancient System."[77] Faivre outlines a
few of the major initiatory societies of this era:

> the 'Swedish System,' founded around 1750 by Karl Friedrich Eckleff; the
> Order of the 'Blazing Star,' whose founder is Théodore Henri de Tschoudy
> (1766); . . . the Asiatic Brethren, for Austria and especially the south of
> Germany (a creation of Heinrich von Ecker-und-Eckhoffen around 1779);
> the Primative Rite of the Philadelphians, founded by F. A. Chefdebien in
> 1780; . . . the Illuminated Theosophers, patterned after Swedenborgianism,
> important in England and the United States. . . . and the Hermetic Rite, es-
> tablished around 1770, inspired explicitly by the teachings of Hermes
> Trismegistus. . . .[78]

From this litany of groups, we can see that many of them appeared precisely
during the time that the United States emerged as a nation. As we shall see, there
are more than coincidental connections between this plethora of European and
English secret societies and those responsible for the founding of the United
States.

There is, of course, a certain inventiveness among some of those responsible for explaining the origins and effects of secret societies, particularly regarding the founding of the United States. One finds, for instance, rampant and
often wildly fictive accounts of connections between some of the German orders, particularly that associated with Adam Weishaupt and the "Illuminati,"
and the founding fathers of the United States. Such accounts feed the popular
imagination, but are often historically inaccurate, even if they are entertaining.
However, the fact remains that some esoteric currents really were influential for
the founding fathers, in particular, Rosicrucianism and Freemasonry. But many
of these influences were somewhat indirect.

To begin to see how this was so, it is important to recognize what
Rosicrucianism and Freemasonry represented in terms of esoteric, pansophic
social movements. Above all, these movements emphasized what later became

the widely accepted values of modernity, especially a universalist tolerance for all religions combined with an emphasis on rationalism and morality. Throughout the seventeenth century, but particularly during the initial years of the Rosicrucian furor that followed the publication of the *Fama Fraternitatis* (1614) and the *Confessio Fraternitatis* (1615), one finds in Europe widespread hope that there is emerging a new era for humanity, a "sixth age" in which all the sciences and arts can be united in a new political arrangement based in religious and social universalism with a spiritual center. In the *Fama*, the author speaks of a "general reformation, both of divine and human things," hastened by the wise who are called to "learn all that which God hath suffered man to know," "all faculties, sciences, and arts, and whole nature, as that which . . . would direct them, like a globe or circle, to the only middle point and *centrum*."[79] The *Confessio* offers a similar certainty that we shall "merrily and joyfully go forth to meet the rising sun."[80]

The nonsectarian universalism of these Rosicrucian treatises derived from Christian theosophy, but in Rosicrucianism took on a pansophic character that emphasized cosmology and universal knowledge over spirituality. Although there may or may not have been any original Rosicrucian order behind these treatises, they did spark such orders all over western Europe, as well as a spate of Rosicrucian illustrations and treatises that emphasized the mysteries of the cosmos, in particular alchemy, astrology, herbalism, magic, and Kabbalistic correspondences. When we recall that Rosicrucianism emerged roughly during the so-called rationalist "enlightenment," the term "Rosicrucian enlightenment" takes on an interesting flavor, for it both participated in and opposed the rationalists. On the one hand, Rosicrucian literature does envision a peaceful, universalist culture rather similar to that of the rationalists, but at the same time it also emphasizes esoteric cosmology, which undoubtedly made uneasy the more hard-boiled rationalists or materialists of the era, not to mention the more conventional Christians of various sects.

Out of the Rosicrucian impulse emerged Freemasonry in the early eighteenth century. Originally, masonry was "operative," meaning that it was one of the trade guilds of the middle ages, but in the early-eighteenth century in England what became known as "speculative" Freemasonry emerged, meaning that the Masons involved were not actually Masons by trade. Important in this transformation from an extension of the medieval guild system to an esoteric association were the Rev. John Desaguliers, a scientist and clergyman, and the Rev. James Anderson, author of the influential *Constitutions, Laws, Charges, Orders, Regulations . . . of the . . . Fraternity of Accepted Free Masons* (London, 1723). Desaguliers's dual interest in science and religion corresponds to the interests of the earlier Rosicrucians; and Anderson's *Constitutions* made it clear that Freemasonry was then speculative in nature and organized hierarchically through a system of affiliated lodges. Masonry had become an esoteric social institution that would grow rapidly in influence and importance.

In little over a decade, a young printer in Pennsylvania named Benjamin Franklin published Anderson's *Constitutions*. This was no coincidence. Freemasonry spread quickly in the American colonies, being especially attractive to those drawn to a semisecret society that was dedicated to self improvement and that encouraged rational scientific exploration, as well as more esoteric pursuits. Relatively soon, Freemasonry's English lodges included many upper class and even royal members; for an ambitious young man like Franklin, Masonry was the perfect way to advance socially. Although on the one hand Masonry was hierarchically organized with a Grand Lodge, numerous subordinate lodges, and ritual degrees up to Master Mason, on the other hand Masonry was also a means for more-or-less democratic social advancement, because when one joined, one became simply a brother Mason regardless of one's social status.

It is interesting that Franklin makes no mention in his famous *Autobiography* of his Masonic membership—indeed, one could not tell from it that he was a Mason at all, much less provincial grand master and the initiator, when in France, of no less a person than Voltaire himself! But such is, in fact, the case. One can tell from Franklin's *Autobiography* that he had sympathies with Masonic values, because he early on began his well-known practice of self-improvement, working on each of the virtues day-by-day. This, of course, is very akin to the Masonic aim of encouraging its members to be "good men and true." Franklin was very interested, as well, in closed or semisecret societies; indeed, he began several, including his "Junto" discussion group. In his autobiography, he writes only that he "esteem'd the Essentials of every Religion" chiefly as they "inspire, promote, or confirm Morality."[81] Franklin also conceived, in 1731, of founding a sect that "should be spread at first among young and single Men only . . . [based in the] Practice of the Virtues" and "kept a Secret till it was become considerable."[82] Such a transreligious "sect" was in fact Masonry, which Franklin joined in Philadelphia in February 1731, becoming grand master of the Lodge in 1734.[83]

Although Franklin was an extremely prominent Mason and capitalized on the fact, he did not write publicly about this. Whenever he visited England or France, he drew on his Masonic connections, and by 1756, he was a member of the Royal Society. When Franklin was initiated into the French *Loge des Neuf Souers* in Paris, there appeared a flurry of etchings with the symbols of America combined with Masonic symbols, and when in 1778, Franklin initiated the aged Voltaire into the same lodge, he made Freemasonry even more famous.[84] In 1779, Franklin was elected grand master of the *Loge des Neuf Souers*, and brought in numerous other famous political, literary, and scientific figures. At exactly the same time that Franklin organized Freemasonry in France, it had emerged as a powerful force in America.

That Masonry quickly permeated the American colonies, however, is obvious. Out of the fifty-six signers of the Declaration of Independence, fifty-three were Masons. George Washington became a Mason on 4 November 1752, and what is more, he strongly encouraged his generals, officers, and soldiers in the Continental Army to join also, so much so that he actually appeared in full Masonic regalia before the troops while celebrating the retaking of Philadelphia in 1778.[85] It is difficult to underestimate how important Masonry was to the founding of America. As Bernard Fay writes,

> All the staff officers Washington trusted were Masons, and all the lead-
> ing generals of the army were Masons; Alexander Hamilton, John Marshall,
> James Madison, General Greene, General Lee, General Sullivan, Lord
> Sterling, the two Putnams, General Steuben, Montgomery, Jackson, Gist,
> Henry Knox, and Ethan Allen were Masons. They all gathered around their
> Master Mason Washington and they all met at the "Temple of Virtue," . . . a
> rude structure flanked by two Pillars Jachin and Boaz. The monument had
> been built by order of the Commander-in-Chief as an assembly hall for the
> meeting of the [military] field lodges.[86]

Furthermore, whereas Franklin officiated in French Freemasonry, and Washington officiated at American military Freemasonry, the center of the revolutionary movement in America was the St. Andrew Lodge, which met in Boston and was led by Dr. Joseph Warren—a close friend of Franklin who died at the Battle of Bunker Hill—and which included among its members Paul Revere, who later became grand master of Massachusetts.[87] This lodge met at "The Green Dragon, or the Arms of Freemasonry," a Mason-owned tavern near the Boston Harbor, from which emerged the Boston Tea Party of 1773, as well as the chain of events that lead to the Declaration of Independence in 1776.

Although the importance is obvious of so many prominent Masonic figures in the American Revolution, perhaps of greater significance is the influence of Masonic governance and ideals on the establishment of the United States. The governmental structure of the United States, with local, state, and federal levels, parallels in some respects the Masonic structure of individual lodges and Grand lodges. As soon as the thirteen colonies organized themselves into thirteen states, there were also Masonic lodges in all thirteen states. We have already alluded to how Masonry in its modern forms emerged from or shared Rosicrucian ideals of universalist nonsectarianism, and the union of science, the arts, and religion to bring about a new era in human affairs via a cosmopolitan republic of educated and wise men, free of both monarchic and clerical control. It is hardly an accident that in Europe the Declaration of Independence was largely viewed as a document of Masonic principles, or that the strongest defenders of the colonies in the British Parliament included William Pitt and Edmund Burke, both Freemasons themselves. The dream of the American republic emerged in no small way from the ideals of Rosicrucianism and Freemasonry.

By the early-nineteenth century, Masonry had become so prevalent in the United States that it was regarded by many, especially in evangelical Christian circles but also among many non-Mason citizens, as dangerous to civic well-being. This resentment of Masonry, and in particular of Masons' undue political and social power via their connections, coalesced and become widespread due to the notorious disappearance of William Morgan on 14 September 1826. Morgan was a stonemason living in western New York state who intended to publish a book entitled *Illustrations of Masonry*, in which he planned to unveil the secrets of Masonry that he had taken an oath to keep. A group of Masons set fire to the printer's shop where the book was being printed, and when the fire was subsequently put out, the Masons had Morgan and his printer, David Miller, arrested. When Mrs. Morgan went to the jail to find her husband, he was gone, and was never seen again. Citizens became incensed at Morgan's disappearance, and out of this anger emerged the Antimasonic party, the first third party in American history. In a number of states, chiefly in New England, the Antimasonic party rivalled and in some instances surpassed the Democrats and Republicans in votes.[88]

Antipathy toward Masons in the United States did not stop at creating a political party—there was also violence, on both sides, and a great deal of mutual recrimination, suspicion, and even hatred. In March 1830, Antimasons forced their way in to the Knights Templar order in Boston, expecting to find an arsenal sufficient to arm two thousand Masons who, it was supposed, were preparing a coup d'état! Instead, they found forty-three ritual swords and some spittoons. Elsewhere, Masonic buildings were defaced, and angered Masons in turn shouted down and drove away Antimasonic speakers. As Paul Goodman writes, "both sides played for keeps. Antimasons sought the total destruction of American Freemasonry . . . [and] by the early 1830's, American Freemasonry was in retreat."[89] Although Masonry did recover from this period of attack, the hostility toward Masonry did not vanish, but remained an undercurrent in American society, as well as a spur toward the creation of competing quasi-Masonic fellowships like the Grange association for farmers, the Odd Fellows, and the Elks, Moose, and other lodges.

The emergence of Antimasonry goes a long way toward explaining why, although Masonry was immensely important in the founding of the United States and its ideals influential for the writings of many of the first great American literary-political figures, Masonry had very little to do with what has become known as the American Renaissance: the period that began immediately after the Antimasonic furor drew to a close in the 1830s. Yet even if we do not find the major literary figures of the mid-nineteenth century to be Masons, they were certainly influenced by the Masonic ideals that informed the founding of the United States. Masonry preserved, in its symbols, rituals, and writings, aspects of the prior European esoteric currents, and it was to these same currents that many writers of the American Renaissance returned. To this reemergence of European esotericism in mid-nineteenth century America we now turn.

four

The Esoteric Ambience of the
American Renaissance

There is a European witticism to the effect that America is where European traditions go when they die. Of course the actual relationship between European esoteric traditions and American esotericism is much more complex and reciprocal. One could as easily say that America is where European traditions go to be reborn, for this more accurately expresses the movement back and forth from Europe and England to the United States, and from North America back to Europe and England. Such a movement is precisely what we find when we survey the history of Western esotericism in the United States during the mid-nineteenth century: it is quite closely intertwined with the history of European and English esotericism. As always, however, this history is rarely if ever one of social movements so much as of remarkable individuals.

When discussing the American Renaissance, we may use the word "Renaissance" in at least two ways. First, there is the more parochial sense of the first wave of great American authors who brought about the founding of the United States, including Washington, Hamilton, Jefferson, and the others, which is followed by the second wave, the American Renaissance of the mid-nineteenth century. But there is a second, wider sense in which we might also speak of an American Renaissance, and this one is more pertinent to our present theme: that just as esotericism played an important role in the earlier European Renaissance, so too esotericism was a significant influence in the American Renaissance. We might recall that the Italian Renaissance was inspired chiefly by two giant intellectual figures, Marsilio Ficino (1433–99), and Pico della Mirandola (1463–94), who were themselves inspired by their rediscovery of the great Western esoteric traditions of Jewish Kabbala, Hermeticism, and Neoplatonism. As we shall see, the American Renaissance had related origins.

Those origins, however, are for the most part not to be found in broad social movements or in secret societies, but in the rediscovery of esoteric traditions by remarkable individuals. This is particularly true in America, where individualism and self-reliance have always been primary among American values. It is for this reason that we will have to examine the major figures of the American Renaissance one-by-one, for although in some cases there may have been mutual interests and shared investigations, as in the case of Bronson Alcott and Ralph Waldo Emerson, for instance, even here there are real differences in these authors' predilections and works, particularly when it comes to esoteric interests.

At the same time, we would do well to consider first the larger history of esotericism in America in the nineteenth century, within which context we can then place more clearly each of these individual figures. During this period, many of the major currents of Western esotericism that had been so prominent in colonial America had waned, gone underground, or for the most part disappeared. There were still farmers' almanacs being printed and used, and undoubtedly here or there one could find a lone figure who still pursued alchemical work. However, esoteric currents continued primarily through oral or folk traditions; and publications of annual almanacs waned, while there were no major alchemical works published at all.

It is true that there were some extensive astrological works published in America during the nineteenth century, including continuations of the earlier Germanic forms of esotericism that emerged in Pennsylvania, as well as English and other continental streams. One finds, for instance, Eberhart Walpern's *Glucks-Rad, oder Würfel-Buch: durch welches man nach astrologischer Art auf unterschiedliche Fragen, so den zwölf himmlischen Hausern nach, abgeheilt sind, eine Antwort finden kann. . . . [Wheel of Fortune,: through which one can find an answer to different questions via the astrological art]* (Reading, Pa.: Heinrich Sage, 1820), or *Hague's Christian Almanac* for 1846, in which the Philadelphia author, an Englishman who arrived in America in 1832, proclaims himself the first U.S. astrologer and includes a letter to President James Polk, while closely tying his astrological almanac to Christianity, with each day devoted to a saint or important Christian figure. But Hague's efforts are, of course, merely strategies to bolster the importance of astrology in a society that no longer paid it nearly the attention it had a hundred or more years previously, whereas Walpern's work is obviously intended for an ethnic German audience only. There is also *Egyptische Geheimnisse, oder das Zigeuner-Buch gennant. . . . [Egyptian Mysteries, or the Gypsy-Book]* (Harrisburg, Pa.: Gustav Peters, 1844), which includes numerous remedies for man and beast, remedies attributed to the gypsies, therefore exoticised.

A more extensive work, published in Boston by the author in 1854, was Dr. C. W. Roback's *The Mysteries of Astrology and the Wonders of Magic, including A History of the Rise and Progress of Astrology and the Various Branches of Necromancy*. Roback's book drew on his Swedish family's background in esotericism, and he included a wide range of esoteric traditions, including geomancy. *The Mysteries of Astrology* includes some general historical discussion, but is also meant as a kind of esoteric primer and shows that there certainly were some people in the United States who kept alive various forms of European esotericism. Such works reveal what is more an undercurrent than a primary current in American society at the time: there were astrologers and perhaps even a few alchemists, but the days when major political and social figures engaged in such pursuits were, for the most part, long past.

There were three major avenues, outside of folk tradition, by which esoteric currents continued in America, albeit in new forms: spiritualism, variant forms of Mesmerism and healing, and various experimental forms of Christianity. At least the first two, and arguably the third as well, were more popular movements than esoteric ones, but all of them continued or derived from earlier Western esoteric traditions. Spiritualism was of course represented in earlier magical traditions as necromancy (i.e., summoning of the dead to interrogate or control them). However, what before the nineteenth century was the practice of the individual magician or a secret esoteric lodge, in the nineteenth century became much more widely known and practiced. The same is true of Mesmerism and various forms of alternative healing that became popular during the nineteenth century: if before, these had been the province of one or another esotericist or secret lodge who experimented privately, in nineteenth-century America these movements entered into society as a whole, chiefly as products or services for sale. The same rule even holds for the various forms of Christian sectarianism of the nineteenth century: whereas in English theosophy of the early eighteenth century, for example, one finds esoteric circles espousing millennialism and visionary spiritual practices, in America in the nineteenth century, one finds similar movements except on a much larger and more exoteric scale.

In the first sentence of his book *Mediums, and Spirit-Rappers, and Roaring Radicals*, Howard Kerr asserts that spiritualism in America began in 1848 with the Fox sisters, thus echoing a long critical tradition of ignoring European and even American esoteric precedents for this phenomena of spirit manifestation. In fact, there is a long history of such phenomena in both Europe and North America. In 1696, English author John Aubrey published his *Miscellanies*, which included sections on apparitions, voices, impulses, omens, knockings, blows invisible, prophesies, marvels, and magic, and 1651 had seen the publication of the English translation of H. C. Agrippa's *Three Books of Occult Philosophy*, an earlier and influential compendium of magical lore that includes sections on how spirits can be called up, on prophetic dreams, and so forth.[1] From the sixteenth to the nineteenth centuries, Western esoteric traditions were already long since based upon connections between the invisible realms of spirits and the physical world.

One of the specific esoteric traditions that provided precedent for spiritualism was crystal or mirror gazing, like that of Dr. John Dee and Edward Kelly, recorded in magical diaries and published by Meric Casaubon as *A True and Faithful Relation of What Passed for many Yeers between Dr. John Dee and Some Spirits* (London, 1656). Dee and Kelly developed a very complex and intricate set of revelations out of Kelly's visionary contacts with spirits, and their revelations, taken as a whole, form a very interesting comparison to the later nineteenth-century American spirit revelations of figures like Andrew Jackson Davis and Thomas Lake Harris. It is true that Casaubon published Dee's account, but this was primarily to discredit them: Dee and Kelly were more or less solitary and esoteric in their practices, which corresponds more generally to what we find in the European esoteric traditions that preceded American spiritualism. Practitioners tended to keep their scrying secret.

So, too, in the eighteenth century one finds numerous instances of European esoteric groups or lodges that practiced communication with spirits, including, as Wouter Hanegraaff points out, "illuminist orders such as Martinez de Pasqually's *Elus-Cohens*, Dom Antoine-Joseph Pernety's *Illuminés d'Avignon*, and Jean-Baptiste Willermoz's *Chevaliers Bienfaisants de la Cité Sainte*."[2] Such esoteric orders' practices included both what they regarded as angelic communications as well as communications with departed spirits, the latter of which of course technically falls under the category of necromancy.

Possible links between European necromantic magical traditions and the emergence of nineteenth-century spiritualism have not yet been carefully considered, at least so far as I know, but it seems a natural subject for inquiry.[3] That there are links between at least one British esoteric lodge and the emergence of American spiritualism is certainly suggested by the remarks of Emma Hardinge Britten (1823–99) in her autobiography. There, she alludes to a secret British group of "occultists" called the "Orphic Society" that awakened her own capacity to be a medium.[4] Britten then became a great proselyte for spiritualism, traveling, lecturing, and giving demonstrations throughout America, where she met such luminaries as Fenimore Cooper, the poets Longfellow and Whittier, Washington Irving, and many other "writers, poets, and celebrities."[5]

Was nineteenth-century American spiritualism in fact directly inspired by European secret lodges? C. G. Harrison, who wrote in the late-nineteenth century on esotericism of his day, proposed an interesting hypothesis about how the spiritualist phenomena began that swept Europe, England, and most of America in the nineteenth century.[6] According to Harrison, in the words of Christopher Bamford, "occult groups, faced with the increasing materialism of Europe in the nineteenth century, *instigated* the phenomena of spiritualism in order to drive a breach in natural science's understanding of reality; that this ploy was undermined by its own success and the firm conviction that arose almost immediately accounting for the phenomena in terms of the dead."[7] This is, of course, a rather startling assertion, but although at first it might seem implausible, there have been others who speculated along similar lines, most notably René Guénon. What separates earlier esoteric forms of spiritualism or necromancy from the form that swept America during the nineteenth century is that earlier forms were clearly limited to one or a small group of individuals and kept secret. Examples of such phenomena in the eighteenth and early nineteenth century are now fairly well known, but at the time were kept quiet; whereas American spiritualism was nothing if not exoteric and widely publicized.

In other words, whether or not we accept the hypothesis of Harrison that some occult lodge or lodges brought about spiritualism, we can be certain that spiritualism as it emerged in the America of the nineteenth century was very different from its esoteric origins precisely because it was so public. The conspiracy hypothesis is somewhat questionable because spiritualism in America for the most part did not take place among esotericists, but among relatively common folk. Probably the most famous of the spiritualist cases involved the young daughters (twelve and thirteen years old) of a Methodist farmer named John Fox, in 1847 in Hydesville, New York. The daughters, Katherine and Margaret, developed a simple code to understand the rapping of the spirits, and people flocked from the surrounding countryside to see them "perform." Indeed, it shortly became a performance, after P. T. Barnum got involved as their promoter, and the girls became celebrities.

There were countless other similar cases, with séances springing up all over the United States in the mid-nineteenth century. Spirit seers vied for public attention with fortune-tellers and with the new efflorescence of psychic phenomena, including table lifting, mysterious writings on slates, ectoplasmic manifestations, and marvels of clairvoyance. Spiritualism was sensational, that is true, but it was also a quasi-religious phenomenon, for as conventional Christianity was assaulted not only by new biblical criticism but also by materialism and scientific rationalism, people increasingly looked for some confirmation that there was something in this world beyond the merely physical. Spirit rapping and the like provided people with the assurance that there were invisible beings, and that personalities survived death. It may also be noted that spiritualism cut across classes in America: one found it in the wealthier upper classes, but also among middle- and lower-class people, for it spoke to many peoples' need to believe in spiritual survival and paranormal phenomena. Although spiritualism may have had predecessors in European esoteric lodges, in America, it was not very esoteric at all.

The second primary American movement derivative of European esotericism during the mid-nineteenth century was Mesmerism, or "animal magnetism," now known chiefly as hypnotism. Here again, as with spiritualism, it is true that there were definite antecedents in eighteenth-century European esotericism to these more public nineteenth-century phenomena. The peculiar phenomena associated with animal magnetism are, of course, associated with Friedrich Mesmer (1734–1815), an Austrian physician and astrologer who became well known in Paris for the miraculous healings and weird psychic phenomena that accompanied his stage shows. Mesmer was certainly not the first to discover the powers of hypnosis and animal magnetism, but he was one of the first to capitalize on it and make it a public affair. Prior to Mesmer one finds some esoteric orders that incorporated similar phenomena into their rituals; what distinguished Mesmer was that, with the infallible instinct of the showman, he made animal magnetism the talk of the town, a stage event. Yet somewhat true to the origins of what he practiced, Mesmer also began a more-or-less esoteric "Society of Harmony" in 1783 that drew its symbolism chiefly from Masonry.[8]

Animal magnetism, or Mesmerism, spread far beyond Mesmer's society, however, particularly when in America it became linked with the "New Church" of the followers of Emanuel Swedenborg, and with the homeopathy of Samuel Hahnemann (1755–1843). It is easy for us today to underestimate the appeal of animal magnetist phenomena during the mid-nineteenth century, but in fact its wide appeal derived not least from the fact that it joined, seemingly inseparably, science and religion under the banner of a new religious or spiritual science. Animal magnetism looked scientific enough, with its use of iron and water and theories of universal fluids and vitalism, but at the same time drew upon the pre-existing theosophic "theology of electricity" while offering the miraculous healings often associated only with religious shrines or saints.[9] Wouter Hanegraaff, in his major study *New Age Religion and Western Culture* (1998) rightly concludes that "the continuity between esotericism, Mesmerism, and occultism is therefore not in any doubt, and Mesmer's theory may legitimately be regarded as a modern presentation of *magia naturalis*," yet at the same time was seen as "the triumph of science over nature."[10]

One of the most important of the American Mesmerist subjects was Andrew Jackson Davis (1826–1910), known as the "seer from Poughkeepsie, New York." In 1843, at the age of seventeen, Davis was a volunteer for a stage presentation of Mesmerism by one Professor Grimes of Castletown Medical College. Although Grimes's experiment with Davis was a failure, it was followed by a successful effort by a local tailor named Levingston, and Davis subsequently reported that it was a nightmarish experience: "Horrid thoughts of disorganization continued to distress me. Naught but an eternal midnight clothed my tender spirit, and I was filled with teror. . . . I sank to the lowest depths of forgetfulness."[11] Despite this unpromising beginning, Davis soon became an accomplished trance subject with clairvoyant abilities that included the capacity to diagnose and prescribe for various ailments. His prescriptions reveal their resemblance to European folk medicine and witchcraft, with such remedies as applying rats' skins behind the ear to cure deafness, or chewing chamomile flowers to alleviate a sore throat.

Davis soon began to publish books on his spiritual illuminations via Mesmerism, among them *The Principles of Nature, Her Divine Revelations, and a Voice to Mankind* (1847), the title of which shows clearly enough how Davis's work conjoined science (the principles of nature), a kind of nature religion (its divine revelations), and millennialism (a voice to mankind). This millennialism, however, differed rather strikingly from much of the Christianity to which it was indebted, for Davis and his followers anticipated a coming golden age, as when he wrote with a kind of shrieking "the tide of intelligence is rising, and is flowing to and over all nations, even as an ocean of truth and knowledge. . . . IT EBBS NOT AGAIN!"[12] Davis in his later work never tired of deriding the Christian clergy, of which he considered "none is absolutely more unenviable and more corrupting."[13] Over time, Davis developed a group of followers that included many figures also prominent in what came to be known as the spiritualist movement.

The admixture of influences in Davis's work is quite evident and fairly complex, even if he, like Swedenborg before him, claimed that he was uninfluenced by any other writer. This claim of not having read the works of any seers prior to himself is, of course, a fairly common refrain among western visionary figures and is meant to emphasize the originality of the seer's own work, but one finds in Davis's work an unmistakeable indebtedness to the socialism of Charles Fourier, as when Davis insists on the "law of association," to European folk medicine, to Mesmerism, but above all to the writings of his predecessor, Emanuel Swedenborg. The relationship of all this to Christianity is somewhat vexed, for although on the one hand Davis and most of the spiritualists rejected conventional forms of Christianity, they not only drew upon Christian traditions like millennialism, but also often termed themselves Christian, as well.

An example of this self-definition as Christian is to be found in the work of Thomas Lake Harris (1823–1906), who has been insufficiently studied. Harris was born in England and emigrated to America in 1828. In 1845, he became a Universalist minister, a career that served him for less than two years, for in 1847 he joined the group of Andrew Jackson Davis. Shortly thereafter, Harris left that group as well, resigning because of Davis's endorsement of "free love," and joining the Swedenborgian "Church of the New Jerusalem." Although Harris lived with a group of spiritualists from 1850 to 1853, he subsequently returned to proselytizing for Swedenborgianism, and traveled to England to do so. There he announced his own esoteric millennialist group called the "Brotherhood of the New Life," intended for the "reorganization of the industrial world."[14] Harris established his group at Brocton, Salem-on-Erie, New York, and finally in California. His Brotherhood was known for its avant-garde views on sexuality, and drew heavily in later years on the Western esoteric traditions, particularly on Freemasonry and Rosicrucianism, as well as on Asian religious traditions.

Harris's primary influences were Swedenborg and the Böhmean theosophic tradition. Naturally, Harris insisted that his thought and vision was original to him, and wrote that "It was my privilege to behold the Lord, whom I saw in his divine appearing, and who laid upon me the charge of receiving and unfolding such of those arcana of the celestial sense as are contained within this volume."[15] The language here, as in much of Harris's work, is Swedenborgian in origin; whereas Swedenborg wrote of "conjugial" relations between men and women, Harris wrote of "counterparts," and so forth. There also are striking parallels between some of Harris's writings and Böhmean theosophy, as when Harris later began to insist on the individual being in a divine marriage not with an earthly counterpart, but with the "Lily Queen" of heaven. This term is derived from Böhme's prophecies of a coming *lilienzeit*, or time of the lily, and from the Böhmean tradition of the soul's marriage to Sophia, or divine Wisdom.

A particularly interesting passage about one of Harris's spiritual groups is to be found in a letter published in the *New Jerusalem Messenger*, now the *New*

Church Messenger. This group, which numbered about fifty and met in an old schoolhouse, was led by S. E. Reynolds, whom Harris had ordained.:

> Speeches are given by influx. To those whose interiors are quickened, this influx is both visible and sensible. When intelligence and faith are treated of, it is through the left temple. When love to the Lord and His Kingdom, through the top of the head and extending to the heart and lungs. When the Word is illuminated the influx is through the forehead. Those who are in self-love will soon be pervaded by an influx from the hells, passing in at the back of the head and neck, opening interior sight and pervading the entire back. These will soon deny the Lord, or imagine that they are filled with the Holy Ghost. . . . For my part I think that but the few will attain unto inspiration, while the great mass of mankind who have spiritual manifestations, will receive them from spirits in self-love, filling the world with a literature vastly inferior to that of the ordinary schools of the day.[16]

This description is remarkable because it almost exactly matches the Böhmean theosophic illustrations and text of Johann Georg Gichtel, whose book *Eine kurze Eröffnung [A Brief Opening]* includes several important illustrations that show the spiritual centers of the human body. Just as in Harris, in Gichtel's illustrations the forehead and top of the head are shown as divine centers, whereas the back of the head and neck and the entire back are depicted as filled with the hellish smoke of, yes, self-love.[17]

Although he remains relatively little known, Harris was a prolific author who also wrote and published a number of hymns and songs. Among his many books are *Arcana of Christianity: An Unfolding of the Celestial Sense of the Divine Word* (1858–67); a collection of extemporaneous lectures entitled *The Millennial Age: Twelve Discourses on the Spiritual and Social Aspects of the Times* (1860); a monograph on "universal religion" entitled *The Breath of God with Man* (1867); and, in the book *The Golden Child* (1878), the daily chronicle of life in the California community Harris founded. In essence, Harris joined together Christian millennialism with Swedenborgian thought, but also drew on a range of other esoteric traditions. Harris is a fairly important figure whose work deserves fuller study than it has yet received. Perhaps his closest twentieth-century analogue is the Christian esotericist Valentin Tomberg, author of the magisterial *Meditations on the Tarot*, a book in which the Tarot provides a launching point for esoteric explication.

The book *The Millennial Age*, by Harris, is not in fact his writing, but rather a record of his extemporaneous remarks in England at the Marylebone Institute in London in February and March 1860. As a result, the book is frustrating because it consists of what now appears to be much blather and little substance. Only occasionally does one gain a sense of what made Harris a strikingly attractive figure for those of his contemporaries who became part of his circle, and who perhaps enjoyed being awash in Harris's flood of verbiage. In a rather nasty little book of gossip entitled *Religious Fanaticism* (1928), Hannah Whitall Smith, who apparently spent her life gathering rumors about nineteenth-century American utopian visionaries whom she obviously despised, wrote that Harris had spent several years "in the Orient, where he learnt a strange vocabulary" and attracted adherents from as far away as Japan.[18] Whatever "the Orient" means here, Smith's comment suggests that Harris may have had some contact with Buddhism, and at first glance one might think that one had found some allusions to Buddhist meditation in *The Millennial Age* when Harris talks about one of his pet themes, "internal respiration." "Redemption of the body," he tells his audience, "is to begin with internal respiration."[19] Here it is clear that Harris alludes to a particular kind of breathing discipline, undoubtedly a kind of esoteric practice. But that Harris knew nothing about Buddhism is quite obvious some pages later, when he speaks of Buddhism's goal as "'nigban,' the utter cessation of active faculty," and of "heaven as eternal stagnor" that "ends at last in the stagnation of the inner man even here below."[20] It seems clear, given his total ignorance concerning Buddhism, that Harris's esotericism was thoroughly European in origin, emerging almost totally out of Swedenborgianism and Böhmean Christian theosophy.[21]

We should not neglect to mention here the remarkable figure of Paschal Beverly Randolph (1825–74), a black American spiritualist, self-styled Rosicrucian, and sex magician who was very influential for many subsequent European, English, and American esoteric groups even if in his own lifetime he was relatively little known. John Deveney's definitive study of Randolph offers a vast amount of new information about Randolph and connections between numerous other figures of the time including Ethan Allen Hitchcock, whom Randolph very probably met and whose library Randolph claimed to have visited.[22] Randolph had traveled in the Middle East and claimed not only to have access to various "Eastern" techniques of magic, sexual and otherwise, but also to be the designated founding figure of Rosicrucianism in America, upon which others built a subsequent fictional American Rosicrucian mythology. Randolph sought out well-known figures, for instance, Abraham Lincoln, and lived in Boston for some years, so it is theoretically possible that he met at least one or another Transcendentalist during that time, but I have not found any direct proof of this. Randolph was quite influenced by the writing of Poe, sought to imitate Poe's poetry (with execrable results), and like many spiritualists of the time, believed he was in touch with Poe's discarnate spirit.[23] Randolph came to a tragic end in 1874, when he committed suicide in Toledo, Ohio, but his subsequent underground influence (partly through his writings) on the history of various magical groups was immense, especially his emphasis on various kinds of sexual magic.[24]

Another point on the spectrum of American figures who continued or transformed European esoteric traditions is represented by John Humphrey Noyes (1811–86), founder of the well-known Oneida community in western New York state. Noyes was from a fairly wealthy merchant family and graduated from Dartmouth. A first cousin to President Rutherford B. Hayes, Noyes was converted in the great revival of 1831 and went to divinity school at Yale, where he entered into radical causes. Endorsing William Lloyd Garrison's abolitionism, Noyes also began to endorse "perfectionism," the idea that Christians should move toward attaining complete salvation from sin in this life. One could recall here that this approach to Christianity has a long history, and often was persecuted in Europe—one thinks, for instance, of the Cathar heretics of Provençal France, whose highest level was that of the *perfecti*. Like the Cathars, Noyes aimed for the perfect life on earth, and like the Cathars and similar groups, he and his community were not exactly welcomed by society-at-large.

Early on, Noyes began to see exclusive wedlock as an unhealthy institution, and as he gathered a perfectionist community in Putney, Vermont, he began to publish his views, which scandalized his neighbors and ultimately caused his community to flee to Oneida in 1848. There, they practiced an interesting and relatively well-organized kind of socialism in which matters of procreation and sexual intercourse—as well as most other decisions—were subject to community judgement. The community at Oneida, which by 1851 numbered 205, was controversial for its sexual views, but in fact was fairly conservative in many respects, not least in its business practices, which included in addition to farming and logging, the production of dinner silverware. Indeed, when the community effectively disbanded in 1881, it did so by forming the Oneida corporation, which today still is responsible for manufacturing Oneida silverware.

Most controversial of Noyes's contentions was his affirmation of "complex marriage" and male continence. His particular version of male continence deserves to be examined more closely for a moment. As practiced at Oneida, it consisted in sexual intercourse without male ejaculation, which Noyes insisted transformed intercourse from an animalistic rutting into, at least potentially, a vehicle of spiritual experience. That this view has parallels in both Hindu and Buddhist Tantrism is more or less widely known, but Noyes almost certainly did not get his approach to sexuality from Asian traditions. Rather—and this is little-known or explored—there are European precedents for such a view, both medieval, as in the Cathari, and more modern, in particular among the Christian theosophers.[25] It is entirely possible that at Yale Noyes had read works that inspired his later views of sexuality and religion, but precisely which works remains to be uncovered.

What makes Davis, Harris, and Noyes interesting vis à vis Transcendentalism is that their writings and for that matter their lives correspond in many respects to what we also see among the Transcendentalists. When Harris left Universalism, he walked in the footsteps of Emerson, who had left his post as a Unitarian minister some dozen years before. Harris, Davis, and Noyes's efforts at establishing ideal communities certainly parallel similar efforts by the Transcendentalists at Brook Farm and Alcott's Fruitlands. What is more, these Transcendentalist attempts at establishing utopias derived from the same European esoteric and socialist origins as the spiritualist or semievangelical ones (i.e., from such figures as Swedenborg and Fourier) and, by a circuitous route, from such movements as Rosicrucianism, Freemasonry, theosophy, and Christian millennialism, all draped in fundamentally secular garb. On top of that, the Transcendentalists insisted upon the importance of divine poetic inspiration, on listening to the inward voice, and of course this is precisely what Harris and Davis also emphasized, as did the spiritualist movement more generally.

This is not to say that there were no differences between the spiritualists or Harris's Brotherhood or Noyes's Oneida and Emersonian or Fourierist Transcendentalism—obviously there were differences, not least of which was the fact that the Emersonian Transcendentalists did not care much for the spiritualists nor, for that matter, did the Fourierists. Emerson referred to spiritualism as the "rat hole of revelation." Rather, it is only to point out that the various Transcendentalisms emerged in a specific context of other more or less millennialist movements that not only share similar influences, but also resemble the Transcendentalists in many of their writings and social manifestations. Likewise, it is important to recognize that Hawthorne's, Poe's, or Melville's stories about Mesmerism or spiritualism exist in the context of well-known figures like Davis. There is no doubt that the writings of the Transcendentalists or the other luminaries of the American Renaissance are much superior in literary quality to that of such bizarre authors as Laurence Oliphant in his *Sympneumata* (Edinburgh, 1885), not to mention the writings of Oliphant's mentor, Harris, or of Andrew Jackson Davis or John Humphrey Noyes. But we would do well to recognize that American Transcendentalism, and the American Renaissance more generally, emerged very much out of origins in Western esotericism similar to those of much lesser-known figures like Davis, Harris, Oliphant, and Noyes.

Hitchcock

Before we discuss some of the more well-known figures of the American Renaissance, we should take a look at the work and life of a remarkable man whose inner and outer lives, more than most, are depicted as falling neatly into two categories rarely if ever discussed together. This man, Ethan Allen Hitchcock, is most well-known as a prominent American military figure and as an eminent advisor to President Lincoln during the entire Civil War—in short for his outward life, which was certainly exciting and eventful. Hitchcock is also well known in another vein entirely, for although he led an unusually active life, he also pursued esoteric studies throughout at least his last twenty years and published books on topics that ranged from Shakespeare to Swedenborg to alchemy. Hitchcock is important for us not only because he knew personally a number of major American literary figures with similar interests—including Emerson and Poe—but also because he is a representative figure for understanding how esotericism was transmuted into literary forms during the mid-nineteenth century.

Hitchcock's eventful outer life is chronicled in great detail in the unfortunately highly edited version of his diary entitled *Fifty Years in Camp and Field*.[1] General Ethan Allen Hitchcock was the grandson of the Revolutionary war hero Ethan Allen, and after he graduated from West Point not long after its founding, he became an an instructor there, and then commandant of the Corps. Thereafter he was engaged in the removal of the Seminole tribe from Florida, and in the Mexican War he was deployed with General Zachary Taylor and then General Winfield Scott, with whom he was inspector-general. At the inception of the Civil War, Hitchcock was to be given command of the field, but on account of ill health he insisted that command go to General Ulysses S. Grant, and instead became the chief military advisor to President Lincoln. He kept up a voluminous correspondence and a massive diary in which he made entries throughout his life, while also publishing so much that he became known as the "Pen of the Army."

From early on, Hitchcock was as much given to reading and scholarship as he was to an active life. An unusually philosophical military man, he wrote during his time at West Point that as much as he liked being among cultured people interested in science and literature, he felt that his duties "did not tax [his] faculties at all," and so read a vast range of works, including Thomas Browne's *Religio Medici*, Hobbes, Lucretius, and Benjamin Franklin's works. It was during this time that he "determined to regard [himself] impersonally—that is, as an impartial observer. . . . I was constantly inquiring of myself about myself."[2] Much can be made of Hitchcock's having been Edgar Allan Poe's instructor at West Point during this time (1830–31), which certainly alters the usual depiction of Poe languishing in the military life while there. Poe was first in Hitchcock's class during his first six months at West Point, and when we take into account their common interests in Mesmerisim, Swedenborg, Hermeticism, and other arcane topics, it does seem that Hitchcock was an important source for Poe's later writings. We will look more carefully at this question when we turn to our section on Poe himself.

Hitchcock was on numerous occasions nominated to be governor of Liberia, but declined, and instead went with Zachary Taylor into Indian Territory, where he soon became Indian agent to the tribes. His accounts of his time among the various tribes and his meetings with them are well worth perusing; he wrote: "The presence of the whites is a blight upon the Indian character, which, in its own native simplicity, is far less objectionable than is generally supposed."[3] It is hard to imagine how Hitchcock traveled into the field, often under very crude conditions, while maintaining his voluminous reading habits, but he did. In 1845, near Fort Jesup and in the field, Hitchcock decided to count his books, and there were 761, not including over sixty volumes of music (he played the flute).[4] During this time, he was certainly interested in secret societies, Mesmerism, Swedenborg, and Spinoza, but his reading was voracious.

Hitchcock had some passing interest in esoteric matters from relatively early in life, but these interests did not blossom until the 1850s. In 1853, he was reading Emerson's *Essays* and wrote in his diary that the *Essays* seemed to him "a series of self-examinations. The thoughts are uttered mostly in proverbs, but many of them need explanations, except to readers of Plato, Swedenborg, and Tom Paine. . . . A distinct consciousness of the love of fame has never crossed my mind, but in reading Emerson I have been led to think of being myself. I must of necessity fall into oblivion, and the thought gives me something like a pang such as I do not remember ever before experiencing. Emerson *over-saw* multitudes of people."[5]

It is self-evident that Hitchcock had been reading Swedenborg—indeed, he subsequently published a book on Swedenborg the Hermetic philosopher— but it was during this same time that he began assiduously purchasing, reading, and taking copious notes on alchemical and Hermetic works. In late May 1854, Hitchcock purchased from a bookshop in New York several books on alchemy almost two centuries old, probably books that American alchemists in the colonies had once owned. These "very old worm-eaten little volumes, much soiled and worn," fascinated him, and he quickly came to believe that "all true alchymists pursued not gold but wisdom."[6]

On alchemy and related topics, chiefly mysticism and Neoplatonism, Hitchcock wrote in his diary many hundreds of pages, but of these Croffut, the editor, gives us almost nothing. Croffut does, however, give us this entry: "The universe is all in all, and it makes no difference whether we call it God or Nature. This, if anything, is what the alchymists considered their 'secret.' It is an interesting point of view, showing that in ages past there was a class of men, not very numerous, indeed, and widely scattered, who were not affected by the common theological or even metaphysical disputes. There were men, as I have often suspected, who stood equally above Martin Luther and the Pope."[7] Thus it is clear here, and is borne out by Hitchcock's subsequent book *Remarks Upon Alchemy and the Alchemists* (1857), that Hitchcock considered alchemy to be chiefly spiritual in nature, and not at all literal or laboratory work. This is, of course, not the case, in that there unquestionably is such a thing as alchemical work in the laboratory, but this kind of alchemy simply did not interest Hitchcock.

It was at this critical juncture in his life that Hitchcock, who already was considering resigning his commission, was ordered to travel into Sioux country near Fort Laramie with an officer Hitchcock considered to be ignorant and brutal, "the man whom I hold least in respect of all men in the army."[8] This expedition resulted in the bloody massacre of the Brulé tribe, and Hitchcock refused to participate. His resignation was regretfully accepted by the president, and subsequently the *New York Tribune* characterized the massacre as "shameful, detestable, and cruel," whereas the *St. Louis News* wrote that the commander had "divested himself of the attributes of civilized humanity and turned himself into a treacherous demon, remorseless and bloodthirsty."[9] Hitchcock, on the other hand, was widely praised for his moral stature and strength of character.

Although leaving the army was in some respects difficult for Hitchcock, his newfound freedom allowed him to delve much more deeply into his esoteric research. He purchased numerous works from London and New England booksellers, many on alchemy, including such authors as Agrippa, the American alchemist Eirenæus Philalethes, the Thomas Taylor translations of Neoplatonic works, Paracelsus, van Helmont, Jacob Böhme, Roger Bacon, Ramon Lull, and some Hindu translations, including the Vishnu Purana and the Bhagavad Gita.[10] On March 28, 1856, Hitchcock remarked in his diary that "[I] received a letter from my book-buyer saying that he has obtained for me some 80 volumes on Alchemy, Hermetic philosophy, etc., ordered some weeks since on a London catalogue."[11] Hitchcock probably had at that time the best collection of these kinds of works in America. During this time he completed *Remarks Upon Alchemy and*

*the Alchemists Indicating a Method of Discovering the True Nature of Hermetic
Philosophy; and Showing that the Search After the Philosopher's Stone Had Not For
Its Object the Discovery of An Agent for the Transmutation of Metals. Being Also
an Attempt to Rescue from Undeserved Opprobrium the Reputation of a Class of
Extraordinary Thinkers in Past Ages* (Boston: Crosby, Nichols, 1857).

The title of Hitchcock's most well-known book reveals a great deal of its
thesis. Hitchcock argued in contradiction to the general belief that alchemy was
a "pretended science by which gold and silver were to be made," and chiefly a
delusion or fraud, that in reality "Man was the subject of Alchemy, and that the
object of the Art was the perfection, or at least the improvement, of Man,"
whose salvation "was symbolized under the figure of the transmutation of metals." In short, "the writings of the Alchemsts are all symbolical, and under the
words gold, silver, lead, salt, sulphur . . . may be found the opinions of the several writers upon the great questions of God, nature, man."[12] At present, spirituality is central in what we may call laboratory alchemy, and there is an
alchemy that is chiefly spiritual and does not involve the laboratory.[13] However,
in Hitchcock's work we see a different tendency than either of these, which is
to ignore the laboratory elements even when they are self-evident, in order to
make the argument that alchemy is totally symbolic and a kind of religious discourse only.

Undoubtedly, in a broad sense Hitchcock's thesis is right, because alchemy
depends upon human labor—it requires an alchemist—but he goes far beyond
this simple observation to argue that all the major alchemical terms, including
technical terms like Antinomy, refer not at all to chemical substances but only
to humanity. This statement, of course, goes too far, for there is a vast amount
of historical evidence that reveals the use of complicated laboratory equipment
and mineral and vegetable substances, not to mention the fact that there are still
working laboratory alchemists today.[14] Hitchcock's refusal to acknowledge
laboratory alchemy is especially interesting given the prevalence of laboratory
alchemy in colonial America: it is as though, laboratory alchemy having largely
disappeared from the scientific landscape by the nineteenth century, the only
way Hitchcock saw to rescue alchemy from the widespread denigration to
which he alludes in the beginning of his own book was to spiritualize it completely.

To explain what Eyrenæus Philalethes (the American alchemist with whom
we earlier became familiar) meant, Hitchcock goes to Plotinus and to a then recently published book that discussed Vedanta. The terms employed as Vedantic
in the work are in fact strange linguistic distortions, but the basic idea is clear:
"the philosophy of the followers of the Vedanta school is founded on the contemplation of one Infinite Being, existing under two states or modifications.
The first, that of a simple, abstract essence, immovable and quiescent; the second, that of Being displaying motion, or active qualities."[15] Hitchcock tells us
that he hopes the reader does not imagine he is trying to convert him to "Hindoo
philosophy or mysticism for his faith," but "simply to indicate a correspondence of thought, by which it may seem probable that the genuine Alchemist

had some mode of conceiving all things as *one*, in some sense, and that his speculations had no reference whatever to making gold."[16]

That Hitchcock in 1857 drew upon Vedanta to explain alchemy certainly reveals the breadth of his learning, because his was undoubtedly at the time cutting-edge knowledge. One can see how Hitchcock's use of Vedanta here parallels the reception of Hinduism by Emerson and Thoreau detailed in my book *American Transcendentalism and Asian Religions*. There I argue that Transcendentalism consisted in essence in what I call a literary religious universalism. Hitchcock's approach to Western esotericism, and specifically to alchemy, very much corresponds to the Transcendentalists' approaches to world religions, which had in common a jettisoning of cultural specifics in favor of their common denominators, chiefly ethics and, for Emerson and Thoreau, self-transcendence. Hitchcock here accomplishes a very similar kind of cultural jettisoning, in this case of laboratory alchemy in favor of an abstract kind of spiritualized and purely symbolic alchemy.

Some of the historical origins of Hitchcock's dismissal of laboratory alchemy in favor of a spiritual and purely symbolic alchemy can be seen in his companion book to *Remarks Upon Alchemy*: *Swedenborg: A Hermetic Philosopher* (1858). Hitchcock offers the following précis of *Swedenborg*:

> [The author's] purpose has been to suggest the opinions of others, especially of a class of men scarcely recognized as existing in the world. The art they profess, called after the name of Hermes, *Hermetic* Philosophy, is so little known at the present day that the name of it by no means indicates it. The adepts profess to be, or to have been, in possession of a secret, which they call the gift of God. The art has been prosecuted under many names, among which are Alchemy, Astrology, and even Chiromancy, as well as Geomancy, Magic, &c., under all of which names it has had *deluded* followers, who have been deceived, as those who claim to be true artists say, not by the art itself, which never "did betray the heart that loved it," but by their own selfish passions.[17]

Hitchcock's focus here, in other words, is chiefly Hermeticism, and only secondarily Swedenborg, whose work he sees as introductory to and exemplary of the art of Hermes.

However, in his fascination with Swedenborg, as in his analysis of Hermeticism, Hitchcock also reveals much in common with Emersonian Transcendentalism.[18] Emerson, as we shall shortly see, was himself fascinated with the writings of Swedenborg and owned a great many of the prolific visionary's works. Hitchcock not only was strongly attracted to the works of Swedenborg, just as Emerson was, but also approached Hermeticism in a very transcendentalist fashion. After putting together his library of more than three hundred rare volumes on alchemy, Hitchcock became convinced that "the *matter* of the philosophers was man, and that the *soap* referred to, the *vinegar*, the *oil*, &c., was no other than the conscience; but the conscience, acting freely and not under external and violent influences."[19] In brief, "the object of the Hermetic philosophers was the perfection of man . . . [through] some knowledge of God in a peculiar sense."[20] In his view of both Swedenborg and of Hermeticism, Hitchcock is very much aligned with the Emersonian Transcendentalist emphasis (shared by Emerson, Thoreau, and Alcott) on the conscience and on human perfection.

That Swedenborg could be interpreted by way of Hermeticism is Hitchcock's primary thesis, however. In making this argument, he is careful in his phrasing, as when he remarks that "Swedenborg's mystical writings are modelled after those of the hermetic writers, and may be interpreted from the standpoint of hermetic philosophy; and this, too, without assuming that Swedenborg was what was called an *adept* in the fullest sense."[21] In other words, Swedenborg was in essence derivative of Hermeticism. Hitchcock takes part of his thesis (that Swedenborg meant his visionary works to be taken symbolically, not literally, just as Hermeticists do) to surprising lengths: halfway through his book, Hitchcock writes that he "conversed with Swedenborg myself in the spiritual world, and it is only necessary for me to 'relate' the particulars of what passed between us. I have in fact had not merely one conversation with him, but have met him many times, and have questioned him very closely."[22] At first glance, Hitchcock's assertion is startling, but eventually we realize that he does not say that he literally held conversations with Swedenborg, any more than Swedenborg literally held conversations with the disciples Peter and Paul, but rather that both he and Swedenborg, like the Hermeticists, held "conversations" by meeting intellectually.

Hitchcock's interpretation of Swedenborg—that he always speaks figuratively—is highly questionable, for it seems quite clear from Swedenborg's own writings that he did indeed undertake visionary journeys. But Hitchcock refuses to accept the possibility that Swedenborg actually saw angels in vision or went on out-of-body spiritual journeys, claiming instead that "The best of men Swedenborg describes as angels, and speaks of them as of another earth than ours; but he is speaking of men nevertheless, in our midst . . . who love to think of God and of eternal things."[23] On Swedenborg's—or anyone's!—undertaking ecstatic journeys, Hitchcock writes, "It is very plain that no one while in the body can ever, in any strict sense, be said to be out of the body. . . . Hence no man will ever travel, we may be sure, to another world, while in the body, and bring back thence any thing but what he carries with him, or may find here before he sets out on his journey."[24] It is one thing to deny that Swedenborg spoke literally; but it is quite another to claim that no one at all can go on a visionary journey!

Thus we can see that Hitchcock goes rather far in his refusal to take Swedenborg literally, and in so doing he is in fact strikingly aligned with Emersonian Transcendentalism. Like Emersonian Transcendentalists, Hitchcock laid primary emphasis on the individual human conscience, and like Emerson, maintained that Jesus was a supreme example of what humanity can achieve. What Jesus achieved has also been achieved by "the genuine Hermetic Philosophers," and "in this class I recognize the Swedish Philosopher, Emanuel Swedenborg."[25] In other words, Hermeticism offers the way to the true realization of Christianity. Emerson does not often speak directly in Hermetic terms, as Hitchcock obviously does, but in their approaches and perspectives, Emerson and Hitchcock are very much in agreement. Hitchcock and Emerson both insist on moral perfection leading to the transcendence of egotism, which they see as the heart of Christianity. Hitchcock's alchemy and Swedenborg may be rather far from their originals, but they represent perfectly the abstraction or intellectualization of esotericism that took place in America in the mid-nineteenth century.

Of course, to say this is not to call into question Hitchcock's sincerity, or for that matter, his certainty that he had really understood something fundamental about alchemy. Indeed, on 12 November 1866, four years before his death, he wrote the following entry in his diary:

> I wish to say that I saw, a moment since, what the Philosopher's Stone signifies.
> I do not omit a statement of it from any desire to make it a mystery. My relation to it is still to be determined. A great number of passages in books of alchemy seem perfectly clear now. I have nowhere told what it is or even what I think it is. It is a kind of revelation, but, when seen, has an effect something like looking at the sun. Personally I have much to fear from it, before I can look forward to its benefits. I have nothing to unsay in my books, and have but this to add that they are studies to reach the One Thing.[26]

Similar affirmations that Hitchcock had realized some essential spiritual truth are scattered through his diary entries subsequent to this, as are extensive further meditations on subjects that range from Cabala to Masonry and the symbolic nature of Christianity. It is evident that he believed he had realized something essential about the nature of alchemy that confirmed what he had written in his book.

However, what he wrote corresponds in striking ways with the general import of American Transcendentalism, in particular with the thought of Emerson and Alcott. Like them, he insisted on the importance of inward, immediate intuition of spiritual truth. In *Nature*, Emerson wrote in a famous passage about how he had experienced self-transcendence and become like a "transparent eyeball." Alcott, though his language was often abstract and sometimes almost impenetrable, also refers to such experiences. Indeed, their mutual insistence on the importance of direct spiritual intuition is why Alcott and Emerson were so attracted to the English Böhmean mystic James Pierrepont Greaves's work, about which we shall say more later.[27] Like Emerson and Alcott, too, Hitchcock saw the life of Jesus and the New Testament chiefly in terms of their symbolic import, all three of them being very much influenced by a Hermetic way of understanding Christianity.

Thus it comes as no surprise that Hitchcock more than once visited Concord, Massachusetts and the Emersons and the Alcotts. Hitchcock had been reading Emerson's writing at least as early as 1843.[28] In 1861, in August, Hitchcock went to Concord to visit "Mr Emerson, the 'Mystic,'—author of the essay on 'Circles,'"[29] and again, in 1862, while Hitchcock recuperated from ill health, he visited Horace Mann, Nathaniel Hawthorne, the Peabodys, the Lowells, and the Winthrops, not to mention "Ralph Waldo Emerson and his oracle, Mr. Alcott."[30] It is also not surprising that the conversations between Emerson, Alcott, and Hitchcock centered on mysticism. Although Hitchcock had met Emerson and Alcott on several occasions, however, one cannot therefore conclude that Hitchcock's own views derived from the Transcendentalists, for it is quite clear that Hitchcock came to his understanding of alchemy and Hermeticism independently via his own voluminous reading and his own meditation upon them. It is rather the case that Hitchcock found in Emerson and Alcott kindred spirits.

We can have no doubt that Hitchcock was an extraordinary man. Famous in his own time for his military career—at West Point, he had taught virtually all the major Union generals of his day as well as Jefferson Davis and Robert E. Lee, and even after leaving the army, was a close advisor to President Lincoln—still he is remembered today perhaps more for his rich inner life, revealed in the numerous books on Hermetic topics that he wrote in his later years. He knew and corresponded with virtually all major American literary figures of his day, and as Marsha Schuchard has pointed out, given Hitchcock's documented interest in secret societies and his uncharacteristic silence about certain periods of his life (his stay in New Orleans for six weeks in 1849 and his travels in Europe during the same year), it may indeed be the case that he was a member of at least one secret society, perhaps, as has been claimed, a Rosicrucian one.[31] However, Hitchcock's importance does not rest on whether he was a member of one or another secret society, interesting though such a possibility may be. His importance lies rather in his place as an independent Hermetic thinker, an esotericist in the American military whose significance in American literary and religious scholarship has yet to be fully assessed.

Poe

Although there have been many books and articles written about Edgar Allan Poe (1809–49), there has been startlingly little work done on the esoteric sources from which he drew so much of his work. In the first issue of the *Poe Newsletter* in 1968, its editor, J. Albert Robbins, remarked on the contradiction between the enormous quantity of critical work published about Poe, and its mostly poor, unsophisticated quality. Robbins called Poe a "critical orphan." As Kent Ljungquist noted in 1995, various academic theoretical fashions contrived to make this situation worse, if anything, chiefly by encouraging a tendency to examine Poe's works without reference to the existing body of Poe scholarship, or to Poe's specific historical antecedents.[1] Although it is obvious that our discussion of how Western esoteric traditions informed Poe's thought and work cannot remedy this larger problem, we can certainly begin to shed light on an important, indeed, a central aspect of Poe's work that has not yet been adequately explored.

Here there is little point in reiterating Poe's biography, which is well known: his life, from his unfortunate marriage to his very young cousin, Virginia, to his "tomahawk" reviews of countless other writers, to his obvious erudition and feverish, erratic, often overwrought writing, to his alcoholism and early death, all suggest a kind of nineteenth-century American tragedy. That Poe's work is uneven is obvious from even a cursory glance over his voluminous work for popular magazines. Poe was forced to struggle for a living as a writer and it is little wonder that he could not afford to write only the short stories and poems for which he is famous. Yet as we shall see, among these lesser known, often popular writings is much that will interest us.

One aspect of Poe's life has received relatively little attention, and that is his stay at West Point as the place where, oddly enough, he almost certainly was introduced to a wide range of classical authors, as well as many esoteric topics

and writers. Generally speaking, Poe's stay at West Point is depicted as somewhat unhappy, although at first he seemed to excel in the military life there, and
for the first six months was near the head of his class.[2] What is rarely, if ever,
remarked upon is that among Poe's teachers at West Point was none other than
Ethan Allen Hitchcock, without doubt one of the most, and perhaps the most
important of nineteenth-century American esotericists. Hitchcock himself remarked in his diary during this time that he enjoyed very much the cordial atmosphere at West Point and the erudite discussions among the young scholars
employed there, discussions that sometimes also included the students. It was,
wrote Hitchcock, one of the most wonderful periods of his life, when to his relief he could be among people of similar intellectual inclinations: "I can never
forget the joy with which I mingled with the young assistant professors of the
Academy. . . . The amount of culture among them was considerable; their conversation was enlightened—turning upon subjects of science and literature . . .
It was something like a transition from earth to Heaven."[3]

It is true that Hitchcock, during this time Poe was at West Point (1830–31),
was not yet totally immersed in his esoteric studies in Swedenborg, animal magnetism, alchemy, and Hermeticism. These interests he developed chiefly from
the 1850s onward, during the time that he published the majority of his books
on these subjects. However, it is clear even from the bowdlerized diary edited
by W. A. Croffutt that Hitchcock was throughout this period reading very
widely and that he maintained a constant interest in "speculative metaphysics."
Hitchcock's later writings on esoteric topics had roots in lifelong reading, some
of which he did while at West Point. What is more, it is remarkable how much
Hitchcock's esoteric interests, which flowered later in life, mirror what we find
reflected in Poe's stories. Every single one of the esoteric topics to which
Hitchcock devoted books also can be found clearly represented in Poe's short
stories, poetry, and non-fiction. This may be coincidence, but one certainly has
to doubt it.[4]

The first and most obvious place to look for Poe's esoteric interests is, of
course, his short stories, for which he is most renowned. One does not have to
look far or hard. We might begin with "Von Kempelen and His Discovery,"
which is characteristic of Poe's style not least in its tongue-in-cheek approach
to documentation. The story of Von Kempelen that Poe relates is one of
alchemy—in essence, Von Kempelen, we are told, "has actually realized, in
spirit and in effect, if not to the letter, the old chimera of the philosopher's
stone," and consequently soon enough gold will be as commonplace as lead and
"of far inferior value to silver." Poe plays with two additional conventions in
addition to that of the real possibility of alchemy. The first is journalism—the
story purports to be setting the record straight, for so many errors have appeared in *Silliman's Journal* and the *Courier and Enquirer* that the narrator needs
to set the record straight because (Poe sneeringly writes) "it does not *look* true.
People who are narrating *facts*, are seldom so particular as Mr. Kissam seems to
be, about day and date and precise location."[5] This of course is ridiculous, and
clearly Poe's gleeful taunting of journalism. The second convention he violates

is scientific: Von Kempelen's discovery is supposedly based upon the "Diary of Sir Humphrey Davy," which the great scientist had intended to be burned, and which gave Von Kempelen the keys to alchemical transmutation. Thus, instead of science succeeding alchemy, we have science giving way, in the end, to alchemy!

Hence we have the account of Von Kempelen's arrest on charges of "counterfeiting" because of his newfound, mysterious wealth, and the subsequent discovery by police of a ten-by-eight-foot closet that included "a very small furnace, with a glowing fire in it, and on the fire a kind of duplicate crucible— two crucibles connected by a tube. One of these crucibles was nearly full of *lead* in a state of fusion."[6] Poe concludes the story by claiming that it very much appears gold can easily be made from lead or other substances, that this undoubtedly would have changed the settling of California, and that the price of lead, on this news, has gone up two hundred percent. Now all of this is mightily amusing, but without substance—even the description of the alchemical apparatus is bogus, and the effect of the whole is to suggest that Poe was simply fooling around with the notion of alchemy and what might happen if the alchemical transmutation of lead into gold took place regularly and could even be industrialized.[7]

Poe's treatment of mesmerism is similar: he draws on it in order to elaborate his own fancies; an esoteric tradition provides a basis for his cosmic fancy. In "Mesmeric Revelation," Poe writes about mesmerizing an ill man named Mr. Vankirk, who expresses an interest to the narrator in being mesmerized so as to investigate death, mesmerism supposedly creating a condition similar to death. Much of the story is devoted to a dialogue between "P.," the narrator, and "V.," the mesmerized patient, who when mesmerized launches into a cosmological description of how "there are *gradations* of matter of which man knows nothing. . . . [T]hese gradations of matter increase in rarity or fineness, until we arrive at a matter *unparticled*. . . . The ultimate or unparticled matter not only permeates all things, but impels all things; and thus *is* all things within itself. This matter is God."[8] Thus, mesmerism forms a vehicle for Poe's proposition that what we call "spirit" is in fact a rarified kind of matter. "V." goes on to assert that "divested of corporate investure man were God. But he can never be thus divested."[9] Hence, Poe has his mesmerized patient deny a central premise of many Christian mystics and of Neoplatonism: that man's purpose is to return to God or to realize the One. It is interesting, and characteristic, that Poe's mesmerized patient immediately dies, and the narrator ends the story by wondering whether the speaker had been addressing him "from out of the region of the shadows." For Poe, the afterlife is indeed a matter, not of heaven or hell, but of "shadows" of the material world.

This brings us naturally to Poe's other well-known story of mesmerism, "The Facts in the Case of M. Valdemar." In this story, Poe tells of how M. Ernest Valdemar, of Harlem, New York, sometime after 1839, was mesmerized during his terminal moments, died, and continued to be mesmerized after death, in which state he continued for some seven months. Eventually, the mesmerist narrator sought to awaken him, during which ministrations a revolting yellow-ish ichor flowed from beneath his eyelids, and he said "For God's sake!—quick!—quick!—put me to sleep! . . . *I say to you that I am dead*!" Within a few moments, Valdemar's whole body rotted away on the bed into a nearly liquid mass of loathsome putrescence, and thus the story ends. In some respects, this story is a continuation of the first, except, of course, that instead of cosmic revelations, the denouement reveals only repugnant decay.

Poe wrote about mesmerism, or animal magnetism, in his *Marginalia* of November 1846, remarking on a book by W. Newnham on the subject. However, Poe's assertion is rather unexpected: he argues that Newnham's claim for magnetism's reality is spurious because Newnham argues that the existence of the counterfeit proves that there must be a genuine. If there is a fraudulent mesmerism, there must also be the real thing. This, says Poe, is a false argument.[10] In an even more apropos observation, Poe wrote in his "Marginal Notes" of August 1845, "The Swedenborgians inform me that they have discovered all that I said in a magazine article, entitled "Mesmeric Revelation," to be absolutely true, although at first they were very strongly inclined to doubt my veracity—a thing which, in that particular instance, I never dreamed of not doubting myself. The story is a pure fiction from beginning to end."[11] Thus, Poe's own views on mesmerism seem at the least more skeptical than his stories might suggest.

At the same time, Poe was taken by many, including Baudelaire, as being very much a believer in mesmerism, and in what we have seen was often affiliated with mesmerist phenomena in America during that time, that is, with Swedenborgian thought. Patrick Quinn wrote that Baudelaire erred in his remarks on Poe's "Revelation Magnetique" because although Poe "knew or pretended to know a great many rather obscure and esoteric authors," "Swedenborg does not appear to have been one of them." Poe, he continued, was "probably relying mostly on his own individual imagination and not on a thorough acquaintance with that tradition of esoteric knowledge in which the name of Swedenborg occupies a capital place."[12] It is true that Poe probably did not have a "thorough acquaintance with that tradition of esoteric knowledge," Swedenborgian or otherwise, but then again, he was only drawing from Swedenborgian, mesmerist, alchemical, and other sources what he needed to inspire or compose his stories. It is quite clear that Poe was quite familiar with mesmerism; and that he knew Swedenborg's thought, at least in a general way, is also certain.

Poe's notorious failure to acknowledge his sources is always problematic, not least of all here. Poe delighted to cite authors in his stories, but often as not, the citations are either false or misleading, as in "Von Kempelen," in which nothing cited is real or as he uses it. It is true that, as he himself pointed out, his stories are purely fiction, but even given Poe's mischievous sense of humor, sometimes his drawing upon sources without citing them goes beyond the merely amusing. Probably the most well-known example is Poe's sneering attack on Nathaniel Hawthorne, in which he explicitly accused Hawthorne of plagiarizing Poe's story "William Wilson."[13] Of course, as more than one critic has remarked, this attack might very well disguise Poe's plagiarism of Hawthorne! Poe repeats the claim of plagiarism more slyly in his *Marginalia* of December, 1844: "Mr. Hawthorne ... is not always original in his entire theme—(I am not quite sure, even, that he has not borrowed an idea or two from a gentleman whom I know very well, and who is honored in the loan)."[14] All of this goes to suggest that the fact Swedenborg is not cited by Poe may in fact mean that he was drawing upon him, even if to sneer at him.

Probably the story closest to Swedenborgian visionary experiences or thought is "The Domain of Arnheim." In "The Domain of Arnheim," we are introduced to one Mr. Ellison, the friend of the narrator, who was intelligent, graceful, and handsome, and from an illustrious and, it turns out, incredibly wealthy family. Ellison, upon receiving several hundred million dollars, set out to "landscape arranging," the most exalted of arts. Why? Ellison explained: "There *may* be a class of beings, human once, but now invisible to humanity, to whom, from afar, our disorder may seem order—our unpicturesqueness picturesque; in a word, the earth-angels, for whose scrutiny more especially than our own, and for whose death-refined appreciation of the beautiful, may have been set in array by God the wide landscape-gardens of the hemispheres."[15] Ellison believed that art surpasses nature by far, and that a strangely built landscape, made by "angels that hover between man and God" is certainly the most beautiful of all. This, he set out to create, and did. We then are treated to the narrator's visit, in which he sees not a leaf out of place, not a dead branch or a withered leaf, but crystalline water, alabaster pebbles, all perfect as if the creation "of a new race of fairies," the glittering, Gothic, "Paradise of Arnheim."

We should be clear, however: this is not Swedenborgian but, if anything, anti-Swedenborgian. Swedenborg was certainly pious in what he wrote: he believed earnestly that he had seen the heavens and the hells in vision, and was unquestionably Christian. His visionary experiences intensified his piety. By contrast, let us think about the implications of "The Domain of Arnheim." In this story, we find emphasized Ellison's great wealth as the means for his power; and his insistence that art in the form of the "phantom" creations of "Sylphs ... Fairies ... Genii, and ... Gnomes" is far superior to nature itself. In essence, Poe claims the superiority of human fantasy to nature, and of the creations of an intermediate class of invisible beings to those of God himself. There is in all of this nothing Christian or pious—quite the reverse, in fact. By any and all of these propositions Swedenborg would have been revolted, and certainly would have regarded them as demonic—that is, as emerging from self-love or the egotism and vanity of what he called the *proprium* (the ego), the very thing that must be transcended in order to enter heaven.

It is clear that Poe was not merely proposing these ideas in a single idle fancy of a story when we turn to the dialogues "The Power of Words." In "The Power of Words" we are introduced to Oinos, "a spirit new-fledged with immortality," and Agathos, a wiser spirit or angel. It rapidly becomes clear from their dialogue that, although at first they may seem orthodox angels and this a kind of Swedenborgian dialogue from paradise, in fact Agathos almost immediately proceeds to the claim that "the Deity does not create," but did so "in the beginning *only*."[16] Oinos replies that among men this idea would be considered "heretical in the extreme," but Agathos goes on to say that the true creation comes through "*the physical power of words*." As they pause before a "wild star," Agathos exlaims that, three centuries before, "I spoke it—with a few passionate sentences—into birth. Its brilliant flowers *are* the dearest of all unfulfilled dreams, and its raging volcanoes *are* the passions of the most turbulent and unhallowed of hearts."[17] It seems clear, in other words, that this Agathos is what in Christianity is termed a fallen angel, who seeks to create on his own, and whose creation is of "the most turbulent and unhallowed of hearts." To say these ideas are un-Swedenborgian is, of course, an understatement.

Perhaps the most anti-Swedenborgian of Poe's works is "The Colloquy of Monas and Una." This dialogue begins with Monas remarking on the term "born again," "the words upon whose mystical meaning I had so long pondered."[18] At first, of course, it would seem that this dialogue will be the most Swedenborgian, for it is apparently about two spirits, male and female, who love one another and who have survived death together. The mystical marriage is certainly one of Swedenborg's pet themes, and he invented a word for it: "conjugial." Although the dialogue between Monas and Una at first appears Swedenborgian, the last half is dominated by the monologue of Monas, who tells the story of how he died, his pulse stilling, and how, after death, sight, hearing, touch, and all the senses were intensified and transformed, but then died away. A sixth sense then emerged: that of time. "By its aid," Monas continues, "I measured the irregularities of the clock upon the mantel."[19] On the "threshold of the temporal Eternity" Monas remained, as he lay rotting in the grave, and then remained conscious after the worms had no more food, and the story concludes, "For *that* which was *not*—for that which had no form—for that which had no thought—for that which had no sentience—for that which was soulless . . . for all this nothingness, yet for all this immortality, the grave was still a home, and the corrosive hours, co-mates."[20] This is far indeed from the rich visionary experiences of Swedenborg; in fact, it seems evident that Poe is mocking the Swedenborgian view of the afterlife, and sneeringly proposing in its stead—soulless nothingness, more or less akin to the horror of being buried alive.

The likelihood that Poe held opposite views is a reasonable interpretation of why Swedenborg's name is signally absent from Poe's writings, and is supported by some remarks Poe once made apropos Hawthorne. In assessing Hawthorne's work, Poe snidely concludes that his fellow author "with these varied good qualities . . . has done *well* as a mystic. But is there any one of these qualities which should prevent his doing doubly as well in a career of honest, upright, sensible, prehensible, and comprehensible things? Let him mend his pen, get out a bottle of visible ink, come out from the Old Manse, cut Mr. Alcott, hang (if possible) the editor of 'The Dial,' and throw out of the window to the pigs all his odd numbers of 'The North American Review.'"[21]

This less than cordial advice to Hawthorne, published in *Godey's Lady's Book*, November 1847, reveals clearly enough Poe's well-known distaste for the Transcendentalists, in particular for Bronson Alcott and Ralph Waldo Emerson. Alcott, of course, was known for his often impenetrable prolixity, but one finds little enough of Alcottian prose to cut from Hawthorne's work in any case. Emerson is another matter. As we shall see shortly, Swedenborg was extremely important for Emerson's work, much more than generally has been recognized. I believe that Poe's distaste for Emerson derives at least in part from Poe's distaste for mysticism or spirituality in general, and for Swedenborg in particular.

There is a passage in Poe's "Autography" devoted to Emerson that certainly reveals Poe's distaste for Emersonian mysticism, which Poe associated consistently with Thomas Carlyle, as well. Poe wrote:

> Mr. Ralph Waldo Emerson belongs to a class of gentlemen with whom we have no patience whatever—the mystics for mysticism's sake. Quintilian mentions a pedant who taught obscurity, and who once said to a pupil, "this is excellent, for I do not understand it myself." How the good man would have chucked over Mr. E.! His present role seems to be out-Carlyling Carlyle.
>
> His love of the obscure does not prevent him, nevertheless, from the composition of occasional poems in which beauty is apparent by flashes. . . .
>
> His MS. is bad, sprawling, illegible, and irregular—although sufficiently bold. This latter trait may be, and no doubt is, only a portion of his general affectation.[22]

Poe's ill humor here is both unpleasant and typical, but interesting for us because it reveals not what Poe disliked about Emerson, necessarily—probably in reality most of all Emerson's success and brilliance—but what he chose to attack in Emerson's work: mysticism. Because this is the theme Poe returns to in sneering also at Hawthorne, one has to suspect that Poe sees the attacking of obfuscation as the most effective way of denigrating these other writers, the means of attack most likely to succeed with the public.

Yet with what does Poe propose to replace what he perceives as the mysticism of Hawthorne and Emerson? In his own stories, we find a fascination with death and decay, and a morbid attraction to psychic extremes, particularly those associated with insanity and murder. It is true that Poe draws on esoteric themes, but it is oftentimes, and perhaps almost always, to undermine their meanings by supplanting transcendence or even esoteric meanings with mere terror. Thus, for example, in Poe's famous story "The Cask of Amontillado," a man walls up in a cellar an acquaintance of his upon whom he seeks revenge. This story may indeed reflect the well-known history, told earlier, of the killing of William Morgan, a Mason who was threatening to tell all about Masonry, and whose mysterious death helped foster the cause of Antimasonry in the United States. After all, Poe does have his victim walled up by masonry, brick-by-brick. Thus it may be that Masonry plays a limited role in Poe's story, but only in what must be recognized as the worst possible light, and merely as a vehicle for terror.[23]

Or again, when we find references to astrology in Poe's work, it is with a similar aim. In "Shadow—A Parable," Poe writes of a "year of terror, and of feelings more intense than terror for which there is no name upon the earth." There were many signs or omens, pestilence was abroad in the world, and to those "cunning in the stars," it was not unknown "that the heavens wore an aspect of ill." For "now had arrived the alternation of the seven hundred and ninety-fourth year when, at the entrance of Aries, the planet Jupiter is conjoined with the red ring of the terrible Saturnus. The peculiar spirit of the skies, if I mistake not greatly, made itself manifest, not only in the physical orb of the earth, but in the souls, imaginations, and meditations of mankind."[24] This bizarre fragment of a story concludes with a portentous shadow resting on the surface of a brass door and announcing to the seven people in the room that it is "SHADOW," at which point everyone leaps up in horror because its voice was actually the thousand voices of their dear departed friends.

As astrology, this is dubious indeed. Aries traditionally is the first of the astrological signs, but Jupiter is generally considered benefic, not malefic, and Saturn is not usually regarded as red. Here again, Poe draws on a prior esoteric tradition, but only for effect, for the sound of the language in the service of terror. One can be sure that he would have sneered at the astrological almanacs of early America, yet it is to them that Poe was indebted; and it is through the farmer's almanacs still printed at that time, and for that matter still printed today, that people were familiar with the idea that the planetary movements could signify benefic or malefic times for various activities. For Poe, the question of astrology in its broader context is not of interest; like the other esoteric traditions we have seen, astrology is used here chiefly for its negative connotations, at best to add a Gothic note to his tale.

There is one more theme in Poe's work that we ought to touch upon, and that is Gnosticism. In *Gnosis and Literature*, I discussed a wide range of authors while tracing the various threads of "Gnosticism" through ancient, medieval, and modern literatures.[25] One of those authors is in fact Poe, whom several scholars have identified as having a perspective strikingly parallel to heretical anticosmic Gnosticism.[26] One problem with such an identification, however, is that little or no effort is made to disentangle the various strands of esotericism in question: Hermeticism, Kabbalism, and Gnosticism are all confused, as if they form one thing. They do not. What is more, although there are some themes in Poe's work that resemble what have been denoted in the interpretations of scholars like Hans Jonas as Gnostic themes—the alien, dread, homesickness, intoxication—this seems more coincidence than a direct indebtedness. In addition, more recent scholarship has shown ancient Gnosticism to be far more religious than Poe ever was. Thus it seems somewhat bizarre to claim Poe's elaborate anticosmological joke screed *Eureka* as a "supreme act of knowing, or *gnosis*," when it so clearly is a parody of modern knowledge and cosmology.[27]

Still, there is some truth in the observation of Barton Levi St. Armand that the fundamental antipathy between Poe and Emerson is "almost a reincarnation . . . in mid-nineteenth century America" of the ancient debate between the Gnostics and the Neoplatonists, exemplified in Plotinus's well-known treatise labeled, rightly or wrongly, "Against the Gnostics."[28] In the chapter on Melville I will make this case more strongly, using Melville as the Gnostic and Emerson as the Platonist, but as I wrote in *Gnosis and Literature*, "To consider Transcendentalism and anti-Transcendentalism in light of Platonism and Gnosticism respectively is most illuminating, and does indeed suggest that Gnosticism and Platonism represent fundamental ways of viewing the cosmos reappearing in different eras."[29] It is probably true that Poe's antipathy to Emerson derived chiefly from his own venomous temperament, but this opposition may also correspond to a deeper division that we will explore further in our final chapters.

When we take all of these stories and observations of Poe together with the poems, what we find is that, on the whole, Poe's work resembles a phosphorescent mushroom: its light is always sickly, and if its color is sometimes brilliant, that brilliance is always tinged by decay. This is true even of his poems, which from very early on were, like his stories, often enough about death. One thinks, for example, of the early poem (pre-1827) "The Spirits of the Dead," which consists in advice for the spirit that finds itself in solitude, surrounded by the spirits of the dead, whose "will / Shall overshadow thee; be still."[30] Here, as in many of Poe's stories, we can see the influence of spiritualism, the movement that swept America throughout the mid-nineteenth century. As to the poetry itself, it is little wonder that Emerson termed Poe "the jingler," given the relentless rhyming. There is always in Poe's work a feverish and sickly quality, even in the poems, a nervous jumpiness that borders on terror or settles back into nameless anxiety.

From what did all of these—the macabre stories, the bizarre dialogues and fragments, even some of the poems—emerge? Often enough, Poe's inspiration was Western esotericism. Mesmerism, Swedenborgianism, spiritualism, alchemy, astrology, all are here, but never affirmed, only as points of inspiration and as means for effect. There are two aspects to this absorption and use of esoteric themes by Poe. One is that he absorbed them often enough only in a general way—he was inspired by and used such themes as astrology or alchemy, but he did not believe in them. The other is that esotericism refracted through the prism of Poe becomes tainted with a gloomy, even sickly and almost always morbid light. Nonetheless, we can certainly say that it is extremely difficult to imagine Poe's works without these various themes, and that without Western esotericism, many of his stories could not exist at all.

seven

Hawthorne

We have already encountered Hawthorne's work, albeit via the unpleasant comments of Poe. It is little surprising that Poe would accuse Hawthorne of plagiarism, for the two authors share a great deal. Above all, for our purposes, the work of both features many of the various currents of Western esotericism. Whereas Poe's use of esoteric themes is relatively unexplored, however, Hawthorne's is much more well known and has been discussed in much more scholarly detail. One of the most useful books for understanding Hawthorne's use of some esoteric themes is William Bysshe Stein's *Hawthorne's Faust* (1953), which as its title suggests, is essentially about the Faust archetype as central to much of Hawthorne's work. The Faust archetype is revealing here because it suggests much about the particular way Hawthorne drew upon many of the same esoteric currents as Poe or the Transcendentalists. For Hawthorne, the esoteric traditions represent something to be feared or mistrusted, and it is thus that they are, for the most part, incorporated into his fiction.

Earlier, we discussed the longstanding traditions of folk magic or witch-craft that were common in the New England colonies. Hawthorne, whose ancestors were themselves involved in some of the witch trials, came by his knowledge of these folk magic traditions in two ways, then: from books, it is true, but also from family and local oral traditions. There is no doubt that Hawthorne was haunted by the Puritan imagination, and his stories are imbued with a sense that pacts with the devil are possible, that mankind is driven to desire more than is permissable, and that this desire is at the root of the human tragedy, whether it be expressed in terms of Faustian science or Faustian pacts with the devil. In his book *Nathaniel Hawthorne and the Romance of the Orient* (1989), Luther Luedtke discusses the great importance that images of Asia had for Hawthorne in formation of his novels and tales. Although these Asian images were important for him, far more important in forming Hawthorne's work is what may be called the dark side of Western esotericism.

Before we consider in detail some of Hawthorne's major tales and novels, we should first remark on the striking absence of esotericism from his letters, notebooks, and journals. Although these topics inform and even govern his fiction, they do not seem to have intruded at all on his daily life or thought; indeed, it seems that he may even have gone out of his way to avoid them. For instance, he wrote a brief letter that recommended "the bearers of this letter," William Pike and Increase Hill, to George Ripley at Brook Farm on 11 October 1846.[1] Hawthorne remarks that they wish to converse with Ripley, almost certainly on religious topics, Hill being a Swedenborgian. But there is in the letter not the slightest inkling of interest in Swedenborgian topics on Hawthorne's own part. Hawthorne did entrust his wife's health to the ministrations of Dr. James John Garth Wilkinson (1812–98), a Swedenborgian homeopathic physician whom Emerson and Henry James Sr. regarded highly.[2] This may have been more Sophia's idea than Hawthorne's, for it appears that she was much more sympathetic to esotericism in practice than Hawthorne himself. When Ethan Allen Hitchcock came to Massachusetts to visit Emerson, the Peabody sisters, and others, it was Sophia who had a "private talk with the Hermetic Philosopher" on 14 August, 1863.[3] Hawthorne himself only remarked, in a July letter, on Hitchcock's political views.

Hawthorne, it seemed, wanted to keep practical forms of esotericism at arm's length. Characteristic is his entry on spiritualism, dated 1 September 1858. Hawthorne shows himself familiar with some of the authorities on spiritualism, as well as with contemporary mediums, and then adds that "what most astonishes me is, the indifference with which I listen to these marvels. They throw old ghost-stories quite into the shade; they bring the whole world of spirits down amongst us, visible and audibly; they are absolutely proved to be sober facts by evidence that would satisfy us of any other alleged realities; and yet I cannot force my mind to interest itself in them. . . . The whole matter seems to me a sort of dreaming awake."[4]

Although he "cannot sufficiently wonder at the pigheadedness both of metaphysicians and physiologists, in not accepting the phenomena, so far as to make them the subject of investigation," and indeed regards spiritualism as in some sense "genuine," yet at the same time he is uncertain whether to devote any time whatever to them in his "not very important journal," so "idle and empty" is spiritualism to him.[5]

It is obvious that Hawthorne is supremely ambivalent about such themes, and this ambivalence makes its way into almost all of his fiction. Indeed, it is as if his work is driven by the tension between his fascination with various forms of esotericism and his aversion to or fear of them. Hawthorne's ambivalence toward esoteric themes, in other words, is not merely a matter of his indecision about them, but rather one of marked polar opposite tendencies that exist side-by-side in his work. If alchemy appears in his works, it is not in order to suggest the noble or transcendent aspects of that tradition, but to show human frailty and the dangers of such experimentation beyond the proper bounds of human society or nature. So, too, it is with magic and the arcane in general: Hawthorne constantly recurs to such themes, finds them indispensable for his art, yet always mistrusts them.

Characteristic of this tension between fascination and aversion is his early story "Dr. Heidegger's Experiment," from *Twice-told Tales*, first published in 1837. Here we find a theme that occupied Hawthorne until the end of his life: that of the alchemical elixir of life. In this relatively early story, the German Dr. Heidegger, owner of a "ponderous folio, bound in black leather, which common report affirmed to be a book of magic," invited four elderly friends to his home in order to offer them the elixir of life.[6] The four friends, three men and a women, partake of the elixir while Dr. Heidegger observes, and they immediately grow younger and turn to flirting, then, fighting. In the fighting, the vase was shattered that contained the elixir from the Fountain of Youth in Florida, and subsequently all four returned to their elderly condition, determined then and there to travel to Florida and find the elixir again. Dr. Heidegger, on the other hand, has learned his lesson and has no intention of touching the elixir himself.

In "The Birthmark," Hawthorne again treats the theme of the scientist-alchemist who wishes to perfect human nature. In this story, the scientist-alchemist Aylmer seeks to remove the birthmark of Georgiana, to whom he is devoted, with a potion described as "bright enough to be the draught of *immortality*." Thus, we are in the realm of alchemy—and for that matter magic—because Aylmer calls himself jokingly a sorceror and wishes to "draw a magic circle" around Georgiana. But when Aylmer has removed the birthmark and perfected Georgiana, he has of course also so purified her that she dies—and Aylmer describes her as perfect precisely at that moment. As R. B. Heilman pointed out in his classic "Hawthorne's 'The Birthmark': Science as Religion," this story can be read as a parable on scientific "progress," but it also can be read as an entirely characteristic Hawthornean tale about the magus-alchemist whose Faustian dream brings sorrow in its wake.[7]

The idea of gaining earthly immortality or human perfection recurs again in the Elixir of Life manuscripts on which Hawthorne was still working when he died. These include the novels *Septimius Felton*, *Septimius Norton*, and *The Dolliver Romance*, all of which involve permutations of alchemy and the consequences of the quest for immortality. In his own documentation from this time, around the middle of 1861 onward, and from a letter written in 1852, it is clear that the genesis of Hawthorne's focus on the elixir of life was his purchase of "The Wayside," a house on the eastern edge of Concord, Massachusetts, about which Thoreau had told him "it was inhabited a generation or two ago by a man who believed he should never die."[8] Initially, the two *Septimius* manuscripts emerged from Hawthorne's meditations about a room in his home that he imagined held an ancient and indecipherable manuscript. Later, the story emerged from the American Revolution, and from a dying British soldier at the

Battle of Concord who, having taking a liking to Septimius, gives him a recipe for the elixir of youth (or that Septimius finds on his body). *The Dolliver Romance*, on the other hand, is about an apothecary who has such an elixir but is forced to relinquish it to a bullying man, who then swigs from the bottle and promptly dies.

What makes these manuscripts interesting for our purposes is the fact that alchemy is reduced from its multivalent symbolism and spiritual significances, to a form of pharmaceutical production for the indefinite extension of earthly life. Hawthorne's notebooks reveal that he associated such efforts with the work of modern science, and he remarked in a magazine article of August 1836 that God had "absolutely debarred mankind from all inventions and discoveries, the results of which would counteract the general laws, that He has established over human affairs."[9] In other words, Hawthorne maintained a more or less conservative Christian disapproval of alchemical experimentation on the grounds that it was Faustian, an effort to violate the laws of nature. Of course, this is precisely what we see illustrated in Hawthorne's various stories: those who attempt to violate the laws of nature by way of alchemy or other means come to a bad end. Clearly the "alchemy" portrayed in Hawthorne's fiction has little to do with the actual esoteric traditions we have earlier surveyed; traditionally, there are various forms of European alchemy, including laboratory alchemy, but they all have spiritual connotations (especially an insistence upon humility) that are wholly absent from Hawthorne's portrayal.

The *Septimius Felton* manuscript is the most fully plotted, and tells the story of how Septimius killed a young British officer and found a manuscript recipe for immortality. As he attempts to decipher the manuscript, he becomes increasingly alienated from his family and friends, except for his part-Indian aunt, first called Keziah, but later called Nashoba, and an ethereal, somewhat sinister young woman named Sybil Dacy. Septimius eventually does decode the recipe and concoct the elixir, after which Sybil drinks the full glass and falls down dying from poison because the elixir contained a wrong ingredient. *Septimius Norton* follows more or less the same plot, but with so much expansion that it never arrives at the climactic moment where the elixir itself is imbibed. *The Dolliver Romance*, a story about an apothecary who gets his hands on an elixir of life but is forced at gunpoint to hand it over to a red faced, volcanic claimant, is also incomplete, although it reads very well.

One interesting addition found in the much-expanded *Septimius Norton* manuscript has to do with Aunt Nashoba, the part-Native American herbalist. Septimius, called "Hilliard" in this version of the story, discovers to his surprise that his old aunt had had the same recipe for immortality all along, and that indeed, he had grown up smelling it.[10] However, she, too, lacked the central ingredient, and so could not help him complete his own recipe. He was astounded by the "strangeness of the coincidence between Aunt Nashoba's despised mixture which he might have tasted, any day, and nourished himself upon from boyhood, and that rare medicine which the old manuscript had revealed to him."[11] Thus, we find that the European alchemical tradition is wedded with

Native American lore, so that one finds the first in "the archives of an ancient and noble family," and second, "by transmission from one old woman's hand to another." "Who could tell," he wonders, "what far antiquity it came down from?"[12]

Yet there was in the brewing mixture something that reminded Septimius of the devil, and there are enough references to broomsticks, "aerial jaunts," and Aunt Nashoba's isolation and reputation, to assure us that she fits the usual description of the witch. She describes herself, sadly, as a "bitter, venemous thing, all my life, out of place, lonely, one whose race, and blood, was gone, a poor yellow creature, whom nobody loved." Yet she shortly turns to talk of how she and Septimius represent a "strange new blood made out of two races, and so that we are a kind of monster in the world." With that one missing herb, she garrulously goes on, "I would have no more died than Satan can." Aunt Nashoba had once thought that the "Great Sagamore" from whom the recipe came "had won the blessing of endless life; now I see that he had got the curse of never dying."[13] When Septimius tells some of this to Sybil Dacy, she starts, and goes on to tell him that her uncle, Dr. Portsoaken, was rumored also to have such a medicine, but could not find quite the right manuscript description, despite all his efforts.

All of this bespeaks Hawthorne's own continual ambivalence about this topic of alchemy and herbalism. On the one hand, he allies Aunt Nashoba pretty clearly with Satan or the devil in her own comments, as well as in those of the neighbors who come to her deathbed. She and Septimius both have "witch-blood," which is somehow allied with their Native American heritage, and which is depicted as sinister. Yet at the same time, Nashoba is a somewhat pathetic figure, lying there on her deathbed and blathering on about her miserable life. In Sybil's comments about her uncle, Dr. Portsoaken, we see acknowledged an English alchemical tradition that isn't denigrated by her at all, but is seen as quite real and not at all necessarily bad. In depicting such a wide range of perspectives on alchemy, Hawthorne is undoubtedly reflecting a range of views in New England, as well, but here, near the end of his life, Hawthorne also seems almost willing to acknowledge the view that alchemy might not necessarily be of the devil. Almost, but not quite. After all, in the *Septimius Felton* story, it is Sybil who dies when she impetuously drinks Septimius's potion, and it is Sybil who is depicted as somewhat sinister. Thus, Sybil's acceptance of alchemy taints her and brings about her death, and so in the end, the elixir of life remains one of the devil's temptations.

When we turn to the novels, we find a similar denigration and horror of witchcraft, yet at the same time a sense that witch-hunting itself was a delusion. In *The House of the Seven Gables*, we are introduced to the Pyncheon line, which began by taking over a disputed piece of land occupied by a man named Matthew Maule. Maule is described as a "wizard" and his witchcraft is represented as a terrible and ugly crime, in which description there was perhaps a bit of irony. Colonel Pyncheon was among the most vocal of those accusing Maule of witchcraft, and Hawthorne takes care to describe Maule as "one of the martyrs to that terrible delusion" that characterizes "the maddest mob."[14] Maule, on the scaffold, curses Pycheon by saying "God will give him blood to drink!"[15] Pyncheon, of course, dies mysteriously, and in every generation or the next another Pyncheon like the old one is born, always haunted by the "evil influence" of the "Evil Genius" of the family, the old patriarch, Colonel Pyncheon. Although the book comes to a happy conclusion, with "Maule's Well" "throwing up a succession of kaleidoscopic pictures, in which a gifted eye might have seen fore-shadowed the coming fortunes of Hepzibah, and Clifford, and the descendent of the legendary wizard, and the village-maiden, over whom he had thrown love's web of sorcery,"[16] the reader feels the dissonance between this happy ending and the novel's more morose beginning. Witchcraft is transformed into "love's web of sorcery."

Numerous critics have remarked upon the prevalence of alchemical symbolism in Hawthorne's stories, and certainly it is visible in *The House of the Seven Gables*, which Randall Clack terms Hawthorne's "last full-length treatment of the alchemy of love."[17] In Clack's view, the Pyncheon house is the alembic of the heart in which the "transmutation and redemption of the corrupt past, symbolized by the legend of the Pyncheon curse, occur through the union of Phoebe and Holgrave."[18] The same idea is outlined in another article by Jeffrey Meikle, who offers an even more extended reading of the alchemical symbolism in *The House of the Seven Gables*.[19] Judge Pyncheon is consistently associated with the metals iron and lead; Hepzibah, an old maid, is somewhat ironically associated with copper, the metal of Venus; and at the novel's end, a branch of the family's elm tree glistens golden. However, as Meikle remarks, the novel's ending does not entirely ring true: Hawthorne himself observes in passing "how soon the heavy earth-dream settled down again."[20] It is true that *The House of the Seven Gables* includes some alchemical allusions, but in the end this symbolism is associated with the suddenly prolific egg production of hens as "guardian angels" of the Pyncheon house! Hawthorne's use of alchemical symbolism is clearly ironic here, and the force of the novel comes from the brooding darkness of the Pyncheon curse, not from its brief, inconclusive lifting at the novel's end.

One also finds alchemical allusions in *The Scarlet Letter*, for which a somewhat more persuasive case can be made that the novel is alchemical at its heart. One can make such a claim because Hawthorne directly connects Roger Chillingworth to alchemical research. As Luther Martin points out, Chillingworth was "heard to speak of Sir Kenelm Digby" [a seventeenth century English alchemist], and had been seen in the company of a "famous old conjurer." The novel illustrates the major alchemical colors of black, white, red, and gold with the characters Chillingworth (black), Dimmesdale (white), and Hester (red-gold), and finally, the product of Dimmesdale's and Hester's illicit union, the daughter Pearl, the alchemical child.[21]

Although *The Scarlet Letter* does contain alchemical allusions that help to illuminate the novel's inner meanings, it is in the end a tragedy, not a comedy. The numerous critics who have pointed out the alchemical symbolism of this novel have often failed to note how ambivalent this symbolism actually is. Chillingworth, who is directly connected to alchemy by Hawthorne, is an "unhappy man" who had "made the very principle of his life to consist in the pursuit and systematic exercise of revenge," an "evil principle," that at the novel's end is likened to an "uprooted weed."[22] Although by the novel's end "hatred and antipathy" "may" have been "transmuted into golden love," Pearl is immediately thereafter described as an "elf-child" and even as "demon offspring," which adds a certain ambivalence to her symbolism. Likewise, Hester at the novel's end is no "destined prophetess" of some brighter future for women, but instead is host in her cottage to numerous other wounded, wronged, erring and wretched women who come to her for consolation.[23] The novel, like *The House of the Seven Gables*, does indeed draw on alchemical symbolism, but toward a very ambivalent end.

Indeed, when we look more closely at the alchemical symbolism in *The Scarlet Letter*, we could well read the novel as a lesson in staying away from alchemical pursuits, and even from herbalism. It is true that Chillingworth had pursued "my old studies in alchemy," and that he knew a very great deal about herbalism and the preparation of simples.[24] He even set up a laboratory in his house, and is frequently seen gathering herbs and "examining a bundle of unsightly plants."[25] But Chillingworth is associated with blight and evil herbs like deadly nightshade—with "vegetable wickedness"—he is the only character explicitly associated with alchemy, and like so many of Hawthorne's alchemist characters, he is largely a negative example, yet another example of Hawthorne's simultaneous attraction to and repulsion from esoteric themes.

In *The Blithedale Romance*, we encounter not witchcraft and alchemy, but the mesmerism and "rapping spirits" of the day, and once again, they are presented in a far from good light. *The Blithedale Romance* is, of course, loosely based on Hawthorne's own experience at Brook Farm, a relatively short-lived Transcendentalist effort to establish an earthly utopia. It is interesting, therefore, that central to Hawthorne's novel is a chapter entitled "A Village-Hall," in which we see an exhibition of mesmerism by a man named Westervelt. In this chapter, Hawthorne allows his narrator, Miles Coverdale, to comment at length about the phenomena of animal magnetism and spiritualism. Coverdale remarks that "there was a great deal of talk going on, near me, among a knot of people who might be considered as representing the mysticism, or, rather, the mystic sensuality, of this singular age."[26] The term "mystic sensuality" is in fact fairly accurate: mesmerism and spiritualism, after all, do represent strikingly physical phenomena presented as having spiritual causes, and it is quite clear that Coverdale finds these phenomena not only disturbing, but a kind of degradation.

Hawthorne, in the voice of Coverdale, goes on to attack all of these spiritualist phenomena at once. He writes:

> The epoch of rapping spirits, and all the wonders that have followed in their train—such as tables, upset by invisible agencies, bells, self-tolled at fu-

nerals, and ghostly music, performed on jewsharps—had not yet arrived. Alas, my countrymen, methinks we have fallen on an evil age! If these phenomena have not humbug at the bottom, so much the worse for us. What can they indicate, in a spiritual way, except that the soul of man is descending to a lower point than it has ever before reached, while incarnate? We are pursuing a downward course, in the eternal march, and thus bring ourselves into the same range with beings whom death, in requital of their gross and evil lives, has degraded below humanity.[27]

This rather lengthy diatribe, which continues on well past what is quoted here, may or may not represent the thoughts of Hawthorne himself. The question of Hawthorne's narrator's voice is always problematic: Coverdale, here, is a persona imposed between the reader and Hawthorne himself, and yet given Hawthorne's own remarks in his journal already quoted, one suspects that there is more than a little of Hawthorne himself in these remarks.

It is, of course, well-known that *The Blithedale Romance* is in large part inspired by the Transcendentalist effort at utopia in Brook Farm, but not as frequently noted are its possible connections to other utopian American communities of the same era, especially mesmerist-spiritualist ones. One might recall that another ill-fated utopian community of the period was that founded by Bronson Alcott, at least to some degree along Christian theosophic lines; but Hawthorne also might have had in mind the sexual tension of John Humphrey Noyes's Oneida community (founded in 1848) where sexual practices (in particular, "male continence," or sexual relations without ejaculation) played a significant role. Certainly *The Blithedale Romance* is permeated with sexual tension, as well (one thinks of Coverdale's reference to the "mystic sensuality" of the day). Furthermore, we should not forget that there were spiritualist communities with strong interests in mesmerism that surrounded such prolific and charismatic figures as Andrew Jackson Davis and Thomas Lake Harris. These groups, too, which also had millennialist leanings and (in the case of Harris) rumored sexual practices, may well have figured in the creation of *The Blithedale Romance*. All of them sought to realize on earth what they saw as "the one true system," and all these groups saw some human casualties as a result.

The powerful, fascinating woman character Zenobia, in taking her leave of Coverdale, remarks that she is "weary of this place [Blithedale]. Of all varieties of mock-life, we have surely blundered into the very emptiest mockery, in our effort to establish the one true system."[28] Zenobia then, having been rejected by Hollingsworth, drowns herself, and at the funeral gathering we see Coverdale meeting with the other principal characters, including Westervelt, whom Coverdale regards as Zenobia's "evil fate." Westervelt tells Coverdale that he regrets that Zenobia wasted her life, and Coverdale blames him for her death, although Westervelt cannot discern why. Coverdale exclaims: "Heaven deal with Westervelt according to his nature and deserts!—that is to say, annihilate him. He was altogether earthy, worldly, made for time and its gross objects, and incapable—except by a sort of dim reflection, caught from other minds—of so much as one spiritual idea."[29] Of course this condemnation does not spare Coverdale himself, either. Shortly thereafter he remarks that he himself was a "colorless" man who took his hues from other peoples' lives. It seems clear that behind the condemnations of the mesmerists and spiritualists in the book is a condemnation of human efforts to control hypnotized people or spirits because such control is a violation of natural law, degrading, and affiliated with prostitution and even rape.[30] By implication, efforts at utopianism are, at least to some extent, extensions of such practices to a larger group and therefore intrinsically suspect.

Certainly one finds also in *The House of the Seven Gables* a distrust of mesmerism. Here, as Samuel Chase Coale points out in his book *Hawthorne and Mesmerism*, the Maule family curse centers on variants of mesmerism. Young Matthew Maule, for instance, "had taken a woman's delicate soul into his rude gripe, to play with—and she was dead!"[31] "The Maule curse," Coale observes, "continues through Holgrave, a secret Maule himself."[32] Holgrave has not only lectured on mesmerism, he remarks that it is "in my blood," "which might have brought me to gallows hill, in the good old times of witchcraft." Thus Holgrave is redeemed by breaking with his innate tendency toward mesmerism in his relationship with Phoebe—his redemption comes about by relinquishing his power in favor of love.

It is noteworthy that the kinds of esotericism that appear in Hawthorne's fiction are not the kind of esotericism we traced earlier. Rather, what we find in Hawthorne's fiction is invariably a kind of literalized esotericism. Alchemy is never the spiritual practice that we find described in alchemical texts; instead, in Hawthorne's fiction, it is always the illegitimate and vain search for earthly immortality, or the pursuit of a sinister figure like Chillingworth in *The Scarlet Letter*. Likewise, the spiritualism and mesmerism that Hawthorne denigrated in *The Blithedale Romance* itself was a kind of literalization and bastardization of prior esoteric traditions. Whereas in the esoteric lodges of Europe during the eighteenth century, spiritualist or mesmeric phenomena were incorporated into a larger spiritual-religious context, in nineteenth century America and as depicted in Hawthorne's work, they were exhibited in stage shows and vulgar exhibitions for entertainment.[33] Hawthorne drew on these literalized esoteric traditions for fictional purposes, but it seems clear that he also wanted to keep them at arm's length. Perhaps in this tactic Hawthorne is very much aligned with the practices of Puritan predecessors like Edward Taylor and Nicholas Noyes, who drew upon alchemical language chiefly to illustrate Christian themes, thus bringing their esoteric subjects safely into a literary and Christian fold.

When we scan Hawthorne's work as a whole, it is evident that he regarded the various forms of esotericism that emerged in his novels and stories with a kind of fascinated horror. In some respects, placing spiritualism, mesmerism, alchemy, and witchcraft in the novels and stories might be seen as a way of keeping these subjects under control, of making them safe by transposing them into the realm of literature. At the same time, there is no doubt that these topics, precisely because they are extreme, bring a kind of fascinating power into Hawthorne's fictional worlds. In *The Scarlet Letter*, for instance, Hester

Prynne's out-of-wedlock child Pearl is described as a "demon" at one point, as an "elf-child" often, and innocently inquires of her mother about a "black man" who roamed the forest with a large book, which he has those he meets sign in their blood.[34] Such references add irony to the novel, because the black man is in fact the man in black, the minister, not the devil, but they also intensify the fiction by incorporating charged religious and esoteric symbolism, even as that very symbolism is to some degree tamed by safe placement in the fictional world.

eight

Melville

Without doubt, Herman Melville remains one of the most enigmatic figures of the American Renaissance. Not surprisingly, then, whereas most of the authors whose work we are considering have a fairly clear relationship to various esoteric traditions, for the most part this cannot be said of Melville's work, still subject as it is to often wildly varying interpretations by literary scholars. Clearly, as one surveys Melville's writings, one finds in them some direct allusions to esoteric traditions. In his fiction, in his poems, and in his letters, we find Melville alluding or referring to such traditions as Freemasonry, Rosicrucianism, Neoplatonism, and perhaps most notably of all, Gnosticism. But what can we conclude about Melville's attitudes toward these esoteric traditions? Does he endorse, doubt, fear, or draw upon them? Has he any certain attitudes at all toward any of them? To answer questions like these, we must delve into Melville's various works with each of these particular traditions in mind. What we will find is that Melville's closest self-identification was probably with Gnosticism.

Melville's attitude toward spiritualism is rather clear from his story "The Apple-Tree Table," published in 1856. In it, he plays on the image with which Thoreau finishes *Walden*: that of an old applewood table from which insects emerge rather noisily after a long hibernation.[1] For Thoreau, the image signifies spiritual rebirth; for Melville, the story evokes all of what he regards as the foolishness that surrounded the table rappers of contemporary spiritualism. In Melville's version, his narrator's daughters are convinced that the insects' noise as they emerge are in fact evil spirits, whereas his wife sees the noises as entirely natural and a professor finally identifies the insects properly. Although it is true that Melville draws on allusions to the Salem witch scare and the writings of Cotton Mather, the import of the whole is that spiritualism and Thoreau's Transcendentalism both are fanciful interpretations of what is, in the end, a bug crawling out of a table.

Certainly, Melville was familiar with Rosicrucianism. Indeed, he wrote a poem entitled "The New Rosicrucians" that suggests the poet's identification with this esoteric movement. The poem reads:

> To us, disciples of the Order
>   Whose rose-vine twines the Cross,
> Who have drained the rose's chalice
>   Never heeding gain or loss;
> For all the preacher's din
> There is no mortal sin—
>   No, none to us but Malice!
> Exempt from that, in blest recline
>   We let life's billows toss;
> If sorrow come, anew we twine
>   The Rose-Vine round the Cross.[2]

This poem is one among a cluster of Melville's poems in which roses are prevalent, many in a less obvious way than this one, which also contrasts the order of the Rosy Cross with the conventional moralistic preaching of contemporary Christianity. In this poem, there is no hint of Melville's often sardonic attitude toward various forms of esotericism; the narrator's voice (perhaps or perhaps not that of Melville) expresses the viewpoint of "us, disciples of the Order," who "in blest recline" "let life's billows toss."

However, the poem could be read in light of another, entitled "Rose Window," which tells of a parishioner's revery as a preacher gave a sermon on "Solomon's Song," and "Four words for text with mystery rife— / The Rose of Sharon."[3] The parishioner slumbers during the sermon, and dreams of "An Angel with a Rose." Then the parishioner awakens, and sees above a "great Rose-Window high, / A mullioned wheel in gable set," casting down a "Transfiguring light on dingy stains / While danced the motes in dusty pew." Read in concert with "The New Rosicrucians," "Rose Window" suggests that perhaps the order of the rose emerges from revery and little more; if the sermon of conventional Christianity is so boring that one falls asleep, one is left to wonder if the dream of an angel with a rose is any more ultimately salvific than the boring sermon. Or, one could read "Rose Window" as suggesting that the "dingy stains" and "dusty pew" of the church are merely the outward shadow or shell of what one can encounter in dream or vision, and what is figured in the Rose Window itself: the true, rosy, heart of Christianity. No settled interpretation is possible, and in light of its companion rose poems, "The New Rosicrucians" is by no means enough to claim Melville (whose poetry often has narrators that are clearly not Melville himself) as a New Rosicrucian.

As one examines Melville's poetry and prose, it becomes increasingly difficult to claim Melville as having any fixed perspective regarding esotericism. For instance, when we turn to his late novel *The Confidence Man* (1857), we do find reference to Rosicrucianism, but of what sort? Quite possibly the most ambiguous and frustrating novel of the nineteenth century, *The Confidence Man* was an absolute commercial failure and resists virtually any attempts to explicate clearly its meaning. But the novel is about confidence, or trust, and its main character is a strange, pale, confidence man of whom little that is certain may be said. A bachelor on the boat with the confidence man speculates about him, and we read that "Before his mental vision the person of that threadbare Talleyrand, that impoverished Machiavelli, that seedy Rosicrucian—for something of all these he vaguely deems him—passes now in puzzled review."[4] What or who is the confidence man? As we have seen, Melville's poem "The New Rosicrucians" offers a noble image of the Rosicrucians; here, that nobility is crossed with a kind of seediness. But we are left with no certain sense either of the confidence man or, for that matter, of how he is a "seedy Rosicrucian."

The Confidence Man seems to be about how people impute to others—in particular the confidence man—what they want to see. Thus, when we are introduced to the confidence man, we are treated to a list of the other passengers' unattributed comments about him. Here are the majority:

"ODD FISH!"
"Poor fellow!"
"Who can he be?"
"Casper Hauser."
"Bless my soul!"
"Uncommon countenance."
"Green prophet from Utah."
"Humbug!"
"Singular innocence."
"Means something."
"Spirit-rapper."
"Moon-calf."
"Piteous."
"Trying to enlist interest."
"Beware of him."[5]

The "green prophet from Utah" probably refers to Mormonism, which in its origins incorporated a great deal from Masonic rituals; "spirit-rapper" and "moon-calf" suggest spiritualism and gullibility. Taken as a whole, however, this series of comments implies nothing so much as that whatever people conclude about the confidence man reflects their own predilections and nothing else. People see what they are inclined to see.

It is also true that Masonry appears in The Confidence Man, shortly after the passage above, when the confidence man meets a businessman named Mr. Roberts. He shakes his hand and says "If I remember, you are a mason, Mr. Roberts?" "And would you not loan a brother a shilling if he needed it?"[6] Eventually, Roberts is won over and becomes compassionate enough to offer the confidence man some money, after which the stranger imparts advice on the possibility of investing in the "Black Rapids Coal Company." Placing one's confidence in the coal company is, of course, another example of the confidence games that pervade the novel, but so too, upon reflection, is Masonry. The well-known preference of Masons for their fellow Masons, by implication, is itself a kind of confidence game as well: one places confidence in one's fellow Masons.

Of course we are not finished with such allusions in *The Confidence Man*. Perhaps the most well-known figure in the novel besides the confidence man himself is the transcendentalist figure Mark Winsome, who is pretty clearly modeled on Ralph Waldo Emerson. Winsome, whose physical description is strikingly close to that of Emerson in the 1850s, like Emerson is fond of Neoplatonism, and even quotes Proclus in the original Greek. Winsome's conversation with the Confidence Man offers some amusing turns on well-known Transcendentalist sentiments, as when the stranger remarks that "death, though in a worm, is majestic; while life, though in a king, is contemptible."[7] This is a fairly anti-Transcendentalist remark, and the sense of anti-Transcendentalism is intensified by the approach of a "shatterbrain" with a "look of picturesque Italian ruin and dethronement" (perhaps meant to remind us of Margaret Fuller's husband Ossoli), who offers Winsome and the stranger a tract "quite in the transcendental vein," but Winsome refuses to give him a penny. The clear implication is that Transcendentalism is the philosophy of a madman and that Emerson is far from compassionate, to boot. Both Transcendentalists and the would-be "shatterbrain" are engaged in a confidence game, too.

At last, we come to the final chapter, "Increase in Seriousness," in which we are introduced to the "Wisdom of Jesus, the Son of Sirach," one of the apocryphal books of the Bible. The confidence man reads from it: "With much communication he will tempt thee; he will smile upon thee, and speak thee fair, and say What wantest thou? If thou be for his profit he will use thee; he will make thee bare, and will not be sorry for it. Observe and take good heed. When thou hearest these things, awake in thy sleep."[8] The confidence man himself continues: "Give me the folly that dimples the cheek, say I, rather than the wisdom that curdles the blood. But no, no; it ain't wisdom; it's apocrypha, as you say, sir. For how can that be trustworthy that teaches distrust?"[9] It would seem that, because the novel's final chapter turns on the apocryphal book of Sirach, there is a final confidence game going on here, and that, of course, is an old man's trust in Jehovah and in his fellow passenger. Christianity, too, the chapter strongly implies, is a confidence game, and the wisest books—like the book of Sirach, which advises us to trust not even our friends—were left out of the Bible.

All of this suggests that Melville's mature view of esotericism—of which he certainly knew at least enough to make all of the various specific references we have outlined in *The Confidence Man*—was as jaundiced as his view of anything else. Elizabeth Foster offered a good hypothesis regarding Melville's mature views: "Perhaps he felt that, because of the profound antagonism between his views and most of the dominant faiths of his America, it was dangerous or hopeless to try to make himself heard, but that he must nevertheless stubbornly record his convictions; if readers deplored pessimism and allegory, then parabolic meanings could be shifted beyond their focus. Perhaps he felt that what he had to say about religion was too radical for the many but that by using esoteric symbols he could convey it to the few."[10] Foster was right, I think, to see that Melville's religious views differed very much from those of most mid-nineteenth-century Americans, who held to a familiar conventional Christianity. That Melville did not agree with them is abundantly clear not only in *The Confidence Man*, but also in the rest of his writings.

How esotericism helped illustrate Melville's most closely held views can be discerned from one of the well-known letters that he wrote to Hawthorne, this one in 1851. About this letter, Sophia Hawthorne, in sending a copy to her sister Elizabeth, wrote "as it is wholly confidential *do not show it*. The fresh, sincere, glowing mind that utters it is in a state of 'fluid consciousness,' & to Mr Hawthorne speaks his innermost about GOD, the Devil, & Life if so be he can get at the Truth . . . & it would betray him to make public his confessions & efforts to grasp—because they would be considered perhaps impious, if one did not take in the whole scope of the case."[11]

Sophia Hawthorne's concern that Melville's innermost thoughts would be perceived as impious and that they should not be shown to anyone underscores what one has to suspect when looking at Melville's work as a whole: that a kind of jaundiced, heretical, anticosmic Gnosticism is at its center. What was in this "wholly confidential" letter to Hawthorne? In it, Melville wrote about the "secret of the universe" that "Perhaps, after all, there is *no* secret. We incline to think that the Problem of the Universe is like the Freemason's mighty secret, so terrible to all children. It turns out, at last, to consist in a triangle, a mallet, and an apron,—nothing more! We incline to think that God cannot explain His own secrets, and that He would like a little information upon certain points Himself."[12] In other words, just as Freemasonry is in the end humbug, so, too, is conventional Christianity. This is an opinion not likely to sit very well with most people in nineteenth-century America, and it is little surprise that Melville felt obliged to keep his views somewhat disguised in his fiction. What sort of views were these? Above all: Gnostic.

Probably the most exhaustive study of Melville's Gnosticism is that of Melanie Bloodgood, whose survey of critical literature and of Melville's works not only takes into account the views of major critics, but also discusses most of Melville's novels and considers contemporary scholarly views of Gnosticism. Bloodgood argues, in essence, that Melville's was not an antinomian Gnosticism, but rather represented a visionary Gnosis along Valentinian lines. Although she presents an extensive case, Bloodgood is not entirely convincing when she ignores Melville's "darkness," his dualism, and his anticosmism.

As an example, Bloodgood attacks Thomas Vargish's pessimistic reading of Melville's poem "Fragment of a Lost Gnostic Poem of the 12th Century," which reads as follows:

Found a family, build a state
The pledged event is still the same:
Matter in end will never abate
His ancient brutal claim.
Indolence is heaven's ally here,

And energy the child of hell:
The Good Man pouring from his pitcher clear,
But brims the poisoned well.

Bloodgood tries to interpret this poem as saying that if man overcomes his ignorance, "Nature . . . [can] exist in a condition of health and harmony."[13] She
vehemently attacks Vargish's much more sensible reading, which holds that the
poem means precisely what it says: that here, caught in matter as human beings,
we are subject to matter's "ancient, brutal claim," and only when we die do we
escape it. Doing good means nothing—it only "brims the poisoned well" that
is earth. Here is a clear example of Melville's Schopenhauerian pessimism, yet
Bloodgood still tries to deny that the poem says "material existence is categor-
ically evil." Bloodgood tries to make Melville a Valentinian Gnostic even when
he explicitly refers to the Cathari, a world-rejecting medieval heretical sect.

If Bloodgood represents an over-interpretation of Melville's Gnosticism
to make it conform to contemporary scholarly views of Gnosticism, the work
of Lawrance Thompson represents an exaggerated emphasis on Melville's dark
side. In his classic study *Melville's Quarrel With God*, Thompson said that it
would be more appropriate to call Melville a "descendentalist" than a transcendentalist, a witticism that manifests a deeper truth than one might expect.
Thompson wrote of Melville: "The turn which his life had taken translated him
from a transcendentalist and a mystic into an inverted transcendentalist, an inverted mystic. To this extent, then, he was consistent, in spite of all his con-
comitant inconsistencies, to the very end of his life. Like his own Captain Ahab,
he remained a defiant rebel, even in the face of death."[14] And the focus of
Melville's rebellion? Not so much man, or even society or Nature—though
these were certainly impugned in his vision—but God himself. According to
Thompson, Melville's vision "narrows down to the sharp focus of a misan-
thropic notion that the world was put together wrong, and that God was to
blame. The gist of it was that simple. He spent his life not merely sneering at
the gullibility of human beings who disagreed with him, but also in sneering at
God, accusing God, upbraiding God, blaming God, and (as he thought) quar-
reling with God."[15]

This description closely resembles twentieth-century existentialist depic-
tions of ancient Gnosticism. Hans Jonas, in his seminal work *The Gnostic
Religion*, says the following in a most provocative discussion of Gnostic exegesis:

The elevation of Cain, prototype of the outcast, condemned by God to be a
"fugitive and a vagabond" upon earth, to a pneumatic symbol and an honored position in the line leading to Christ is of course an intentional challenge
to ingrained valuations. This opting for the "other" side, for the traditionally
infamous, is an heretical method, and much more serious than a merely sen-
timental siding with the underdog . . . [for] allegory, normally so respectable
a means of harmonising, is here made to carry the bravado of nonconfor-
mity.[16]

Indeed, Jonas continues, the Gnostics hardly claimed to bring out the meaning of the original, because its author was their great adversary, the benighted creator-god. Rather, they said, the blind author unwittingly embodied something of the truth in his partisan version of things, and this truth can be brought out by inverting the intended meaning.

The connection here with Melville cannot be overlooked: the central place of Ishmael and of Ahab as societal outcasts has been noted before, as has the Cainite theme that recurs throughout *Moby Dick*.[17] By placing these outcasts at the novel's center, Melville does valorise them, just as the Gnostics valorised outcasts throughout history, the most radical example being Marcion, who taught that Christ descended into hell solely to redeem those who, like Cain, denied the God of the Jews, while those who obeyed the deluded creator-God—Noah, Abel, Abraham, Moses—were left below.[18]

In fact, Ishmael and Ahab are overtly Gnostic, Ahab's speech in "The Candles" being incomprehensible without reference to Gnostic doctrines. As Thomas Vargish has shown, the "sweet mother" to whom Ahab calls is the Gnostic Sophia, from whose anguish his benighted father is born.[19] Says Ahab, vauntingly, precisely as did the Gnostics before him: "certainly [thou] knowest not thy beginning, hence callest thyself unbegun. I know that of me, which thou knowest not of thyself, oh, thou omnipotent. There is some unsuffusing thing beyond thee, thou clear spirit, to whom all eternity is time, all thy creativeness mechanical."[20] Here is the Gnostic distinction between the true, hidden God, and the jealous, mechanical demiurge, The deluded demiurge is identified with fire, "whom on these seas I as Persian once did worship, till in the sacrificial act so burned by thee that to this day I bear the scar."[21] This is an allusion to the scar borne by Cain, who was also burnt in the sacrificial act. Note, too, that the reference is in the past tense—for Ahab has gained in knowledge: "I now know that thy right worship is defiance" for "To neither love nor reverence wilt thou be kind; and e'en for hate thou canst but kill; and all are killed."[22] The God is fire, says Ahab, but to the end he will deny its complete "unintegral mastery in me." "I own thy power," he says, "yet while I earthly live, the queenly personality lives in me and feels her royal rights." Though ruled by the demiurge, Ahab still knows of the true knowledge, which is the Sophia. Note, too, that in all these references to the demiurgic God, the address is in lower case, hence absolving Ahab of the "flunkeyism" in the usage of upper-case references to which Melville alluded in his letter to Hawthorne. Surely Jonas could be paraphrasing Ahab, as he is the Gnostics, when he says the Gnostics held that "man's inner self is not part of the world, of the demiurge's creation and domain, but is within that world as totally transcendent . . . as is its transmundane counterpart, the unknown God without.[23]

There is one central aspect of Gnostic thought that manifests in the characters Ishmael and Ahab, and that must be pointed out if we are to see the full scope of Melville's Gnosticism in *Moby Dick*, that being the deterministic nature of the cosmos. Jonas writes: "the preëminent character of the cosmos for the Gnostics was the *heimarmene*—that is, universal fate."[24] In the Greek tradition—and especially in the Pythagorean and Platonic strain, which is its essence—the stars and planets were seen as the harmonious reflexion of the Intelligible order, which is precisely how Emersonian Transcendentalism viewed them.[25] However, for the heretical Gnostics, the stars and planets "now stared man in the face with the fixed glare of alien power and necessity. [Their] rule is tyranny, not providence." Moreover: "Under this pitiless sky, which no longer inspires worshipful confidence, man becomes conscious of his utter forlornness, of his being not so much a part of, but unaccountably placed in and exposed to the enveloping system."[26]

Ahab symbolizes and manifests precisely this consciousness of man's subjection to an implacable fate. This is made quite explicit near the end of *Moby Dick* when, in "The Symphony," the "natural man" is contrasted with the demiurgic madness. In this chapter, Ahab is reminded of his wife and child back home, but recognizes his entrapment in the *heimarmene*: "What is it, what nameless, inscrutable, unearthly thing is it; what cozening, hidden lord and master, and cruel, remorseless empreror commands me . . . recklessly making me ready to do what in my proper, natural heart, I durst not so much as dare?"[27] And his answer? "By heaven, man, we are turned round and round in this world, like yonder windlass, and Fate is the handspike."[28] Then it is that we are reminded, again, of the Cainites, for here again Cain is implicitly absolved of his guilt: "Where do murderers go, man! Who's to doom, *when the judge himself is dragged to the bar*?"[29] How can God condemn, when it's God who's responsible? Once again, the demiurge is impugned. Again, says Ahab, in the fierceness of the chase: "This whole act's immutably decreed. 'Twas rehearsed by thee and me a billion years before this ocean rolled. Fool! I am the Fates' lieutenant; I act under orders. Look, thou underling; that thou obeyest mine."[30]

This last statement finally reveals one aspect of the subtle allegorical meaning to which Melville referred in his correspondence with Hawthorne; that is, throughout the novel Ahab is identified with fire, so much so that in at least one scene his very soul seems to dissolve into a chasm lit with forked flames.[31] Because "The Candles" suggest that the deluded demiurge is identified with fire, one must wonder if Ahab himself, in his relentless tyranny over the crew, is not himself a type of the demiurge. In the passage above, we see the resolution of the question: as Ahab himself says, he is to the crew as Fate is to him. The demiurge, the *heimarmene*, the delusion and entrapment that is this world hold him, but still, still despite all this he knows his queen Sophia—he is above it. This gnosis saves him, as it cannot the deluder himself.

The demiurge is the fated, entrapped aspect of every man; delusion is not external to us. Ahab is to the crew as the demiurge is to each one of us and as our own tyrannical reasoning is to our being seen whole: a raging tyrant. Yet there is more to Ahab, just as there is more to man; hence the captain cannot be seen only as an allegorical figurehead, for he, too, is finally a victim of the botched world.

Interestingly, that chapter most overt in its antiworldly references is that in which Melville himself seems most in the foreground: "The Whiteness of the Whale." Note, for instance, the authorial presence in the caveat, midway through the chapter: "But thou sayest, methinks this white-lead chapter about whiteness is but a white flag hung out from a craven soul; thou surrenderest to a hypo, Ishmael."[32] In this, as in the author's two notes on the white shark and on Coleridge, one senses Melville intruding more than usual into the text; there is a self-conscious sense that reinforces the novel's fluidity, the permeability of the characters. Ishmael, after all, only says "Call me Ishmael," and, as Viola Sachs observes, "The reader may well wonder if Ahab is really Ahab's name, or if he has one or perhaps several names, or even no name at all."[33]

There is absolutely no question that in this chapter, as in "The Candles," the reigning understanding is antinomian Gnosticism. Here, however, the speaker is not Ahab, but at least nominally Ishmael, whoever he might be. Although the chapter begins with references to the valuation of white among various peoples, it quickly turns to white as an instrument of terror, citing the primal fear of a young colt when a buffalo robe is shaken behind it, though it had never seen a buffalo. Concludes the narrator: "here thou beholdest in even a dumb brute, the instinct of the knowledge of the demonism in the world."[34] And, he continues: the muffled rollings of a milky sea; the bleak rustlings of the festooned frosts of mountains; the desolate shiftings of the windrowed snows of prairies; all these, to Ishmael, are as the shaking of that buffalo robe to the frightened colt: "Though neither knows where lie the nameless things of which the mystic sign gives forth such hints; yet with me, as with the colt, somewhere these things must exist. *Though in many of its aspects this visible world seems formed in love, the invisible spheres were formed in fright.*"[35]

This last statement is profoundly Gnostic in character: this is a restatement of the Valentinian teaching that the Sophia, glancing down at her reflection in the waters, in matter, recoiled, and from that fear the various emanations that culminated in this world were formed, successively distant from the supernal Origin.[36] However, Melville does not stop merely with a restatement of Gnostic cosmology: he goes on to say that whiteness "is at once the most meaning symbol of spiritual things, nay, the very veil of the Christian's Deity; and yet should be as it is, the intensifying agent in things the most appalling to mankind."[37] Observe the careful distinction, most Gnostic in character, implied between the "Christian's Deity," and God. Another implication, of course, is that there is not so great a difference between the orthodox Christian deity and things "most appalling to mankind." "Is it," he asks, "that by its indefiniteness it shadows forth the heartless voids and immensities of the universe, and thus stabs us from behind with thoughts of annihilation when beholding the white depths of the milky way?"[38]

All of this speculation, disturbing in itself, is preparatory for the final spiraling crescendo of the passage, in which the narrator states outright that Nature is a fraud, that all sensual perceptions are "but subtile deceits," and that ultimately all deified Nature absolutely paints like the harlot, whose allurements cover nothing but the charnel-house within; and when we proceed further, and consider that . . . the great principle of light, forever remains white and colorless in itself, and if operating without medium upon matter, would touch all objects, even tulips and roses, with its wan blank tinge—pondering all this, the palsied universe lies before us a leper . . . so the wretched infidel gazes himself blind at the monumental white shroud that wraps all the prospect around him. And of all these things the Albino whale was the symbol. Wonder ye then at the fiery hunt?[39]

Is this the voice of Ishmael, of Melville, or of Ahab? Stylistically, it is perhaps the last, while nominally it is the first—but one suspects above all it is that of Melville himself. This suspicion is underscored by the following two chapters, which have no reference whatever to Ishmael, and which depict events of which Ishmael himself could have no knowledge (as of Ahab in his cabin, say). This narrative ambiguity underscores—as does the wordplay in the following chapter[40]—the prevalent Melvillean gamesplaying involved here and allows him to state profoundly disturbing, heretical thoughts to a predominately Christian audience without having to take complete responsibility for what he wrote. There is a characteristic authorial coyness here, as throughout *Moby Dick*, which masks the questioning of our most basic assumptions about the nature of the cosmos.

At the same time, the narratorial fluidity of *Moby Dick* highlights the general fluidity of Melville's thought itself: there is no doubt that Gnostic elements permeate *Moby Dick* and that, in a sense, it could well be called a Gnostic novel. Yet even so, just as the narrator of *Moby Dick* could well be said to exist upon a spectrum, along which Ishmael, Ahab, Starbuck, and Mapple are arranged, so, too, Melville himself was possessed of myriad, at times bewilderingly different personae and perspectives. One must beware of taking any single perspective as the only one.

Yet Melville's understanding was very much conditioned by previous scholarship and interpretation, as well as by Gnosticism.[41] Significantly, late in life Melville became a voracious reader of Schopenhauer's pessimistic works, and it is especially interesting that he should have marked in those works many passages.[42] Of course, Melville's own pessimistic, Gnostic tendencies were manifest long before he read Schopenhauer, but it is revealing that he should have felt such an affinity with an author who took an anticosmic, pessimistic position. This is not, again, to restrict Melville to only this understanding— *Clarel*, for instance, contains some surprisingly traditionalist statements—but to point out an area upon the spectrum across which Melville's mind worked, an area to which he returned again and again.

There was a traditional element of sorts in Melville's complexity, as well, manifested perhaps most clearly in *Clarel*, in passages like the following, from "The Dominican," which argues that

Whatever your belief may be—
If well ye wish to human kind

Be not so mad, unblest and blind
As, in such days as these to try
To pull down Rome. If Rome could fall
'Twould not be Rome alone, but all
Religion. All with Rome have tie
Even the railers which deny
All but the downright Anarchist.[43]

One must remember that these are only the words of a character in a poem with many characters—yet Melville could have chosen to undermine them with irony, and did not. Moreover, he places in the mouth of the Dominican a refrain recurrent throughout the poem:

Shall science then
Which solely dealeth with this thing
Named Nature, shall she ever bring
One solitary hope to man?
'Tis Abba Father that we seek
Not the Artificer. I speak
But scarce may utter.[44]

One may note the implied division here betwen "Abba Father," the Gnostic hidden God, and the demiurgic "Artificer." Similar thoughts recur in the voices of Ungar, and of Mortmain, among others.[45] What is more, there is one signal place in which they recur without the intermediary character: in a canto entitled "The High Desert" the narrator considers

Abel and Cain—Ormuzd involved with Ahriman
In deadly lock. Were those gods gone?
Or under other names lived on?
The theme they started. "Twas averred
That, in old Gnostic pages blurred,
Jehovah was construed to be
Author of evil, yea, its god;
And Christ divine his contrary:
A god was held against a god
But Christ revered alone. Herefrom

. . . .

The twofold Testaments become
Transmitters of Chaldaic thought
By implication. . . .[46]

The narrator goes on to wonder whether, even if "no more / Those Gnostic heretics prevail," yet with the proliferation of new sects, does not that "old revolt" now reappear?

This change, this dusking change that slips . . .
Over the faith transmitted down:
Foreshadows it complete eclipse?
Science and Faith: can these unite?

Or is that priestly instinct right
(Right as regarding conserving still
The Church's reign)? . . .[47]

As if to underscore the narrator's torment, he continues:

Is faith dead now,
A petrification? Grant it so,
Then what's in store? what shapeless birth?
Reveal the doom reserved for earth?
How far may seas retiring go?[48]

And again:

Shall Science disappoint the hope
Yea, to confound us in the end
New doors to superstition ope?[49]

The question: "How far may seas retiring go?" marks the queries as Melville's—for him the sea represented adventure, life itself.[50] Yet here, if taken as such, these qualities would be allied with faith and tradition—a curious juxtaposition, given the anti-Christian aspects of Melville's other works.[51] The resolution of this dilemma may well be found in Gnosticism, which with its concept of the "two Gods," the demiurge and the true God, allowed Melville to attack orthodoxy while remaining, more or less, Christian.

Even within *Clarel* there are subtle signs that Melville had not left heretical Gnosticism wholly behind, as when in the section entitled "In Confidence," Dawn is described not as serene but as

Cloven and shattered, hushed and banned.
Seemed poised as in a chaos true
Or throe-lock of transitional earth
When old forms are annulled and new
Rebel and pangs suspend the birth.[52]

Surely there are echoes here of the Valentinian mythos, which details Sophia's fright at her own reflection, that fright giving birth to the present "aborted" world, with its ignorant demiurge.[53] We see here no serene Greek *Eos*, no rosy cheeks. One can see how adherence to the Gnostic mythos that this world is, in essence, a cosmic error would lend itself to an heightened awareness of the darkness and confusion of the present era: for is not materialistic Science (as Melville implies throughout *Clarel*) but an infatuation with the very Nature which marks man's Fall?

The ambiguity of Melville's Gnosticism cannot be resolved without acknowledging the multivalent complexity of Melville's mind and his love of complex, perverse jibes. Melville's position is always to some degree ambivalent—he plays games with his readers, as when in *Moby Dick* he has Starbuck say of the *Pequod*'s crew that the whale is their "demigorgon," a Melvillean cross between the demiurge of Gnosticism and the Demogorgon to which

Shelley alludes, a word of especial significance when one considers Shelley's attitude toward Christianity as practiced.[54] Finally, though, one cannot help but recognize the rebellious, Romantic, Shelleyan tinge of Melville's Gnosticism: like Shelley's semi-Platonic visions in "Epipsychidion," Melville's vision tends downward. When Pip, in *Moby Dick*, has a mystical vision, all is inverted and he sees not the heights but the depths of the Divine, seeing "God's foot upon the treadle." Little wonder Pip went mad, for his was the antithesis of the mystical ascent to the Divine.[55]

As Hawthorne said, Melville was never settled in his unbelief—but there are patterns, foci in his unsettlement. Melville recurred, again and again, to the Gnostic, pessimistic vision. What is more, these patterns inhere in and reflect patterns in western culture as a whole. In Melville's opposition to Transcendentalism, one can see echoes of the tension between Plotinus and the Gnostics, between the medieval Church and the Cathari, between Shelley and "this world," between the Schopenhauer-like, pessimistic interpretation of eastern teachings, and the Transcendentalist understanding.[56]

Perhaps all Gnostics—whom Melville himself invokes, after all—have in common, finally, not a pessimistic view of this world so much as a need for perfection envisioned in another, spiritual realm. Of course, the Church and Plotinus and the Transcendentalists have been accused of world rejection, as have Buddhism and Hinduism, and every religious tradition. But the difference is one of degree, I think.

As we shall shortly see, Emerson, and the Transcendentalist movement more generally, were deeply indebted to the Neoplatonic and Hermetic currents in European tradition. Chief among the American Transcendentalist affirmations was the assertion that evil has no real power, that evil is only the privation of the good, the traditional Neoplatonic view and the very part of Transcendentalism with which Melville took most exception. It is inappropriate to place Melville and Emerson together, as if both of them were members of the same literary Hermetic Club, for in fact they were in opposition, much as were the Neoplatonists and the Gnostics in antiquity. One denied the ultimate existence of evil, the other acknowledged its presence in the cosmos as a real force.[57]

In her study *The Demiurge: A Study of the Tradition from Plato to Joyce*, Meredith Bratcher argues that

> the ambivalence of Plato's demiourgos in creating imperfect human beings is dramatized more vividly in [heretical] Gnostic accounts of the demiurge as an incompetent cosmocrator, and as a prison-guard who, having in ignorance trapped portions of the eternal spirit in human flesh, subject to pain and mortality, refuses to free them when he learns of the true pleromatic home. The responsibility the demiurge bears for deliberate trapping human beings in a sense-world, a condition of mortality, and a physical body, all of which will inevitably be vehicles of suffering for the human immortal spirit, is his distinctive mark in his appearances in Western culture from the classical to the modern period. To realize that one lives in the demiurge's world is to long for escape, as the Gnostic myths and rituals dramatized so plainly.[58]

Melville's novels, short stories, and poetry also dramatize this desire to escape the world and the clutches of an ignorant demiurge, and thus Melville's Gnosticism harks back clearly to ancient heretical predecessors.

I do not wish to diminish Melville's work: his imagination worked on a vaster scale than most writers' and he sought to incorporate in his work a panoramic view of life. There is a grandeur to Melville's fiction, and this grandeur draws readers back again and again. Nevertheless, his works remain ultimately as a testimony to what must be called modern, essentially areligious or existentialist Gnosticism. In this divorce of Gnosticism from religion, Melville remains a forerunner of twentieth-century fiction, and perhaps it is for this reason that he retains such an attraction for modern readers. Melville's work represents for us the possibilities of the rebellious modern soul without religion: the hell-bent Ahab, the naïf Ishmael, the passive Billy Budd, the nefarious Confidence Man. There are, in such a world, those who take advantage, and those who are taken advantage of; it is a world from which one can imagine escape via death. It is a world from which complete religious tradition is absent, esotericism merely provides various kinds of blind alleys; its gnosis is only insight into the ties that bind us, and in all this perhaps it represents all too well the world in which most people live today.

Greaves

In 1842, Emerson wrote in his journal a passage with a startling reference to a little-known English author and mystic. The passage reads: "And yet there are books of no vulgar origin but the work & the proof of faculties so comprehensive, so nearly equal to the universe which they paint, that although one shuts them also with meaner ones, yet he says with a sigh the while, this were to be read in long thousands of years by some stream in Paradise. Swedenborg, Behmen, Plato, Proclus, Rabelais, & Greaves."[1] Plato and Proclus come as no surprise and need no introduction, nor, probably, do Swedenborg, Jacob Böhme and Rabelais. It is a peculiar list, made more peculiar by its concluding name, Greaves. Who on earth is this, and what is he doing in this list of luminaries, Emerson's literary-religious pantheon of writers to be read in Paradise? To answer this question is to understand how American Transcendentalism was deeply influenced by Böhmean German theosophy—filtered through the English author Greaves.

Very little has been published about Greaves—I found no articles on him listed in any of the major databases. However, there are in fact several articles and books that at least refer to Greaves. Among them are the entry in the British *Dictionary of National Biography* and a 1994 article by Jackie Latham called "Emma Martin and Sacred Socialism: the Correspondence of James Pierrepont Greaves." Latham sneers at Greaves's "turgid" prose and, much more interested in the socialist politics of Emma Martin, pays little attention to the significances of Greaves's work.[2] More about Greaves, Alcott, and others in Greaves's circle can be found in Joel Myerson's 1978 article "William Harry Harland's 'Bronson Alcott's English Friends.'"[3] For the most part, however, Greaves's significance (and that of Christian theosophy generally) for American Transcendentalism has been ignored.

In a previous article, I have shown that Bronson Alcott's often incomprehensible writing becomes far more understandable when seen in light of Jacob Böhme's works. Böhme, who was so influential that Christian theosophy can also be called "Boehmean theosophy," was unquestionably a hidden influence on American Transcendentalism. The impact of his visionary works spread throughout Europe, ramifying through philosophy and literature, but most of all 'underground' through 'Pietist' religious circles, whose history and impact has yet to be fully chronicled. Böhme has often been misunderstood and maligned for his complex terminology and dense style, but his work has nonetheless fascinated and inspired countless others, including many writers, among them Alcott.

It is undeniable that Alcott was inspired by Böhme and we need not reconsider this subject, but it is important to point out here that Alcott was the medium by which Böhme and Greaves came to Emerson and to American Transcendentalism generally. If, as I noted elsewhere, Emerson was responsible for introducing Alcott to the Bhagavad Gita and Hindu sacred writings, Alcott in turn was responsible for introducing Emerson and anyone else who was interested to Böhme and European theosophy, which remained central for Alcott's work from the 1830s to the end of his life. Alcott recognized in Böhme and in Christian theosophy more generally the spark that has inspired radical spirituality time and again throughout modern times, and that in fact is visible in a diffused way throughout American Transcendentalism as a result of Alcott's own efforts.

Bronson Alcott's personal history is readily available through his voluminous letters and extensive biographical documentation, but one chapter of his life has not been adequately documented, and perhaps never will be. This is, of course, the period in 1842 when Alcott visited England in order to meet the English theosopher James Pierrepont Greaves and other theosophically influenced people. Alcott had corresponded with Greaves and others in English theosophic circles since the late 1830s and must have been immensely excited to be able actually to visit with them. But alas, Greaves himself, who had been quite ill and in reclusion, died before Alcott arrived, so the two, who had so much in common, never met.

What sort of man was Greaves? Just to examine his biography will reveal how much he and Alcott had in common. Born in 1777, Greaves became a London businessman who somehow lost a fortune, ended up relinquishing his property to his creditors, and lived on a minimal subsequent income. In 1817, he traveled to Yverdun, Switzerland, where he stayed for some time with the educational reformer Pestalozzi, and in 1825 became secretary of the London Infant School Society. In 1832, he settled in Gloucestershire, but eventually returned to London, where he began a philosophical group called the Aesthetic Society that met at his house in Burton Crescent. He had many friends and acquaintances who admired him immensely: A. F. Barham claimed him "a unique specimen of human character . . . an absolute undefinable," intellectually and spiritually far superior to his contemporary, Coleridge.[4] Eventually, Greaves's circle established a school called Alcott House, in Ham, Surrey, to embody his educational views, and there he died in 1842.

Like Alcott, Greaves was a lifelong vegetarian; like Alcott, Greaves spent much of his life concentrating on educational reform; and, like Alcott, Greaves was profoundly influenced by Böhme. Little wonder that they recognized one another as kindred spirits. In recently published journals of 1838, Alcott wrote that he received various books from Greaves and that Greaves received a dozen copies of Alcott's own *Conversations on the Gospels*, which Greaves held to be "invaluable." "There must be a circle of persons in London," Alcott muses, "of free opinions, with which one would like to become acquainted."[5] "I intend to write immediately to Mr. Greaves. I should have done this in answer to his letter of September 1837." But Alcott refrained from writing Greaves until 26 April 1839, mainly because he was upset over the failure of his own Temple School as a result of the uproar over his *Conversations*.

Despite what their sometimes sporadic exchange of letters might suggest, Alcott and Greaves were strikingly similar, not only in the ways already mentioned, but also in their ways of expression. Alcott has always been notorious for his impenetrable diction, but if he could be topped for "orotund vacuity" Greaves was probably the only one capable of doing so. Of course, at times Alcott, in his journals especially, could be quite inspired and clear. On the last day of 1838, Alcott wrote an oration that spurred himself to higher, more profound spiritual experience: "I have lived:——lived at times, days, hours, minutes, during the passage of this vale around the orb of day. I have had light, heat, sight, for brief and fitful moments: and memory yet reverts to these living hours wherein I rose from the sepulchres of sense, and was in God. Alas! how few and transient, these quickenings of the divine life, in the soul! How <much of the time> [often] I have been buried, and dead to the true, living, eternal, facts, that are the joy, the beatitude, the knowledge, the apotheosis, of the soul." Here Alcott reveals the central focus of his life, the drive for direct spiritual experience. It was this that attracted Alcott and Greaves to Böhme, who both had and enjoined such experiences. In a subsequent entry, Alcott wrote:

> Grow wise. Attain to a clearer insight of the angel that is cherishing in its bosom, Thyself. Time! Time! what is time to thee? what years? what millenniums, but the ebb and flow of God through thy soul, into the shows of nature; that so thou mayst chronicle the great facts within thee, for a while, upon the images and objects of the senses! Space! space, is but the flexile self that thou art, ever shaping to thee Idols of thy thought, in its objects, that so thou mayst catch some glimpse of thy great nature, by beholding thy shadow! Penetrate through the world of things, into the world of thoughts, and thence, into the innermost life of instincts. Live in thy love. Come back to thyself. Retreat into life. . . . Exist in all thy faculties. Put on the Perfect. Become the Ideal . . . conform thine Actual to the Ideal Beauty, that <shall> [would] make thee *one with the Perfect and fair Godhead* . . . within thy faculties . . . whose Image is God; transcending, Times and Spaces; without beginning or end; Chronicle, or History.——[6]

Here Alcott's language is more characteristically Alcottian: archaic, peculiar, and in places less than clear (as when he exhorts himself to "Retreat into life"), but at its best exalted and exalting.

Before we delve further into this new chapter of American Transcendentalism's indebtedness to Böhmean theosophy, it may be helpful to consider the role of language in this hidden theosophic tradition of modern Christianity. Theosophic writers, especially Böhme himself, are often chided for being needlessly obscure; his latinate terms and baroque, circuitous language seem hopelessly impenetrable to many modern readers. But those who dismiss Böhme because of his style fail to recognize that for Böhme, and for many theosophers, language can have different functions than direct communication of facts. Rather, for Böhme (and to some degree for Alcott and Greaves) language is a means of pointing readers toward direct spiritual experience, of exhorting them to it, of advising them on dangers along the way, and inasmuch as possible, of conveying the inexpressible.

The kind of language one chooses or requires depends upon one's aims, and I think that Böhme, Alcott, and Greaves are often denigrated for very much the same reason: their critics do not recognize that these authors' aims in writing were not like those of a journalist or even of most writers on theological subjects. As with Böhme in much of his writing, Alcott's aim in the passages just quoted is to point us toward "transcending, Times and Spaces," toward "attaining a clearer insight of the angel that is cherishing in its bosom, *Thyself.*" It is not surprising that Alcott was derided by many journalists when in 1840 the first issue of the Transcendentalist periodical *The Dial* published his "Orphic Sayings:" his mysticism was light years from the mundane world of Yankee newspapers, and an easy target to boot.

However, there is another reason Alcott and Greaves have been sneered at for their "turgid" language, and it is central to my argument here: both authors were devotees of Böhme and independently represented in their works a modernized, abstracted German theosophy without much of its characteristically Christian Hermetic vocabulary. I have already traced how much Alcott was indebted to Böhme—the key to all of Alcott's work and thought—but precisely the same was true of Greaves. Greaves and Alcott's language is strikingly similar because they were up to the same thing: attempting to adapt Böhmean theosophy to contemporary expression. This meant jettisoning much of Böhme's overtly Christian exhortations and phrasings, as well as virtually all of his obscure alchemical and latinate terminology. What is left? Precisely what we see in Alcott and Greaves's writing.

Let's turn to some samples of Greavesian prose, beginning with *Spiritual Culture; or Thoughts for the Consideration of Parents and Teachers*, a Boston 1841 reprint of Greaves's "Three Hundred Maxims on Education." The copy I consulted was signed by Alcott himself, and bears prefatory remarks by "a mother" that urges us to pay attention to this book. In the London preface, Greaves tells us "I have . . . not confined myself to the common mode of expression, but have used such as appears to me calculated to awaken internal consciousness, which generates thought, and corresponding energies."[7] This more or less plainly demonstrates our earlier point: that Greaves's aim in writing was to awaken dormant qualities in his readers, to make of reading a means to spiritual awakening.

When we read Greaves's "Thoughts for the Consideration of Parents," the first section of this little book, we can see just why his work would have appealed to Alcott and Emerson, both of whom also delighted in aphorisms. The "Thoughts" begin with the admonition: "Mother! The maternal instinct in you, is the representative of divine paternal love to your child." This seems clear enough, and undoubtedly harmonized perfectly with Alcott's own views, but we soon enter into Greavesian territory: "Let the child's exterior vocation be corresponding to its interior vocation, or else it will not be able to receive the love fulfillment."[8] Yet we can see immediately how Greaves's writing must have been received by American Transcendentalists when he writes, less obscurely, "To educate your child *for* God, you must dedicate yourself like a child *to* God." Or "Let not the child study *your* doings but study the *child's* doings with respect to the inner mover."[9]

Like Emerson and Alcott, Greaves insists upon the primacy of the "inner mover," of founding outward action upon inward spiritual awareness. Greavesian educational philosophy consists in nurturing the whole child and in preserving its right relationship to nature and to the divine, so that "the in-creating spirit will never vanish from its will."[10] Most contemporary educational philosophy is based upon informing the child—filling it with information—but Greaves, like Alcott, insisted that it was much more important to "Let the child constantly inform you, and itself, what it is, what it does, and what it experiences."[11] In this respect, Greaves, like Alcott, bore an affinity with the Platonic recognition that true education consists not in pouring information in, but in awakening and drawing forth nascent understanding already there.

This first book of Greaves to be published in America—and undoubtedly one of the works Emerson referred to when he placed Greaves among his luminaries—is remarkably clear and succinct in expression. In the appended essay called "Doctrine of Spiritual Culture," Greaves writes in strong, declarative sentences: "Man is the noblest of the Creator's works. . . . The Art which fits such a being to fullfil his high destiny, is the first and noblest of arts. Human Culture reveals to a man the true Idea of his being—his endowments—his possessions—and fits him to use these for the growth, renewal, and perfection of his Spirit. It is the art of completing man."[12] Alcott and Emerson must have read these words with delight, as also Greaves's exhortation to revive and renew the "Idea" of Jesus in order that "by its quickening agency, it may fructify our common nature, unfold our being into the same divine likeness, and reproduce Perfect Men. It is to mould anew our Institutions, our Manners, our Men; to restore Nature to its rightful use; purify Life; hallow the functions of the Human Body, and regenerate Philosophy, Literature, Art, Society."[13]

As I have pointed out elsewhere, Emerson also called for such a transformation of human society; and in a slightly different form, this same idea underlay the American Transcendentalist attempts at utopia like Brook Farm and Alcott's own Fruitlands (the project of Alcott and the English disciple of Greaves, Charles Lane), as well as *The Dial* and its aims to bring about an American literary-religious awakening.[14]

Indeed, so much in this work of Greaves resonates with Alcott and Emerson's views that one can hardly believe the three never met. Imagine, for instance, Alcott's response to the following: "This preference of Jesus for Conversation, is a striking proof of his comprehensive Idea of Education."[15] If ever there was a proponent for the Art of Conversation, it was Alcott, who would actually have cards printed up announcing the subjects of his Conversations, and accounts of later Transcendentalist Conversations were published in American newspapers. It is, of course, hard to tell who influenced whom, but many of the correspondences between Greaves and the American Transcendentalists were probably not so much the result of influence as of arriving at similar conclusions independently.

Of course, not all of Greaves's works were as succinct as his aphorisms, nor as strikingly similar to American Transcendentalist thought. In his *New Theosophic Revelations*, for instance, extracts from Greaves's voluminous journals published in London, 1847, the editor forewarns us that "The ideas and language in this volume are of an extraordinary *esoteric* character, and, therfore, may not be easily apprehended nor appreciated by many in their exoteric *States of Being*."[16] There is no doubt that the editor is right: the book's epigraph is "The soul has a preparatory process to go through in an outward dispensation before it is in an efficient state to bear the Divine Essence, or *Love's* powerful Incarnation." We are not in for an easy read. On the very first page of Greaves's text we see that

> With every death degree there is a corresponding Life degree, one circle of the regenerate seven-fold Life puts to death one circle of the seven-fold evil Life, and Satan, when dislodged from his stronghold in us, soon becomes weaker and weaker.
>
> He himself is insecure in us when driven from his castle into his secondary fortification; but we are never secure till he is dead in us constitutionally.
>
> The less Satan holds in us, the more the Spirit holds; and as we are to be held, and cannot hold any thing, our business is to see by whom we are held, and co-operate in accepting *the right holder*.[17]

This is a rather uncompromising beginning, but it clearly reveals the origins of Greaves's writing in Böhmean theosophy, some remarks on which may help clarify it.

Greaves here draws upon a fairly abstruse tradition within Böhmean theosophy, one elaborated most by Johann Georg Gichtel, editor of the first complete edition of Böhme's writing in German and author of several thousand pages of letters published under the title *Theosophia Practica* (1722) that consists of spiritual advice to his followers and friends. Perhaps more relevant is a concise book by Gichtel, often also published under the title *Theosophia Practica*, but actually entitled *Eine kurze Eröffnung und Anweisung der dryen Principien und Welten in Menschen* (1696/1779), [A Little Opening into and Demonstration of Three Principles and Worlds in Man]. Here Gichtel elaborates his doctrine of the seven planets as corresponding to bodily centers and shows in illustrations and commentary how "fallen man" is ruled by the seven planetary forces (emotional forces), as well as how in "regenerated man" these same points are transmuted into spiritually illuminated centers.

Greaves's language here very much reflects the theosophic tradition as manifested in the works of Gichtel, in the Netherlands, and in those of the English theosophers, as well. His is a deeply Christian terminology, insistent upon battling with Satan and with penetrating into the "Love-fire." When he speaks of being "held," or of a "right holder," Greaves refers to what he insists upon throughout his work: that the individual has to surrender himself to God, to be "held" by God rather than succumbing to his constitutionally fallen nature and be "held" by Satan. From the way he writes, one can tell that Greaves was not writing scholarly advice to his correspondents about topics on which he had read, but rather had direct experience of his subject.

At the same time, even in those writings clearly influenced by theosophy, Greaves sought a language that would also speak to modern people. If one compares Greaves's prose with that of Böhme or Gichtel, one will find his stripped of Böhme's arcane latinate terms and of Gichtel's Pietist vocabulary, as well. Instead, we find Greaves closer to a scientific language, with many abstract words that at first may seem impenetrable. For instance, Greaves writes that "The higher faculted we are within, the more our outer doings will be for others and not for ourselves." This is clear enough, and close to the Buddhist *bodhisattva* ideal, but this sentence is followed by another less clear:

> This Spirit, by the sounding string, causes the passive string and air to vibrate.
> The Spirit, by the pre-causative faculties, causes the receptive faculties and the circulating sap to produce external results. . . .
> So far as the pre-causative faculties are initiated into activity, they incite the branches to external results. . . .
> Life or Light or Love can initate, by their own pre-causative faculties, the re-productive faculties into fruitfulness.
> He who can magnetize another, does it from the pre-causative ground, and not from any of the re-productive faculties. . . .
> It is necessary that the *pre-causative faculties* be opened before the virtue, which is within the Spirit, can pass through them into the causative faculties, and manifest its Universal results.[18]

What on earth is he writing about?

Essentially, Greaves is explicating Böhmean theosophy without using Böhmenist language. The "pre-causative faculties" refer to the principles of consciousness that precede and transcend individual human existence, and one can only "magnetize" others or manifest the Spirit's "Universal results" by realizing these principles that transcend the individual self. The analogy Greaves uses here, that of the plucked string, is one found in Pythagoreanism and throughout the European tradition—and it illustrates Greaves's desire to integrate science, music, and spirituality. Indeed, Greaves even refers directly to Ptolemy and Copernicus in his conclusion to this work. His final aphorisms are simple, fairly clear affirmations of life (the contracting principle), light (the expanding principle), and love (the centering principle). The greatest of these, says Greaves, is love, for "it is not knowledge that is wanted by man, but Love."[19]

Like earlier theosophers, Greaves had a circle of followers with whom he corresponded. A prolific correspondent not unlike the eighteenth-century theosopher Gichtel, Greaves's letters focus on several major themes, chief among them marriage. Indeed, the first letter in his book *Letters and Extracts from the MS. Writings* (1845) sets the tone for many others:

> Dear Friend,—Your remarks on Marriage are indeed excellent, and won my deepest attention. We must acknowledge that education, even when rightly conducted, can only be viewed as remedial, not as regenerative or re-formative. Education cannot repair the defects in birth.[20]

Greaves insists again and again in his letters that parents should enter into a sacred marriage, and only then can children be truly well born. "Evil will only end," he argues, "when none but divine pre-paired parties marry."[21] Sacred marriage, he holds, must become the basis for society, which in its organization should in turn be based on "sacred socialism." In other words, the natural must be preceded by the theosophic, the mortal by the immortal. If we pay attention to the immortal, when we turn to the mortal, all will fall into place; if we ignore the immortal, the mortal will be in chaos.

In his letters, Greaves shows another side, for he wrote not only aphoristic observations, but also individual spiritual advice. What appear at first to be utterly abstract statements, Greaves himself reveals to be spiritual advice to a particular correspondent:

> Every letter that I write to you, I consider a sacred deposit put in your hands, to be offered up whenever an opportunity offers to the divine end, that it may apply the same to others as it has done to you. You will be blessed indeed if you are allowed to use all I have written to you with a whole heart and with unbroken sincerity. . . . All your questions are answered in my letter, if you can discover the same. It is more my duty to ask you questions than to answer any directly, and to correct your answers. May you be led to turn inwards more and more, so that you experience may be more and more celestial and divine, and less and less earthly.[22]
>
> J. P. G.

Of course, Greaves himself admits the distance between his abstract formulations and their application to his correspondent's life when he adds that all questions are answered in the letter, "if you can discover the same."

When we turn back to the American Transcendentalists, we can easily see what in Greaves must have been appealing, particularly to Emerson. Like Emerson himself, Greaves drew upon the great tradition of European mysticism but sought to express himself in modern language for a modern audience. What's more, Greaves held that there was an approaching new era in which humanity would realize its full potential, conjoining spirituality with its new scientific understanding, a belief that Emerson himself set forth in his very first major publication, *Nature*. Greaves encouraged a refining of the "spiritual sight" (seeing and eyes are immensely important for Emerson), and insisted upon its actualization.

Most important, from their perspective, Emerson and Alcott believed that Greaves had himself realized the spiritual ideals about which he wrote. This actualization was of immense significance for both of the Americans, as we can see in the following entry by Emerson about Alcott and others, including Greaves:

> Alcott was good, so qualified & so strong. I said to him what is really A's distinction, that, rejoicing or desponding, this man always trusts his principle, never deserts it, never mistakes the convenient customary way of doing the thing for the right & might, whilst all vulgar reformers, like these community people, after sounding their sentimental trumpet, rely on the arm of money & the law. It is the effect of his nature, of his natural clearness of spiritual sight which makes this confusion of thought impossible to him. I have a company who travel with me in the world & one or other of whom I must still meet, whose office none can supply to me: Edward Stabler; my Methodist Tarbox; Wordsworth's Pedlar; Mary Rotch; Alcott; Manzoni's Fra Cristoforo; Swedenborg; Mrs Black; and now Greaves, & his disciple, Lane.[23]

Stabler and Rotch were Quakers; the laborer Tarbox helped Emerson understand prayer when they worked together in 1825; and all of these people had in common an inward focus, what Emerson recognized as a "natural clearness of spiritual sight."[24] They had not merely written about spirituality, but had also realized it. Hence it is not surprising that Emerson speaks of Greaves's "disciple," Charles Lane, nor that he holds all these as "supreme people."

In fact, whereas Emerson himself did not always measure up to Alcott's standards, Greaves did. In May 1837, Alcott had visited his friend Emerson once again, and came to the following conclusion. Emerson, he confided to his journal, "writes and speaks for effect. Fame stands before him as a dazzling award, and he holds himself somewhat too proudly, nor seeks the humble and sincere regard of his race. His life has been one of opportunity, and he has sought to realize in it more of the accomplished scholar than the perfect man.—A great intellect, refined by elegant study, rather than a divine life radiant with the beauty of truth and holiness. He is an eye more than a heart, an intellect more than a soul."[25] By contrast, consider what Alcott wrote of Greaves: "Nobody remained the same after meeting him. . . . His influence was not unlike that of Jesus."[26] And this although Alcott had never met Greaves! Greaves indeed must have been a powerful presence, for a man who had met him claimed that he "impressed a stranger with the inescapable conviction that a man of genius was pouring out his deep central heart into your ears."[27]

From all this, we can see that Emerson's accolades to Greaves with which we began—placing him in such company as Plato, Proclus, or Böhme—are not nearly as strange as they first appear. Seen in context, in fact, Greaves represents an important link between German theosophy and American

Transcendentalism. In all his main interests—educational reform, mysticism, a union of science and spirituality, a new era, and "sacred socialism"—Greaves corresponds strikingly to the interests of the American Transcendentalists. What is more, Greaves's main effort—to make his spiritual insights accessible via modern language—was very much parallel to the work of Alcott and Emerson. Greaves was more influential as an independent confirmation of Emerson and Alcott's views than as a source for what they thought, but nonetheless he represents a direct conduit between German and English theosophy and American Transcendentalism whose significance should not be overlooked.

Alcott

None of the American Transcendentalists was so ridiculed as Amos Bronson Alcott. Throughout his life, Alcott was a thoroughgoing religious radical whose pronouncements often were too much even for Transcendentalists like Emerson, although they themselves had abandoned Unitarian liberalism as too conservative. Although many critics have noted and lampooned Alcott's eccentric modes of "prophetic" expression from his "Orphic Sayings" in *The Dial* onward—some considering him deluded and even insane—much in Alcott's work becomes far more comprehensible when one considers a central hidden source of his inspiration: German mysticism exemplified in the work of seventeenth-century Protestant mystic Jacob Böhme.

This is not to defend Alcott completely from the charge of unfortunate expression, of course. It is no accident that Alcott, with his often incoherent "Orphic Sayings," inspired more derision of the early Transcendentalist peridical *The Dial* than anyone else. Even Alcott's friend Emerson criticized the "Sayings," published in the first issue of *The Dial* in 1840, as containing Alcott's "inveterate faults:" verbosity, imprecise expression, extreme abstractness, and incoherence. Emerson suspected that his friend would never write so well as he talked, but Emerson still encouraged Margaret Fuller—who shared his assessment of Alcott—to publish "Orphic Sayings" because they would distinguish *The Dial* from other publications.[1]

Distinguish it they did. Newspaper writers ridiculed *The Dial* as "the ravings of Alcott and his fellow zanies," even though Alcott's was the only genuinely eccentric writing in the new magazine. *The Knickerbocker*, in its issue of November 1840, parodied Alcott's contribution to *The Dial* with its "Gastric Sayings," and such pronouncements as "The popular cookery is dietetical. . . . Appetite is dual. Satiety is derivative. Simplicity halts in compounds. Mastication is actual merely." One sees how close Alcott's writing was to this mockery in this genuine "Orphic saying:"

> The popular genesis is historical. It is written to sense not to the soul. Two principles, diverse and alien, interchange the Godhead and sway the world by turns. God is dual. Spirit is derivative. Identity halts in diversity. Unity is actual merely. The poles of things are not integrated: creation globed and orbed. Yet in the true genesis, nature is globed in the actual, souls orbed in the spiritual firmament. Love globes, wisdom orbs, all things. As magnet the steel, so spirit attracts matter, which trembles to traverse the poles of diversity, and rests in the bosom of unity. All genesis is of love. Wisdom is her form: beauty her costume.

Another newspaper wag said Alcott's prose was like "a train of fifty cars going by with only one passenger."[2] Margaret Fuller's assessment was apt: "The break of your spirit in the crag of the actual makes surf and foam but leaves no gem behind. Yet it is a great wave Mr. Alcott."[3]

What on earth was Alcott trying to say in such a passage? Without reference to German mysticism, it makes no sense whatever. However, consider this excerpt in light of medieval and Protestant German mysticism. The classical medieval mysticism of Johannes Tauler and Meister Eckhart emphasizes the imageless transcendent divine unity, toward which the contemplative ascends. The Protestant mysticism of Böhme likewise emphasizes this divine unity, but also includes a cosmological dualism seen in the antinomy of divine love and wrath, both of which derive from transcendent divine unity. The English Böhmean mystic John Pordage (whose work Alcott had read, as we shall see) speaks of the contemplative ascent to the divine unity using the visionary image of a globe. For Alcott to write "Nature is globed" or that souls are "orbed" is for him to rephrase Pordage and to reiterate the traditional mystical understanding of correspondences between man as microcosm and nature as macrocosm, both of which have their origin in the divine, the perfection of which is symbolized by the orb or globe.

No question that Alcott's phrasing here is cryptic, to say the least. Indeed, without a thorough knowledge of such writers as Böhme and Pordage, one can only regard Alcott's writings as a complete cipher. But the key to this cipher is definitely found in the Protestant mystics, especially in Böhme. Alcott is contrasting historical Christianity with spiritual or mystical Christianity in this passage. He compares the dualistic, materialistic understanding of God, man, and nature seen in historical, literalist religion, with the transcendent unity of God, man, and nature seen in a mystical light as found in the writings of Böhme. Alcott's passage implicitly urges us to "traverse the poles of diversity, and rest in the bosom of unity."

Unfortunately, as is more often the case than not, Alcott's phrasing is grotesque and virtually incomprehensible even for those familiar with his sources. Why say that "two principles, diverse and alien, interchange the Godhead?" The verb is not only unfamiliar but imprecise as well—and worst of all, unnecessary. Later, what he writes is "The poles are not integrated: creation globed and orbed." What he apparently means is: "In fallen nature, polarities are not integrated in a greater harmony, nor is creation seen in the light of its transcendent unity." However, with the utterly unnecessary use of the colon, he makes the sentence incoherent and grammatically wrong. This kind of imprecise expression—and the incompetent attempts at grandiloquence or oracular utterance it represents—meant that Alcott met with little success even among Böhmenist mystics, much less among the general public.

Böhmenist mysticism appears overtly in virtually all of Alcott's books, especially in *Tablets* (1868), *Concord Days* (1872), and *Table-talk* (1877). In *Tablets*, Alcott writes on what was to become his own central attack on Darwinist evolutionism using an emanationist mysticism based in Genesis and Böhme: "Boehme, the subtilest thinker on Genesis since Moses, conceives that nature fell from its original oneness by fault of Lucifer before man rose physically from its ruins." But Alcott corrects Böhme as well: "We think it needs no Lucifer other than mankind collectively conspiring, to account for nature's mishaps, or man's."[4] Regardless of Alcott's anthropocentrism, however, his Christian emanationism opposed to Darwinian evolutionism drew much on Böhme's *Mysterium Magnum*, his enormous commentary on the first book of the Old Testament.

In *Concord Days* (1872), Böhme again reappears, here in a section that Alcott wrote about him, along with a lengthy letter from the British Böhmenist Christopher Walton that praised Böhme to the skies and explained his own never-completed project of publishing many works of Böhme and his disciples. Alcott's comments on Böhme here say volumes about his indebtedness:

> Mysticism is the sacred spark that has lighted the piety and illuminated the philosophy of all places and times. It has kindled especially and kept alive the profoundest thinking of Germany and of the continent since Böhme's first work, "The Aurora," appeared. Some of the deepest thinkers since then have openly acknowledged their debt to Boehme, or secretly borrowed without acknowledging their best illustrations from his writings. It is conceded that his was one of the most original and subtlest of minds, and that he has exercised a deeper influence on the progress of thought than anyone since Plotinus.[5]

Implied here, but not said outright, is that American Transcendentalism also is indebted to Böhme.

Perhaps most illustrative of how Alcott saw himself as an American Böhmean—as a deep thinker who at times acknowledged his debt to Böhme, and at times did not—appears in Alcott's 1877 book, *Table-talk*. Here, as in "Orphic Sayings," Alcott is at his most oracular. "Instinct, intuition, volition, embosom and express whatsoever the Spirit vaticinates and verifies in experience," Alcott wrote in *Table-talk*. Why use a word like vaticinate; what does this sentence mean? It is unclear, to say the least. However, in the same book, we find an illustration entitled "Orbis Pictus" that very much echoes similar illustrations Alcott had seen adorning Böhmean books in England. (See Figure 1, p. 118)

Figure 1. "Orbis Pictus." From Bronson Alcott, *Table-talk*, 1877.

While in England more than thirty years before, Alcott had read the works of Böhmenists John Pordage and Dionysius Andreas Freher and had seen the numerous alchemically based diagrams and illustrations that accompany not only those English works, but also many German Böhmenist works. Not surprisingly, Alcott, as a kind of fresh American Böhme, included in *Table-talk* this quasi-Böhmenist illustration "Orbis Pictus," along with the following words that strongly remind us of "Orphic Sayings" and its "orbed thoughts:" "To the senses, things appear linear, orbed to thought. The lines of genesis, like flames, show spirally and aspirant. The spiral includes all known figures. / Principles, like fountains, flow round ceaselessly, / Whirling in eddying evolutions of wavelets."[6] This is Alcott's brand of American Böhmenism; admittedly incoherent, by and large, but definitely finding its inspiration in Böhmean thought, especially of the English variety. The references here to "figures" and "orbed," to "fountains" and "flames" reflect quite precisely the visionary nature of Böhmean thought, which works like alchemy in images, not in logical succession of thought.

We can see that Alcott was intensely drawn to Böhmenist mysticism not only in his search for books by such authors as Law and Pordage while in England in 1842 and by references in his books to Böhme, but also in his later attempts to forge connections between the American Transcendentalist movement and British Böhmenist disciples Christopher Walton and Edward Burton Penny. However, despite their common love for Böhme's works, Alcott and the British mystics only made a sporadic alliance. In 1867, Alcott wrote to Christopher Walton—editor of a proposed massive series of theosophic writings called the *Cyclopaedia of Pure Christian Theology and Theosophic Science*, or *Law's Memorial*—warmly proposing that Walton contribute to the New England Transcendentalist publications and organizations like the Free Religious Association. Alcott wrote: "My studies for many years have lain in the direction of the Mystic authors, Jacob Behmen being a favorite, and, as I judge, the master mind of these last centuries. I was fortunate, when in England in 1842, to find not only his works in Laws' [*sic*] edition, but most of the works of his disciples; Taylor, Pordage, Frances Lee, Law, and others."[7] Walton replied with an extensive letter, but it was a year before Alcott responded.

Alcott's belated reply revealed how much he was interested in Böhme and in the publications Walton and Penny were bringing out in England. Alcott had been able to read copies of the English Böhmenists's translations and other works through the Harvard library and his friend Fernald; he had, he writes Walton, read them all.[8] This intensive reading of the letters of Louis-Claude de Saint-Martin (1743–1803), an ardent French Böhmenist, and other works "deepened" Alcott's "conviction" "of the exceeding importance of giving to the world full accounts of the lives of Behmen's illustrious desciples [*sic*]."[9] "I hope nothing will defeat your purpose of doing this," Alcott wrote, for "it is a kind of thought with which our advanced thinkers should be familiar in order to justify any claims to a real knowledge of spiritual things." "I wish I could add that any considerable number of our advanced thinkers had penetrated the core of the Mystery."[10]

Alcott did what he could to cement connections between W. T. Harris's *Journal of Speculative Philosophy*, a chiefly Hegelian organ of St. Louis Transcendentalism with which Alcott was affiliated, and the British Böhmenists, coaxing Penny or Walton to write articles about Böhme for it. "You will see by his table of contents how comprehensive his [Harris's] range is, and yet that without Boehme it is not inclusive," Alcott writes. By 1873, however, Alcott was still writing Walton, trying to coax him to write an article about Böhme for Harris's journal. Although Alcott took the liberty of having Harris publish a letter from Walton as a sort of advertisement for him—and even sent Walton copies of the journal, as well as of Alcott's latest book—the bonds between American Transcendentalism and British mysticism never really materialized, save in Alcott himself.

When in 1878, Thomas Johnson—a young Platonist from Osceola, Missouri—wrote Alcott about establishing a "Journal of Mysticism and Idealism," Alcott wrote back enthusiastically, hoping that in Johnson's publication he would find a vehicle for American publication of Böhmenist and other mystical writers. Revealingly, Alcott wrote that

> I think much of republications of authors now little known, but whose thoughts must find acceptance with our religious and thinking public once brought to their notice. The religious element has always attached the liveliest significance to the mystic and Ideal in life and thought, and we have no Journal, or newspaper even, doing any justice to its force and power.
>
> And biographical sketches of the great founders of these schools would form a most attractive feature of your magazine.[11]

Johnson's proposed journal became *The Platonist*, published from 1881 to 1888. It continued Alcott's love for Platonism, but did not become a vehicle for Böhmenist mysticism.

During Alcott's last years—when his dream, the Concord School of Philosophy, became a reality—there was considerable public confusion about whether he had reverted or converted to "Christian orthodoxy" more amenable to the Unitarian and other Protestant clergy of his day, and here again Böhme provides an explanation. Especially as a result of his association with the popular Congregationalist clergyman Joseph Cook, Alcott found himself answering letters and questions from many people who wondered what his precise sectarian or doctrinal position was. In his lectures at the Concord School and elsewhere, Alcott propounded a "Christian theism" that fiercely opposed Darwinist materialism, and even underwent several doctrinal examinations by various Protestant clergy, who concluded that Alcott was more or less doctrinally sound.[12] All of this drove *The Index*, a radical Transcendentalist publication, to condemn Alcott as having become "orthodox."

In fact, Alcott had been deeply drawn to universalist Protestant Böhmean mysticism more than forty years before, and he had not undergone a great change in attitude. In the 1870s and 1880s, as much earlier, Alcott sought to propogate a nonsectarian Christianity rooted in Protestant mysticism, especially that of his "Arch-mystic," Böhme. But circumstances had changed. Whereas during the 1840s Alcott's mysticism was perceived as part of Transcendentalist radicalism, and hence as a threat to more conservative Protestantism, by the 1880s his views were opposed to Darwinist evolutionism and materialism— and hence his mysticism was allied with more conservative Protestants, who also opposed the Darwinist evolutionism that had permeated postbellum Transcendentalist religious radicalism.

Almost all of the "second cycle" Transcendentalists who embraced "Free Religion" radicalism also fervently embraced Darwinist science, their most fanatic apostle being John Fiske. However, Alcott adamantly opposed Darwinism in all its social and other applications, recognizing in it, and in the dogma of "progress," an antispiritual sentiment that Böhmenist mysticism effectively countered.[13] In fact, Alcott was able effectively to exclude proponents of Darwinism from the Concord School of Philosophy and never failed to rail against Darwinism from his "Christian theist" position, which he drew from such authors as St. John, Plotinus, Tauler, Eckhart, and Böhme.[14]

Because it is clear that Alcott was drawn to Böhmean theosophy and arguably knew more about it than anyone else in America at that time, it is not surprising that Alcott's interests also included alchemy and other esoteric traditions. But to explain how this was so requires some further background. I have already discussed how Alcott and Emerson drew on the work and thought of James Pierrepont Greaves. However, there is more to the story. When Greaves died in 1842, Alcott was on his way to meet him, and instead met his follower Charles Lane, who with Alcott boxed up Greaves' extensive library of esoteric works and brought it to New England with them. To Greaves's own books, Alcott and Lane added many others in a similar esoteric vein, and thus the Concord Transcendentalists suddenly had the best library of Western esoteric books in America.

This remarkable library was announced in *The Dial* in April 1843, along with a partial list of the books included. Unaccountably, this announcement and list were deleted from the twentieth-century republication of *The Dial* and scholars of the American Renaissance have not remarked about its deletion, but it is an event of considerable importance from our angle of inquiry. Fuller and Emerson, editors of *The Dial*, undoubtedly recognized the value of this collection, and in fact the announcement concludes that "the arrival of this cabi-

net of mystic and theosophic lore is a remarkable fact in our literary history."[15]
It is clear from the announcement that Alcott and Lane intended the establishment of a library as "an institution for the nurture of men in universal freedom of action, thought, and being," but before we consider what became of this project, we must look at the contents of this catalog.[16]

It is a remarkable catalog. What sorts of books were included in this library? Among the many titles are *The Divine Pymander of Hermes Trismegistus* (London, 1650), the entire works of Böhme in English, including the so-called William Law edition, as well as numerous other individual titles in various editions. Edward Taylor's *Theosophick Philosophy Unfolded* (London, 1691) is included, as is Johann Georg Gichtel's *Eine Kurze Eröffnung* (Berlin, 1779), Heinrich Khunrath's *Amphiteatrum Sapientiæ Æternæ* (Magdeburg, 1602), Miguel Molinos's *Spiritual Guide* (Dublin, 1798), John Pordage's *Theologia Mystica* (London, 1683), Thomas Bromley's *The Way to the Sabbath of Rest* (London, 1761), the works of Jane Leade, various histories of Pietism or theosophy; the works of Antoinette Bourignon, the works of William Law, Swedenborg, and Novalis; the works of Plato and major Neoplatonists including Plotinus, Proclus, and Iamblichus, all in the translations of Thomas Taylor. Also, there were various translations of Hindu works, including Sir William Jones's *The Laws of Menu*. But it is clear from this list that theosophy predominated, and that anyone with access to this library could have an extremely thorough understanding of English and German theosophy, as well as a good general understanding of Neoplatonism.

Yet there is still more to this story. I have not mentioned another wing of this library, which included some magical, and many alchemical works. Among those works are Henry Cornelius Agrippa's *Occult Philosophy* (London, 1651); Roger Bacon's *Opus Magus* and *Mirror of Alchymy* (1597), E. Sibley's *Key to Physic and the Occult Sciences* (London, 1821), and Paracelsus's *Archidoxis* (London, 1663). These books are on the border between magic and alchemy, but incline toward alchemy, and there are numerous other books that are completely alchemical, including *Centrum Naturæ Concentratum, or the Salt of Nature Regenerated* (London, 1696) (probably the work of Thomas Bromley), numerous books by Van Helmont, and George Starkey's *Pyrotechny Asserted and Illustrated* (London, 1658).

Knowing about all of these books, one would be delighted to travel to Fruitlands, where they once were held, and view them. But alas, the entire collection was dispersed, and the contemporary scholar is hard pressed to find any of them. Some of the losses are irreplaceable, like the twelve-volume collection of Greaves's manuscripts, or the marginalia that Alcott, Emerson, or perhaps Fuller or Lane might have added to any of them. I have managed, however, to trace the whereabouts of some of these books, which were donated to Harvard University's Widener Library by F. Alcott Pratt sometime during the twentieth century. Apparently, at least some of the books (in particular the alchemical ones) were retained within the family and only donated or sold long after Alcott's death. Among these is the copy of George Starkey's *Pyrotechny*

Asserted and Illustrated mentioned above, which includes numerous markings near passages. Although we cannot be sure who made these markings, it is entirely possible that they are from the hand of Alcott.

These alchemical books and their markings are particularly interesting because they unquestionably represent the practical or laboratory alchemy that we found in colonial America, and indeed, George Starkey is one of the more important colonial American alchemists. In *Pyrotechny*, we find underlinings of passages like this one: "The Liquor Alcahest is a Salt of an exquisite fiery nature, the like of which is not in the world beside, *not mineral nor metalline*, circulated till it become a very Spirit."[17] Also underlined are references to the "*noisomness*" of the subject in its first preparations and to the "*gentle heat of the Balneum Mariæ.*" There are passages underlined that refer to more metaphysical questions, as well, as in this definition of the alchemical body: "*one in essence or kind, two in number or apparency*," for "*that which is above is like that which is beneath.*"[18] Underlined, this succinct statement of one of the primary Hermetic maxims could not be overlooked easily by subsequent readers, so even if the markings were made by Greaves or someone else, it is certain that this book was at one time in Alcott's hands and very likely that he read these instructions on alchemical work.

Another of the books listed in this catalog and to be found now in Harvard's library is Paracelsus's *Archidoxis*. Paracelsus occupies a position of great importance in Western esotericism, not least because he offered an Hermetic-alchemical form of medicine called "spagyric," which, in turn, influenced many esotericists after him. What makes this particular book especially interesting as part of the Transcendentalist collection is its unrelenting practicality: this is not a book of Hermetic philosophy, but of spagyric medicine. Thus in it we find marked the following recipe: "Take of *Ginger*, one pound; *Long-pepper* and *Black* of each, half an ounce; *Cardamomes*, three drams; *Granes of Paradise*, one ounce; and put them in a Glass . . . with two Ounces of *Aqua Solvens* or the dissolving water, Seal up the Glass, and let it remain in Sand the time of finishing its digestion. . . . Afterward presse it out, and keep it; this is the best and most potent *Diaphoretick.*"[19] This is far from theoretical Hermetic philosophy, or even spiritual alchemy. In the appended "Book of Renovation and Restauration," we also find many marginal notations, chiefly in the form of a squiggly pointing hand and finger. For instance, there is a passage marked on the following: "Likewise the quintessence of Pearls, or *Unio's*, of the Smaragdine, the Saphire, Ruby, Granate, Jacynth, do *renovate* and *restore* the body into all perfection."[20] Or again, there is a passage on the "*Tincture*, the *Arcanum*, or *Quintessence*, in which the very Fundamentals of all Mysteries and Operations do lye hid."[21] All of this clearly is practical or laboratory Hermetic alchemy, and in this respect surprising to find among the Transcendentalists. But there it is.

It is unlikely that Alcott himself ever indulged in laboratory work, not least because to do so would have required money that he simply did not have, particularly after the Fruitlands experiment collapsed. When one visits Fruitlands

Figure 2. "Double Triangle and Serpent With Rays." From Margaret Fuller, *Woman in the Nineteenth Century*, original 1844 edition.

itself, a wonderful farmhouse on a high ridge with a stunning view of the Massachusetts countryside, and considers that in it Alcott probably had many of these theosophic and Hermetic books, one can see why he would have been so disheartened by losing it. Moving back to Concord must have been difficult indeed. However, for a time it undoubtedly seemed to him that his dream would be fulfilled—a remote and beautiful retreat in which he, his family, and friends could actualize theosophy and Hermeticism. That practical matters of money and farming income dashed such hopes does not alter the fact that Alcott remains alone among the Transcendentalists and, for that matter, in the entire American Renaissance, for of all things, his interest in practical esotericism and in making theosophy a part of lived experience.

In sum, then, we may say that the theosophy of Jacob Böhme was extremely important for Bronson Alcott from the beginning to the end of his career. Indeed, like Böhme himself, Alcott has often been mocked for his incomprehensibility. Yet his attraction to Böhmean theosophy or Hermeticism has been little explored, either as a key to his often otherwise inexplicable oracular writings, or as a reason for his later attacks on evolutionism and his association with more conservative Protestant clergy. What is more, this little-known association between Alcott and Protestant Böhmean mysticism, and possibly alchemy, suggests a deeper filiation between Emersonian Transcendentalism and earlier Protestant nonsectarian theosophy—including filiations between Alcott's Fruitlands experiment and earlier American Böhmean communities like Ephrata, in the eighteenth century—that certainly could bear further exploration.

eleven

Emerson

Of all the authors of the American Renaissance, arguably the most influential
was Ralph Waldo Emerson, and a vast body of critical discussion has arisen
about his work. Yet the influences on his writing remain difficult to pinpoint,
not least because Emerson himself hid them. I have elsewhere analyzed at
length his indebtedness to Asian religious traditions, and here will concentrate
on what it was in the European intellectual inheritance that predisposed
Emerson toward Asian religious traditions.[1] Although Emerson's reading was
vast, and one certainly needs to avoid claiming any one influence on him as the
primary one, still it is the case that much in Emerson's work reflects his reading
of Hermetic, theosophic, and Swedenborgian esoteric texts. It was out of this
reading that he developed not only his cosmological, but also his metaphysical
perspectives.

From the very beginning, Emerson's work reflects esoteric premises.
Those who claim Emerson as a "prophet of piratical industrialism" in the manner of Ivor Winters do him a disservice, for Emerson recognized that nature
"ministers" to man only because man, in turn, is responsible to redeem the
world and to become fully human himself.[2] He wrote in his first book, the 1836
Nature, that "all the parts [of nature] incessantly work into each other's hands
for the profit of man. The wind sows the seed; the sun evaporates the sea; the
wind blows the vapor to the field; . . . and thus the endless circulation of the divine charity nourish man."[3] He adds later, man is "placed in the centre of beings, and a ray of relation passes from every other being to him. And neither
can man be understood without these objects, nor these objects without man."[4]
From where did he derive such ideas?

In such observations, Emerson reflects the European theosophic tradition
that runs through such pivotal authors as Jacob Böhme, Franz von Baader, and
Louis-Claude de Saint-Martin, all of whom also drew on the fundamental

Hermetic doctrine of the relationship between the microcosmic individual and the macrocosmos. Saint-Martin, for example, wrote that "things must be known through man, and not man through things," and espoused very much the same doctrine that Emerson is here elaborating: that man serves a profound purpose on earth, that we are here to "crown" creation through our capacities to know and to love.[5] One could multiply parallel quotations from many esoteric (particularly theosophic) authors, but the point remains: as we shall see, European esoteric traditions influenced Emerson deeply.

At the same time, Emerson is an American, and even more than this, a mid-nineteenth century American, who therefore participated in what instead of "the American Renaissance" might be termed an "American dawn." One sees this clearly enough in Thoreau's *Walden*, when the author implies that the living dog of American culture is better than the dead lion of Europe, again when Thoreau tells us that he wishes to make a clarion morning call like Chanticleer the rooster, again in Whitman's brash brag in *Leaves of Grass*, but most of all in this bold little book of Emerson's, with its insouciantly vast titles, titles like those of nearly all his essays: "Beauty," or later in his life, "Farming," or "Solitude." Here we are with an American, who is willing to tackle the whole of life in his writing. However, rarely in all of literature do we see a man who read so much, and hid it so well.

We know that Emerson read extremely widely, that he was well versed in all the classics of the European tradition, and that further he had read whatever of the Asian classics, like the Bhagavad Gita, he could lay his hands on. But one only rarely sees glimpses of this vast reading directly because, as a general rule, Emerson does not cite or even quote others in *Nature* or elsewhere; his evident aim is to reveal or embody in his writings what one might well call a new American classicism, if one may so put it, rooted in the whole of world literature and on exactly the same level—but on his own terms and in his own American words. Emerson saw all the great spiritual writers of the world as friends or colleagues, whose number he—and we—can join simply by doing so.

This extraordinary openness is characteristic of Emersonian esotericism, and in it there is something uniquely American and Transcendentalist. The very highest of which man is capable, the soaring truths of the Bhagavad Gita and Plato, of Sufism and Christianity, are in Emerson assumed at once to be entirely ours. He blithely affirms that the "relation between the mind and matter is not fancied by some poet, but stands in the will of God, and so is free to be known by all men."[6] Everyone possesses intrinsically the possibility for this knowledge—here we have no one excluded from knowing except if they choose not to be. I think that the exhilaration one often feels when reading the work of Emerson comes from just this openness; it is like when one steps out of doors and suddenly the sky is open above.

Traditionally, esotericism, as initiatory traditions are rather closed—the discipline of alchemy, for instance, is couched in relentlessly riddling language and symbol, designed to drive off all but the most persistent seekers, and even those are very often led astray by their own predilections or worse, by deliberately misleading works. One generally needs to find an elder who can guide one in such matters, and this, too, is difficult. All these difficulties are by and large characteristic of European esotericism—in a sense, even a primary attraction, for one expects that profound truths or illumination must be somewhat difficult of access, and worth the trouble of overcoming obstacles inherent in cryptic texts.

This premise of Western esotericism, however, Emerson turns on its head: his Hermeticism is open to all. His language direct, he writes forthrightly that "when in fortunate hours we ponder this miracle" (of the profound relation between mind and matter) "the universe becomes transparent, and the light of higher laws than its own, shines through it." *Anyone* can ponder this miracle of consciousness, and to do so is simply miraculous good fortune worthy of wonder. What in esotericism is hidden in the traditional formulation from the *Tabula Smaragdina*—as above, so below—in Emerson becomes delightfully straightforward, in his proposition that "nature is the symbol of spirit," and that therefore "the visible creation is the terminus or the circumference of the invisible world."[7] Everything we see is a manifestation of spirit.

This openness and directness is Emerson's uniquely American contribution to the Western esoteric stream broadly conceived, stretching from "the era of the Egyptians and the Brahmins, to that of Pythagoras, of Plato" up to that of Swedenborg and of Emerson himself.[8] In his work, we are urged to read the secret texts of Nature for ourselves, so that "the world shall be to us an open book, and every form significant of its hidden life and final cause."[9] Nothing is unavailable to us; everything is open before us if we would merely allow the scales to fall from our eyes. There is in this affirmation a breathtaking assuredness that Eden can again be ours, that we can live in a primordial harmony with the cosmos, and that we can fulfill what it means to truly be human. This, I submit, is the American Revolution of consciousness.

Among the most well known and critically discussed chapters of *Nature* is that entitled "Language," which begins with the remarkable assertion that "Nature is the vehicle of thought," and with these simple propositions: (1) Words are signs of natural facts. (2) Particular natural facts are symbols of particular facts. (3) Nature is the symbol of spirit. Of all these assertions, the first and the last—that nature is the vehicle of thought and the symbol of spirit—are the most striking, and the most profoundly Hermetic. Here Emerson is affirming quite explicitly that "every natural fact is a symbol of some spiritual fact."[10] In other words, and this is the fundamental basis of Hermeticism: everything in the natural world "corresponds to some state of the mind." Consciousness precedes and informs all that we see, and spirituality consists in becoming conscious. Language is the medium of consciousness, of the translation of spirit into matter, and matter into spirit. Thus, to find Hermes, the god of communication, in Emerson, we ought to look at the chapter entitled "Language."

To use the formulation of St. John, "in the Beginning was the Logos," the Word. If as Emerson claims, the visible world is "the dial plate of the invisible,"[11] it is so because it is preceded by and informed by spiritual archetypes (in the Logos), which the world of appearances embodies for us. "Day and night, river and storm, beast and bird, acid and alkali, preëxist in necessary Ideas in the mind of God . . . in the world of spirit."[12] These Ideas are in the Logos, which is also the means of translation between spirit and matter, and whose function we see symbolized exactly in the magical functions of language. Language can invoke changes in consciousness and changes in the world; it is exactly the point of translation between above and below, between archetypal dynamic power and its incarnation.

When this world of archetypes is closer to our direct experience, the world around us becomes synchronistic and dreamlike; it reveals more clearly than usual its transcendent meanings. This is what Emerson means when he writes that "the universe becomes transparent, and the light of higher laws than its own, shines through it."[13] Miracles can indeed happen. In the face of such miracles, "the wise man doubts, if, at all other times, he is not blind and deaf." Our purpose as human beings is to become divine and to incarnate this world of archetypes. If "every scripture is to be interpreted by the same spirit which gave it forth," this can only mean that we are called to attain the same state of consciousness that brought the Scripture (and the world) into being. Such consciousness means that we see the miracle of ordinary life.

We come to realize this miracle through the Imagination, which is the human supersensible faculty. Of Imagination, Emerson wrote in his journal that whereas "the Fancy takes the world as it stands & selects pleasing groups by apparent relations, the Imagination is Vision, regards the world as symbolical & pierces the emblem for the real sense."[14] The Imaginative faculty in the human being is closely akin to the Logos in the cosmic realm: to perceive truth, Emerson argues, quite in line with the Hermetic tradition represented by Jacob Böhme, one's intellect enters the archetypal realm of the Logos; hence, one's clearest thoughts are always accompanied by images as their incarnations. Translation from Logos to individual thought is accomplished by the Imagination, precise and pure.

Emerson's distinction between Fancy and Imagination reflects a distinction upheld by Jacob Böhme, about whom Emerson wrote "Jacob Behme is the best helper to a theory of Isaiah & Jeremiah. You were sure he was in earnest & could you get into his point of view the world would be what he describes. *He is all imagination.*"[15] This passage in Emerson's journals immediately precedes his discussion of Imagination, as well as the following, used in *Nature* about a year later: "There sits the Sphinx from age to age, in the road Charles says, & every wise man in turn that comes by has a crack with her."[16] In fact, in this same entry Emerson copied out the title page and a quotation from Böhme's *Aurora*, published in English translation in London, 1656. It is quite evident from all this that Emerson was reading Böhme closely before he wrote *Nature*, that he admired the German mystic, and that some fundamental concepts informing Emerson's thought derived from Böhme.

In 1841, for instance, Emerson copied from Auguste Theodore Hilaire's history of German philosophy, published in 1836, the following quote: "According to Boehmen the world was nothing else than the relievo the print of a seal of an invisible world concealed in his own bosom." To this Emerson added that "His world was a bible in relief."[17] This is the essential doctrine of Emerson's own *Nature*, and Emerson was undoubtedly gratified to find such external confirmation of his own Hermetic doctrines. We might again recall here that after his death, James Pierrepont Greaves's private library of nearly a thousand volumes, chiefly Böhmean mysticism, was brought over by Charles Lane and Bronson Alcott from England.[18] The significance for American Transcendentalism and for Emerson in particular of this library, announced in *The Dial*, has not yet been widely recognized.

Böhme's doctrines are too elaborate to consider here in any detail, but we can point out at least that central to Böhme's profound cosmology founded in gnostic revelation and spiritual regeneration is the human spiritual Imagination, and its function in revealing the profound, secret significance of sacred language. In fact, many of Böhme's major works explicate the hidden cosmological significances of what might well be called the European equivalent of Sanskrit seed-syllables in Hindu and Buddhist spiritualities. For instance, Böhme will break a word like "Mercurius" down into its fundamental parts, and then explicate the meanings of each element in relation to its spiritual origin and implications. Generally speaking, these expositions rely on striking visual images—for example, the "flaming" or "fiery" nature of a given syllable might be emphasized.[19]

I have no intention of arguing that Emerson's observations on "language" in *Nature* are due solely, or even primarily to the works of Jacob Böhme. However, there is no doubt that Emerson was influenced by Böhme's revelatory Hermetic view of language as being much more than simply syllables arbitrarily assigned as mental "signifiers" of this or that object in the physical world. Emerson, like Böhme, understood that language is far more mysterious than we generally recognize. Indeed, both authors affirm that language is really intermediate between heaven and earth, that in a very profound sense, "in the Beginning was the Logos,"and that to understand truly the mystery of language requires spiritual insight, not just grammatical or analytical facility.

Hence, Emerson tells us that all of Nature exists like a great book, in order to be read—that all of Nature is emblematic, a language of the Spirit. In the chapter of *Nature* entitled "Spirit," Emerson tells us directly that "the noblest ministry of nature is to stand as the apparition of God. It is the great organ through which the universal spirit speaks to the individual, and strives to lead back the individual to it."[20] Perhaps it is only coincidence that this paragraph begins with an aphorism that refers to Jacob Böhme in Emerson's journal: "Of that ineffable essence which we call Spirit, he that thinks most, will say least."[21] Certainly Böhme's work exemplifies through language better than most how nature is the "apparition of God."

"Spirit," this penultimate chapter of *Nature*, is in fact its rhetorical peak, and this is demonstrated by its extraordinary sentence structure—especially remarkable for Emerson, the man of short sentences. We saw earlier how *Nature* began abruptly and jerkily. Compare the work's beginning with its penultimate conclusion, from "Spirit."[22] If we enquire into the nature of matter, Emerson tells us here,

> We learn that the highest is present to the soul of man, that the dread universal essence, which is not wisdom, or love, or beauty, or power, but all in one, and each entirely, is that for which all things exist, and that by which they are; that spirit creates; that behind nature, throughout nature, spirit is present; that spirit is one and not compound; that spirit does not act upon us from without, that is, in space and time, but spiritually, or through ourselves. Therefore, that spirit, that is, the Supreme Being, does not build up nature around us, but puts it forth through us, as the life of the tree puts forth branches and leaves through the pores of the old.[23]

In brief, "the world proceeds from the same spirit as the body of man," is "an incarnation of God," and for us is nothing less than the language of the Divine calling us home. It is no wonder that Emerson actually considered publishing a book to follow *Nature*, called *Spirit*.[24]

Chief among these who inspired Emerson to write *Nature* were the German Romantics, and from among these Emerson was undoubtedly especially influenced by Friedrich von Hardenberg (1772–1801), the brilliant young poet and author with the pen name "Novalis" whose mysterious aphorisms are so captivating and provocative still. Emerson and Novalis shared extraordinary insight into all aspects of human life—it is not for nothing that Novalis could entitle one work "The Encyclopedia" whereas Emerson could write a book with the amusing title "The Uses of Great Men" and essays with titles as vast as "Nature" or "Books" or "The American Scholar." Whatever else one may accuse these writers of, one cannot accuse them of lacking scope, and at the center of both writers' works is the Hermetic tradition.

It would not be appropriate, however, to say that Emerson was influenced only by Novalis among the Germans. Stanley Vogel, in his *German Literary Influences on the American Transcendentalists* (1955), wrote that

> before the publication of *Nature* Emerson read for the first time or reread, excluding Goethe's works, the writings of Novalis, the Schlegels, Karl Müller, Jung-Stilling's *Autobiography*, Mendelssohn's *Phaedo*, Herder's *Outlines of the History of Man*, Heeren, Fichte, Tieck, Lessing, Schleiermacher, Schelling. . . . Richter [Jean Paul], Wieland (whose letters to Merck he found charming), Boerne, Winckelmann, Zelter's *Correspondence with Goethe*, Schiller's *Correspondence with Goethe*, Friedrich Wolf, Camper, and Tischbein. By 1838 he added to his reading list the names of Spinoza, Niebuhr, Herschel, and Bettina von Arnim.[25]

In short, as Kristin Pfefferkorn has written, "It is remarkable with how few exceptions this list could have been drawn up also by Novalis. While in part this is due to the literary climate of the time, it is also a reflection of some basic similarity of intellectual temperament between Emerson and Novalis."[26]

However, there is more we can say about this agreement between Emerson, Goethe, and Novalis, the brilliant young German author of the late eighteenth century.

As early as 1830, Emerson was reading Goethe, Fichte, and Novalis—and of course among these authors, Goethe was enormously significant. Goethe, whose work included not only literary but also religious, philosophical, and scientific dimensions, was indisputably the great figure of Europe for Emerson, representing the natural philosopher or scientist, just as Shakespeare represented the poet, and Plato the philosopher. But there is a side of Goethe not often recognized these days: Goethe as Hermetic philosopher. This is the aspect of Goethe most closely allied to Novalis and to Emerson.

There is certainly ample evidence that Goethe had studied the Hermetic tradition. Early in his writing life, Goethe had read widely in Hermetic, Rosicrucian, and alchemical source works, and this reading was to influence deeply the rest of his life. There is, as we shall see, much to suggest that Goethe's scientific interests, especially in color theory and optics, had their philosophical origins in Hermeticism. But one sees the influence of the Hermetic tradition most clearly in two works: Goethe's "fairy tale," a wonderful, complex symbolic story that has recently been published in English, and, of course, Goethe's lifelong work, *Faust*, especially *Faust, Part Two*.

Emerson had read Goethe's works fairly early in his writing life, and undoubtedly had drawn some of his own worldview out of Goethe's, but it is in Novalis that we find the closest correspondences with Emerson's own writing. These correspondences derive, I think, mainly out of a similarity in intellectual proclivity: both Novalis and Emerson wrote and thought with aphoristic clarity, whereas Goethe—though he, too, was fond of aphorisms—tended to write densely symbolic literary works. Indeed, Emerson's essays often seem more a collection of aphorisms grouped into paragraphs; and of course Novalis wrote mainly in aphorisms, collected under various subtitles and published posthumously as *Pollen and Fragments*, though he also wrote Hermetic fairy-tales like *Die Lehrlinge ʒu Sais*, or *The Disciples at Sais*.

However, there is much more than a merely formal parallel between Novalis's aphoristic writings and Emerson's *Nature*. Several scholars have already recognized the indebtedness of Emerson to Novalis's work, and Henry Pochmann goes so far as to claim that every major element of Emerson's *Nature* can be traced back to Thomas Carlyle's article on Novalis: "Indeed, except for the illustrations drawn from natural science, and the homespun phrases and figures, Emerson's *Nature* contains few ideas that have not their counterparts in Carlyle's words on Novalis or in the quotations from Novalis that are adduced for illustrative purposes."[27]

There can be no doubt Emerson was familiar with Novalis's work before he wrote *Nature*. In his journals, Emerson quoted from Novalis's works frequently during the time he wrote his first major work. Some of these quotations came from a series called "Specimens of German Genius" in *New Monthly Magaʒine*, which he withdrew from the Boston Athenaeum in 1832, but most indeed came from Carlyle's article, which evidently Emerson examined numerous times, for he drew upon it again and again over several years.[28] For example, from Carlyle's article Emerson copied the following: "What is Nature? An encyclopedical systematic Index or Plan of our spirit. Why will we content us with the mere Catalogue of our Treasure? Let us contemplate them ourselves & in all ways elaborate & use them."[29] The relevance of such a quotation to Emerson's work is self-explanatory, and there are many others.[30] It seems hardly coincidental that Emerson called his quotation book "Encyclopedia," the precise name of a large section of Novalis's aphorisms from which Emerson was himself quoting.

We can note the parallels between Emerson's *Nature* and Novalis's work in more detail. Although it is not quite fair to Emerson to lay the entire inspiration for his work at Novalis's feet, it is certainly true that Carlyle's essay, laid down next to Emerson's *Nature*, is strikingly apropos. Carlyle places considerable emphasis upon Nature in this essay. Carlyle writes that "One character to be noted in many of these, often too obscure speculations, is [Novalis's] peculiar manner of viewing Nature: his habit, as it were, of considering Nature . . . as a self-subsistent universally connected Whole."[31] Indeed, "He loves external Nature with a singular depth; nay, we might say, he reverences her, and holds unspeakable communings with her: for Nature is no longer dead, hostile Matter, but the veil and mysterious Garment of the Unseen; as it were, the Voice with which Deity proclaims himself to man."[32]

However, there is another aspect of Novalis's work as portrayed by Carlyle that Emerson must have loved: his appreciation of life's fleeting quality, what Emerson, drawing on Asian religious doctrine, called Maya. According to Carlyle, Novalis held that "the Invisible World is near us: or rather it is here, in us and about us; were the fleshly coil removed from our Soul, the glories of the Unseen were even now around us; as the Ancients fabled of the Spheral Music."[33] Novalis, like Emerson, recognized that "the Earth and all its glories are in truth a vapour and a Dream, and the Beauty of Goodness the *only* real possession." This is not to denigrate the earth, however—quite the reverse, for we ought to cherish all the more what is so evanescent and yet so beautiful, precisely because it reflects the Beautiful.

It is noteworthy that the excerpts Carlyle chose from Novalis's work tend to refer to Nature in ways that must have been congenial to Emerson. Indeed, *Die Lehrlinge zu Sais* begins:

> Men travel in manifold paths: whoso traces and compares these, will find strange Figures come to light; Figures which seem as if they belonged to that great Cipher—writing which one meets with everywhere, on wings of birds, shells of eggs, in clouds, in the snow, in crystals, in forms of rocks, in freezing waters, in the interior and exterior of mountains, of plants, animals, men, in the lights of the sky, in plates of glass and pitch when touched and struck on. . . . In such Figures one anticipates the key to that wondrous Writing, the grammar of it.[34]

Undoubtedly one sees in this passage—particularly in the description that follows of the idyllic, nature-loving childhood and youth of the Disciples' Teacher, who "gathered stones, flowers, insects, of all sorts," who "wandered far and wide" in the wild, who saw how "stars were men, now men were stars, the stones animals, the clouds plants"[35]—something of Emerson's "Orphic poet" whose parable concludes *Nature*. Emerson, like Novalis, saw that natural phenomena reflected a spiritual origin and meaning.

In fact, after reading Carlyle's essay on Novalis—and in particular the excerpts from *Die Lehrlinge zu Sais*—it is very hard to read the "Orphic poet" section of *Nature* without Novalis in mind. Certainly it is plausible that the "certain poet" who sang the quoted section to Emerson was Novalis, for the second excerpt Carlyle quoted from *Die Lehrlinge*, like Emerson's poet, speaks of time's cycles and of how "history is but the epoch of one degradation." Today—both Emerson's and Novalis's poets tell us—"we distrust and deny inwardly our sympathy with nature." Today, in Emerson's memorable phrase, "man is a god in ruins."[36] But we are called to restore "to the world original and eternal beauty" "by the redemption of the soul."[37]

This redemption of nature through the soul's redemption is the fundamental task to which both Emerson and Novalis call us. We must, Emerson insists, see the world with new eyes. We must return to a childlike innocence, both authors urge. Central to Novalis's fairy tale of Sais is the innocence of childhood, and Emerson, too, tells us that "Infancy is the perpetual Messiah, which comes into the arms of fallen men, and pleads with them to return to paradise."[38] Although this is the language of Christian rebirth, in fact Emerson and Novalis are calling even more on the language of the Mystery traditions upon which Christianity itself drew, and that were encapsulated in the Hermetic tradition that both writers embody.

Surely it is not coincidental that Novalis's second chapter of *Die Lehrlinge zu Sais* is entitled "Nature," or that just as Emerson speaks of both the destructive and the beneficent sides of Nature, so, too, before him in his chapter "Nature" Novalis writes of how Nature appears "a frightful Machine of Death" everywhere, and adds "Hail to that childlike ignorance and innocence of men, which kept them blind to the horrible perils" all around them. There Novalis delineates several classes of men: those who seek refuge from the world in "their ancient Father," those who degenerate "into Beasts," those who seek to "build us a new Fairyland," those who have a "serene consciousness," and finally he who is "lord of the world," who realizes that the moral sense alone makes one "forever Master of Nature."[39] It is no accident that Emerson ends his *Nature* by claiming likewise through his "Orphic poet" that "The kingdom of man over nature, which cometh not with observation,—a dominion such as now is beyond his dream of God,—he shall enter without more wonder than the blind man feels who is gradually restored to perfect sight."[40] Both Emerson and Novalis urge mastery of the self and of nature, but they also reverence nature.

It is something of a commonplace today to say that "Nature is the great teacher," and usually this is meant only in the most vague way. However, for

Novalis—and even more for Emerson in *Nature*—the concept of Nature as our teacher takes on a special power and precise meaning. For Emerson and Novalis, and for authors of the Hermetic tradition more generally, Nature is the great human teacher in a way perhaps best understood by way of Platonism. According to Platonism and Hermetism both, everything that we see in the physical world reflects its hierarchic celestial archetypes. Thus it is possible to trace all phenomena back to origins—or better, to see in all nature the patterns that inform it and that reveal to us the unseen world of Forms or archetypes that dynamically create what we see.

We see this understanding reflected in the works of both Novalis and Emerson. Indeed, the whole of Novalis's *Pollen and Fragments* is rooted in the Hermetic tradition, expressed in aphorisms like this one from "The Encyclopedia:" We owe all the greatest truths of our day to contact with the long-separated limbs of total-knowledge."[41] This "total-knowledge" or holistic knowledge, in the Hermetic tradition, refers to the archetypal origin of all the various and only apparently discrete forms of human knowledge. Philosophy, Literature, Science, Mathematics: all can be traced back to Language, or the Word; and in the Word we see the primordial relationship between Man and Nature. The Word mediates between the archetypal realm and the realm that we see.

This mediation or movement between the archetypal or spiritual realm and the earthly world is central to Novalis's worldview—and to Emerson's. Novalis writes that "Our thought is simply a galvanization—a touching of the earthly spirits—through the spiritual atmosphere—of a heavenly unearthly spirit. All thinking is thus already a sympraxis in a higher world."[42] Hence "The higher philosophy deals with the marriage of nature and spirit." Exactly the same ideas Emerson conveys in the chapter "Spirit," when he writes that although "the world proceeds from the same spirit as the body of man," "as we degenerate, the contrast between us and our house is more evident."[43] By implication, then, "regeneration" means reunion between us and nature, a reunion in which we again understand the speech of birds, the meanings of all Nature.

In Western esotericism, there is a profound correspondence recognized between the physical world and its spiritual archetypes. Novalis writes, echoing the Hermetic *Tabula Smaragdina*, or *Emerald Tablet* ["I am a child of earth and starry heaven"]: "Magic of the star-like power. Through it man becomes as powerful as the stars; he is, above all, related to the stars."[44] Indeed, "the world is the macroanthropos," so there is an intimate relationship between ourselves and our world—"formation of the soul is also at the center of formation of the world-soul—and thus indirectly is a religious obligation."[45] Likewise, according to Emerson, virtue is "the golden key / Which opes the palace of eternity," a truth that "animates me to create my own world through the purification of my soul."[46]

This relationship between the realm of spirit and the realm of nature takes place through soul, which is "bound, enclosed, contracted spirit (Novalis)"[47] and is elucidated through the Word. There is, therefore, a great mystery in language for both Novalis and Emerson. Novalis remarks on "grammatical mysticism," "at the root of which" lies "the primal astonishment over speech and writing." In fact, "All that we experience is a message. So the world . . . is a message—revelation of the spirit." Hence "in the end, all becomes poetry," just as "the world, in the end, proves itself to be heart-felt spirit."[48] For Novalis as for Emerson, "The world is a universal trope of the spirit, a symbolic image therefrom."[49]

However, at the absolute center of both Novalis and Emerson's work is spiritual awareness, self-transcendence, which they express in startling, vivid terms. Novalis writes that "We will come to understand the world when we understand ourselves, since we and it are integrating in the center. God's children, Godly embryos are we. One day we are to become what our Father is."[50] "Our spirit," Novalis holds, "is a connecting link to the wholly incomparable," for "nothing is more attainable to the spirit than the infinite." Carlyle included in his essay Novalis's aphorism that "The true philosophical act is annihilation of self; this is the real beginning of all Philosophy. . . . This act alone corresponds to all the conditions and characteristics of transcendental conduct."[51] Emerson likewise writes in *Nature* of transcendent exhilaration, of becoming translucent, and of how this selfless experience in turn allows realization of the profound unity between us and the natural world.

I do not think we should neglect this point: the connection between self-transcendence, and unity between us and nature is critical. Emerson, an American closer to the woods than his German predecessor, wrote that "In the woods, is perpetual youth. . . . [W]e return to reason and faith." Here, "all mean egotism vanishes." In the woods, "The currents of the Universal Being circulate through me; I am part or particle of God. The name of the nearest friend sounds then foreign and accidental."[52] Here is the central point: in the wilderness, there is "an occult relation between man and the vegetable"—trees "nod to me and I to them." When we rise above our petty selves, we enter into an Edenic state of union with nature. Selflessness is greater consciousness of our world.

Surely it must have struck Emerson with special force when he read Novalis's assertion, translated by Carlyle in his essay, that "Man announces himself and his Gospel of Nature; he is the Messiah of Nature."[53] Man is the Messiah of Nature: this is the key to Emerson's little book, for Emerson is urging us to redeem both ourselves and our world. It is also a key to the power of Emerson's affirmation—for we are each potential messiahs in his vision, able if we rise to the challenge, to restore meaning to ourselves and to our world. This was why Emerson so powerfully challenged the lukewarm rationalist Unitarianism of his generation: he brought to his time the same kind of radical Christianity that we see preceding him in Novalis.[54]

For Emerson, as for Novalis, the type of the redeemer is the poet, because, as Novalis writes, "the true Poet is all-knowing; he is an actual world in miniature." To redeem the self is to redeem the world; and to do this is to be poet and priest at once. The highest example of this is Shakespeare, for both Novalis and

Emerson, and as Novalis writes, Shakespeare "was a mighty, many-gifted soul, whose feelings and works, like products of Nature, bear the stamp of the same spirit; and in which the last and deepest of observers will still find new harmonies with the infinite structure of the Universe. . . . They are emblematic, have many meanings, are simple and inexhaustible."[55] The poet—and here Rilke comes to mind as a modern exemplar—gathers the pollen of the visible and creates the honey of the invisible.

In the works of both Emerson and Novalis, we are called through the paradoxical medium of words to see the cosmos through new eyes: every aspect of life is to be redeemed, all of nature and all human endeavor is seen in a primordial light. Here "words cannot cover the dimensions of what is in truth." "Finite organs of the infinite mind," words "break, chop, and impoverish" truth.[56] We are meant as humans to see the world anew, as it is in the reality of "universal Spirit." These words of Emerson express the paradoxical nature of his work and that of Novalis and indeed of Western esotericism more generally. For we are called through words to that which is beyond words; communication is meant to communicate the incommunicable, what must and in fact can be only directly experienced.

This is American literature at its most breathtakingly universal: through Emerson's prose we are introduced to the world seen anew, and this introduction can only take place in the same way as a Hermetic initiation by a master—by one who has already directly seen truth—to a disciple, to an individual who wishes also to see the world in this way. Emerson and Novalis are both initiatory writers in at least this way: they communicate to us as individuals and can be understood only when we are as if engaged in a dialogue or conversation with them, much like the Hermetic dialogues of the *Corpus Hermeticum*. Each of us must grasp or receive individually the multiplex implications of Emerson's aphorisms.

Through these individual revelations—which happen for each of us in different ways, spontaneously and dependent upon our own background, predilections, and personality—we in a sense recreate for ourselves that original spontaneous insight of Emerson. To use an analogy, I have drawn elsewhere to describe the work of Novalis, an aphorism requires us to "leap a gap" between ourselves and it, rather like a spark, thrown off by an incandescent electrical source, arcs from one point to another when a connection is made. We as readers are the only means by which a written work can "arc" in this way, and it is only through this kind of receptive reading that a work like Emerson's is completed. *Nature* exists in order to be read, and not just read as if one were processing information, but read as a living being can be read. This is the only way true education can take place, Plato told us in his seventh letter.[57]

Like life itself, a work like *Nature* is multifaceted, and Emerson was acutely aware of this truth. Indeed, he tells us "*Omne verum vero consonat*: Every universal truth which we express in words, implies or supposes every other truth. . . . Every such truth is the absolute Ens seen from one side. *But it has innumerable sides*."[58] This is the crystalline center of Emerson's work, not only in *Nature*, but also in the rest of his writings. His essays are profound exactly because they have "innumerable sides," because his work incorporates the paradoxical and multiplex nature of nature. Novalis, too, sought to do this, but here the age of Emerson—who began his writing career in his early thirties, while Novalis died before he was thirty—gives Emerson an advantage: Emerson's work is rounded, more complete, not just "pollen and fragments," but completed essays.

So Emerson is not just an American writer—his deep awareness of world literature, which my discussion of Goethe, Shakespeare, Novalis, Carlyle, and Emerson only underscores—places him among authors whose work truly possesses universal qualities and cannot be relegated only to the more parochial field of "American writers" subject only to "American influences."[59] But of course precisely this universalism reveals Emerson's work as profoundly American in its vast scope and its primordialism, its embrace of the whole of human history, of the entire human literary and religious inheritance at once. Like Hermes, Emerson's purview includes all books, all writing, the whole realm of Mercury under whose sign all communication takes place, and in this great embrace Emerson is indisputably American, exactly because of his universalism, common also to Whitman, Melville, and Thoreau, to name only a few among many.

Although Emerson's focus on natural science in *Nature* has often been remarked upon and examined, not so much attention has been paid to the precise nature and implications of the science that Emerson advocates. For Emerson is indeed advocating rather than simply discussing. In fact, Emerson in the final chapter of *Nature*—"Prospects"—calls for a new science, one far more than simple cataloging or theorizing, but that consists in a "contemplation of the whole" through "sallies of the spirit." He calls, in short, for a "*metaphysics* of conchology, of botany, of the arts." This metaphysical science for which Emerson calls already existed in his day as in ours, and is, put simply, the Hermetic science of soul and spirit. How we engage in this science is the subject of Emerson's last chapter in *Nature*.

In order to understand what Emerson was trying to achieve in *Nature*, we should recognize the historical epoch in which he lived and which we share with him. In his day, as in ours, a materialistic, quantifying worldview prevailed. Science consisted in the examination, categorization, and quantification of phenomena, chiefly with an eye to technological exploitation, and largely without regard for the implications of the whole, certainly without recognizing the spiritual significance of scientific exploration. Indeed, from the eighteenth century onward, science and technology were severed from their religious or spiritual implications and pursued as if they were themselves "objective," without spiritual ramifications for people or for the world.

Historically speaking, this materialistic isolation of science is a very strange, virtually unprecedented situation. After all, it is not as though traditional cultures around the world had no sciences of their own; indeed, every traditional culture consists in explaining the significance to people of the cosmos in which they exist. In Tibetan Buddhism, to take only one example, one finds very developed medicinal and astrological systems. But here, as in other traditional cultures, medicinal and stellar and planetary observation are integrated into a complete worldview that includes the spiritual significance of both external (sidereal) and internal (psychophysiological) phenomena. In a tradition, one does not study stars or planets solely to calculate distances between them; one endeavours to elaborate what they *mean* for us as human beings.

In Emerson's day, as in our own, science had become separated from its religious origins, and although the disastrous ecological and human consequences of this divorce had not yet become apparent in mid-nineteenth century America, Emerson foresaw where things were headed. Thus he begins "Prospects" by noting that the "problems to be solved are precisely those which the physiologist and the naturalist omit to state. It is not so pertinent to man to know all the individuals of the animal kingdom, as it is to know whence and whereto is this tyrannizing unity in his constitution, which evermore separates and classifies things."[60] Only spiritual insight can provide the answers to the questions posed to the soul of whence it is come, and where it is going.

Carlyle immediately recognized what Emerson was up to. In a letter to Emerson, Carlyle said he was delighted with the little "azure-coloured *Nature*," lent it to many friends, and always heard the same verdict when it came back:

> You say it is the first chapter of something greater. I call it rather a Foundation and Ground-plan on which you may build whatsoever of great and true has been given you to build. It is the true Apocalypse, this where the 'Open Secret' becomes revealed to a man. I rejoice much in the glad serenity of soul with which you look out on this wondrous Dwelling-place of yours and mine,—with an ear for the *Ewigen Melodien* which pipe in the winds round us and utter themselves forth in all sounds and sights and things; not to be written down by gamut machinery, but which all right writing is a kind of attempt to write down. You will see what the years will bring you.[61]

Most important here are the keywords—*Nature*, Carlyle said, represents "the true Apocalypse," in which "the 'Open Secret' becomes revealed to a man." This is the language of Christian Hermeticism, of the tradition of Jacob Böhme in particular, about whose work exactly the same words could be used.

What is the "Open Secret" to which Carlyle referred? This term, combined with the phrase "true Apocalypse," (meaning inward revelation, presumably, rather than outward catastrophe) is characteristic of Hermeticism, which is based in the spiritual discipline and illumination of an individual through contemplative praxis in a broadly Christian context. One sees this clearly in examining, for instance, the collection of Hermetic texts called *The Hermetic Museum*, published in Latin in Europe in successive editions of 1625 and 1678. In a particularly valuable text in this collection called "The Sophic Hydrolith," we read of how in antiquity the Hermetic "secret" was known by a few adepts, who transmitted this "hidden truth," in turn, to only a worthy few. Among those who knew this "Open Secret" are listed Hermes Trismegistus, Pythagoras, Plato, Dionysius, Raymond Lull, Thomas Aquinas, and Paracelsus.[62]

Traditionally, this "Open Secret" is said to be everywhere visible, but spurned by the foolish who do not recognize it. Only those who are truly virtuous are given God's grace to realize it:

> For itself is the universal and sparkling flame of the light of Nature, which has the heavenly Spirit in itself with which it was animated at first by God, Who pervades all things, and is called by Avicenna, the Soul of the world. . . . In short, it is a Spiritual Essence which is neither celestial nor infernal, but an aerial, pure, and precious body, in the middle between the highest and lowest, the choicest and noblest thing under heaven. But by the ignorant and the beginner it is thought to be the vilest and meanest of things. It is sought by many Sages, and found by few: . . . 'Men have it before their eyes, handle it with their hands, yet know it not, though they constantly tread it under their feet. It is the greatest wealth, and he who knows the Art may rival the richest.'[63]

It is most interesting to read Carlyle's words to Emerson—and even more Emerson's *Nature*—with a Hermetic passage like this in mind. Carlyle's congratulations, we should note, are not so much for Emerson's *words* as for his *state of consciousness*: Carlyle "rejoice[s] much in the glad serenity of soul with which [Emerson] look[s] out on this wondrous Dwelling-place of yours and mine,—with an ear for the *Ewigen Melodien* which pipe in the winds round us and utter themselves forth in all sounds and sights and things; not to be written down by gamut machinery."

In the modern era, we have a surfeit of "gamut machinery," but we could perhaps benefit from a bit more "glad serenity of soul." Emerson, in his "Prospects," is pointing us toward exactly this, toward a transformed state of consciousness that does not merely quantify the world, but is able to see that as the Christian poet George Herbert wrote

> All things unto our flesh are kind,
> In their descent and being; to our mind,
> In their ascent and cause.[64]

Ascent to what Plotinus called "Authentic Being" takes place through the mind, and only such an ascent can truly reveal the significance of human existence in the cosmos; without it, we are like dethroned Nebuchadnezzar, Emerson tells us, "eating grass like an ox."

Here, in Emerson's final famous passage in the words of an "Orphic poet," based as I have argued earlier, on Novalis, we find Emerson's most profoundly Christian Hermetic and most beautiful formulations. Listen to the magnitude of his claims and the power of his rhetoric: "A man is a god in ruins. When men are innocent, life shall be longer, and shall pass into the immortal, as gently as we awake from dreams."[65] Of course, this is strikingly close to Novalis's aphorism, translated in Carlyle's essay, that "Our life is no Dream, but it may and will perhaps become one." Or again, when Emerson claims that "Infancy is the perpetual Messiah," he is not far from Novalis's affirmation of his "Gospel of Nature" calling man to be "Messiah of Nature." But the rhetoric is certainly powerful, and stands on its own.

In order to unveil Emerson's sources and his intent in *Nature*, it may be useful to consider more deeply the significance of Emerson's indebtedness to Jacob Böhme, that source of inspiration for Novalis, as well. As Elisabeth Hurth has so nicely documented for us, Emerson was undoubtedly fascinated with the work of Böhme, and although his journals record occasional doubts about the German mystic, on the whole they demonstrate Emerson's sustained interest in the many remarkable books of this autodidact who also saw the profound meanings of the natural world, saw it as transparent, revealing its spiritual origins and implications for those with eyes to see.[66]

Exactly here, in this New Testament allusion to "eyes to see," do we find the central metaphor of Emerson's *Nature*—a metaphor that many readers have recognized as essential in Emerson's thought—the theosophic metaphor of the eye. Although many critics have remarked on Emerson's preoccupation with sight and especially with eyes, no one to my knowledge has recognized Emerson's indebtedness to the Böhmean theosophic tradition in this regard. I know of no other tradition that places so great an emphasis on the symbolic meanings of the eye, making this image central to many if not all of the countless beautiful illustrations and diagrams that adorn the various editions of Böhme's works, and many other theosophic publications, as well. One finds eyes in hearts, an eye in the center of the world, rings of eyes encircling globes, paradise depicted as a veritable swarm of disembodied eyes—the list goes on. When one looks into the symbolism of the eye in the works of Böhme and the later English Philadelphians like Dr. John Pordage, we find that the number of references to eyes becomes almost unmanageable.

We do not have room here to elaborate the entire significance of this profound theosophic subject, on which I have written extensively elsewhere in any case.[67] Rather, we can only consider the fundamental implications of this image of the eye for the Böhmean theosophers. The theosophers—who represent a definite self-identified school—were essentially interested in experientially penetrating into paradise while alive on earth. Their aim, and by their own accounts many of them achieved it, was to experience gnosis, or direct insight into the spiritual origins of nature and of humanity. Thus their goal was really to unite the worlds, to in Emerson's words "make the axis of vision" "coincident with the [true] axis of things," so things appear not "opake," but "transparent."[68]

Various critics have pointed out how striking are these references to the "axis of vision," but their antecedent in theosophic illustrations has gone unrecognized.[69] The theosophers, following in ancient Christian custom, used the symbol of the eye to indicate exactly the coincidence of two realms, conceived as spheres or circles. Where these circles overlap one has the geometrical figure known as the *vesica piscis*, which resembles at once the image of an eye and of a fish, hence part of the meaning behind the ancient Christian symbol of the fish—the meeting point of two realms, of paradise and earth. We see this symbolism explicitly in almost every major Böhmean illustration, and in words it is implied quite well in Emerson's references to the axes of vision and of things.

It is not for nothing that Böhme is known as a Christian *visionary*, for if anyone ever was, Böhme was a *seer* (hence Emerson's continual fascination with him). Böhme saw the fundamental principles within the cosmos, he saw paradise and hell, he saw angels, and all these he elaborated in much detail in his many works. Emerson in *Nature* is insisting on the primacy of this Böhmean theosophic or spiritual vision over mere natural vision. Some time thereafter, in "Man the Reformer," Emerson quoted the Neoplatonist Thomas Taylor, another oft-maligned mystic, on "the venerable counsel of the ancient Egyptian mysteries, which declared that 'there were two pair of eyes in man, and it is requisite that the pair which are beneath should be closed, when the pair that are above them perceive, and that when the pair above are closed, those which are beneath should be opened.'"[70] In the final chapter of *Nature*, Emerson tells us that we must open the upper pair of eyes before we can see aright below; we must have spiritual eyes before we can have an authentic science. This is a message undeniably well illustrated by Jacob Böhme.

Thus, we are not too surprised to find Emerson calling, at the end of *Nature*, not for a "knowledge of man," which is "an evening knowledge, *vespertina cognitio*, but that of God," "a morning knowledge, *matutina cognitio*."[71] After all, it had only been a short while since Emerson had been reading the English translation of Böhme's first and seminal book, *Aurora*, whose title page and a quotation he carefully copied into his journals on 1 August 1835, along with a query into "why the world exists" and the answer, "it exists for a language or medium whereby God may speak to Man."[72] Emerson recognized that Böhme was precisely an interpreter of this divine language or medium, and that he offered a "morning knowledge," an *Aurora* as a means of "reading" the book of nature through, to use the title of one of Böhme's books, *The Signature of All Things*.

There is yet more. Indisputably, one of Emerson's primary concerns in "Prospects" is to point toward a new science, a science that is not mere quantification or cataloging, but is a visionary or Hermetic science, one with not just lower eyes, but upper, spiritual eyes, as well. Hence, it is remarkable that in the late-twentieth century one finds a French physicist named Basarab Nicolescu publishing a book entitled *Science, Meaning and Evolution: The Cosmology of Jacob Boehme*, in which he explicitly and with remarkable humility expresses his indebtedness to Böhme, and calls for a "new scientific and cultural approach—one which is transdisciplinary—in which all branches of knowledge, both the so-called 'exact' sciences and the so-called 'human' science, as well as art and tradition, must cooperate."

This "transdisciplinary" "new science" of nature Nicolescu finds embodied in the work of Böhme, and in particular in *Aurora*, the very book Emerson was also reading before he, too, envisioned a new transdisciplinary Hermetic science. Nicolescu tells us that Böhme's Hermetic works will inevitably be rediscovered, for "Boehme shows us how the multiple splendor of Being is reflected in the mirror of Nature," and that "The time for a truly new alliance—that of man with himself—has come. In our quest, Jacob Boehme is present among us, bodily present, a friend, a divine cobbler, a living witness to this new alliance."[73] Nicolescu is far more open in his endorsement of Böhme than Emerson was—Emerson elided his indebtedness wherever he could, as I have elsewhere documented.[74] But the correspondence between Emerson and Nicolescu's visions of a new Hermetic science founded in Böhme remains clear.

Hence, Emerson's final words in *Nature* take on a particular significance in their affirmation that "The kingdom of man over nature, which cometh not with observation,—a dominion such as now is beyond his dream of God,—he shall enter without more wonder than the blind man feels who is gradually restored to perfect sight."[75] The "kingdom of man over nature" to which Emerson here looks forward does not represent a *rejection* of the entire modern worldview, with its technological sophistication. Nor does Emerson here *embrace* modern science, or what some perceptive authors have called "scientism," meaning a quasi-religious faith in scientific dogmas.[76]

Rather, Emerson tells us that we shall one day enter "a dominion such as now is beyond [our] dream of God," and that only this illumination, only this restoration to authentic vision, can create a complete science—a science of true Hermetic knowledge that encompasses and directs wisely all its various branches or technologies. We are called to attain this illumination not gradually—as if a banished king were to try and reclaim his kingdom inch by inch—but by vaulting at once into the throne.[77] Yet even if this is not possible, we can through prayer or inward contemplation slowly open those upper or spiritual eyes, and eventually we will nonetheless be able to see how we too are "present at the sowing of the seed of the world," and how "with a geometry of sunbeams the Soul lays the foundations of nature."[78] We, too, can see how all the various sciences—including "poetry & music & dancing & astronomy & mathematics"—derive from the most essential science of all, the Hermetic illumination of soul and revelation of spirit.

I have concentrated thus far almost exclusively on the origins of Emerson's first book, *Nature*, primarily because *Nature* includes so much of what was to come in Emerson's writing. But we should recognize how esoteric currents continued to be important for Emerson throughout his career, chiefly under the auspices of one synthesizing figure: Swedenborg. If Emerson early on was familiar with Hermeticism and Christian theosophy, by the 1840s, he had become intimately familiar with Swedenborg's writing, as well, so much so that some of his contemporaries speculated that he and his second wife Lidian had become Swedenborgians. This was, of course, not at all the case, as Emerson made entirely clear in his 1838 journal entry, remarking that "the instant the defining lockjaw shuts down his fetters & cramps all round us, & we must needs think in the genius & speak in the phraseology of Swedenborg, & the last slavery is worse than the first."[79] Without doubt, Emerson was not a Swedenborgian churchgoer.

However, there is no question that Emerson was fascinated by the figure of Swedenborg and made constant references to him in his writing. His own personal library included many volumes by the prolific Swedish visionary, from both his scientific and his religious periods.[80] Works Emerson owned and read included translations of Swedenborg's *The Economy of the Animal Kingdom* (Boston, 1843–44), *The Apocalypse Revealed* (Boston, 1836), and *The True Christian Religion* (Boston, 1843). References to Swedenborg in Emerson's journals and published works were frequent, particularly during the 1840s, and often in essays where one might not expect the visionary to crop up, like, for instance, "The Poet."

Of course, Emerson defines "poet" widely, for he includes the following in his list: "Orpheus, Empedocles, Heraclitus, Plato, Plutarch, Dante, and Swedenborg."[81] Emerson can define Swedenborg as a poet (even though he acknowledges the seer to be singularly unpoetic) because the poet is "representative," "a man of genius." Swedenborg figures highly in Emerson's definition and discussion of the poet not least because Swedenborg understood the "universality of the symbolic language;" he understood that the universe is the "externization of the soul," and that "the world is a temple, whose walls are covered with emblems, pictures, and commandments of the Deity."[82] In other words, the poet is one who shows us the symbolic true nature of the world, and in this sense is Swedenborg as a visionary very much a poet.

Yet there are more than Swedenborgian allusions in Emerson's discussion of the poet, for he overtly refers us to European esoteric currents. When Emerson offers his famous dictum that "The poets are thus liberating gods," he cites such esoteric luminaries as "Pythagoras, Paracelsus, Cornelius Agrippa," "Swedenborg, Schelling, Oken, or any other who introduces questionable facts into his cosmogony, as angels, devils, magic, astrology, palmistry, mesmerism, and so on."[83] Why is Emerson citing such esoteric figures as these in an essay ostensibly on the poet? "I think nothing is of any value in books," Emerson announces, "excepting the transcendental and extraordinary." The poet "unlocks our chains," and "admits us to a new scene."[84]

But there is a deeper connection between Emerson's wide definition of the poet and esotericism, even beyond Emerson's high valuation of what is "transcendental and extraordinary." This deeper connection is found in the imagination. As we will recall, Antoine Faivre remarked that one of the main characteristics of European esotericism is the emphasis placed upon the imagination not merely as fantasy, but as a means of seeing into the spiritual realm. For this kind of imaginative seeing, Henry Corbin invented the term "imaginal," to distinguish spiritual sight from fantasy or daydreaming.[85] Emerson himself defines "Imagination" in a very particular way, calling it "a very high sort of seeing, which does not come by study, but by the intellect being where and what it sees, by sharing the path, or circuit of things through forms, and so making them translucid to others."[86] This is an enormously important definition of imagination because it emerges quite clearly from Emerson's knowledge of the European esoteric traditions he has referred to: it is a definition of imagination not as human fantasy, but actual seeing by becoming. The separation between subject and object that characterises modern forms of knowledge, and particularly the sciences, is here jettisoned by Emerson in favor of the "intellect being where and what it sees," in favor of a union, in other words, of subject and object that precisely characterizes Western esoteric traditions like magic, alchemy, and astrology.

Now we can begin to see the magnitude of what Emerson is about when he includes and endorses such "occult" figures as Agrippa and Paracelsus in an essay on poetry. Emerson not only redefines poetry to *include* an essentially magical relation to the cosmos (which is precisely what we see in Agrippa and Paracelsus), he is in fact defining the Imagination and poetry as *being* magical. This redefinition reflects the kind of often-remarked "American Adamism" that we see also in Whitman, an American Adamism in which Emerson, by insisting on the primal unity of the poet with the cosmos, is in essence making of America a kind of new Eden. Emerson's new American poet is a primeval poet somehow "earlier" than his British or European predecessors by being more primal, that is, more in touch with the essential Adamic relation of humanity to the cosmos that is found in esoteric traditions, particularly in magical ones, but also in many of the others, even derivatives like animal magnetism. In all of these, there is a profound relationship between subject and object, a deep connection, even a union.

Emerson found Swedenborg representative of such a profound union between subject and object, and so it was that he delivered in 1845 his lecture on Swedenborg that subsequently became part of the collection *Representative Men*. In 1845, Swedenborgianism had become influential in New England, and particularly in Boston, where a number of Emerson's friends and acquaintances were quite enamored of the visionary's writings. Indeed, there was an American Swedenborgian periodical, *The New Jerusalem Magazine*, and a large new Swedenborgian church in Boston, not to mention the intellectual dispersion of Swedenborg's writings via a new set of translations published during the 1840s. Thus, it is perhaps not too surprising that in "Swedenborg, or the Mystic," Emerson was to assert that "by force of intellect, and in effect," Swedenborg "is the last Father in the Church, and is not likely to have a successor."[87]

However, Emerson did not agree wholeheartedly with Swedenborg, and his assessment of the visionary includes numerous criticisms. Emerson was critical of Swedenborg's doctrine of celestial, eternal marriages, and argued that all such unions are temporary, that when we pass out of one another's purview, divorce is inevitable.[88] What's more, Emerson was highly dubious about Swedenborg's visionary literalism and his wallowing in imagery of various hells. "These books should be used with caution," Emerson warns, for if such images of the spiritual realm become "fixed," they become false. An ardent young man might one day read them, but then discard them for good—thus they would serve their proper use. Emerson despised the idea of "Swedenborgizing," and insisted that one not serve as satellite of another man's system. Naturally, such an attitude raised the ire of doctrinal Swedenborgians like Prof. George Bush, who lambasted Emerson for his criticisms of Swedenborg, but even when he was in England and met a number of Swedenborgians, Emerson did not change his fundamental assessment of the visionary or of his followers.

It is interesting that Emerson contrasts Swedenborg, "strange, scholastic, didactic, passionless, bloodless man, who denotes classes of souls as a botanist disposes of a carex," with Jacob Böhme, whom Emerson much favors:

> How different is Jacob Behmen! *he* is tremulous with emotion, and listens awestruck with the gentlest humanity to the Teacher whose lessons he conveys, and when he asserts that, 'in some sort, love is greater than God," his heart beats so high that the thumping against his leathern coat is audible across the centuries. 'Tis a great difference. Behmen is healthily and beautifully wise, notwithstanding the mystical narrowness and incommunicableness. Swedenborg is disagreeably wise, and with all his accumulated gifts paralyzes and repels.
> It is the sign of a great nature, that it opens a foreground, and like the breath of morning-landscapes invites us onward. Swedenborg is retrospective . . . he could never break the umbilical cord which held him to nature and he did not rise to the platform of true genius. . . . I think sometimes, he will not be read longer.[89]

Emerson's penetrating observation here—that Swedenborg's literalist visions of heaven and hell do not entice like the complex gnosis of Jacob Böhme— leads up to his passing thought that Swedenborg may be more a fashion of the day, for "he could not break the umbilical cord which held him to nature." Such an Emersonian view of nature—as holding one back from spiritual greatness—provides an interesting contrast with other Emersonian remarks on nature and suggests something of Emerson's underlying gnostic perspective.[90]

With all of these criticisms of Swedenborg aside, though, it is obvious that Emerson nonetheless thought highly of the Swedish seer, enough that he could devote a chapter of *Representative Men* to him. One might say that the importance of Swedenborg to Emerson lay, not in Swedenborg's visionary works in themselves, so much as in what remarks they inspired in Emerson. In the end, it is not possible to disentangle Emerson's influences from his own writing, for all is so profoundly intertwined as to be inseparable and, in Emerson's own view, part of a single continuous current. For Emerson, a writer does not exist in isolation from, but in communion with all predecessors; the writer's work is not his own possession, but that for which the writer is a conduit. In this sense, even though Swedenborg's work was undoubtedly flawed, and perhaps not truly great, still it adds to the writer's "magazine of power;" it is of great use to the future writer that Emerson is, and in turn may be of use to us.

Swedenborg, for Emerson, was a representative man, representative for not only Western esotericism more generally, but specifically for what Emerson called "the mystic," along with the philosopher, the poet, and the soldier-leader, one of the main types of humanity. Certainly, Emerson knew of other such figures: in his essay "Books," published in the 1870 *Society and Solitude* but written earlier, Emerson mentions Henry Cornelius Agrippa twice, and emphasizes his love of the Neoplatonists. Here, of course, esotericism and philosophy overlap, because Neoplatonism is itself not only a major stream in the western European tradition, but also a stream close to various esoteric traditions, including magic. One thinks here of such major Renaissance figures as Pico della Mirandola and Marsilio Ficino, who represent links between Neoplatonism and Kabbalism, and Neoplatonism and white magic, respectively. If Swedenborg represents a broadly mystical "type," nonetheless there remain numerous other subcategories, each with its representative figures, as well.

Emerson's Neoplatonism deserves mention here because of the prominence of the translator Thomas Taylor for him. Taylor was a prolific English translator of and author on Neoplatonic traditions and writings during the early nineteenth century, and was central for Emerson's understanding of Platonism. In his essay "Books," Emerson specifically mentions Thomas Taylor's translation of Synesius, and cites also as important "Plotinus, Porphyry, Proclus . . . Jamblichus."[91] When he traveled to England, Emerson inquired about Taylor and his translations, and was astounded to find that virtually no one in England knew of him. Taylor was not widely liked by his contemporaries because not only was he an independent translator who barely eked out his living by translating (rather than being a university professor), but also he was outspoken as an advocate of Platonism/Neoplatonism and as a critic of Christianity. Yet about Taylor's work Emerson writes that reading it is like "walking in the noblest of temples," and that "the imaginative scholar will find few stimulants to his brain like these writers. He has entered the Elysian Fields; and the grand and pleasing figures of gods and dæmons and dæmonical men, of the 'azonic' and the 'aquatic gods,' demons with fulgid eyes . . . sail before his eyes."[92]

At the conclusion of his essay "Books," Emerson writes of the "Bibles of the world," among which he includes not only the Vedas and the Upanishads and the Bhagavad Gita, as well as the Buddhist classics, but also the works classed under the name "Hermes Trismegistus." For Emerson, the *Corpus Hermeticum* takes its place next to all the other books sacred to various peoples; it does not occupy a higher place, but neither does it occupy a lower one. Hermeticism, Neoplatonism, and the various other streams of esotericism, all feed along with Buddhism and Hinduism and Confucianism and whatever other traditions are revered by one or another culture, into our own time and into ourselves. What matters to Emerson is how these works inspire us now, how they open up new vistas for us in the present. He is not a scholar of the dry bones of the past, nor does he write for such people, but is instead an "imaginative scholar," one who draws on all the various traditions available to him in order to generate a new synthesis.

Certainly one cannot say that Emerson was an esotericist in the sense that he closely studied any single esoteric tradition and became a representative of it. At the same time, however, our understanding of his work and what he was about would be incomplete if we did not recognize the importance that various streams of esotericism played in it. Neoplatonism and Hermeticism provided Emerson with long-standing philosophico-religious perspectives independent of Christianity that in turn gave him the foundation from which he could as a universalist survey all the Bibles of the world. It is true that Emerson's work cannot be fully understood without reference to the Asian religious traditions on which he drew, but it is also true that Emerson's understanding of Asian religious traditions was very much grounded in his knowledge of many European esoteric currents and major figures. Emerson was not a practicing esotericist, but his work was certainly deeply informed by European esotericism, an indebtedness whose importance is only now beginning to be recognized.

twelve

Fuller

The Hermetic and theosophic library brought to New England by Charles Lane and Bronson Alcott certainly influenced Alcott and Emerson, but there were other Transcendentalists who also reveal a very Hermetic understanding of nature—perhaps most importantly and surprisingly, Margaret Fuller. One might have surmised that Fuller had some Hermetic leanings from Hawthorne's depiction of Zenobia in *The Blithedale Romance*, but there has been relatively little scholarly attention paid to this subject. The original edition of Fuller's *Woman in the Nineteenth Century* is preceded by an obviously Hermetic illustration—a serpent biting its own tail and forming a circle, within which are two superimposed triangles, one black, point upward, another white, point downward, behind the first. The entire image is amid rays going outward like the sun's. But the later edition of the same book, edited by Fuller's brother, is *sans* this very illustration, which unquestionably has occult origins and significance.[1] The disappearance of such a Hermetic illustration from Fuller's work could be seen as symbolizing a general scholarly disregard for such esoteric themes in Fuller's writing. As we shall see, however, there is good reason to recognize the place of esotericism in Fuller's work.

Without doubt, Fuller had strong and, one might say, practical interests in what could well be described as "occult" subjects. In the highly edited edition of Fuller's *Memoirs*, there are a number of extremely interesting passages that shed an unexpected light on Fuller's practical esotericism. In the section entitled "Arcana," for instance, we read that "It was soon evident that there was somewhat a little pagan about her." In particular, she had a "taste for gems, ciphers, talismans, omens, coincidences, and birth-days. She had a special love for the planet Jupiter, and a belief that the month of September was inauspicious to her."[2] What is more, Fuller went so far as to put on certain gems in order to write letters to various friends—one an onyx, another an amethyst.

"Coincidences, good and bad . . . seals, ciphers, mottoes, omens, anniversaries, names, dreams, are all of a certain importance to her," her brother Robert wrote.[3] Indeed, she surrounded herself with a kind of "personal mythology," marked by a "seal-ring of the flying Mercury," by a personal symbol of the *Sistrum*, by a series of interconnected dreams, and by occasional times of spiritual ecstasy.[4]

In the summer of 1840, Fuller, who had since childhood believed that she was psychic, and who held that by turning her head a little she could see into the inner nature of some people, began to experience a kind of spiritual illumination. She was at the time familiar with the literature of mysticism, and in 1840 also met "certain mystics, who had appeared in Boston about this time," but none of these were directly responsible for her plunging "into the sea of Buddhism and mystical trances."[5] During the summer, she entered into "a sort of ecstatic solitude," of which in 1842 she wrote that "inward life [was] more rich and deep, and of more calm and musical flow than ever before."[6] Her brother doubted that this was a profound or lasting condition, however, and his doubts irritated her. Regardless of how one assesses her spiritual experiences, though, it is certain that Fuller was familiar not only with the esoteric correspondences between planets, gems, and people, but also with what we may call trance literature.[7] Her work *Summer on the Lakes* (1844) is worth mentioning here, for it represents a peculiar combination of an account of Fuller's travels about the Great Lakes, with the well-known story of the "Seeress of Prevorst" (one of the most well-known cases of European trance literature of the nineteenth century).[8] It is abundantly clear that Fuller had carefully scrutinized Justinius Kerner's account of the German "seeress," her trances, and the paranormal phenomena that surrounded her.

All of these connections between Fuller and European esotericism suggest that only Bronson Alcott among the authors of the American Renaissance was as inclined not only to be inspired by, but also to practice esoteric traditions. It is not that Fuller was exclusively interested in esotericism, any more than any of these writers was, but one cannot consider Fuller's life and work *in toto* without acknowledging esotericism as one of its primary influences. In the various traditions of Western esotericism, including not only astrology and gemology, but also oneiromancy, trance literature, and Rosicrucianism, Fuller found inspiration for her own daily life, as well as for her writing. It is certainly possible to write a biography of Fuller and not offer a single reference to any of these esoteric traditions, but to do so is to ignore completely an important aspect of Fuller's life, which she saw woven out of an intricate web of correspondences.[9]

Little attention has also been paid to Fuller's poetry, which although it is not exactly the finest poetry one might find, still is rife with Hermetic allusions. In "Winged Sphynx," Fuller wrote

> Through brute nature upward rising,
>   Seed up-striving to the light,
> Revelations still surprising,
>   My inwardness is grown insight.

The poem moves from darkness and seed to "nature virgin mother queen" who "Assumes at last the destined wings, / Earth & heaven together brings." The "riddle" of the poem is not to be solved from "intellectual wells, / Cold waters where truth never dwells." Instead, the poem concludes, "Seek her in common daylight's glow."[10] This latter advice is in fact commonplace in alchemical treatises, where we are often told that Wisdom or the *materia* of the Philosopher's Stone is to be found in common places, discarded and ignored.

In another poem with clear Hermetic implications, "My Seal Ring," Fuller writes that "Mercury has cast aside / The signs of intellectual pride, / Freely offers thee the soul, / Art thou noble to receive? Canst thou give or take the whole?"[11] We have already seen Emerson's insistence on the Understanding, and on self-transcendence—and this is precisely what this poem is also about. Casting aside intellectual pride, and taking the whole: then alone "thou wholly human art" for "the golden chain of love / Has bound thee to the realm above." One wonders whether Fuller, who was formidably learned, had run across reference to, or even a copy of, the widely influential eighteenth-century Hermetic alchemical work *Aurea Catena Homeri, The Golden Chain of Homer*. Certainly Mercury in the poem, as traditionally, is equivalent to Hermes, the revealer.

Then, too, there is the rather interesting poem "Sub Rosa-Crux." "Sub Rosa-Crux" refers quite explicitly to the "Knights of the Rosy Cross," or Rosicrucians, who "knew the secret of the sacred oil / Which, poured upon the prophet's head, / Could keep him wise and pure." Alas, Fuller writes, "The pasword now is lost / To that initiation full and free." But the new dawn will come, and in it we will find ourselves surrounded by angels. There is in this poem at least echoes of Novalis's famous poem "Hymns to the Night," and of course the title and explicit references make clear that it is a poem about the esoteric Rosicrucian movement that flourished in Europe from the early seventeenth century onward. Rosicrucianism drew upon Hermetic and theosophic currents in order to create its plethora of groups and intricate cosmologies.

There is even more evidence that Fuller drew consciously on Western esoteric traditions, as we can see in the poem named for the esoteric illustration that preceded *Woman in the Nineteenth Century*: "Double Triangle, Serpent and Rays." Here is the poem itself:

> Patient serpent, circle round,
> Till in death thy life is found;
>   Double form of godly prime
> Holding the whole thought of time,
>   When the perfect two embrace,
> Male and Female, black & white,
>   Soul is justified in space,
> Dark made fruitful by the light;
>   And, centred in the diamond Sun,
>   Time & Eternity are one.[12]

That this is a poem full of esoteric allusions is obvious. Poetically, it is about as good as Fuller's poetry gets, and it is worthy of closer examination. The figure of the serpent biting its own tail can be traced back to early Christianity, when some Gnostic and Hermetic circles used it as an esoteric symbol of the world cycle of suffering, and of rebirth. The two superimposed triangles are also virtually ubiquitous in esotericism, often being called "Solomon's Seal," and common in magical traditions. Here the two triangles are emphasized over the six-pointed star that they together form; Fuller refers to the triangles as "male and female," and they are in her illustration black and white, or dark and light.

Let us consider the broader implications of Fuller's poem in relation to Alcott and Emerson's work. The poem "Double Triangle" emphasizes the complementary nature of existence, the union of male and female, dark and light, of time and eternity. This union, condensed symbolically in the illustration, reflects what we have seen as central also to the views of nature in Alcott and Emerson's works: duality (man and nature) is resolved by the presence of a third (spirit). In this illustration and poem, there is duality (black and white, male and female), but this duality is not oppositional. Rather, it forms a greater whole, the union of time and eternity. There is in this union no reference to self; there is no intruding ego, no reference, as there is in for instance the maudlin "Leila," to the "dim wood of regret" rhyming with "Margaret." What is more, Fuller evidently did experience some kind of unitive illumination, an ecstatic self-transcendence that she confided to Emerson, no doubt recalling his own account of self-transcendence in *Nature*.[13] In short, this Hermetic poem represents, like the illustration it accompanies, the union of humanity and nature with the divine.

Fuller drew some of her esoteric views from Goethe, whose work she studied more extensively than anyone else's. Above all, from Goethe she drew the idea of the dæmon and of the dæmonological. Dæmon is a peculiar word drawn from the Greek word *daimon*, which refers to a class of being intermediate between humans and gods, and in Goethe's (and Fuller's) usage does not precisely mean "demon," but rather a kind of spontaneous force that can be either negative or positive. In its negative form, according to Fuller, it is obstructive power, and when "the dæmon works his will," "nothing succeeds with me." Yet it can also be positive power. Fuller wrote

> As to the Dæmoniacal, I know not that I can say to you anything more precise than you find from Goethe. There are no precise terms for such thoughts. The word *instinctive* indicates their existence. . . . When conscious, self-asserting, it becomes (as power working for its own sake, unwilling to acknowledge love for its superior, must) the devil. That is the legend of Lucifer, the star that would not own its center. Yet, while it is unconscious, it is not devilish, only dæmoniac. In nature, we trace it in all volcanic workings, . . . in deceitful invitations of the water, . . . and in the shapes of all those beings who go about seeking what they may devour. We speak of a mystery, a dread; we shudder, but we approach still nearer, and a part of our nature listens, sometimes answers to this influence. . . .
>
> In genius, and in character, it works, as you say instinctively; it refuses to be analyzed by the understanding, and is most of all inaccessible to the per-

son who possesses it. We can only say, I have it, he has it. . . . It is most obvious in the eye. As we look on such eyes, we think on the tiger, the serpent, beings who lurk, glide, fascinate, mysteriously control. For it is occult by its nature, and if it could meet you on the highway, and be familiarly known as an acquaintance, could not exist. The angels of light do not love, yet they do not insist upon exterminating it.

It has given rise to the fables of wizard, enchantress, and the like; these beings are scarcely good, yet not necessarily bad. Power tempts them. They draw their skills from the dead, because their being is coeval with that of matter, and matter is the mother of death.[14]

Fuller's remarks here reveal quite clearly that she had thought a great deal about this subject.

These remarks are extremely interesting, perhaps most for their refusal to make any distinction between natural and supernatural. Rather, in Fuller's view, the word "dæmonic" can be said to refer at once to natural phenomena like volcanoes or winds, to predators like serpents or tigers, or to the fallen angels and to wizards and enchantresses—or to a person possessed of genius. Thus the natural, the supernatural, and the artistic genius are all manifestations of the same force, which "refuses to be analyzed by the understanding." When we turn from these remarks back to the poems, we can see how Fuller often chose her subjects because they automatically were linked to this "dæmonism," which "is occult by its nature." Goethe himself wrote that this power was not human, not natural, not angelic, and not devilish, but inexplicable, and precisely this indefinability made the dæmonic attractive to Fuller. Indeed, when one considers how influential she was in her own circles, and what an impact she made upon those she knew, one has to suspect that Fuller had some dæmonism in herself that helps account also for her profound interest in the topic.

With these remarks in mind, let us turn again to Fuller's *Woman in the Nineteenth Century* with its esoteric frontispiece. Fuller begins this work with a quotation from Shakespeare's Hamlet—"Frailty, thy name is Woman."—which she proposes to change to "Frailty, thy name is MAN." She then goes on to refer to the "prodigal son," man, who "feels himself called to understand and aid nature, that she may, through his intelligence, be raised and interpreted; to be a student of, and servant to, the universe-spirit; and king of his planet that as an angelic minister, he may bring it into conscious harmony with the law of that spirit."[15] It is obvious, when one looks closely at this passage, that Fuller's language comes not only from the socialist idealism of Charles Fourier, but even more from western magical traditions. Nature is to be "raised" and "interpreted;" man is meant to be "king of his planet" as an "angelic minister." Fuller's ambitious vision of what humanity can be is couched in the language of magic, and it is all the more important that this passage is from the first page of Fuller's work.

In fact, Fuller's esoteric vision in *Woman in the Nineteenth Century* is evident even in her preface to the work, where she asserts that it is the "destiny of Man, in the course of the Ages, to ascertain and fulfil the law of his being, so that his life shall be seen, as a whole, to be that of an angel or messenger . . . [and his] holy work . . . is to make the earth a part of heaven." She continues, "By Man I mean both man and woman: these are the two halves of one thought. I lay no especial stress on the welfare of either. I believe that the development of the one cannot be effected without that of the other."[16] These words do not correspond well to much of twentieth-century feminism, which focused precisely on the sociopolitical welfare of women. But they make sense if one recognizes that they reflect esoteric ideas, especially the concepts, found in alchemy and in Böhmean Christian theosophy alike, that humanity is meant to restore both earth and humanity to a heavenly or paradisal state, and that in paradise man and woman are not separate sexual beings, but androgyne, "two halves of one thought." This concept of the paradisal androgyne is present throughout Böhmean theosophy, and is, I believe, of central importance to Fuller's vision.

Certainly Fuller was not understood by some of her contemporaries. Orestes Brownson, editor of the *Boston Quarterly Review*, and a prominent Roman Catholic spokesman, was entirely baffled by Fuller's *Woman in the Nineteenth Century*. In an amusing review, Brownson remarks that the book "has neither beginning, middle, nor end, and may be read backwards as well as forwards, and from the centre outwards each way, without affecting the continuity of the thought or the succession of ideas."[17] Brownson writes that all in Fuller's book is "profoundly obscure," and that "as we read along in the book, we keep constantly asking, What is the lady driving at? What does she want? But no answer comes."[18] Brownson's is perhaps a more extreme reaction than that of many critics, but nonetheless is not an uncommon one for many readers.

Yet I think that if we consider the movement of Fuller's book in light of several esoteric currents of thought, her work makes considerably more sense. We have already seen how the preface, the frontispiece, and the first page have esoteric implications. The poem that accompanies the frontispiece illustration, "Double Triangle, Serpent, and Rays," corresponds precisely to the themes that emerge from the beginning of Fuller's book, and in particular to the confluence of magic, sexual embrace, and the forming of a greater whole out of the meeting of man and woman. The poem, once again, reads:

> Patient serpent, circle round,
> Till in death thy life is found;
>   Double form of godly prime
> Holding the whole thought of time,
>   When the perfect two embrace,
> Male and Female, black & white,
>   Soul is justified in space,
> Dark made fruitful by the light;
>   And, centred in the diamond Sun,
>   Time & Eternity are one.[19]

The "whole thought of time" here corresponds to the language in the preface that refers to how man and woman correspond to a "single thought," and the union of Time and Eternity here corresponds to the making of earth into heaven through the embrace of the "perfect two," "Male and Female."

When we read *Woman in the Nineteenth Century* with these esoteric themes in mind, we are able to see the entire work in a striking new light. It is no accident that early in the work, Fuller remarks that "no doubt, a new manifestation is at hand, a new hour in the day of man."[20] This is a millennialist statement, tinged with the language of magic by the use of the term "manifestation." Immediately thereafter, Fuller offers the following extensive quotation from Louis-Claude de Saint-Martin, the most prominent French Böhmean theosopher:

> The ministry of man implies, that he must be filled from the divine fountains which are being engendered through all eternity, so that, at the mere name of his master, he may be able to cast all his enemies into the abyss; that he may deliver all parts of nature from the barriers that imprison them; that he may purge the terrestrial atmosphere from the poisons that infect it; that he may preserve the bodies of men from the corrupt influences that surround and the maladies that afflict them; still more, that he may keep their souls pure from the malignant insinuations which pollute, and the gloomy images that obscure them; that he may restore its serenity to the Word, which false words of men fill with mourning and sadness; that he may satisfy the desires of the angels, who await from him the development of the marvels of nature; that, in fine, his world may be filled with God, as eternity is.[21]

Saint-Martin's vision of the restoration of nature, of the purification of humanity, and the union of time and eternity, expresses very well the esoteric implications of the beginning of *Woman in the Nineteenth Century* and Fuller's poem "Double Triangle, Serpent, and Rays."

One might note also that Fuller's image of a triangle, a serpent, and rays can be found in another Transcendentalist work, as well—the 1877 *Table-Talk* of Bronson Alcott, where Alcott includes an illustration called "Orbis Pictus," a feature none other than a triangle within which is a serpent, both surrounded by a circle of rays.[22] Alcott's illustration, though published after Fuller's death, undoubtedly reflects Alcott's 1842 trip to England to meet the theosopher James Pierrepont Greaves, and his return to New England with the finest theosophic library in America. Alcott and the Greavesian esoteric library are undoubtedly the origins of Fuller's quotation from Saint-Martin.

Thus, it can hardly be surprising that Fuller follows this quotation from Saint-Martin by pointing to another "obscure observer of our own day and country, to draw some lines of the desired image." This next "obscure observer" is in fact none other than Bronson Alcott, whose "Orphic Sayings" Fuller had published in the Transcendentalist periodical *The Dial* during her time as its editor (1840–42). We might recall that Alcott was the most knowledgeable concerning Böhmean theosophy of all the Transcendentalists, and that theosophy represents a hidden key to Alcott's own thought. It is not unexpected, then, that after quoting Saint-Martin, Fuller should make an only slightly veiled allusion to Alcott as an American Orpheus. Fuller's language here, which refers to drawing "some lines of the desired image," also is magical: one draws an image of that which is desired.

What is the image that Fuller desires? She envisions "every arbitrary barrier thrown down" for women, "every path laid open," not for political reasons only, but because then "the divine energy would pervade nature to a degree unknown in the history of former ages, and that no discordant collision, but a ravishing harmony of the spheres would ensue."[23] This is a kind of millennialist feminism, and we are not surprised to find that Fuller's alter ego immediately after this passage is none other than Miranda, daughter of the magician Prospero in Shakespeare's *The Tempest*. Miranda, according to Fuller, is a "child of the spirit;" she represents the sacred marriage, or *hieros gamos*, that represents a "brave new world" and concludes the greatest of Shakespeare's plays. Fuller thus writes also in favor of the purity of marriage as a "meeting of souls," not as a mere "contract of convenience and utility."[24] Yet she has in mind not only a pure marriage, but the transmutation of the world.

This transmutation of the world Fuller associates with the mysticism of Jacob Böhme, to whom she directly refers in another striking passage later in the book. "Mysticism," she writes,

> which may be defined as the brooding soul of the world, cannot fail of its oracular promise as to woman. . . . Whenever a mystical whisper was heard, from Behmen [Böhme] down to St. Simon, sprang up the thought, that, if it be true, as the legend says, that humanity withers through a fault committed by and a curse laid upon woman, through her pure child, or influence, shall the new Adam, the redemption, arise. Innocence is to be replaced by virtue, dependence by a willing submission, in the heart of the Virgin Mother of the new race.[25]

Fuller is not impressed by intellect alone, which she sees as masculine; intellectual men are often blind, whereas women recognize "the fine invisible links which connect the forms of life around them." These "fine invisible links" are none other than the hidden correspondences between all things that is one of the cornerstones of Western esotericism, and to which Fuller believes women are more sensitive than men. Fuller hence prefers the union of man and woman in one person, the "high idea of love, which considers man and woman as the two-fold expression of one thought. This the angel of Swedenborg, the angel of the coming age, cannot surpass, but only explain more fully."[26] Thus, Böhme and Swedenborg, two primary sources for Western esotericism, are central for the vision, the magical image of the divine androgyne, that Fuller evokes in her book.

Nearer the end of the book, Fuller exclaims: "Let us be wise and not impede the soul. Let her work as she will. Let us have one creative energy, one incessant revelation. Let it take what form it will, and let us not bind it by the past to man or woman."[27] This realization of one creative energy that is both masculine and feminine Fuller sees as a kind of "Rosicrucian lamp" to which each age has borne witness in its own way and that will one day soon be realized in America. Her book teases out of the past examples of those who point toward the spiritual blossoming of man and woman—Böhme, Saint-Martin, Swedenborg—but she points above all toward a future era in which her vision can be realized fully. Fuller's vision is one of millennialist esotericism in a literary guise.

I have mentioned the magical allusions in *Woman in the Nineteenth Century*, but it is in Fuller's bizarre quasi-autobiographic work "Leila" that we find the merging of Fuller's millennialist esotericism with magic. "Leila" was a name Fuller took for herself, a kind of magical alter ego, a dream or magical self. The essay "Leila" was published first in *The Dial* in 1841, and of its name Fuller later wrote in her *Memoirs* that "I knew, from the very look and sound, that it [the name "Leila"] was mine; I knew that it meant night,—night which brings out stars, as sorrow brings out truth" (I.219).[28] The essay begins with a peculiar epigraph—"In deep vision's intellectual scene"—which implies a kind of trance state of "deep vision" in which one sees not just abstract thoughts but an "intellectual scene," in other words, images. "Leila" is an enigma riddled with clues, many hidden in the images that populate its "intellectual scene."

Fuller's unconventional essay begins with allusions to the mysterious, ungraspable nature of Leila, who "is one of those rare beings who seem a key to all nature. Mostly those we know seem struggling for an individual existence." Instead, Leila is "the *fetiche*" that suggests "all the elemental powers of nature," the French word *fetiche* meaning "an object filled with magical power." Leila represents "eternity," and most men cannot bear to look upon her; she is "boundlessness"; she is "the clasp to the chain of nature."[29] All of this allusive language suggests that Leila represents a juncture between time and eternity; she represents also the point at which humanity and nature are joined. She is, in other words, a "spirit under a mask," in reality transcending "sex, age, state"—she is pure spirit in human form.

Very quickly the essay "Leila" becomes a description of what Fuller calls the "art magic." When she can no longer look at Leila's living form, the narrator avails herself of the "art magic," and

> at the hour of high moon, in the cold silent night, I seek the center of the park. My daring is my vow, my resolve my spell. I am a conjurer, for Leila is the vasty deep. . . . At night I look into the lake for Leila.
>
> If I gaze steadily and in the singleness of prayer, she rises and walks on its depths. Then know I each night a part of her life. . . . In the night she wanders forth from her human investment, and travels amid those tribes, freer movers in the game of spirit and matter, to whom man is a supplement.[30]

The narrator sees Leila among the Sylphs in the air; she sees Leila in the secret veins of earth; she sees Leila burst up in fire. Then the narrator herself becomes free from the fear of death, and Leila offers the blessing of "rivers of bliss." Prison walls turn into Edens, serpents into Phoenixes, and Leila is revealed as the narrator's "wild-haired Genius."

One can certainly read all this as simply Fuller's reverie, an imaginary journey, but there is the disconcerting first sentence of "Leila"'s final section: "Could I but write this into the words of earth, the secret of moral and mental alchymy would be discovered, and all Bibles have passed into one Apocalypse; but not till it has all been lived can it be written."[31] Here Fuller directly undercuts the possible interpretation of all this as simply poetic reverie, insisting that one must live it before one can write it down. What is more, this sentence suggests that Fuller has already lived at least some of what she is writing about. At the very least, it is clear that Fuller has been thinking much about magic. Leila, we find out in the final passage, is the "wondrous [magical] circle, who hast taken into thyself all my thought." The narrator hopes at the end that she and Leila, who has taught her to "recognize all powers," will become one. "Arise!" Fuller writes at the end of her essay: "let us go forth!"

When we consider all of these aspects of Fuller's works and life, we cannot help be struck by how seldom they turn up in books and articles about her. It is true that Jeffrey Steele has devoted much effort to uncovering this aspect of Fuller's work, but it is also true that from Thomas Wentworth Higginson's biography of Fuller right through to the present, the esoteric aspects of Fuller's work has been for the most part assiduously ignored.[32] Given how important esoteric correspondences were in Fuller's daily life, as her brother and Emerson attested, it is nothing less than shocking to discover in biographies of her not a single word about, or at best only a brief allusion to and dismissal of her esoteric interests. Such an obvious omission leads one to speculate about how, even though esoteric interests were common to the European and English Romantics, as well as to the authors of the American Renaissance, these interests have been almost totally omitted from subsequent accounts of their work.

Yet the truth is, Fuller's esotericism is at the forefront of many of her writings and changes the way we see them. What does it mean that Fuller's esoteric emblem is the frontispiece for *Woman in the Nineteenth Century*? Why is the "Seeress of Prevorst" so prominently featured in Fuller's midwestern travel book, *Summer on the Lakes*? And what is the significance of Fuller's clear interest in astrology, temporal patterns, oneiromancy, and gemology in connection with her personal life and poetry? How central is magical "Leila" to Fuller's own self-image? All of these questions are in part answered by Fuller's remarks about the dæmonic, which suggest that for her the supernatural was simply part of a continuum, that for her the esoteric was not excluded from the rest of life, but an intrinsic part of it. When we see her esoteric interests in this way, as part of a continuum that includes the whole of life, suddenly her work takes on very different implications. Her social and political interests cannot be separated from her literary, religious, philosophical, and, yes, esoteric interests. Indeed, one wonders whether in the end it is esotericism, so long excluded from consideration of her work, that is at its center, and whether without this key, one really understands Fuller's life and work at all.

thirteen

Whitman

Walt Whitman, author of *Leaves of Grass*, deliberately set out to be the quintessential American poet. As we have seen, however, to be a nineteenth-century American intellectual was to draw upon the traditions of the world, and Whitman was no exception to this tendency. Indeed, as the inclusive poet par excellence, he illustrates it better than anyone except Emerson. Like Emerson, Whitman incorporated Asian religious traditions, especially Hinduism, into his writings and, like Emerson, he was indebted to prior Western esoteric traditions. But Whitman's personality was of a very different character from that of Emerson or, for that matter, anyone else in the American Renaissance. More than anyone else of the time, Whitman represented an antinomian, world-embracing mysticism of a kind that had a fair number of European manifestations, but was in Whitman made particularly American.

Whitman's use of Asian religious traditions—chiefly Hinduism—in his poetry has not been fully examined yet, but there are a number of books and articles on the subject, most published in India. Among these are such works as V. K. Chari's *Whitman in the Light of Vedantic Mysticism* (1964), T. R. Rajasekharaiah's *The Roots of Whitman's Grass* (1970), as well as comparative criticism like V. Sachithanandan's *Whitman and Bharati* (1978). That there are many parallels between Whitman's poetry and Vedanta has been recognized by many readers stretching back to Emerson's assessment of *Leaves of Grass* as a combination of "the Bhagvat Geeta and the *New York Herald*," and to Thoreau's initial reading of the same poems, which he called "wonderfully like the Orientals." When Thoreau visited Whitman in Brooklyn, however, he asked Whitman if he had read any Indian religious works, and Whitman replied "No: tell me about them."[1] This probably somewhat disingenuous reply tells us a great deal about the difficulty studying, not only Whitman's indebtedness to Hinduism, but also his relation to any previous traditions, including European ones.

Whitman—with his effort at universality, combined with what was perceived both at the time and later as his efforts to create a "New Bible" with himself as its prophet—certainly did know something about Hinduism, as he also knew something about at least some Western esoteric traditions. However, these were utterly subordinated in Whitman's poetry to Whitman himself and to his own religious perspective. It is hardly surprising that, when Whitman's disciple Edward Carpenter remarked that the west had "much to learn from India," Whitman replied "I do not myself think there is anything more to come from that source. . . . We must rather look to modern science to open the way. Time alone can absolutely test my poems."[2] Rajasekharaiah seeks to explain this remark away by saying that "a note of natural pride is hardly the explanation," but pride or self-referentiality is an entirely reasonable explanation, especially given the quasi-religious fervor of what David Kuebrich has called the "Whitman cult."[3]

Kuebrich, in his important book *Minor Prophecy* (1989), which deals with Whitman's "new American religion," sketches the intensity of the "Whitman cult," the Whitman disciples who held him to be "the most divine of men." One book by such a disciple declared Whitman the "Prophet of the New Era" and "The Christ of Our Age," and one of its chapter titles called him "The Carpenter of Brooklyn."[4] Kuebrich convincingly argues that these disciples, some of whom Whitman himself declared insane, responded to something that really existed in Whitman's poetry. As Kuebrich remarks, "Whitman did want to begin a new religion. He wanted his poetry to serve two functions: to promote the spiritual development of his readers and to provide them with a coherent vision which would integrate their religious experience with the dominant modes of modern thought and action—science, technology, and democracy."[5]

Kuebrich outlines the basic elements of Whitman's new religion, which included his "progressive millennialism" (an incorporation of the Darwinian notion of evolution and mid-nineteenth century sciences), as well as his indebtedness to Quaker and other Protestant religious traditions that emphasize direct individual intuition of divine truth. "Progressive millennialism" does not expect an apocalypse on a given day, but rather, in the manner of many Protestants of the mid-nineteenth century, holds that individual conversions generate a kind of critical mass of spirituality that ushers in a new age for humanity. This kind of evolutionary millennialism, as well as the individual intuition of divine truth, was maintained by major spiritualist figures of Whitman's day like Andrew Jackson Davis. Indeed, there are striking parallels between Davis's writings and the views visible in *Leaves of Grass*, particularly in common emphasis on individual and societal spiritual progress, and radical denial of evil. Whitman was also influenced by a Quaker named Elias Hicks, whom Whitman's parents took him to hear at the age of ten. Hicks, Whitman later recalled, pointed hearers to "the fountain of all naked theology, all religion, all worship . . . namely in *yourself*."[6]

Of course, there was a difference in emphasis between Hicks and

Whitman. Hicks emphasized *all religion* in yourself, whereas Whitman emphasized all religion in *yourself*. This is a larger difference than might at first seem apparent, and highlights what I believe is the fundamental division between Whitman's poetry and Vedanta or, for that matter, Quaker spirituality. Vedanta has at its center the equation *atman* is *Brahman*, meaning that the individual self is ultimately divine. The emphasis here is not on *self* being divine, but on the self being *divine*. This distinction is sometimes translated as the difference between self (as in selfish or egotistic) and Self (as in the transcendent Self). Vedanta insists on Self over self, if one may put it that way. Such a distinction is also expressed in, for instance, Quaker spirituality, which emphasizes divine inspiration, not the expansion of the self to include everything, even God. Whitman's poetry, on the other hand, represents precisely such a gigantic self-extension.

Malcolm Cowley remarked on Whitman's astonishing "narcissism" or "auto-eroticism," commenting that Whitman's "early poems are those of a man engaged in a passionate love affair with his own person. 'I have heard what the talkers were talking,' he says, . . . 'while they discuss I am silent and go bathe and admire myself.' I doubt that any other poet has expressed self-love with so much ardor."[7] It is hard to argue with Cowley, given such observations as this from "Song of Myself:" "If I worship one thing more than another, it shall be the spread of my own body, or any part of it. . . . I dote on myself, there is that lot of me and all so luscious."[8] It is here that my own argument diverges from Kuebrich's: it is true that Whitman sought to develop a "new American religion," but it is also true that this new religion was the religion not of the transcendence of the self, as in traditional forms of mysticism either Asian or European, but of self-worship or the infinite expansion of the self.

We can see in virtually every single poem that alludes to Western esoteric traditions that Whitman's religion is self-worship or the infinite expression of self. Whitman's attitude toward the past of all cultures is made clear in his poem "With Antecedents," in which he celebrates "my fathers and mothers and the accumulations of past / ages," "Egypt, Indian, Phenicia [*sic*], Greece and Rome," "the poet, the skald, the saga, the myth, and the oracle." He asserts that "materialism is true and spiritualism is true, I reject no / part," and that "where I am or you are this present day, there is the / centre of all days, all races."[9] In other words, the "I" is the center of and includes all traditions. One sees this attitude in "Chanting the Square Deific," an interesting poem, not least because it has been held forth as having Hindu origins in its adding to the Trinity a fourth. However, when one looks carefully at the poem itself, one finds that its center is not deity, but, as one might expect, the poet who does the chanting. It does not much matter, therefore, whether or not the poem has Hindu antecedents because those antecedents, like European ones, are subordinated to the stupendous Whitman ego.

In "Chanting the Square Deific," the poet takes on the persona of four aspects or "sides" of divinity. Thus, "solid, four-sided (all the sides needed) from this side Jehovah am I, / Old Brahm I, and I Saturnius am; / Not Time affects me—I am Time . . . / Relentless."[10] In the second stanza, we see the poet as the second "side" of divinity: "Consolator most mild, the promis'd one advancing, / With gentle hand extended, the mightier God am I. . . . All sorrow, labor, suffering, I, tallying it, absorb in myself."[11] In the third stanza the poet becomes "Aloof, dissatisfied, plotting revolt . . . crafty, despised . . . with sudra face . . . I, Satan."[12] And in the fourth stanza the poet becomes "Santa Spirita, breather, life., / Beyond the light, lighter than light / Beyond the flames of hell . . . Beyond Paradise . . . I, the general soul, / . . . I the most solid, / Breathe my breath also through these songs."[13]

It is, of course, interesting that Whitman here proposes a fourfold divinity, just as did C. G. Jung in the twentieth century; it is also interesting that, like Jung, Whitman incorporates into this divinity both "Saviour and Satan." Naturally, such a proposal is heretical from any orthodox Christian perspective Whitman could have been familiar with, with one exception. Here we touch on the much discussed "Santa Spirita" of Whitman's fourth stanza, which could easily be attributed to his linguistic ignorance, the Italian form of "Holy Spirit" actually being "Spirito Santo," hence masculine. However, there is another possibility for Whitman's neologism, and that is the immense importance of a feminine aspect of divinity in Western esotericism, Divine Wisdom. By making the Holy Spirit feminine, Whitman could be invoking the feminine figure of Divine Wisdom, traditionally held from the Book of Wisdom onward to permeate creation, and indeed to be "ethereal, pervading all . . . essence of forms."[14] If this is so, and it may well be because he could have encountered reference to Divine Wisdom in countless places, then Whitman is drawing on a preexistent European esoteric tradition.[15]

What makes the poem most interesting for our purposes is that all four aspects of divinity are expressed as "I." Whether Whitman draws on a Vedic tradition of four-sided divinity, or whether he draws on one or another Western esoteric traditions in regard to Divine Wisdom—and both may well be the case—he incorporates such traditions into his omnivorous poetic persona, so omnivorous, in fact, that it is capable of "absorbing" all the aspects of God, and Satan, as well! This is a profoundly different approach to divinity than what we see in Western esoteric traditions regarding Sophia. In the history of Christian theosophy, for instance, detailed in my book *Wisdom's Children: A Christian Esoteric Tradition*, as well as in my *Wisdom's Book: The Sophic Anthology*, we find the theosophers invoking Divine Wisdom, even taking Wisdom as a bride, but never presuming to make Wisdom an aspect of themselves. Even if Whitman draws on the Sophianic tradition in his stanza on "Santa Spirita," he does so in a way completely antithetical to that tradition, in essence making divinity an aspect of himself, or of his own poetic voice.

Whitman's omnivorous persona, admittedly, is not quite as evident in "The Mystic Trumpeter," which certainly includes some esoteric terminology. In "The Mystic Trumpeter," as the title suggests, we find an actual trumpeter that does not turn out to be Whitman himself. On the other hand, the trumpeter plays "to no one's ears but mine, but freely gives to mine / That I may thee translate."[16] Thus, even though the trumpeter does not turn out to be Whitman, Whitman is his sole audience. Listening to the trumpeter, Whitman walks in "cool refreshing night the walks of Paradise."[17] He sees "arm'd knights," "some in quest of the holy Graal," and remarks on how "the immortal phantoms crowd around me!"[18] Whitman writes of how he sees "the vast alembic ever working," "the flames that / heat the world, / the glow, the blush, the beating hearts of lovers;" he sees the "spell" and "conjure" of "war's alarums."[19] All of these are esoteric themes: Christian theosophy has many instances of its practitioners experiencing paradise while alive on earth; the chivalric quest for the Grail is one of the major European esoteric currents; "alembic" and "flames" refer to alchemy; and "spell" and "conjure" draw on the magical tradition.

In the seventh stanza, these are all subordinated to the poet's realization that "O trumpeter, methinks I am myself the instrument thou playest."[20] The mystic trumpeter's playing brings to him shame and humiliation and utter defeat, and yet "'mid the ruins Pride colossal stands unshaken to the last, / Endurance, resolution to the last." It is characteristic of Whitman's poetry that all these esoteric themes or symbols be in turn submerged in Whitman himself as the musical trumpet and that at the stanza's end "Pride" is left standing amid ruins. In the final, eighth stanza, we find a "glad, exulting, culminating song!" in which "A reborn race appears—a perfect world, all joy!" This theme, of a reborn race for which all is become joy, reflects the progressive millennialism common in Whitman's day, visible not only in mainstream Protestant mysticism but also in the spiritualist evolutionism of Andrew Jackson Davis or Thomas Harris, both of whom were Whitman's contemporaries and with whose work he was very likely familiar. This progressive millennialism is a kind of popularized modification of prior esotericism,[21] and here shifts attention from the poet's realization that he is the proud instrument to the outward explosion of that realization in the rebirth of a new world and a new era of joy.

When one looks closely at Whitman's poetry, one is struck, then, by its peculiar combination of extreme egotism that borders on solipsism, in which the entire cosmos and even the various aspects of divinity are subsumed into the poet's voice, and its affirmation of the poor, the humble, the suffering, and the ordinary things of life. Characteristic of this seemingly incongruous mix is the poem "To a Common Prostitute," in which Whitman announces that "I am Walt Whitman, liberal / and lusty as Nature, / Not till the sun excludes you do I exclude you."[22] His immense self-inflation gives him leave to affirm everything else in creation, even the rough, mean, or commonly derided or scorned elements of human life. It is true that such affirmations seem part of a kind of poetic pose, and that Whitman's ecstasies are not so much ecstasies of union with the divine or with nature as they are ecstasies of incredibly expansive self-inflation and absorption.

But there is another aspect of such works as "To a Common Prostitute" and many other Whitman poems that we need to recognize here: his more or less religious emphasis on sexuality. This aspect of Whitman's work was remarked upon from the very beginning: the 1855 *Leaves of Grass* was almost universally seen in America as shockingly frank in its sexual references. Emerson and Thoreau chided Whitman for this reason, and in fact when Whitman went to Concord, he was not allowed to visit the Emerson, Thoreau, or Alcott households because none of the women would allow him in. There are some revealing anecdotes about Whitman from the meetings of Thoreau, Alcott, and Whitman. In 1856, Thoreau wrote to his friend Harrison Blake that he was very impressed with Whitman, but that there were "two or three pieces in the book which are disagreeable, to say the least; simply sensual. He does not celebrate love at all. It is as if the beasts spoke."[23] This well-known remark sums up the reactions of many in the nineteenth century to such poems of Whitman as those under the headings "Children of Adam," or "Calamus."

Whitman's attitude toward sexuality was alluded to a number of times by Bronson Alcott, who in his journals wrote down some perceptive entries on his meetings with Whitman. Alcott, like Thoreau, noted Whitman's astonishing egotism, writing in his journal that "If a broader and finer intercourse with men serves to cure something of his arrogance and take out his egotism, good may come, and great things, of him."[24] But Alcott, in visiting Whitman at home, noted something else: in Whitman's bedroom, unframed pictures of "a Hercules, a Bacchus, and a satyr" were pasted to the wall. Alcott asked which of these was the poet, but Whitman deflected the question, which Alcott interpreted as meaning the poet took to himself "the virtues of the three . . . unreservedly." Thus in his journal entry, Alcott describes Whitman as "Bacchus-browed, bearded like a satyr, and rank . . . in fine, an egotist."[25] These connections to Bacchus and a satyr are important clues to at least part of what Whitman was up to, particularly in the poems comprised under the heading "Children of Adam."

These poems have long been singled out as obscene. A review of *Leaves of Grass* in the 1860 *Boston Post* is as good an example as any. In it, the reviewer begins by referring to the poems not as grass, but as "foul and rank leaves of the poison-plants of egotism, irreverence, and of lust run rampant." These poems, the reviewer continues, are "prurient," "polluted," and represent an "exulting audacity of Priapus-worshiping obscenity, which marks a large portion of the volume."[26] Such reviews were not unusual, nor confined to the United States. The London *Literary Gazette* of 1860 printed the following: "Of all the writers we have ever perused Walt Whitman is the most silly, the most blasphemous, and the most disgusting. If we can think of any stronger epithets we will print them in a second edition."[27] It is not true that, as the *Boston Post* reviewer claimed, the majority of *Leaves of Grass* is some form of "Priapus-worshiping." But there are certainly such passages.

In "Children of Adam," we find the poem "Ages and Ages Returning At Intervals," which reads as follows:

> Ages and ages returning at intervals,
> Undestroy'd, wandering immortal,
> Lusty, phallic, with the potent original loins, perfectly sweet,
> I, chanter of Adamic songs,

Through the new garden the West, the great cities calling,
Deliriate, thus prelude what is generated, offering these, offering myself,
Bathing myself, bathing my songs in Sex,
Offspring of my loins.[28]

There is no doubt that this poem could be termed "priapic" in nature, but what makes it especially interesting is the connection between Adam, the "garden," deliriousness, and sexuality. Here we might think back to the Greek mysteries associated with Bacchus, the bacchanalian revels, and the associations there between sexual activity and renewal. What makes Whitman's poem interesting is that he conjoins these "pagan" associations, in particular the immortality of the god "undestroy'd, wandering immortal, / Lusty, phallic," with the Garden of Eden, Adam, and the American West. Of course the wandering immortal god here turns out to be "I, chanter," but the associations remain.

Whitman's amorousness has been termed homosexual, but I think a more apt description would be omnisexual. In "I Am He That Aches With Love," Whitman writes "Does the earth gravitate? does not all matter, aching, attract all / matter? / So the body of me to all I meet or know."[29] In "Native Moments" he tells us that "I am for those who believe in loose delights, I share the midnight / orgies of young men, / . . . O you shunn'd persons, I at least do not shun you, / I come forthwith in your midst, I will be your poet."[30] Whitman's poetic persona shares the "midnight orgies of young men," it is true, but for him sex is like gravity; it is universal, and not confined to people: "We become plants, trunks, foliage, roots, bark," "rocks," "oaks," "fishes," "the coarse smut of beasts," "hawks," "two resplendent suns," "seas," "clouds," and so forth.[31] This universalization of sex is "Adamic," that is, an almost shamanic reunion with nature at the dawn of time, sharing with the orgiastic rites of the Greek mysteries what Eliade called the primal characteristic of religions, the breaking through of timelessness into time, the reconnection with origins.

In Whitman's "Children of Adam" poems, Whitman claims the power of sex is spiritual: in "singing the phallus," he is "The divine list for myself or you or for any one making." Arousal exists not for its own sake, but for "The mystic deliria, the madness amorous, the utter abandonment."[32] The means by which the poet expands beyond himself is sexual intercourse: in the astonishing poem "A Woman Waits for Me," Whitman's persona tells us that "Sex contains all, bodies, souls, / . . . All the governments, judges, gods, follow'd persons of the earth, / These are contain'd in sex as parts of itself and justifications of itself."[33] And not only does sex contain everything in the cosmos, Whitman's persona makes love to all warm-blooded women in these United States! He is tender, but demanding: "I do not hurt you any more than is necessary for you, / I pour the stuff to start sons and daughters fit for these States, I / press with slow rude muscle, / I brace myself effectually."[34] He drains into these women "the pent-up rivers of myself," and of America. In brief, the poet, in his "mystic deliria," becomes all men in America having intercourse with all women, creating new "perfect men and women out of my love-spendings."

Although I find David Kuebrich's argument in his book *Minor Prophecy* convincing, and do think that Whitman had in mind precisely what he himself said he was doing—which was not simply writing poems but in some sense founding a new American religion—it strikes me as strange that Kuebrich seems unwilling to acknowledge the importance of sexuality in Whitman's new religious vision. Sexuality is at the center of Whitman's "new gospel." It is not merely happenstance that so many critics seized upon passages like those cited above from "Children of Adam" to condemn Whitman. Those passages are central to what Whitman was about: he was quite consciously drawing on the Bacchic, orgiastic traditions that stretch back to Greco-Roman antiquity, but that were also to be found recurring in Europe not only in literature, but also in religion in medieval and modern times. It is no accident that during his life Whitman was often compared to Rabelais, more often by his defenders than his detractors. Rabelais does indeed represent a kindred spirit, exultant, excessive, deliberately shocking, and full of love of life. Nor is it an accident that many critics have found homosexuality a common theme in Whitman's poetry. Whitman's poetry includes homosexual as well as heterosexual passages, and includes passages as well about sex between animals, clouds, and for that matter, rocks and stars. This omnisexuality is at the heart of Whitman's new American religion, as numerous critics have pointed out.[35]

Yet how new is Whitman's new American religion? Paradoxically, his "mystic deliria" of sexuality has a long history in European tradition, and certainly has ancient, medieval and modern antecedents. Plato, of course, had Socrates discussing the various levels of love as spiritual ascent, and we might recall that here, as in Whitman, love might be homosexual or heterosexual. Plato undoubtedly reflected the pre-existent mystery traditions that concerned ecstatic spiritual ascent, but so, too, as we have seen, did Whitman. In my book *The Mysteries of Love: Eros and Spirituality* (1996), I trace the history of eros as a spiritual path from antiquity to the modern period, discussing in addition to Plato and the Mysteries, the chivalric tradition represented by epics like Wolfram von Eschenbach's *Parcival* (which certainly has esoteric content in its astrological, numerological, and Grail references); the troubadour tradition, which celebrated love for a man or a woman as at once sexual and spiritual; the alchemical tradition, especially in reference to the *hieros gamos*, or spiritual marriage of the King and Queen; the theosophic tradition, particularly in its most heretical forms, in which sexual intercourse was celebrated as a religious ritual; and the magical tradition, which included such figures or organizations as Paschal Beverly Randolph, Maria de Naglowska, or the O.T.O. (Ordo Templi Orientis), all of whom espoused sexuality as one part of a magical path in the nineteenth or twentieth centuries.[36]

It is true that many of these traditions—especially the more heretical ones like the medieval Brethren of the Free Spirit, reputed to have included orgiastic practices, or the circle around Eva von Buttlar in eighteenth-century Germany that practiced sexual religious rites, or the sexual rites of Randolph (who lived on the East Coast during Whitman's lifetime)—were for the most part unknown to Whitman. However, there are some striking parallels between Whitman's work and many of these. However, where did Whitman encounter the intersection of religion and sexuality? He was certainly familiar with the chivalric tradition because he alludes to it often in his poetry, and as we have seen he had at least a passing knowledge of alchemy and the Grail literature. Yet none of these is anywhere near as explicit as Whitman's poetry about sexuality as a means of spiritual illumination.

One of the most valuable investigations into contemporary quasi-esoteric influences on Whitman is to be found in Harold Aspiz's *Walt Whitman and the Body Beautiful*. Aspiz investigated the links between Whitman and the numerous figures of his day who espoused animal magnetism, and showed, not surprisingly, that when Whitman sings "the body electric," he is incorporating into his poetry prevalent nineteenth-century ideas concerning sexuality as fundamentally electrical and magnetic in nature. In *Leaves of Grass*, Whitman refers in section 24 to "threads that connect the stars, and of wombs, and of the father-stuff." Aspiz links this passage to a series of early authors that includes Sir Thomas Browne, and Robert Fludd, who referred to "Etheriall Sperm, or Astricall Influences . . . of a far subtiler condition than is the vehicle of visible light."[37] According to Aspiz, Whitman draws on a whole collection of pre-existing links between electricity, magnetism, and the esoteric concept of hidden or "etheriall" links between the woman ["the womb"], man ["the father-stuff"], and the stars.

However, was Whitman directly influenced by the figures that Aspiz cites, major esoteric authors like Paracelsus and Robert Fludd? It is, of course, possible that Whitman knew something of their works, but it is far more likely that Whitman inherited aspects of their thought as they fed into the more popular currents of animal magnetism. By 1842, Whitman had extolled Mesmerism in the *New York Sunday Times* as revealing "at once the existence of a whole new world of truth, grand, fearful, profound, relating to that great mystery, in the shadow of which we live and move and have our being, the mystery of our Humanity."[38] I think that Aspiz is exactly right in finding a central source for Whitman's religio-sexual ideas in mesmerism and in related contemporary ideas concerning electricity in the human body, but find little evidence that Whitman was reading more arcane sources like some of those Aspiz cites.

At the same time, there is no doubt that Whitman's poetic persona as a universal shaman-healer reflects mesmerism just as Aspiz claims. Aspiz cites a passage in which the poet is "jetting the stuff of far more arrogant republics," after which he dismisses the physician and priest, and with "resistless will" "dilate[s]" a dying patient with his "tremendous breath" for "I am he bringing help for the sick as they pant on their backs."[39] Here the Whitman persona is more than full of himself: he is full of magnetic-sexual power that allows him to heal the sick and bring power to those who are strong. He clearly represents the animal magnetist healer who heals by his "resistless will," and whose power comes from his imagined immense sexual vitality, his ability to ejaculate the "stuff of far more arrogant republics."

The other major influence on Whitman that Aspiz cites is also a quasi-esoteric one: spiritualism. Like mesmerism, spiritualism derived from pre-existing esoteric traditions, but as it became a popular movement, it lost most of its ties to them. Still, one finds that in the mid-nineteenth century, mesmerism and spiritualism were frequently combined, along with popular theories of electricity as a kind of invisible spiritual force, in order to form what we might call a kind of popular esotericism. In 1870, a British spiritualist insisted that Whitman was himself "one of us," a spiritualist, and it is true that in 1860 Whitman wrote another "prophetic" work entitled "Mediums," in which he claimed that

> They shall arise in the States—mediums shall,
> They shall report Nature, laws, physiology, and happiness,
> They shall illustrate Democracy and the kosmos,
> They shall be alimentive, amative, perceptive,
> They shall be complete men and women—their pose brawny and
>   supple. . . .
> Of them and their works, shall emerge divine conveyers, to convey gospels,
> Characters, events, retrospections, shall be conveyed in gospels—
>   Trees, animals, waters, shall be conveyed,
> Death, the future, the invisible faith, shall all be conveyed.[40]

One could argue that Whitman, in his efforts to catalog everything, simply included mediums and spiritualists in the mix, but I think there is something more important here. Whitman, in one of his notorious anonymous self-reviews, wrote of himself that "He is the true spiritualist. He recognizes no annihilation, or death, or loss of identity. He is the largest lover and sympathizer that has appeared in literature."[41] The link here between "lover" and "spiritualist" here requires further investigation.

Without doubt, one of the most influential of those who espoused a unified theory of mesmerism and spiritualism was Andrew Jackson Davis, creator of what he called "the Harmonial Philosophy." In his voluminous writings, Davis discusses at length spiritualism and the role of animal magnetism in healing, but of greatest interest to us is what he writes about the generation of the prophetic visionary state. Davis writes of how one can induce a trance state in which one can see visions, and how "the repeated influence of a second person will furnish the required degree of corporeal refinement."[42] The two people become "galvanized," he claims, and one of the two enters into "what is called animal magnetism, but . . . is really a spiritual intercourse operating throughout the organism." In such a condition, Davis claims, one attains "a development of every spiritual power;" it is a "superior condition" of clairvoyance; one "merges into the electricity of universal Nature" and "utters and confirms that which man has taught and believed, if the same are true . . . he reveals new and vaster principles."[43] Davis tells us that this is precisely how he came to write some of his own books.

Davis's writings are of particular interest to us here because they imply the links between sexual polarity, animal magnetism, and visionary or clairvoyant experiences. We will recall that Whitman wrote of himself that he was a "true spiritualist" and the "largest lover" in history, and that electricity and magnetism are vitally important in Whitman's poetry. Very similar language appears in Davis's works, where visionary and prophetic states are said to be generated out of the "galvanic" union of a "positive" "operator" and a "negative" person, sometimes, but certainly not always, a woman. In Davis's view, a male-female or positive-negative polarity when generating "animal magnetic force" is "really a spiritual intercourse operating through the organism." In other words, "spiritual intercourse" or visionary experience comes about through a kind of "spiritual intercourse" between two people, often as not in Davis's practice, two men. But where would Davis have gotten the foundational ideas that join together sexual polarity and visionary insight?

The answer, I believe, lies in the work of a figure immensely influential throughout the nineteenth century, at times an underground influence, but almost omnipresent: Emanuel Swedenborg. Davis was a follower of Swedenborg's, and Davis's writings very strongly reflect Swedenborg's influence. We have already discussed the gist of Swedenborg's visionary works, and his name has cropped up in many of our studies of individual authors. Here, however, it is not Swedenborg's visions that interest us, so much as Swedenborg's view of sexuality in religion. Swedenborg, we will recall, was well known for his emphasis on "conjugial love," meaning that marriage on earth between a man and a woman prefigures their marriage in eternity. True couples complete one another, according to Swedenborg, and in eternity they experience "conjugial" delights that are beyond our earthly imagination. Thus, sexual-spiritual "conjugial" union has its place at the center of Swedenborg's religious vision, even though he, like Whitman, was a bachelor.

In a lengthy article in the journal *Esoterica*, Marsha Keith Schuchard revealed considerable evidence of an eighteenth- and early-nineteenth-century European esoteric tradition that draws on sexual polarity and energy in order to generate visionary experiences.[44] According to Schuchard, sexual practices were quite important for Emanuel Swedenborg in the generation of his visionary experiences, and she provides extensive evidence from Swedenborg's own writings to support this assertion. What is more, Schuchard demonstrates that Swedenborg in turn influenced the poet William Blake, in whose art one finds all manner of sexual imagery combined with visionary experiences expressed in poetry. Without question, evidence Schuchard has collected certainly sheds new light on Swedenborg and Blake, both of whom—like Whitman—drew on sexual polarity to generate or intensify visionary and creative experience, and both of whom were, like Whitman, prophetic in their writings.

It is quite certain that Whitman knew Swedenborg's work rather well. In 1856, Whitman came to know a man named John Arnold, who was a Swedenborgian, and as Helen Price wrote in a letter about her familiarity with Whitman, "although the two men differed greatly on many points, such was the mutual esteem and forbearance between them, that during the many talks they had together . . . [e]ach, though holding mainly to his own views, was large enough to see truth in the other's presentation also."[45] Arnold must have made some headway convincing Whitman of Swedenborg's virtues. In 1858, Whitman wrote an article for the Brooklyn *Daily Times* entitled "Who was Swedenborg?" in which he said that Swedenborg would "probably make the deepest and broadest mark upon the religions of future ages here, of any man that ever walked the earth."[46] This remark, of course, places Swedenborg well above Jesus Christ in influence on the future, and in itself gives us at least a sense of Whitman's respect for Swedenborg.

We have already seen how Whitman envisioned himself as divine procreator, having intercourse with many women and bringing forth a new race in America. But he emphasizes two lovers, "comrades," "companions," in this poetic procreation, which is at once sexual and religious. In "Calamus," in the poem entitled "For You O Democracy," Whitman tells us he will "make the most splendid race the sun ever shone upon, / I will make divine magnetic lands, / With the love of comrades, / With the life-long love of comrades." He continues: "I will plant companionship thick as trees along all the rivers of / America, and along the shores of the great lakes . . . / By the love of comrades, / . . . For you these from me, O Democracy, to serve you ma femme!"[47] These "divine magnetic lands" fashioned from the love of "comrades" or "companions" reminds one strikingly of Swedenborg's visions of celestial paradises made of the love of couples. It is true that "Calamus" has passages that suggest homosexuality, but we might note that here Whitman addresses "Democracy," "ma femme!" whom he is serving, and that it also celebrates "the well-married husband and wife."[48]

It is clear from a close reading of his poems, particularly "Calamus," that Whitman is definitely discussing the generation of immortality in paradise through something like conjugial love. Whitman, in "I Hear It Was Charged Against Me," writes that "really I am neither for nor against institutions," but only will "establish in the Mannahatta and in every city of these / States inland and seaboard, / And in the fields and woods . . . The institution of the dear love of comrades."[49] In "Fast-Anchor'd Eternal O Love!" he writes of "O woman I love! / O bride! O wife!" who "disembodied," "ethereal," is his consolation, and he "float[s] in the regions of your love O man."[50] There is some gender confusion here, to be sure, but for our purposes what matters more is that love creates a disembodied floating in its "region." Or again, in "I Dream'd In A Dream," Whitman writes that he dreamt of an invincible city, a "new city of Friends," where "Nothing was greater there than the quality of robust love."[51]

This was the era of "free love," we might recall, and also the era of numerous attempts at real-life communal utopias in which sexuality figured strongly. Among such efforts were John Humphrey Noyes's Oneida community and Thomas Lake Harris's community in upper New York State. Noyes's community practiced a form of male continence that entailed intercourse without ejaculation and Harris's group, drawing on Swedenborg, held that each man and woman had a divine "counterpart" and that the counterpart completed one in paradise. In Harris's most well-known book, *The Arcana of Christianity*, he wrote about the "conjugial union" of angels, and his description is well worth quoting. According to Harris, the Angel and the Angel's wife are "diffused" together,

> Her members are diffused through his members, her gentle bosom enters into all the organic sensations of his bosom; her blood circulates in all his blood like rosy fire; her fairy thoughts become his thoughts, tripping in music through all his mental sanctuaries; her heart is entranced in the conscious, interior shekinah of his heart; and so her essence is fused in his essence. . . . So is unfolded that great mystery, in which the apostle compares the marriage relation, in its true order, with the mystical union of the Lord with His true and living Church of purified, immortal Spirits. So is fulfilled that infinite prediction, that "they twain shall become one flesh."[52]

Whether or not Whitman read *Arcana* (published in 1858), this passage from a distinctively American visionary of the same period is strikingly parallel to the sexual union as mystical union of Whitman's poetry.

There is more. In the same volume of *Arcana*, Harris refers to the coming of a great poet, and his description is one Whitman would certainly have endorsed. According to Harris, the poetic gift "is a blossom from the tree of the genius of the universal race." In fact, he continues, "there are solar men, of corresponding genius, so vast in lyrical endowments that all the poets of our orb might find place, as it were, their varieties of function, within the organs of a single brain. These, through all the intermediate lyrical monarchs of superior suns, find at last, their point of universal centrality in the arch-solar poets, who hymn the odes of the Divine Creator."[53] These universal poets draw their sustenance from the Word of God, which has "arcana . . . within arcana," contains all truth, and cannot be exhausted. Thus, the true poet occupies a very high place indeed in Harris's visionary scheme of things, a view with which Whitman would undoubtedly have concurred.

The many parallels between Harris and Whitman—especially that both placed sexual / mystical union at the center of their new American religions, that both were roundly vilified for doing so, that both were visionaries, that Whitman included Satan in his "Chanting the Square Deific," whereas Harris included a "Song of Satan" (a dictated poem) in his *Arcana of Christianity*, that both subscribed to a vast evolutionary cosmology that included life on other planets, that both espoused spiritual evolution and immortality in paradises— all of these parallels do not need to reflect direct influence in either direction in order to be quite significant. Seeing Whitman in relation to a figure like Harris is extremely revealing because it tells us a great deal about the American ambience in which Whitman wrote. Both he and Harris drew upon Swedenborg and many other sources, including spiritualism and animal magnetism, and in the process began to reveal a kind of new American religion that has its roots in Western esoteric traditions but that looks forward constantly to a new era for mankind.

Despite detractors—who saw them as degenerates and false prophets— Harris and Whitman inspired their followers with religious devotion. Harris was the spiritual leader of several communities, and Whitman inspired quasi-religious organizations like the Walt Whitman fellowship. About which one was the following written? "Above all else, he was a great religious teacher and prophet . . . [and his work] is a gospel—glad tidings of great joy to those who are prepared to receive it."[54] Although words like these were written of Harris, these were the words of John Burroughs in 1902 that described Whitman. Burroughs was far from alone. R. M. Bucke wrote in 1883 that what the "Vedas were to Brahmanism, the Law and the Prophets to Judaism . . . the Pitakas to Buddhism, the Gospels . . . to Christianity, the Quran to Mohammedanism, will *Leaves of Grass* be to the future of American civilization."[55] Bucke's insistence on Whitman as a religious figure—that *Leaves of Grass* is "the bible of Democracy," and that in it is "a new spiritual life for myriads of men and women"—is especially important because, as is well known, Whitman himself closely edited and revised Bucke's book, cutting out what he disliked and adding what he thought important. Bucke's outlandish claim for *Leaves of Grass* as the replacement for all religious books of the past and as the future of American civilization has the imprimatur of the poet himself!

It is also true that, of all the figures of the American Renaissance except Emerson, Whitman was the one who most intuited the American religious paradigm that emerged during the twentieth century. Far more than Emerson, Whitman is the poet-father of the New Age movement, as also of the so-called sexual revolution of the mid-twentieth century and of the "Beat" and "Hippie" movements. As we have seen, however, despite Whitman's obvious efforts to appear sui generis, he did indeed have many antecedents for his imagined new American religion, and these antecedents are to be found in the Western esoteric traditions, especially in the heretical movements that long preceded him, as well as in literary figures like Rabelais. Perhaps more than any other figure, Whitman illustrates how the American Renaissance was about Adamic origins, about finding the original American self that, coming after so much history that it incorporates, is nonetheless new, Edenic. Paradoxically, this American Adamism always must be understood in relation to the past as much as to the future, as is very much exemplified by Whitman's Americanization of European esoteric currents as they were filtered through the popular movements and figures of his day.

fourteen

Dickinson

At first glance, Dickinson is certainly the most unexpected of authors to encounter in our study of Western esotericism in the American Renaissance. There is only scant evidence of her reading, and none that she read directly on topics like alchemy or mysticism. What is more, there is just a modicum of evidence that she was interested in the vulgarized esotericism of spiritualism or mesmerism, despite the fact that, as Robert Weisbuch observed with only mild exaggeration, "nearly every poem Dickinson wrote has to do with death."[1] Fascinated with death Dickinson certainly was, but how are we to make connections between this fascination and Western esoteric traditions? Here I will argue that even though Dickinson did not read a great deal about Western esotericism, she did nonetheless know something about esoteric traditions, and in her poetry reveals a highly literary form of what emerged elsewhere in American society as spiritualism, as well as what we may call a spontaneously auto-initiatic spirituality.

Comparatively little has been published about Dickinson's interest in esoteric subjects, but there have been a few useful studies. Benjamin Lease's *Emily Dickinson's Readings of Men and Books* includes quite a bit of valuable information, as do several articles by Barton Levi St. Armand.[2] However, the vast majority of authors on Dickinson pay very little or no attention to the ways Dickinson drew on esoteric traditions like alchemy, or quasi-esoteric traditions like spiritualism or mesmerism. Most likely, this oversight has to do at least in part with the more general neglect of such subjects in the American Renaissance as a whole, but it may also have to do with the way esoteric topics are woven into Dickinson's poems.

To begin, we might consider for a moment where Dickinson might have learned anything about Western esoteric traditions properly speaking. To say that we know little about her reading is an understatement, but it seems safe to say that she was not at all like that omnivorous reader Emerson, who had read virtually everything there was to read, and recurred constantly to Swedenborg and Neoplatonism. Nonetheless, Dickinson, with her weirdly jagged letter-writing prose did, in her initial correspondence with Thomas Wentworth Higginson, tell him what she read at the time (25 April 1862). Replying to his first letter, she wrote coyly "You asked how old I was? I made no verse—but one or two—until this winter—Sir—."[3]And then she admits

> I had a terror—since September—I could tell to none—and so I sing, as the Boy does by the Burying Ground—because I am afraid—You inquire my Books—For Poets—I have Keats—and Mr and Mrs Browning. For Prose—Mr Ruskin—Sir Thomas Browne—and Revelations. I went to school—but in your manner of the phrase—had no education. When a little Girl, I had a friend, who taught me Immortality—but venturing too near, himself—he never returned. . . .
>
> You ask of my Companions Hills—Sir—and the Sundown—and a Dog, large as myself, that my Father bought me. . . . My Mother does not care for thought—and Father, too busy with his Briefs—to notice what we do— He buys me many Books—but begs me not to read them—because he fears they joggle the Mind. They are religious—except me—and address an Eclipse, every morning—whom they call their Father. But I fear my story fatigues you—I would like to learn—Can you tell me how to grow—or is it unconveyed—like Melody—or Witchcraft?[4]

Such a letter is strikingly like Dickinson's poetry, but one can only imagine what Higginson made of its style, which she maintained for a number of more years before mellowing into mere abruptness.

It is to be expected that Dickinson read Keats, the Brownings, and Ruskin, but it is more revealing that she spent much time with the Revelation of St. John and Sir Thomas Browne. Revelation is interesting because it is undoubtedly the most arcane of all the books of the Bible. Chock full of esoteric symbolism, its imagery recurs throughout the history of Western esotericism, and indeed, in my book *Western Esotericism, Literature, and Consciousness*, I suggest that Revelation is in many respects the *ur-buch*, or origin, of the Western esoteric traditions. Certainly, at the very least, it is responsible as much as anything for the millennialism that pervaded so many sects in nineteenth-century America, and given that Dickinson's family was conventionally religious, addressing as they did "an Eclipse, every morning—whom they call their Father," one can be sure that she must have been steeped in the esoteric imagery and prophecies of Revelation since childhood. But it was in Sir Thomas Browne that she would have gained some sense of Western esotericism in its more modern forms.

Sir Thomas Browne (1605–82) is undoubtedly one of the most engaging authors of the seventeenth century, and nowhere more so than in his most well-known book, *Religio Medici* (1654). One can see why this book would have appealed to Dickinson, not least because, like her, he was a freethinker in matters of religion and had a special interest in death and what comes thereafter. Like Dickinson, Browne's thought is in the margin between orthodoxy and heresy, and he devotes some time at the beginning of *Religio Medici* to various heresies concerning death and the afterlife. Browne writes that "indeed Heresies perish not with their Authors, but like the River *Arethusa*, though they lose their currents in one place they rise up againe in another," "as though there were a *Metempsuchosis*, and the soul of one man passed into another, opinions doe finde after certaine revolutions, men and mindes like those that first begat them."[5] He remarks on the heresy of the "Arabians" that the soul should perish with the body but be raised again on the final judgment; the heresy of Origen that God would eventually release the damned from their torments; and the heresy of prayers for the dead.

It was in Browne that Dickinson would have learned of Hermetic and Platonic thought. He writes that he is content "to understand a mystery without a rigid definition," preferring "an easie and Platonick description. That allegorical description of *Hermes*, pleaseth me beyond all the Metaphysicall definitions of Divines."[6] Browne remarks that he has "often admired the mysticall way of Pythagoras, and the secret Magicke of numbers." What is more, "the severe Schooles shall never laugh me out of the Philosophy of Hermes, that this visible world is but a picture of the invisible, wherein as in a pourtract, things are not truely, but in equivocall shapes, and as they counterfeit some more reall substance in that invisible fabrick."[7] Browne's emphasis on the invisible world fits well with Dickinson's poetry, where the invisible and visible worlds often are indivisible. And she would have read with delight Browne's insistence that we, like the "heathens," learn our divinity from Nature, "that universall and publik Manuscript, that lies expans'd unto the eyes of all."[8] According to Browne, "the Heathens knew better how to joyne and reade these mysticall letters, than wee Christians, who cast a more careless eye on these common Hieroglyphicks, and disdain to suck Divinity from the flowers of nature."[9] Surely Dickinson, who wrote that "Angels, in the early morning / May be seen the Dews among," would have loved to read in Browne of sucking Divinity from the flowers of nature.[10]

Earlier, we noted in Dickinson's second letter to Higginson her request for him to help her "grow," unless growing be untaught, "like Melody—or Witchcraft." Where would she have been reading of witchcraft and magic? In *Religio Medici*, Browne devotes some time to refuting those who "should so farre forget their Metaphysicks, and destroy the Ladder and scale of creatures, as to question the existence of Spirits: for my part, I have ever beleeved, and doe now know, that there are Witches; they that doubt of these, doe not onely deny them, but Spirits; and are obliquely and upon consequence . . . Atheists."[11] What is more, Browne continues,

> I beleeve that all that use sorceries, incantations, and spells, are not Witches, or as we terme them, Magicians; I conceive there is a traditionall Magicke, not learned immediately from the Devill, but at secondhand from his Schollers; who have once the secret betrayed, are able, and doe emperically practice without his advice, they both proceeding upon the principles of nature. . . . Thus I thinke a great part of Philosophy was at first Witchcraft;

which being afterward derived from one to another, proved but Philosophy, and was indeed no more than the honest effects of Nature: What invented by us is Philosophy, learned from him is Magicke. Wee doe surely owe the discovery of many secrets both to good and bad Angels. . . . I doe thinke that many mysteries ascribed to our own inventions, have beene the courteous revelations of Spirits; for those noble esssences in heaven beare a friendly regard unto their fellow-creatures on earth.[12]

This is an interesting discourse, not least because it neatly encapsulates the nature of Renaissance white magic and reveals the abiding belief in Browne's day not only in magic, but also in the continuum that ranges from contracts with the devil all the way to a "traditionall Magicke" that proceeds from nature and is not illegitimate because its practitioners "doe emperically practice without his [the devil's] advice."

Dickinson frequently depicted in her poetry exactly the kind of world revealed in Browne's writing, a world populated not only by visible creatures, but also by invisible ones, angels and demons, and all manner of friendly spirits. She writes of "Angels in the early morning," and of something "so appalling— it exhilirates— / So over Horror, it half Captivates— . . . To scan a Ghost, is faint—," of "Members of the Invisible, / Existing, while we stare, / In Leagueless Opportunity, / O'ertakeless, as the Air—," or of this extraordinary poem about invisible guests:

Alone, I cannot be—
The Hosts—do visit me—
Recordless Company—
Who baffle Key—
They have no Robes, nor Names—
No Almanacs—nor Climes—
But general Homes
Like Gnomes—
Their Coming, may be known
By Couriers within—
Their going—is not—
For they're never gone—[13]

What are we to make of this poem? Let us read it as written, but with reference to Renaissance white magical tradition with which Browne, and thereby Dickinson, was obviously familiar. The "Hosts" are the heavenly hosts of angels, who certainly would "baffle Key;" and their "Coming" is preceded by "Couriers within," that is, by preliminary spirits. They cannot be understood by astrological "Almanacs," nor have they "Robes, nor Names." They are "never gone," meaning that they are latent within humanity, but can "visit" us in their full glory—like Rilke's Angels, they are absolute Presence.

Dickinson's interest in paranormal phenomena and esoterica is evident in some of her letters. In July 1880, Dickinson wrote to her confidante Mrs. J. G. Holland about how she and her brother Austin "were talking the other Night about the Extension of Consciousness, after Death, and Mother told Vinnie, afterwards, she thought it was 'very improper.'"[14] In another letter, this one to Forrest Emerson in 1879, she wrote "Mother congratulates Mr. Emerson on the discovery of the 'philosopher's stone.' She will never divulge it. It lay just where she thought it did—in making others happy."[15] These two references tell us a fair bit about Dickinson's interest in esoteric topics: she was more than willing to make after-dinner conversation on ideas about the survival of human consciousness after death, and to jocularly refer to the alchemical philosopher's stone as simply "making others happy." Dickinson was most interested in esoteric topics when they intersected with daily life, when they allowed her to see the mundane in unexpectedly new ways, and she was more courageous than most in exploring those new ways of thinking and seeing.

Undoubtedly Dickinson had had experiences unfamiliar to many of us, and more than one commentator has pronounced her mad as a result. John Cody, author of *In Great Pain: The Inner Life of Emily Dickinson*, claimed that "one will inevitably misunderstand and trivialize much of Emily Dickinson's life and poetry if one fails to grasp the full intensity of her suffering and the magnitude of her collapse. For this reason let me state at the onset my thesis that the crisis Emily Dickinson suffered following the marriage of her brother was a psychosis."[16] Although Cody polemically states his assertion as a fact, he immediately follows it by a series of much more qualified questions, like "What can this 'snarl in the brain' be?" surrounded by much more timid qualifiers like "might conceivably constitute," and "seem to be" or "can scarcely be interpreted in any other way."[17] Unfortunately, Cody himself inevitably misunderstands and trivializes Dickinson's life and poetry by flinging the label "psychotic" at her, and then shoring up his charge with poems for which I can suggest an entirely reasonable alternate interpretation that does not require placing Dickinson in the booby hatch.

She herself was already familiar with this charge of insanity and, of course, wrote a poem about it. The poem reads as follows:

Much Madness is divinest Sense—
To a discerning Eye—
Much Sense—the starkest Madness—
'Tis the Majority
In this, as All, prevail—
Assent—and you are sane—
Demur—you're straightway dangerous—
And handled with a Chain.[18]

In this poem, the most important line is the first: "Much Madness is divinest Sense." The word "divinest," here, resonates with a long European tradition of what had come to be known as "enthusiasm," a word that has its origins in Platonism and implies self-transcendence, for the artist as well as for the religious. The idea of "enthusiasm" as the origin of art and religious experience emerged once again among the Cambridge Platonists, and yet again among some of the Romantics, as well, of course, as among the Christian theosophers.

Böhme, for instance, has often been accused of being mad, and to learn the "divinest Sense" of his writings takes a long time. All of this is to say that there is a great deal of historical precedent for the point of this poem, and, although it is unlikely Dickinson knew all of it, it is entirely likely she was familiar with some.

Let us take this poem and, with it in mind, consider another that Cody suggests indicates Dickinson's "psychosis:" "I felt a Funeral, in my Brain." The first stanza reads:

> I felt a Funeral, in my Brain,
> And Mourners, to and fro
> Kept treading—treading—till it seemed
> That Sense was breaking through—

The poem refers to some kind of experience, to be sure, to an almost literal psychic breakthrough. She imagines a kind of funeral service in the soul, during which "My Mind was going numb," when "Space—began to toll, / As All the Heavens were a Bell, / And Being, but an Ear, / And I, and Silence, some strange Race / Wrecked, solitary, here—." Even for Dickinson, who had an astonishing ear for language, these lines are intricately woven together with natural rhymes, and linger strangely in one's memory like an incantation. This brings us to the final stanza:

> And then a Plank in Reason, broke,
> And I dropped down, and down—
> And hit a World at every plunge,
> And Finished knowing—then—[19]

It may well be that Dickinson experienced something like a shamanic initiatory experience, a spontaneous opening of the invisible realms, a dropping down in which she "hit a World at every plunge."

This alternative reading of Dickinson's psychic collapse helps to explain a great many of her poems, not making them out to be exhibits on display for the probing fingers of the psychoanalyst, but recognizing how they emerge from Dickinson's profound and, for most of us, unfamiliar and even eerie experience to become beautifully crafted jewels. If we regard Dickinson merely as having gone insane, then her poems become the inexplicable and perhaps incidental creations of a madwoman, but if we suggest that she went through a kind of spontaneous shamanic initiation, then the poems can be seen as a record of what may look to an outsider as madness, but for the cognoscenti is "divinest Sense." In a later poem, for instance, Dickinson wrote that

> I heard, as if I had no Ear
> Until a Vital Word
> Came all the way from Life to me
> And then I knew I heard.
> I saw, as if my Eye were on
> Another, till a Thing

And now I know 'twas Light, because
It fitted them, came in.
I dwelt, as if Myself were out,
My Body but within
Until a Might detected me
And set my kernel in.
And Spirit turned unto the Dust
"Old Friend, thou knowest me,"
And Time went out to tell the News
And met Eternity [Unto Eternity—*alt. version*][20]

Cody explains this poem as Dickinson's self-estrangement as a result of severe depression, but that interpretation ignores the poem itself. When we look at the poem, what we notice first of all is that it is about the poet's experience with something outside herself, in the first stanza referred to as "a Vital Word" that "Came all the way from Life to me / And then I knew I heard." In other words, the poem is not at all about self-estrangement, but about spiritual illumination. The "Vital Word," the Logos of Christianity, comes from the source of Life to her; the Light and divine Might comes to her, and then she can truly see and hear, just as Jesus said in his parables. Each of the first three stanzas begins with an "as if," so that for example "I dwelt, as if Myself were out," "*Until* a Might detected me / And set my kernel in." The poem is about how one is self-estranged until divine power comes and one is born again, given ears to hear and eyes to see things in the spirit. Ultimately, the poem is about the marriage of Time and Eternity by way of this process of spiritual awakening; hence its conclusion that Spirit and Dust are old friends that know one another, that "Time went out to tell the News / And met Eternity."

Dickinson's poems of interest to us here thus can be roughly sorted into four main categories: there are the poems of terror and psychic dismemberment or dissolution, the poems of divine reconstitution or illumination, the poems of subsequent insight into the nature of death and of invisible beings, and the poems about the ecstasy of one who is spiritually illuminated and looks anew at the ordinary beauties of nature. Poems of psychic dissolution or terror include "I felt a Funeral, in my Brain," "I felt a Cleaving in my Mind—" as well as poems like "It was not Death, for I stood up, / And all the Dead, lie down—." Poems of divine illumination include "I heard, as if I had no Ear," "The Spirit is the Conscious Ear," "The Drop, that wrestles in the Sea— / Forgets her own locality— / As I—toward Thee—," or "Exhiliration—is within," but there are many others. Poems about the nature of death and the presence of invisible beings abound in Dickinson's work, but prominent examples include "What care the Dead, for Chanticleer—," "I died for Beauty—but was scarce," "I heard a Fly buzz—when I died—," "Three times—we parted—Breath and I—," "A Death blow is a Life blow to Some," "You'll find—it when you try to die," and "Alone, I cannot be—." And poems about an ecstatic perception of nature include the poem "There came a Day at Summer's full / Entirely for me— / I thought that such were for the Saints, / Where Resurrections—

be—," as well as "There is a morn by men unseen—," "Angels in the early morning," and of course "I taste a liquor never brewed—."

With this categorization I absolutely am not suggesting that Dickinson's life and poetry can be rigidly classified into stages, but rather that categorizing the poems in this way suggests a process of spiritual disintegration and reintegration that corresponds in a rough way to what we find elsewhere in Western esoteric traditions and in their secularized literary offspring, Romanticism. The poet Novalis (Friedrich von Hardenberg) , for instance, certainly drew on Kabbalah and Christian theosophy in describing the acquisition of new spiritual senses and knowledge of invisible realms. Some of Novalis's knowledge was derived from his readings, but some of it spontaneously emerged from his own experience. Dickinson's esoteric poetry emerged, I think, out of a similar combination, but in her case she relied far more on her own experiences, which led to a process that occurred without her urging or desiring it.

Yet as we have seen, Dickinson did read and think very highly of Sir Thomas Browne, and one can see from her poetry that she was doing some reading on esoteric topics. Here, for instance, is a poem from a manuscript dated roughly 1862:

> Trust in the Unexpected—
> By this—was William Kidd
> Persuaded of the Buried Gold—
> As One had testified—
>
> Through this—the old Philosopher—
> His Talismanic Stone
> Discernéd—still with[h]olden
> To effort undivine—
>
> 'Twas this—allured Columbus—
> When Genoa—withdrew
> Before an Apparition
> Baptized America—
>
> The Same—afflicted Thomas—
> When Deity assured
> 'Twas better—the perceiving not—
> Provided it believed—[21]

This is a poem about the human need for discovery, for tangible results. In the second stanza, the Philosopher's Stone is discerned by the old Philosopher, but it is still withheld from those whose efforts are profane. The stanza that immediately follows is about Columbus's discovery of America, which implies a link between the two: both searches go against conventional wisdom and both insist that there is something real on the other end of the search. Belief is not enough, because these searchers insist on actuality.

Another such poem, this one more curious, was written around 1870, initially as the following two lines only:

> Best Witchcraft is Geometry
> To a Magician's eye—

These lines were extended and slightly altered in another version:

> Best Witchcraft is Geometry
> To the magician's mind—
> His ordinary acts are feats
> To thinking of mankind.[22]

We might note that of the two works of Sir Thomas Browne that Dickinson probably read, *Religio Medici*, and *The Garden of Cyrus, or on the Quincunx*, the argument of the latter bears more on the poem above. Traditionally, European magic often entails the use of geometric forms that include the circle, the square, the hexagram, and so forth, and Browne remarks on this at length in *The Garden of Cyrus*, commenting in particular on how often recur certain numbers and geometric forms based on patterns of five. The other thing we might note about this poem is that it takes witchcraft and magic seriously; it suggests that there is a "best witchcraft," mathematical in its precision, and that what seems ordinary to the magus represents "feats / To thinking of mankind."

Then, too, as Barton Levi St. Armand points out in his important article "Emily Dickinson and the Occult," she was certainly aware of the meaning of the term "Hermetic," as one can see in her poem "Strong Draughts:"

> Strong Draughts of Their Refreshing Minds
> To drink—enables Mine
> Through Desert or the Wilderness
> As bore it Sealed Wing—
> To go elastic—Or as One
> The Camel's trait—attained—
> How powerful the Stimulus
> Of an Hermetic Mind—[23]

It is tantalizing to wonder from whose "Refreshing Minds" Dickinson has been drinking, here, and whose is the "Hermetic Mind" whose stimulus she feels. Most likely it is that of Sir Thomas Browne, although it might be remotely possible she had happened upon a rare copy of Mary Anne Atwood's book *A Suggestive Inquiry into Hermetic Mystery* (London, 1850), a book that would undoubtedly have encouraged Dickinson's conviction that the Hermetic mysteries lay in the human spirit itself, in the enabling elasticity of the "Hermetic Mind."

But this is about as far as we can go in tracing or speculating about Dickinson's reading on esoteric topics, excluding, that is, her constant reading of Shakespeare's works, which are filled with esoteric allusions.[24] Much more important, in the end, is the experiential basis for her poetry. Who could doubt that Dickinson's own experience lies behind a poem like this?

> There is a pain—so utter—
> It swallows substance up—
> Then covers the Abyss with Trance—
> So Memory can step
> Around—across—upon it—
> As one within a Swoon—

Goes safely—where an open eye—
Would drop Him—Bone by Bone.[25]

Anyone who has undergone a traumatic experience is familiar with the way that utter pain is somehow erased by a kind of trance, so that one's memory can pass beyond it, rather like a sleepwalker safely walking over what he would surely fall from were he awake and with open eyes. This may or may not be a poem that alludes to the psychic disintegration we spoke of earlier, but it is noteworthy that regardless of the poem's specific it has central terms—Abyss, Trance—that emerge out of esoteric contexts. Yet the poem is not about these terms; it is about the way human beings safely make their way through utter agony and emerge well on the other side.

Dickinson did emerge well on the other side, if evidently somewhat eccentric. One of the most revealing accounts of a visit with Dickinson is by Thomas Wentworth Higginson, who wrote about his in a letter to his wife. The discription is fascinating, and begins with Wentworth's entry into

> A large county lawyer's house, brown brick, with great trees & a garden—I sent up my card. A parlor dark & cool & stiffish, a few books & engravings. . . .
>
> A step like a pattering child's in entry & in glided a little plain woman with two smooth bands of reddish hair & a face a little like Belle Dove's; not plainer—with no good feature—in a . . . blue net worsted shawl. She came to me with two day lilies which she put in a sort of childlike way into my hand & said "These are my introduction" in a soft frightened breathless childlike voice—& added under her breath Forgive me if I am frightened; I never see strangers & hardly know what I say. . . . Manner between Angie Tilton & Mr. Alcott—but thoroughly ingenuous & simple which they are not & saying many things which you would have thought foolish & I wise.[26]

Especially interesting for our purposes is the fact that Higginson immediately compared Dickinson to Bronson Alcott, widely known for his esoteric interests and for his aphoristic prose, which some considered wise and others foolish. One might note that Higginson had some interest in spiritualist phenomena and ghost stories, and this side of Dickinson's work might have attracted him, as well.[27] Some examples follow of Dickinson's aphoristic observations, which include "I find ecstasy in living—the mere sense of living is joy enough." Perhaps most interesting of all is Higginson's summary of his meeting with Dickinson: "I never was with any one who drained my nerve power so much. Without touching her, she drew from me. I am glad not to live near her. She often thought me *tired* & seemed very thoughtful of others."[28]

Some twenty years later, in the *Atlantic Monthly*, Higginson recalled this interview again:

> The impression undoubtedly made on me was that of an excess of tension, and of an abnormal life. Perhaps in time I could have got beyond that somewhat overstrained relation which not my will, but her needs, had forced upon us. Certainly I should have been most glad to bring it down to the level of

simple truth and every-day comradeship; but it was not altogether easy. She was much too enigmatical a being for me to solve in an hour's interview, and an instinct told me that the slightest attempt at direct cross-examination would make her withdraw into her shell; I could only sit still and watch, as one does in the woods; I must name my bird without a gun, as recommended by Emerson.[29]

"Enigmatical," "draining"—these are interesting terms for description, and lead one to wonder exactly why Dickinson rarely if ever left the house, whether what had happened to her had made her so sensitive that she was like a kind of psychic sponge who soaked up her guests, and thus had made her very wary of allowing visitors. In any case, one gains from Higginson's remarks something of the strangeness of Dickinson's personality.

It is obvious that Dickinson was fascinated with the nature of the afterlife, and it is thus not surprising that she was quite interested in spiritualism, an interest supported by Higginson's own fascination with this subject.[30] Higginson had long had an interest in spiritualist phenomena, having submitted an affidavit that supported the authenticity of spiritualist phenomena he witnessed in séances conducted by a Harvard divinity school student.[31] Indeed, in April 1852, as Benjamin Leach points out, Higginson attended a séance in Boston and inquired of his dead father and brother whether he ought to take a position as minister of the Free Church in Worcester, Massachusetts. When his father's spirit encouraged him to take the position, he did.[32] What is more, Higginson spoke publicly in favor of spiritualism, and so, as Barton Levi St. Armand points out, Higginson's public and private views on spiritualism undoubtedly helped shape those of Dickinson. In a letter to the *Banner of Light*, a spiritualist magazine, Higginson wrote that "Undoubtedly the facts of Spiritualism are the most important yet launched upon the history of humanity."[33]

Strictly speaking, of course, spiritualism as a mid-nineteenth century American phenomenon, although it does not belong to the historical line of Western esoteric traditions that includes alchemy, Christian theosophy, and Rosicrucianism, still was heir to some aspects of Western esotericism, particularly European magical lodges and necromancy. In his monumental study *New Age Religion and Western Culture: Esotericism in the Mirror of Secular Thought*, Wouter Hanegraaff discusses in detail the filiations involved, pointing out that American spiritualism was very much indebted to Swedenborgianism and that, although many scholars habitually date the beginning of American spiritualism to the famous spirit rappings of the Fox sisters in 1848, spiritualist phenomena were found in Europe as early as the late-eighteenth century, as were "illuminist" phenomena of spirit communications in such orders as Martinez de Pasqually's *Elus-Cohens*, or Jean-Baptiste Willermoz's *Chevaliers*.[34]

For whatever reasons, however, many scholars of American literature traditionally have paid scant attention to the complex web of filiations that produced such a widespread movement as American spiritualism, let alone acknowledged the influence of such a movement on literary figures like Higginson and Dickinson. Although there are numerous recent and solid studies on spiritualism, scholarship in this area has frequently remained separate from literary analysis.[35] Jon Butler rightly remarks, for instance, that "Higginson scholars have had little to say about Higginson's spiritualism and its effect on his life and work." To give an example: in Tilden Edelstein's *Strange Enthusiasm: A Life of Thomas Wentworth Higginson*, there is but a single brief allusion to Higginson's interest in this subject.[36] I am not suggesting that an interest in spiritualism is central to Higginson's remarkable and varied life, but clearly it is more important than is implied by a mere passing reference.

Likewise, when we consider Dickinson's poetry and letters as a whole, we must at least acknowledge that there are more references to the Western esoteric traditions than most Dickinson scholars have noted. Furthermore, those references in turn suggest, not that Dickinson read widely or deeply in Western esotericism, but rather that, in addition to what she drew from sources like Sir Thomas Browne and Shakespeare, she had direct experiences of her own that could well be understood not just as the onset of insanity, but as a process of spiritual awakening that entailed great psychic sensitivity. We can see signs of this awakening and sensitivity in her poetry and her life, from which it is clear that she was not interested in conventional or orthodox forms of Christianity, but rather in direct spiritual experience, including but by no means limited to spiritualist encounters with the dead. This focus on direct spiritual experience—be it of what follows physical death, or of angels, or of nature—is central to her poems, just as it is central to the Western esoteric traditions more generally. At the very least, we certainly can conclude that a closer look at Dickinson's poetry in light of Western esoteric traditions and their emphasis on experiential spirituality can yield many new insights into her work.

fifteen

The Esoteric Origins of the
American Renaissance

When we survey the history of esotericism in North America from the colonial period to the late-nineteenth century, we find that a remarkable shift took place. As the colonists came over, especially from England or Germany, they brought with them a great many kinds of practical esotericism that were integrated into daily life. Astrology, alchemy, folk magic, and various esoteric orders or lodges all were prevalent in the lives of many Americans right through to the beginning of the nineteenth century. But gradually, much changed. By the time of the American Renaissance and such authors as Emerson, Poe, Melville, Dickinson, and Fuller, these various currents of esotericism had largely, though of course not totally, vanished from the American scene, and were transposed instead into the creative work of these major American writers. Here, I will begin to account for this momentous shift and to essay its significance.

It is clear from my survey of the material that the New England colonies were pervaded with various forms of esotericism. Alchemy was widely respected and practiced well into the eighteenth century; astrological almanacs were immensely popular; European-derived folk magic was commonplace in the countryside; Böhmean theosophy was extremely influential, especially in Pennsylvania; and Freemasonry, with its Rosicrucian ideals, was instrumental in the founding of the United States, as one can easily see with a glance at U.S. currency that features a truncated pyramid and disembodied eye. By the early nineteenth century, however, every one of these traditions, so prevalent earlier, had waned. None of them disappeared completely, of course. Undoubtedly, each of these currents continued to have its practitioners here or there; yet no longer could any of these be regarded as commonplace in American life by the time that the American Renaissance authors emerged.

Much has been made of the William Morgan kidnapping and the subsequent rise of the Antimasonic party in American politics during the early nineteenth century. It is certainly true that the disappearance and presumed murder of Morgan, supposedly about to become a betrayer of Masonic secrets, did much to galvanize public opinion against Freemasonry. But the Antimasonic movement is a symptom, not a cause, of this larger movement in American society away from esoteric traditions. By the time the Antimasons became prominent, every single one of the esoteric traditions mentioned above, with the possible exception of Freemasonry, had already disappeared from many Americans' lives. The rejection of Freemasonry in early nineteenth-century America followed more than provoked this change. The Antimasonic party could become prominent because it spoke to larger trends in American society as a whole, of which the discarding of esoteric traditions itself is only a part.

It was, of course, not impossible to live on the American frontier and practice alchemy or Christian theosophy or astrology; there were many who did precisely these things. However, settlers practiced these disciplines because they brought them over from the Old World and saw the New World in a millennialist light, as a place where they would be free from persecution and whose primary attraction was precisely such freedom to practice their esoteric interests. It is a truism that many Europeans came to America for religious freedom, but it is not considered often enough just what sort of traditions those immigrants practiced, or how important a role esoteric currents played in their lives. Not everyone who came over from England or Europe was a conventional Christian, and this gave a definite fervor to their lives.

However, this fervor in the New World generally did not transfer from generation to generation. It is rare, though occasionally possible, to find a second generation of practicing alchemists in the American colonies; the various theosophic communities had largely dispersed by the early nineteenth century; various kinds of folk magic had largely become "superstitions;" and sons did not always follow their fathers into Masonry. Many, perhaps nearly all second, third, fourth, and fifth generations of such families were much more preoccupied with the ordinary affairs of life: farming, founding businesses, taking care of families, grappling with the exigencies of life. What in one generation was practiced with exceeding devotion on the frontier, in a later generation was discarded as quaint, backward looking, superstitious nonsense, its books dispersed and virtually all record lost. This, one may say, is a kind of Americanization.

Such Americanization came about through the rise of what became known as modern scientific rationalism and industrialization, which emerge from a worldview quite antithetical to those found in the various esoteric traditions. The rise of the sciences, technology, and industrialism are all linked by their adherents' objectification of the cosmos. By contrast, in the various esoteric traditions, despite their wide range, subject and object are not rigorously separated but rather by way of the tradition itself joined together as deeper meanings are unveiled. Thus, for instance, whereas the practice of herbal alchemy reveals the deeper connections between ourselves and a particular plant or group of plants by way of healing and is necessarily an individual's work, industrialization takes place through objectifying separation of ourselves from that plant in order to process it and make it into a product for the masses that then can be sold and consumed. Alchemy takes place for or between individuals; industrialization is, by definition, for the masses. Alchemy joins, whereas industrialization separates and objectifies for consumption.

Astrology and astronomy also exemplify this shift: astrology is founded in the relationships between and meanings of the planets or stars and the natural and human realms and cycles, but astronomy is based exclusively in quantification or measurement and identification. Meaning, in the senses found in astrology, is almost completely jettisoned from modern astronomy, and out of this absence in turn springs the profound antipathy that many—perhaps almost all—astronomers have had for astrology. Whereas in astrology a planet links together a whole constellation of meanings in the human and natural realms, in astronomy the planet is defined exclusively in terms of its size, density, trajectory, mineral deposits, and so forth.

As the industrialization of America commenced in earnest during the nineteenth and twentieth centuries, so, too, at least for a time, alchemy, astrology, and other esoteric traditions were by and large not only discarded, but also denigrated because they were not at all conducive to the objectification—let alone the consumption—of the natural world. It is certainly true that at least some of the early industrial processes, chiefly concerned with soap, wax, metallurgy, and medicine, emerged out of the efforts of alchemists. Hence, for example, the American alchemist George Starkey was still widely known some time after his death because of the continuing sale of what had become known as "Starkey's Pill."[1] However, these innovations occurred during the period of transition from earlier perspectives colored by alchemical and other esoteric traditions, to modern scientific industrialism. The fact remains that—as we saw in the disappearance of astrological almanacs and practicing alchemists by the turn of the nineteenth century—fundamentally, modern scientific rationalism and earlier Western esoteric traditions appeared incompatible with one another and that, during the nineteenth century in America, scientific rationalism won what seemed a convincing victory in routing various forms of practical esotericism from American society.

Yet this rout of Western esoteric traditions was not nearly so thorough as might first appear. It is true that, by the measure of how many astrological almanacs were published, or how many practicing alchemists there were, such esoteric traditions seem to have vanished from American society by the mid-nineteenth century. However, what we have seen in this survey of major American authors during this time reveals a rather different scenario. Every one of the authors whose works we have considered refer to and draw upon Western esoteric traditions, and a closer examination of this phenomenon suggests the following: that even as Western esoteric traditions by and large vanished from Americans' daily lives, major American authors of the American Renaissance took up their themes. Indeed, we could go further, and suggest that these authors drew upon esoteric themes and traditions that had preoccupied many of their ancestors, so that the American Renaissance may well be seen from this angle as the transference of esoteric traditions from daily life into literary consciousness.

I do not want to appear to overemphasize the importance of Western esotericism in the American Renaissance, but as we have seen, the presence of esotericism in the works of all these authors—from Poe and Hawthorne and Melville to Emerson, Dickinson, Alcott, and Fuller—is undeniable. Furthermore, although each author drew from different particular traditions, we can certainly say that if one were to imagine an American Renaissance without any of these prior esoteric traditions its entire character would be changed and it might very well not exist at all. For instance, one certainly cannot imagine Emerson or Alcott's works without reference to esotericism, nor for that matter would Poe or Hawthorne's works have anywhere near the same resonance. By drawing upon alchemy, astrology, theosophy, Swedenborgianism, Mesmerism, Rosicrucianism, Freemasonry, and so forth, these authors drew upon currents of thought that, even though prevailing scientific or industrialist rationalism in American society had largely abandoned them, still had enormous resonance in the popular mind, still remained living forces in the American imagination.

At the same time, what strikes one most about these authors of the American Renaissance is how not one of them delved into practical forms of Western esotericism, but rather almost without exception limited their contact with esoteric traditions to the realm of literature alone. Whereas in the American colonies the various forms of esotericism practiced, from folk magic to astrology and even to Christian theosophy and alchemy, all represented practices that one actually *did*—one had to purchase and consult an almanac, or accumulate certain kinds of laboratory equipment, for example—for the authors of the American Renaissance, these esoteric traditions were totally a matter of the imagination. Ethan Allen Hitchcock exemplifies this tendency as well as anyone: here was a man who accumulated the finest library of rare alchemical books in mid-nineteenth century America, who published several tomes of his own on the nature of alchemy, yet who had never owned a bit of laboratory equipment and even insisted in his books that such equipment was unnecessary for the true practice of alchemy! Such a contention would have been a shock indeed to his predecessors, the colonial alchemists, who went through a great deal of difficulty to obtain the proper glassware and furnaces.

We might call this transfer of esotericism from the realm of daily life to the sphere of literature a kind of intellectualization, but in the case of the fiction writers especially it also might be called an imaginization of esotericism. Hawthorne, for instance, drew upon many prior esoteric traditions in America, perhaps most notably alchemy, yet at the same time even when Hitchcock (whose own view of alchemy was highly intellectualized!) came to visit, Hawthorne stayed away and it was his wife who entertained the Hermetic scholar. Hawthorne was interested in alchemy as long as it was safely confined to the past and to his own imagination; it could inspire fictional romances, but it was not to be allowed into the realm of actual, daily life. So, too, Poe and

Melville incorporated into their works esoteric themes that ranged from Mesmerism to Masonry—but they did so for dramatic or illustrative reasons and because doing so drew upon images already highly charged in the popular imagination.

Authors of nonfiction like Emerson and Alcott, on the other hand, reveal a intellectualized esotericism. Clearly Emerson's sources include Swedenborg, as well as Böhmean theosophy, Neoplatonism, and Hermeticism—all interests that he shared with his friend Bronson Alcott. In addition, Alcott was drawn to alchemy and, as we have seen, may even have made annotations in rare alchemical works, but his interest in the subject, like Emerson's in any of these traditions, was theoretical nonetheless. For Emerson especially, but also for Alcott, these esoteric traditions remained sources of intellectual inspiration, in this respect very much akin to Asian religious sources like the Bhagavad Gita, the Vedas, and the Upanishads.[2] Emerson was hardly likely to become a practitioner of any of these, and even if Alcott was very much drawn to Böhmean theosophy, still, his books *Tablets* and *Concord Days* remain as evidence of his intellectual uses of theosophy, not of his being himself entirely a theosopher in the thoroughly practical sense that seventeenth-century figures like Johann Georg Gichtel or John Pordage were.[3] Both of these authors wrote books on their spiritual experiences as guides for others, whereas Alcott was much more interested in conversations he held as more or less public events.

In American Renaissance poetry, too, we often find evidence most akin to these various esoteric traditions. Melville allowed his poetry to give voice to views that he did not countenance openly in his fiction, for instance in "Fragments of a Lost Gnostic Poem," "The New Rosicrucians," or "Clarel." Melville was an author known for offering readers many voices rather than one, and it is not surprising that some of his are decidedly esoteric in nature, even if his own views were probably most clearly set forth in that sardonic riddle of a book, *The Confidence Man*. Fuller also wrote poems indisputably esoteric in inspiration, perhaps most notably "Winged Sphynx," "My Seal Ring," "Sub Rosa-Crux," and above all "Double Triangle," probably the best of her poems, whose accompaniment is the esoteric illustration that originally appeared at the beginning of *Woman in the Nineteenth Century*. Surprisingly, however, some of the most experiential esoteric poems were written by Emily Dickinson, who like Melville was very much influenced by the entertaining author on all manner of esoteric lore, Sir Thomas Browne. Dickinson was not inclined toward scholarly inquiry into Hermeticism or theosophy, but she was interested in such topics as witchcraft and posthumous existence, and if her life was outwardly stationary, inwardly she definitely journeyed on a spiritual and psychological path that resembles at times a kind of Christian shamanism not far from Christian theosophy.[4]

Many scholars have come to use the term "American romanticism" to refer to these major figures of the American Renaissance, and when we consider these figures in light of Western esotericism, the term "American romanticism" becomes particularly apropos. These authors of the American Renaissance certainly shared a great deal with the European romantics. Emerson's indebtedness to Goethe and Novalis was, as we have seen, particularly great; and with them, as with the English romantics, Emerson and his fellow American writers of the time shared many central themes. Primary among these themes is that of subjectivity as opposed to the objectification that characterizes scientific rationalism and industrialism. Confronted with the "dark Satanic mills" of modern industry, the English romantics, particularly Wordsworth, counterposed a wholly different understanding of nature as refuge for the individual, one in which the individual aesthetic sense is intensified. Blake, on the other hand, counterposed the industrialist and rationalist views of nature with an imaginative mythology of his own that owed a great deal, as Kathleen Raine and other scholars have shown, to Neoplatonic, Hermetic, and especially theosophic currents.[5]

The American romantics and at least some of the German and English romantics of the late-eighteenth and nineteenth centuries shared an indebtedness to Western esoteric traditions. This indebtedness has not yet been adequately surveyed and analyzed, but it is certainly the case that figures like Blake and Novalis, Emerson, Alcott, and Fuller, were much more familiar with and influenced by Hermetic and theosophic currents of thought than many literary scholars commonly acknowledge.[6] When we consider the emergence of scientific rationalism and industrialism, particularly in the late-eighteenth and nineteenth centuries, we can easily see why some authors—who saw such objectifying worldviews not only as limited but also as destructive to humanity and the natural world—would look for pre-existing traditions that could be seen as alternatives. The various Western esoteric currents are the obvious first choice. In Hermeticism, alchemy, and theosophy, one finds ways of seeing nature—chiefly couched in terms of profound correspondences between humanity, nature, and the divine—far different from those of industrialism.

Yet to say that some English and German romantics, like some American romantics, were indebted to Western esoteric traditions does not make any of them Western esotericists. That Emerson, Blake, and Novalis drew upon esotericism in order to create their literary works is certain; yet they remain literary figures, drawing upon a host of prior traditions in order to create their unique works. What is more, there are some major differences between these authors, or for that matter, between the various authors of the American Renaissance and the Western esoteric traditions on which they drew. Chiefly, romanticism is distinguished from esotericism by its subjectivity or emphasis on individualism. Romanticism is a literary, intellectual, and aesthetic reaction against rationalist-industrialist civilization, and as such fundamentally counterposes subjectification to the objectifying tendency that gave rise to scientific rationalism and industrialism. The romantic takes refuge in the individual psyche, seen most clearly in isolation in nature, in this way opposing to the objectification of the world the subjectivity of the poet.

However, Western esotericism is not about subjectification or objectification, but about the transcendence of both. As such, esotericism could be seen as having given birth both to industrialism (objectification), on the one hand,

and to romanticism (subjectification), on the other. If the predecessors of New England factories are to be found in the laboratories of New England alchemists, so, too, the predecessors of romantic poets are to be found in the poetry and prose of the Hermeticists and alchemists of previous centuries. In some sense, one can say that both extremes—of subjectification and objectification, of romanticism and industrialism—emerge out of what one finds in Western esoteric traditions, which together chart a course between Scylla on the one hand and Charybdis on the other. What is more, the kind of literature that emerges from the Hermetic or alchemical traditions is peculiarly parabolic and enigmatic, and is not easily analyzed in the same way as modern literary works. It is of a different nature: it belongs as much to religion as to literature, and as much to neither as to both.[7]

Thus far, I have focused primarily on literary implications, but now it is time to turn to the religious implications of Western esotericism in the American Renaissance. As we saw in my book *American Transcendentalism and Asian Religions*, as well as in such works as Luedtke's *Nathaniel Hawthorne and the Romance of the Orient* (1989) and in a number of other recent works of scholarship, Asian religious traditions and cultures very much influenced the American Renaissance in general and American Transcendentalism in particular. However, what has not been adequately stressed is how Western esoteric traditions represent hermeneutic means to understand religious traditions other than those of Judaism and Christianity. Antoine Faivre has traced the figure of Hermes throughout western history and shown how the figurations of Hermes emerge again and again in European culture, marking the appearance of Hermeticism and alchemy as spiritual traditions in their own right, as well as meeting points for different religions.[8]

In the first issue (March 1697) of the *Acta Philadelphica*, the official publication of the Philadelphian society in London under the direction of Jane Leade and Francis Lee, the very first page begins with the following sentence:

> We having an Establish'd Correspondency in most parts of *Europe*, relating to the Affairs of Religion, and most specially to such Passages therein Emerging, as are less Heeded, and Known by the Generality of *Christendom* (so called:) and likewise to the Extraordinary Appearances of *God* in Nature, and to the Antient *Mystick Knowledge* of *the Eastern Nations*, which we do esteem no contemtible Key, towards a Right and Fundamental Understanding of [a] great Part of the *Sacred Writings*, both of the *Old and New Testament*: Hereupon . . . we have been mov'd . . . to bring forth our Light.[9]

This emphasis on the "*Antient Mystick Knowledge* of the *Eastern Nations*" as "no contemtible Key" to Christianity is an attitude we find taken up again with even greater vigor by the American Transcendentalists. In his journals, Emerson writes warmly about the thought of "this band of grandees," beginning with Hermes—and including Plato, Proclus, and the other Platonists—whose "truth and grandeur" is "proved by its scope & applicability; for it commands more even than our dear old bibles."[10]

Although Emerson embraces Hermes here, the various Western esoteric traditions have often occupied a precarious place on the margin of mainstream European religions, even in the case of Christian theosophy. Thus, esoteric practitioners always have found themselves attacked by, shunned by, or negotiating a place in relation to more dogmatic, less gnostic forms of Christianity or Judaism. At the same time, one finds Hermeticists, alchemists, Kabbalists, and Rosicrucians all often taking a position not only of tolerance, but also of embracing truth wherever they found it. Esotericists were in contact with and drew not only from Spanish mysticism, but also from Islamic alchemical traditions centuries before one found such cross-cultural or cross-religious possibilities realized in modern society. Yet this very openness to other traditions provided ample cause for more sectarian believers to attack them.

Out of this openness to other traditions, and out of this marginal position of Hermeticism and the other forms of esotericism, emerged the universalism of the American Transcendentalists. It is clear from all that we have seen of the various kinds of American Transcendentalism that the movement was defined both in its antebellum and postbellum forms by its emphasis on the importance of comparative religion and an overarching thesis that inherent in all the various forms of religions around the world is universal human religion. It is true that the later forms of Transcendentalism espoused by authors like Samuel Johnson or William Rounseville Alger had little directly to do with Hermeticism or Neoplatonism, but this was because the earlier Transcendentalism of Emerson and Alcott emerged out of Western esotericism to embrace world religious traditions and such Asian religious works as the Bhagavad Gita or the Upanishads. After Emersonian universalism had been established, it was easy for the later Transcendentalists to write with footings based in it and to ignore its Western esoteric predecessors.

What separates the whole of Transcendentalism from its Western esoteric predecessors is its radical individualism. It is true that alchemical laboratory work, for example, is generally practiced by solitaries, but it represents nonetheless a particular discipline that the individual seeks to understand and practice properly: the individual exists in relation to the particular tradition he practices. By contrast, American Transcendentalism was an individual matter, as well, but it was a radical individualism because the individual existed vis à vis many traditions at once, yet only intellectually, not in practice. Thus, American Transcendentalism is heir to European and English romanticism, not least in its extreme subjectivity. The Transcendentalist individual was free to pick and choose what was important in any world religious tradition, whereas the various Western esoteric traditions were at heart about practice and experience in a particular discipline, whether in a laboratory, with an astrological chart, or in a theosophic spiritual community. Transcendentalism represents a startling departure from previous approaches to various religious traditions because it did not require practice, but was strictly an intellectual affair.

What I have said here about American Transcendentalism in relation to Western esotericism is also true of the American Renaissance more generally.

That is, all of the various writers we have discussed, with the possible exceptions of Alcott and Fuller, have in common the fact that none of them actually practiced any kind of esoteric discipline, but rather extracted from the various esoteric traditions whatever happened to suit their particular kind of writing. Given the prominence of Western esotericism in colonial America, it is reasonable to suggest that the writers of the American Renaissance drew on themes and traditions that were still part of the American ambience in the mid-nineteenth century, even if their actual practice had largely, though certainly not completely, disappeared. The search for an elixir of immortality, knowledge of posthumous conditions, Mesmerism, Hermeticism, Neoplatonism, and Gnosticism all were transmuted into literature that reflected, spoke to, and in some sense immortalized the ambience in which it was created. However, the particular kind of esotericism refracted into this literature was purely a matter of the individual author's inclination, and remained strictly intellectual.

This individual refraction of Western esoteric traditions into broader society via general literature is in some respects a new and peculiarly modern phenomenon. Of course, in the past one finds, for example, the publication of alchemical treatises or poetry or illustrations, but those were in general intended almost exclusively for other alchemists. What defines modern literature is precisely its appropriation of such themes into exclusively literary works—the emergence of literature for its own sake rather than for the specific transmission of any kind of particular esoteric tradition. This transfer of esotericism from daily American experience to the realm of literary imagination has been little remarked upon, but remains one of the primary elements of nineteenth-century American literature. Very probably this transfer prepared the way for the turn of the century, when in all the major American cities semi-secret lodges (Masonic and other) outnumbered churches, and for the twentieth century, when esoteric practices like astrology and even alchemy again became a part of many Americans' lives.[11]

As contemporary scholarship continues to unveil more and more of the hidden connections between the Western esoteric traditions and the European, English, and American literary currents between the seventeenth and twentieth centuries, we undoubtedly will see in ever greater detail just how deeply intertwined are the twin currents of esotericism and literature. Indeed, the extent of modern literature's indebtedness to esoteric traditions ultimately may prove to be of great significance in developing a comprehensive theory of literature and religion. I have made some preliminary effort in that direction in *Western Esotericism, Literature, and Consciousness*, which argues that the Western esoteric traditions, including alchemy, Hermeticism, Kabbalah, Rosicrucianism, and theosophy, all emerge out of and reflect what we may call a gnosis of the written word. Thus, we may see that the influence of the Western esoteric traditions on the American Renaissance is only one episode in a long history, a history whose end is nowhere in sight and the study of which will prove fruitful indeed.

Notes

Chapter 1

1. John L. Brooke, *The Refiner's Fire: The Making of Mormon Cosmology, 1644–1844* (Cambridge: Cambridge University Press, 1994); Michael Quinn, *Early Mormonism and the Magic World View* (Salt Lake City: Signature Books, 1987).

Chapter 2

1. See Antoine Faivre, *Access to Western Esotericism* (Albany: State University of New York Press, 1994); for a less comprehensive and organized, but still stimulating work, see Dan Merkur, *Gnosis: An Esoteric Tradition of Mystical Visions and Unions* (Albany: State University of New York Press, 1993). Very useful are Antoine Faivre and J. Needleman, eds., *Modern Esoteric Spirituality* (New York: Crossroad, 1992); Karl Frick, *Licht und Finsternis*, 2 vols. (Graz, Germany: Akademisches, 1978); and Will-Erich Peuckert, *Pansophie*, 2d ed. (Berlin: Erich Schmidt, 1956), as well as Jean-Paul Corsetti, *Histoire de l'ésotérisme et des sciences occultes* (Paris: Larousse, 1992).

2. See Arthur Versluis, *Wisdom's Children: A Christian Esoteric Tradition* (Albany: State University of New York Press, 1999), the first complete introductory survey of theosophic history and doctrines in English, and *Theosophia: Hidden Dimensions of Christianity* (Hudson, N.Y.: Lindisfarne, 1994).

3. See Garth Fowden, *The Egyptian Hermes* (Cambridge: Cambridge University Press, 1987).

4. On Paracelsus, see Andrew Weeks, *Paracelsus: Speculative Theory and the Crisis of the Early Reformation* (Albany: State University of New York Press, 1997), useful at least for its historical information, if not for a sympathetic understanding of Paracelsian writings.

5. *The Hermetic Museum*, trans. Arthur Edward Waite (York Beach: Weiser, 1991), pp. 313–14.

6. See Arthur Versluis, "Christian Theosophy and Ancient Gnosis," *Studies in Spirituality* 7 (1997), pp. 228–41.

7. Frances Yates, *The Rosicrucian Enlightenment* (London: Routledge, 1972), p. 220.

8. Yates, Rosicrucian Enlightenment, p. 238.

9. Marsha Keith Schuchard, "Freemasonry, Secret Societies, and the Continuity of the Occult Traditions in English Literature," Ph.D. diss., University of Texas, Austin, p. 191.

10. See Edmond Mazet, "Freemasonry and Esotericism," in Faivre and Needleman, *Modern Esoteric Spirituality*, p. 268.

11. Letter of G. A. Beyer, 14 November 1769, in R. Tafel, *Documents Concerning Swedenborg* (London: Swedenborg Society, 1875), 2.279–280.

12. Signe Toksvig, *Emanuel Swedenborg: Scientist and Mystic* (New Haven: Yale University Press, 1948), p. 83.

13. Toksvig, *Emanuel Swedenborg*, p. 234.

14. Tafel, *Documents*, document 314, p. 1035.

15. *New Jerusalem Magazine* (44): 175–76, cited in M. Beck Block, *The New Church in the New World: Swedenborgianism in America* (New York: Holt, 1932), pp. 74–75.

Chapter 3

1. Daniel Leeds, *The Temple of Wisdom for the Little World, in Two Parts* (Philadelphia: Bradford, 1688), preface, p. 1.

2. Leeds, *Temple of Wisdom*, p.1.

3. Leeds, *Temple of Wisdom*, pp. 6–7.

4. Leeds, *Temple of Wisdom*, p. 37.

5. See Arthur Versluis, *Theosophia: Hidden Dimensions of Christianity* (Hudson, N.Y.: Lindisfarne, 1994), and, for an introduction to and survey of the theosophic tradition in Germany, England, and America, *Wisdom's Children: A Christian Esoteric Tradition* (Albany: State University of New York Press, 1999).

6. Leeds, *Temple of Wisdom*, p. 112.

7. Leeds, *Temple of Wisdom*, p. 116.

8. Leeds, *Temple of Wisdom*, p. 124.

9. See, for instance, the section in Versluis, *Wisdom's Children* on "hierohistory" and "metahistory." See also Johann Georg Gichtel's *Theosophia Practica*, 7 vols. (Amsterdam, 1721).

10. See Christian Lehman, Germantown and Roxborough Papers, 1742–1799, MS 61–1498, D-60, HSP No. 362, in the Historical Society of Pennsylvania Library collection.

11. John Heydon, *Theomagia, or, The temple of wisdome: in three parts, spiritual, celestial, and elemental: containing the occular powers of the angels of astromancy in the telesmatical sculpture of the Persians and Egyptians: the mysterious vertues of the characters of the stars . . . the knowledge of the Rosie Crucian physick, and the miraculous secrets in nature* (London: Printed by T. M. for Henry Brome, 1663–64), 1.57–59.

12. Heydon, *Theomagia*, 1.60.

13. Heydon, *Theomagia*, 1.2.

14. H. Tincom and M. Tincom, *Historic Germantown: A Survey of the German Township* (Philadelphia: American Philosophical Society, 1955), pp. 10, 18.

15. See, for example, Jacob Taylor's *Almanack and Ephemeris of the Motions of the Sun and Moon* (Philadelphia: Bradford, 1746), in which Taylor denigrates astrology as spurious and idolatrous, even as he provides an ephemeris for astrological purposes!

16. Jonathan Mitchell, "Continuation of Sermons upon the Body of Divinity," 1655–58, 8 February 1656, in Massachusetts Historical Society collection.

17. Cotton Mather, *The Boston Ephemeris, an Almanack for the Year of the Christian Aera 1683* (Boston, 1683).

18. See David Hall, *Worlds of Wonder, Days of Judgment: Popular Religious Belief in Early New England* (New York: Knopf, 1989), p. 59; see also Marion Stowell, *Early American Almanacs: The Colonial Weekday Bible* (New York: B. Franklin, 1976), and George Kittredge, *The Old Farmer and his Almanack* (Cambridge: Harvard University Press, 1920). Examples of such early almanacs include Samuel Cheever, *An Almanack for the Year of Our Lord 1660* (Cambridge, Mass.: 1660) and Israel Chauncy, *An Almanack of the Coelestial Motions for the Year of the Christian Aera 1663* (Cambridge, Mass., 1663).

19. Samuel Morison, ed., *Charles Morton's Compendium Physicæ*, Colonial Society of Massachusetts Publications, no. 33 (Boston, 1940): 29.

20. P. Boyer and S. Nissenbaum, *The Salem Witchcraft Papers: Verbatim Transcripts of the Legal Documents of the Salem Witchcraft Outbreak* (New York: Da Capo Press, 1977), 2.397.

21. See Samuel Willys Collection, *Records of Trials for Witchcraft in Connecticut*, 7 August 1668, no. 7, Connecticut State Library, Hartford.

22. Deodat Lawson, Christ's Fidelity the Only Shield against Satan's Malignity (Boston, 1692), p. 73.

23. A notable exception to the lack of attention to alchemy in the New World is William R. Newman, *Gehennical Fire: The Lives of George Starkey, an American Alchemist in the Scientific Revolution* (Cambridge: Harvard University Press, 1994). Also important are the numerous articles by Ronald Sterne Wilkinson, chiefly in *Ambix*, from 1960 to 1972. On European alchemy there are numerous publications, many relatively recent. A useful example in English is Claudia Kren, *Alchemy in Europe: A Guide to Research* (New York: Garland, 1990). For an annotated survey of the field, see Antoine Faivre, *Access to Western Esotericism* (Albany: State University of New York Press, 1992), pp. 305–11.

24. Hugh Trevor-Roper, *Religion, the Reformation, and Social Change* (London: Macmillan, 1967), p. 240.

25. See Ronald Sterne Wilkinson, "The Hartlib Papers and Seventeenth-Century Chemistry," *Ambix* 15.1 (February 1968): 54–69; and 17.2 (July 1970): 85–110.

26. Wilkinson, "Hartlib Papers," part 1.57.

27. Wilkinson, "Hartlib Papers," part 1.61.

28. See Ronald Sterne Wilkinson, "The Alchemical Library of John Winthrop, Jr., 1606–1676," *Ambix* 16.1 (February 1963): 33–51.

29. Benjamin Tompson, *A Funeral Tribute to the Honourable Dust of the Most Charitable Christian, Unbiased Politican, and unimitable Pyrotechnist John Winthrope esq.* (Boston, 1676).

30. See Newman, *Gehennical Fire*, for the argument in favor of Starkey as Eirenaeus Philalethes. However, in "The Problem of the Identity of Eirenaeus Philalethes," *Ambix* 13.1 (February 1964): 24–43, Wilkinson outlines a number of reasons why Winthrop may have actually written those treatises.

31. See William C. Black, *The Younger John Winthrop* (New York: Columbia University Press, 1966), p. 196.

32. Jonathan Brewster to John Winthrop Jr., 14 January 1656, *Massachusetts Historical Society Collections* 7 (1865): 72–73.

33. Brewster to Winthrop, 14 January 1656, p. 75, cited by Wilkinson, "Alchemical Library," p. 47.

34. Newman, *Gehennical Fire*, p. 43.

35. See Newman, *Gehennical Fire*, pp. 44–45.

36. Cited from Kittredge's notes at Harvard by Newman, *Gehennical Fire*, p. 48.

37. Translated from Latin in Newman, *Gehennical Fire*, pp. 250–51.

38. Historical Society of Pennsylvania collection, donated by Harold Gillingham, ms. n.d., n.p, under the heading "Rosicrucians."

39. See Ronald Sterne Wilkinson, "New England's Last Alchemists," *Ambix* 10.3 (October 1962): 129; Morison, *Charles Morton's Compendium Physicae*.

40. Franklin B. Dexter, ed., *The Literary Diary of Ezra Stiles* (New York, 1901), 3.266–67.

41. Thomas Thumb, *The Monster of Monsters* (Boston, 1754), p. 15.

42. See Franklin B. Dexter, ed., *The Writings of Benjamin Franklin* (New York, 1907), 6.105–6.

43. See Dexter, *Literary Diary of Ezra Stiles*, 2.216.

44. Quoted in Cheryl Oreovicz, "Investigating 'The America of Nature': Alchemy in Early American Poetry," in *Puritan Poets and Poetics*, ed. Peter White (University Park: Pennsylvania State University Press, 1985), p. 104.

45. On the poetry of Edward Taylor, see Randall Clack, "The Transformation of Soul: Edward Taylor and the Opus Alchemicum Celestial in Meditation 1:8," *Seventeenth-Century News* 50 (1992): 6–10—in part a response to Cheryl Oreovicz, "Edward Taylor and the Alchemy of Grace," ibid., 34 (1976): 33–36. See also Joan Del Fattore, "John Webster's Metallographica: A Source for Alchemical Imagery in the Preparatory Meditations," *Early American Literature* 18 (1983–84): 231–41.

46. *Anonimus' travels throu' Europe and America, and some visions of many heavenly mansions in the house of God. . . . How he conversed with the inhabitants of the other world, and found, that their respective works had actually followed them* (Ephrata, Pa.: 1793) AC 152, in the Julius Sachse Collection, Historical Society of Pennsylvania, p. 4.

47. *Anonimus' travels*, pp. 8–9.

48. This was also a name taken by an earlier Pennsylvania sect, that of the "Newborns" led by Matthias Bauman (d. 1727). See the discussion below.

49. See J. Sachse, trans., *The Diarium of Magister Johannes Kelpius*, in *The Pennsylvania-German Society, Proceedings and Addresses*, vol. 25 (Lancaster, Pa.,: 1917).

50. See for example, J. McArthur Jr., "The Enigma of Kelpius' Cave," *Germantown Crier* 3 (summer 1983): 54–56.

51. See Johannes Kelpius, *A Short, Easy, and Comprehensive Method of Prayer*, trans. Christopher Witt (Philadelphia, 1761).

52. See Julius Sachse, *The German Pietists of Provincial Pennsylvania* (Philadelphia: Sachse, 1895), pp. 72 ff.

53. See Frances Yates, *The Rosicrucian Enlightenment* (London: Routledge, 1972), esp. pp. 144–50.

54. See James Ernst, *Ephrata: A History* (Allentown: Pennsylvania German Folklore Society, 1963), p. 38.

55. See E. G. Alderfer, *The Ephrata Commune: An Early American Counterculture* (Pittsburgh: University of Pittsburgh Press, 1985), p. 35; citing Julius Sachse, *The German Sectarians of Pennsylvania* (Philadelphia, 1900), 1.73.

56. Julius Sachse discusses some aspects of Ephrata magical practices in *German Pietists*, III.372 ff. See also Versluis, *Wisdom's Children*, 3.iii and 3.iv.

57. Sachse, *German Sectarians of Pennsylvania*, 1.112, 1.207.

58. For a general comparison of Ephrata and the Moravian community in Pennsylvania, see Alderfer, *Ephrata Commune*, pp. 78 ff.

59. From Conrad Beissel, *Mysterion Anomias: The Mystery of Lawlessness or, Lawless AntiChrist Discover'd & Disclosed*, trans. M. Welfare. (Philadelphia: Bradford, 1729), p. 20.

60. Beissel, *Mysterion Anomia*, pp. 27, 31.

61. James Bolton's *Treatise on the Universal Restoration* (Ephrata, Pa., 1793), in the Cassell Collection, AC 156, pp. 3–4.

62. Bolton, *Treatise on the Universal Restoration*, p. 7.

63. James Ernst, *Ephrata: A History* (Allentown: Pennsylvania German Folklore Society, 1963), p. 341.

64. "The Cloister Hospital, 1777," (Ephrata, Pa.: Restored Press, 1976).

65. Gichtel in particular denigrated sectarianism and had an esoteric theory to explain why sectarianism prevents spiritual awakening; on which topic, see Versluis, *Wisdom's Children: A Christian Esoteric Tradition* (Albany: State University of New York Press, 1999), III.v, "Penetrating the Merely Astral."

66. Benjamin Franklin, *The Autobiography of Benjamin Franklin* (New Haven: Yale University Press, 1964), p. 157.

67. Franklin, *Autobiography*, p. 190.

68. Franklin, *Autobiography*, p. 191.

69. On the Nova Scotia awakening, see Gordon Stewart, ed., *The Great Awakening in Nova Scotia* (Toronto: Champlain Society, 1982); on New England more generally, see Stephen Marini, *Radical Sects of Revolutionary New England* (Cambridge: Harvard University Press, 1982).

70. Henry Alline, *Henry Alline: Selected Writings*, ed. G. A. Rawlyk (New York: Paulist Press, 1987), p. 173. One might recall that Milton drew on Böhme too, on which see Margaret Bailey, *Milton and Jakob Boehme*, (New York: Haskell, 1964).

71. John Wesley, *The Letters of Rev. John Wesley*, ed. John Telford (London: Epworth, 1931), 8.182.

72. For examples of theosophic books published in America during the nineteenth century, see Elimelech [E. Eckerling], *Die aufehende Lilie, ist ein Theosophischer Discurs und Unpartheyisches Zeugniss zur Behauptung der Bibel und des Welt-Erloeser* (Lancaster, Pa.: Hamilton, 1815); Böhme, *Christosophia* (Ephrata, Pa.: Jacob Ruth, 1811–12); *Ein systematischer Auszug des . . . Theosophi J. Böhmens Sämmt. Schriften* (Ephrata, Pa.: Joseph Bauman, 1822–24); Karl Eckhartshausen, *Die Wolke über dem Heiligthum* (Philadelphia: W. Mentz, 1841). One also finds astrological treatises in German published in Pennsylvania during this time—for instance, Eberhart Walpern, *Glucks-Rad oder Würfel-Buch: durch welches man nach astrologisher Art . . . abeheilt sind, eine Antwort finden kann. . . .* (Reading, Pa.: Heinrich Sage, 1820).

73. What follows is drawn from Karl Arndt, "George Rapp's Harmony Society," in *America's Communal Utopias*, ed. D. Pitzer (Chapel Hill: University of North Carolina Press, 1997), pp. 57–88. Author of numerous studies on the subject, Arndt remains the primary scholar of the Harmony Society.

74. Arndt, "George Rapp's Harmony Society," p. 75.

75. Arndt, "George Rapp's Harmony Society," p. 76.

76. Faivre, *Access to Western Esotericism*, p. 79.

77. Faivre, *Access to Western Esotericism*, p. 79.

78. Faivre, *Access to Western Esotericism*, pp. 79–80.

79. Appendix to Yates, *Rosicrucian Enlightenment*, pp. 242, 249.

80. Yates, *Rosicrucian Enlightenment*, p. 257.

81. Franklin, *Autobiography*, p. 146.

82. Franklin, *Autobiography*, p. 162.

83. See Bobby Demott, *Freemasonry in American Culture and Society* (Lanham, Md.: University Press of America, 1986), p. 15.

84. See on Franklin, Bernard Fay, *Franklin: the Apostle of Modern Times* (Boston: Little, Brown, 1930), p. 167; see also Melvin Johnson, *The Beginnings of Freemasonry in America* (New York: Doran, 1924), pp. 58–60.

85. Demott, *Freemasonry*, p. 17.

86. Bernard Fay, *Revolution and Freemasonry, 1680–1800* (Boston: Little, Brown, 1935), p. 150.

87. Fay, *Revolution and Freemasonry*, pp. 238 ff.

88. See Paul Goodman, *Towards a Christian Republic: Antimasonry and the Great Transition in New England, 1826–1836* (New York: Oxford University Press, 1988), pp. 3 ff.

89. Goodman, *Towards a Christian Republic*, pp. 5 ff., 8.

Chapter 4

1. John Aubrey, *Miscellanies upon the following subjects* (London: E. Castle, 1696); Henry Cornelius Agrippa, *Three Books of Occult Philosophy*, trans. James Freake (London, 1651).

2. Wouter Hanegraaff, *New Age Religion and Western Culture: Esotericism in the Mirror of Secular Thought* (Leiden: Brill, 1996), p. 436.

3. That the connection between necromancy and spiritualism occurred to people of that time is clear from such articles as A. Peabody's "Modern Necromancy," *North American Review* 80 (April 1855): 523–24.

4. Emma Hardinge Britten, *The Autobiography of Emma Hardinge Britten* (London: Heywood, 1900), p. 4.

5. Britten, *Autobiography*, p. 54.

6. This was also the thesis of traditionalist René Guénon, who in his works *L'Erreur Spirite* (1923; rprt., Paris: Etudes Traditionelles, 1952), and *Le Théosophisme, histoire d'une pseudo-religion* (1921; rprt., Paris: Editions Traditionelles, 1982), claims that the occult group the Hermetic Brotherhood of Luxor was responsible for the outbreak of spiritualism, and that Britten was a member; see the first work, p. 50, and the second, p. 95; see also Joscelyn Godwin, *The Theosophical Enlightenment* (Albany: State University of New York Press, 1994), ch. 10.

7. Christopher Bamford, Introduction to C. G. Harrison, *The Transcendental Universe* (1893; rprt., Hudson, N.Y.: Lindisfarne, 1993), p. 13.

8. See Antoine Faivre, *Access to Western Esotericism* (Albany: State University of New York Press, 1994), p. 77.

9. See Ernst Benz, *The Theology of Electricity* (Allison Park, Pa.: Pickwick, 1989).

10. Wouter Hanegraaff, *New Age Religion and Western Culture: Esotericism in the Mirror of Secular Thought* (Leiden: Brill, 1996) pp. 433, 434.

11. See James Webb, *The Occult Underground* (LaSalle, Ill.: Open Court, 1974), p. 27.

12. Webb, *The Occult Underground*, p. 31, from *The Principles of Nature, Her Divine Revelations, and a Voice to Mankind* (London: Chapman, 1847), 2.734.

13. Davis, *Principles of Nature*, 2.699.

14. Webb, *The Occult Underground*, p. 125.

15. Thomas Lake Harris, *The Arcana of Christianity: An Unfolding of the Celestial Sense of the Divine Word*, 2 vols. (New York: New Church, 1858–67), 1.9.

16. *New Jerusalem Messenger*, now the *New Church Messenger*, 1.349–50; 2.108.

17. See Johann Georg Gichtel, *Eine kurze Eröffnung und Anweisung der dryen Principien und Welten in Menschen* [*A Brief Opening and Demonstration of the Three Principles and Worlds in Man*] (Leipzig, 1696/1779), a translation of which Versluis is currently preparing for publication.

18. See Hanna Whitall Smith, *Religious Fanaticism: Extracts from the Papers of Hannah Whitall Smith*, ed. R. Strachy (London: Faber, 1928), p. 121.

19. Thomas Lake Harris, *The Millennial Age: Twelve Discourses on the Spiritual and Social Aspects of the Times* (New York: New Church, 1860), p. 142.

20. Harris, *Millennial Age*, p. 170.

21. I have examined most of the books published by Harris, including *The Arcana of Christianity*, 2 vols. (New York: Brotherhood of the New Life, 1867), and *The Breath of God With Man* (New York: Brotherhood, 1867). There are a number of interesting passages in these works, including Harris's spirit visions of the dead in the hells or heavens. See for instance *Arcana of Christianity*, 1.238, where he meets the dead Margaret Fuller, or 1.434 ff., where he meets dead American Indians from the time of the American Revolution. Or, see Harris's implacable criticisms of contemporary American Christian society, which sent forth a "plague" that "decimates the so-called pagan world." "Wherever there is on the earth a people which the so-called Christian nations have not defiled by lust . . . enslaved for dominion, and extirpated by slavery, and robbed for riches, they are now endeavouring to *exploit* it by a civilized system, which is the scientific combination and final consequence of them all" (*Arcana of Christianity*, 2.323). As for poetry, one might compare Harris's poem in *Breath of God* (p. 96) with Margaret Fuller's poem "Double Triangle." The last stanza of Harris's poem reads:

Heavenly King and Heavenly Queen
Father, Mother, two in one,
First in Deity are seen,
Beaming from the Bridal Sun.

In the same book he also admits that in "the grand old faiths of the Orient" there are indeed varying degrees of veracity and morality (p. 73). Harris is a significant figure in American esotericism, and deserves more detailed study than we can offer here.

22. See John Patrick Deveney, *Paschal Beverly Randolph* (Albany: State University of New York Press, 1997), p. 395.

23. Deveney, *Paschal Beverly Randolph*, p. 440.

24. See, for instance, Paschal Beverly Randolph, *The Ansairetic Mystery, A New Revelation Concerning Sex!* (Toledo: Liberal, [1873]), and *Eulis! The History of Love* (Toledo: Randolph, 1874), as well as the French edition of *Magia Sexualis*, trans. Maria de Naglowska (1931; repr., St-Jean-de-Braye, France: Dangles, 1991), from which stemmed much of Randolph's influence on continental magical circles.

25. See Arthur Versluis, *The Mysteries of Love: Eros and Spirituality* (St. Paul: Grail, 1996), pp. 115 ff., on "Erotic Philosophy" in Christian theosophy, and from pp. 123 ff., on Christian theosophic parallels to Tantrism. In particular, see the discussion of the group that surrounded Eva von Buttlar in Germany, whose scandalous ap-

proach to sexuality is still little explored. This is the only discussion of the group in English.

Chapter 5

1. Ethan Allen Hitchcock, *Fifty Years in Camp and Field*, ed. W. A. Croffut (New York: Knickerbocker, 1909).

2. Hitchcock, *Fifty Years*, p. 51.

3. Hitchcock, *Fifty Years*, p. 71.

4. Hitchcock, *Fifty Years*, p. 189.

5. Hitchcock, *Fifty Years*, p. 404. It is interesting that Hitchcock, like Alcott, thought of Emerson in connection with "love of fame." Hitchcock and Alcott alike were interested in Hermeticism and neither were interested in being famous.

6. Hitchcock, *Fifty Years*, pp. 412–13.

7. Hitchcock, *Fifty Years*, p. 413.

8. Hitchcock, *Fifty Years*, p. 414.

9. Hitchcock, *Fifty Years*, p. 419.

10. Hitchcock, *Fifty Years*, p. 421.

11. Hitchcock, *Fifty Years*, p. 423.

12. Ethan Allen Hitchcock, *Remarks Upon Alchemy and the Alchemists Indicating a Method of Discovering the True Nature of Hermetic Philosophy; and Showing that the Search After the Philosopher's Stone Had Not For Its Object the Discovery of An Agent for the Transmutation of Metals. Being Also an Attempt to Rescure from Undeserved Opprobrium the Reputation of a Class of Extraordinary Thinkers in Past Ages* (Boston: Crosby, Nichols, 1857), pp. iv–v.

13. To see how spirituality and laboratory alchemy are intertwined, one may consult any of the major works of the classical western European alchemical tradition, among which one might cite in particular *The Hermetic Museum* (1678), a collection of major alchemical texts. To see spiritual alchemy without a laboratory context, one can turn to the Böhmean theosophic tradition, either to Böhme's own works like *Signatura Rerum*, or, for instance, to John Pordage's "Letter on the Philosophic Stone," included in Versluis, ed. *Wisdom's Book: The Sophia Anthology* (St. Paul: Paragon House, 2000).

14. A well-known exemplar of modern laboratory alchemy is Frater Albertus, whose *Alchemist's Handbook* (York Beach: Weiser, 1974), is widely used today.

15. Hitchcock, *Fifty Years*, pp. 288–89.

16. Hitchcock, *Fifty Years*, p. 291.

17. Hitchcock, *Swedenborg: A Hermetic Philosopher* (New York: Appleton, 1858), pp. 3–4.

18. On Swedenborg's influence on another American author of this time, see James William Taylor, *The Swedenborgianism of W. D. Howells* (Urbana: [n.p.] 1969).

19. Taylor, Swedenborgianism of Howells, p. 11.

20. Taylor, Swedenborgianism of Howells, p. 13.

21. Taylor, Swedenborgianism of Howells, p. 21.

22. Taylor, Swedenborgianism of Howells, p. 119.

23. Taylor, Swedenborgianism of Howells, p. 126.

24. Taylor, Swedenborgianism of Howells, p. 127.

25. Taylor, Swedenborgianism of Howells, p. 352.

26. Hitchcock, *Fifty Years*, pp. 482–83. See also Versluis, *The Hermetic Book of Nature* (St. Paul: Grail, 1997), esp. pp. 37–54.

27. See Chapters 9 ("Greaves") and 10 ("Alcott") in this volume.

28. Hitchcock, *Fifty Years*, p. 182.

29. Hitchcock, *Fifty Years*, p. 432.

30. Hitchcock, *Fifty Years*, p. 444.

31. See Marsha Keith Schuchard, "Freemasonry, Secret Societies, and the Continuity of the Occult Traditions in English Literature," (Ph.D. diss., University of Texas at Austin, 1975), p. 578.

Chapter 6

1. See Kent Ljungquist, "Prospects for the Study of Edgar Allan Poe," *Resources for American Literary Study* 21 (1995) 2: 173–88.

2. See Ethan Allen Hitchcock, *Fifty Years in Camp and Field*, ed. W. A. Croffut (New York: Knickerbocker, 1909), p. 63.

3. See Hitchcock, *Fifty Years*, p. 50.

4. On some of these themes in Poe, see Barton Levi St. Armand, "Dragon and the Uroboros: Themes of Metamorphosis in 'Arthur Gordon Pym,'" *American Transcendentalism Quarterly* 37 (1978): 57–71.

5. See Edgar Allan Poe, *The Complete Tales and Poems of Edgar Allan Poe* (New York: Random House, 1938), p. 82.

6. Poe, *Complete Tales*, p. 85.

7. See, for more on Poe and alchemy, see Randall Clack, "'Strange Alchemy of the Brain': Poe and Alchemy," in *A Companion to Poe Studies*, ed. Peter White (Westport, Conn.: Greenwood Press, 1996), pp. 367–87. See also Randall Clack, "The Phoenix Rising: Alchemical Imagination in the Works of Edward Taylor, Edgar Allan Poe, and Nathaniel Hawthorne," Ph.D. diss., University of Connecticut, 1994.

8. Clack, "Strange Alchemy," pp. 90–91.

9. Clack, "Strange Alchemy," p. 93.

10. Edgar Allan Poe, *Essays and Reviews* (New York: Library of America, 1984), pp. 1410–12.

11. Poe, *Essays and Reviews*, p. 1367.

12. Patrick Quinn, *The French Face of Edgar Poe* (Carbondale: Southern Illinois University, 1957), p. 93.

13. Poe, *Essays and Reviews*, p. 576, from *Graham's Magazine*, May, 1842.

14. Poe, *Essays and Reviews*, p. 1343.

15. Poe, *Complete Tales*, p. 609.

16. Poe, *Complete Tales*, p. 441.

17. Poe, *Complete Tales*, p. 443.

18. Poe, *Complete Tales*, p. 444.

19. Poe, *Complete Tales*, p. 449.

20. Poe, *Complete Tales*, p. 451.

21. Poe, *Essays and Reviews*, pp. 587–88.

22. Edgar Allan Poe, *The Complete Works of Edgar Allan Poe*, 17 vols., ed. J. Harrison (New York: Society of English and French Literature, 1902), 15.260.

23. See Peter Sorensen, "William Morgan, Freemasonry, and 'The Cask of Amontillado,'" *Poe Studies* 22 (1989): 45–47.

24. Poe, *Works*, p. 457.

25. See Versluis, *Gnosis and Literature* (St. Paul: Grail, 1996), pp. 173 ff.

26. See Barton Levi St. Armand, "Usher Unveiled: Poe and the Metaphysic of Gnosticism," *Poe Studies* 5 (1972): 1–8; see also Michael Auer, "Angels and Beasts:

Gnosticism in American Literature," (Ph.D. diss., University of North Carolina, Chapel Hill, 1976).

27. St. Armand, "Usher Unveiled," p. 1.

28. See Plotinus, *Enneads*, 2.9.

29. Versluis, *Gnosis and Literature*, pp. 174–75.

30. Edgar Allan Poe, *Complete Poems of Edgar Allan Poe* (New York: Heritage, 1943), p. 14.

Chapter 7

1. Nathaniel Hawthorne, *The Letters of Nathaniel Hawthorne*, Centenary edition (Athens: Ohio State University Press, 1965–), 16.181.

2. Hawthorne, *Letters*, 17.382–83.

3. Hawthorne, *Letters*, 18.593.

4. See Nathaniel Hawthorne, *The Heart of Hawthorne's Journals*, ed. Newton Arvin (Boston: Houghton, 1929), p. 307.

5. Hawthorne, Heart of Hawthorne's Journals, p. 307.

6. Hawthorne, *Letters*, 9.230.

7. R. B. Heilman, "Hawthorne's 'The Birthmark': Science as Religion," *South Atlantic Quarterly*, 48 (1949): 575–83.

8. Hawthorne to G. W. Curtis, 14 July 1852, Fruitlands Museum, Harvard, Massachusetts.

9. *American Magazine of Useful and Entertaining Knowledge*, 2 (August 1836): 520, cited in Hawthorne, *Letters*, 13.558.

10. Hawthorne, *Letters*, 13.406.

11. Hawthorne, *Letters*, 13.408.

12. Hawthorne, *Letters*, 13:408.

13. Hawthorne, *Letters*, 13.424–25.

14. Hawthorne, *Letters*, 2.7.

15. Hawthorne, *Letters*, 2.8.

16. Hawthorne, *Letters*, 2.319.

17. Randall Clack, "The Alchemy of Love: Hawthorne's Hermetic Allegory of the Heart," *ESQ* 41 (1995): 331.

18. Clack, "Alchemy of Love," 331.

19. See Jeffrey Meikle, "Hawthorne's Alembic: Alchemical Images in *The House of the Seven Gables*," *ESQ* 26 (1980): 173–83.

20. Meikle, "Hawthorne's Alembic," 182.

21. See Luther Martin, "Hawthorne's Scarlet Letter: A is for Alchemy?" *American Transcendental Quarterly* 58 (1985): 31–42. Martin's reading is helpful, but one has to agree with Clack that Pearl is not the alchemical agent but rather a product of the alchemical union.

22. Hawthorne, *The Scarlet Letter* (New York: Norton, 1978), p. 183.

23. Hawthorne, *Scarlet Letter*, p. 185.

24. See Melinda Parsons and William Ramsey, "The Scarlet Letter and an Herbal Tradition," *ESQ* 29 (1983): 197–207.

25. Parsons and Ramsey, "Scarlet Letter," p. 126.

26. Hawthorne, *The Blithdale Romance*, centenary edition text (New York: Norton, 1978), p. 182.

27. Hawthorne, *Blithdale Romance*, p. 183.

to *Moby Dick: An Authoritative Text*, ed. H. Hayford and H. Parker (New York: Norton, 1967).

21. *Moby Dick*, pp. 416–17.

22. *Moby Dick*, pp. 416–17.

23. Jonas, *The Gnostic Religion*, p. 252.

24. Jonas, *The Gnostic Religion*, p. 255.

25. See, for instance, ch. 7 of *Nature*, entitled "Spirit," which includes in its beginning: "The aspect of nature is devout. Like the figure of Jesus, she stands with bended head, and hands folded upon the breast. The happiest man is he who learns from nature the lesson of worship." One can only imagine how the author of "Whiteness," in *Moby Dick*, would have scoffed at this.

26. Jonas, *The Gnostic Religion*, p. 255.

27. *Moby Dick*, ch. CXXXII, pp. 444–445. Note the inversion of the Neoplatonic "natural" versus the "spiritual" man here. The "natural" heart is "proper;" the "spiritual" heart is a "cozening" and "inscrutable" master, "cruel" and "remorseless." One imagines St. Augustine's reaction to this.

28. *Moby Dick*, pp. 444–45.

29. *Moby Dick*, pp. 444–45 (italics added).

30. *Moby Dick*, ch. CXXXIV, p. 459.

31. *Moby Dick*, ch. XXIX, XXXVI, pp. 111–14, 142.

32. *Moby Dick*, ch. XLII, pp. 168–69.

33. Cf. Sachs, *The Game of Creation*, app. I, ch. 7: "Ahab's Name," pp. 203 ff.; see also *Moby Dick*, ch. XVI, p. 77, vide Peleg's warning: "Look ye, lad: never say that name (Ahab) on board the *Pequod*. Never say it anywhere. Ahab did not name himself."

34. *Moby Dick*, ch. XLII, p. 169.

35. *Moby Dick*, p. 169 (italics added).

36. See Jonas, *The Gnostic Religion*, pp. 174 ff.

37. *Moby Dick*, ch. XLII.

38. *Moby Dick*, ch. XLII. Cf. Melville's talk with Hawthorne in Melville, *Melville Log*, p. 925, in which he says that he has not quite made up his mind to be annihilated. Parallel to this, cf. Jacques LaCarriere, *The Gnostics* (New York: Dutton, 1977), pp. 34 ff.

39. *Moby Dick*, ch. XLII, 169–70. The rant here against nature painting as a harlot seems a direct counterpoint to the lyricism of Emerson's *Nature*. That Emerson's own view is not so simple can be seen in "Illusions," which treats first of Platonic, then eastern perspectives of the world and of nature.

40. *Moby Dick*, ch. XLIII, pp. 170–71, a chapter that begins and ends in wordplay on "Tish" and "Hist"—anagrams for "Shit," says Sachs, in *The Game of Creation*, pp. 21, 77. Perhaps.

41. As discussed elsewhere, as an adolescent Emerson was taken in by popular accounts of Buddhism as annihilationism, as can be seen from his journal entries. When Thoreau translated part of the *Lotus Sutra* from the French in 1844 (it appeared in the *Dial* of that year), he translated "transcendence" as "annihilation," following the French translation of Burnouf. Temperamentally and logically, this annihilationism did not sit well with the Transcendentalists, as it did with Melville. Both Thoreau and Emerson changed perspectives. By the 1860s, Emerson was reading primarily eastern works and Thoreau had incorporated into *Walden* aspects of Hinduism and Buddhist monasticism, the latter of which Thoreau had taken from Hardy's work on that subject that he had in his own library. See especially "Higher Laws."

28. Hawthorne, *Blithdale Romance*, p. 209.

29. Hawthorne, *Blithdale Romance*, p. 222.

30. See B. F. and A. B. Lefcowitz, "Some Rents in the Ve:
Blithdale Romance, pp. 341–50, for links between prostitution and r

31. Samuel Chase Coale, *Hawthorne and Mesmerism* (Tuscalc
Alabama Press, 1998), pp. 92 ff.

32. Coale, *Hawthorne and Mesmerism*, p. 93.

33. On spiritualism and mesmerism as vulgarizations of prior
see Hanegraaff, *New Age Religion and Western Culture: Esotericis*
Secular Thought (Leiden: Brill, 1996), pp. 435–41, 484–90.

34. See the chapter "A Forest Walk" in Hawthorne, *Scarlet Le*

Chapter 8

1. Herman Melville, "The Apple-Tree Table," *Putnam's* 7 (M
Melville, *The Complete Stories*, ed. J. Leyda (New York, 1949): 409–

2. Herman Melville, *Collected Poems of Herman Melville*, e
(Chicago: Packard, 1947), p. 297.

3. Melville, *Collected Poems*, p. 299.

4. Herman Melville, "The Confidence Man: His Masquerade,"
Herman Melville (Evanston, Ill.: Northwestern Newberry, 1984), 10.

5. Melville, "Confidence Man," p. 7.

6. Melville, "Confidence Man," p. 21.

7. Melville, "Confidence Man," p. 194.

8. Melville, "Confidence Man," p. 242.

9. Melville, "Confidence Man," p. 243.

10. Quoted in Melville, "Confidence Man," p. 336, "Historical

11. Melville to Hawthorne, 1851, in Melville, *Writings of Melvi*

12. Melville to Hawthorne, 1851, in Melville, *Writings of Melvi*

13. Melanie Bloodgood, "Gnostic Nature of the World Vie
Themes of Herman Melville," Ph.D. diss., Oklahoma State Universi

14. Lawrance Thompson, *Melville's Quarrel with God* (Prin
University Press, 1952), p. 425.

15. Thompson, *Melville's Quarrel*, p. 425. Curiously, however, 1
little mention of Gnosticism, or of Melville's ambiguity toward natt
and, yes, toward God in this regard. Yet, demonstrably, Gnosticism
Melville's perspective.

16. Hans Jonas, *The Gnostic Religion* (Boston: Beacon, 1963), p.

17. Cf. Viola Sachs, *The Game of Creation: The Primeval Unlett*
Moby Dick, or, The Whale (Paris: Editions de la Maison des Sciences de
pp. 67–73, *passim*.

18. See, on the so-called hylic race, Jonas, *The Gnostic Religion*,
pp. 44 ff. See also the *Nag Hammadi Library*, ed. J. Robinson (New Yo
ticular "The Gospel of Philip," II.3:131–151, as well as the "Hy
Archons," 134:27–135:4, which begins, "Their lord is blind. Because c
norance and conceit, he says in the midst of his creation, "I am God."

19. Thomas Vargish, "Gnostic Mythos in Moby Dick" *PMLA* (.
276.

20. *Moby Dick*, ch. CXIX, pp. 416–17. All subsequent reference

42. Thompson, *Melville's Quarrel*, p. 350.

43. Melville, *Clarel: A Poem and Pilgrimage in the Holy Land*, vol. 12 in *The Writings of Herman Melville* (Evanston, Ill.: Northwestern University Press, 1991), I.276.

44. *Clarel* I.275.

45. Cf. Ungar's speech, *Clarel* II.249 ff., to wit:

Know / Whatever happen in the end,
Be sure "twill yield to one and all / new confirmation of the fall
Of Adam . . . In glut of all material arts
A civic barbarism may be:
Man disennobled, brutalised
By popular science—atheised / Into a smatterer—.

46. *Clarel* II. 20 ff.

47. *Clarel* II.22.

48. *Clarel* II.22.

49. *Clarel* II.24.

50. See *Moby Dick*, p. 13: "Meditation and water are wedded forever." See also Viola Sachs, *The Myth of America* (The Hague: Mouton, 1973).

51. Consider, for instance, the utter incongruity between Thompson's work and Nathalia Wright's *Melville's Use of the Bible*: we are suggesting here that the juncture between the two may well be Gnosticism, which allowed Melville to attack orthodoxy while remaining, more or less, Christian.

52. *Clarel* II.100.

53. Cf. Kurt Rudolph, *Gnosis: The Nature and History of Gnosticism*, trans. Robert McLachlan Wilson (San Francisco: Harper and Row, 1983); see also on Valentinian cosmology Jonas, *The Gnostic Religion*; Melville learned about Gnosticism in part by reading the strange and labyrinthine works of Pierre Bayle, the French Enlightenment scholar who brought Gnosticism to western attention again.

54. Cf. Thompson, *Melville's Quarrel*, pp. 179–80.

55. Cf. Melville's "Black Angel" in "The Trap," in *Moby Dick*; for a discussion of this, see Sachs, *Myth of America*, p. 53.

56. See Adrian Snodgrass, "Stellar and Temporal Symbolism in Traditional Architecture," (Ph.D. diss., University of Sydney, Australia, 1985), pp. 7 ff. Snodgrass writes that Platonism is "perhaps, more readily accessible to a Western mentality than are the doctrines of the Asian traditions, characterised as those doctrines are by the unfamiliar concept of non-dualism."

57. Bloodgood, *The Gnostic Nature of the World View*, p. 105; Werner Berthoff, *The Example of Melville* (Princeton: Princeton University Press, 1962), p. 9.

58. Meredith Bratcher, "The Demiurge: A Study of the Tradition from Plato to Joyce" (Ph.D. diss., Duke University, 1985), p. 199.

Chapter 9

1. Ralph Waldo Emerson, *Journals and Miscellaneous Notebooks*, ed., W. Gilman (Cambridge:, Harvard University Press, 1960), 8.254–55, hereafter cited as *JMN*.

2. See also Jackie Latham, "Emma Martin and Sacred Socialism: the Correspondence of James Pierrepont Greaves," *History Workshop Journal* 38 (fall 1994): 215–17.

3. Joel Myerson, "William Harry Harland's 'Bronson Alcott's English Friends,'" *Resources for American Literary Study* 7 (spring 1978): 24−60; see also Versluis, "Bronson Alcott and Jacob Böhme," *Studies in the American Renaissance* 16 (1993): 153−59.

4. See L. Stephen and S. Lee., eds., *Dictionary of National Biography* (London: Smith, 1890), 23.37.

5. See Larry Carlson, ed.,"Bronson Alcott's Journal for 1838," *Studies in the American Renaissance* (Charlottesville, Va.: University Press of Virginia, 1994): 143−44.

6. Carlson, ed., "Bronson Alcott's Journal," p. 183.

7. James Pierrepont Greaves, *Spiritual Culture; or Thoughts for the Consideration of Parents and Teachers* (Boston: Smith, 1841), xii.

8. Greaves, *Spiritual Culture*, p. 15.

9. Greaves, *Spiritual Culture*, pp. 16−17.

10. Greaves, *Spiritual Culture*, p. 21.

11. Greaves, *Spiritual Culture*, p. 19.

12. Greaves, *Spiritual Culture*, pp. 79−80.

13. Greaves, *Spiritual Culture*, p. 84.

14. See Arthur Versluis, *American Transcendentalism and Asian Religions* (New York: Oxford University Press, 1993), Emerson chapter; on Lane, see also, Priscilla Brewer, "Emerson, Lane, and the Shakers: A Case of Converging Ideologies," *New England Quarterly* 55, no. 2 (1982): 254−75.

15. Brewer, "Emerson, Lane, and the Shakers," p. 87.

16. James Pierrepont Greaves, *New Theosophic Revelations* (London: Strand, 1847), p. iv.

17. Greaves, *New Theosophic Revelation*, pp. 1−2.

18. Greaves, *New Theosophic Revelation*, pp. 256−57.

19. Greaves, *New Theosophic Revelation*, p. 292.

20. James Pierrepont Greaves, *Letters and Extracts from the MS. Writings*, ed. Alexander Campbell (London: Chapman, 1845), 1.3.

21. Greaves, *Letters and Extracts*, 1.7.

22. Greaves, *Letters and Extracts*, 1.51.

23. Emerson, *JMN*, 7.465.

24. See Emerson, *JMN*, 2.388.

25. Bronson Alcott, *The Journals of Bronson Alcott*, ed. O. Shepard (1938; rprt., Port Washington: Kennikat, 1966), 2.90−91.

26. Alcott, *Journals*, 1.144.

27. H. G. Wright, cited by Latham, "Emma Martin," p. 217; see H. G. Wright, in *The New Age*, (December 1843), 1:12.

Chapter 10

1. See Frederick C. Dahlstrand, *Amos Bronson Alcott, An Intellectual Biography* (Rutherford, N.J.: Fairleigh Dickinson University Press, 1982), pp. 182−83.

2. See Joel Myerson, "'In the Transcendental Emporium': Bronson Alcott's 'Orphic Sayings' in the *Dial*," *English Language Notes* 10 (September 1972): 31−38; and Harry de Puy, "Amos Bronson Alcott: Natural Resource or Consecrated Crank?" *American Transcendental Quarterly* 1 (March 1987): 55. Myerson points out that the *Dial* omitted the bracketed word in the following sentence: "The poles of things are not integrated: creation [not] globed and orbed" (33n.).

3. Dahlstrand, *Amos Bronson Alcott*, p. 183.

4. Alcott, *Tablets*, Genesis (1868; rprt., Philadelphia: Saifer, 1969), p. 181.

5. Alcott, *Concord Days* (1872; rprt., Philadelphia: Saifer, 1962) p. 237.

6. Alcott, *Table-talk* (1877; rprt., Philadelphia: Saifer, 1971), p. 132.

7. Bronson Alcott, *The Letters of A. Bronson Alcott*, ed. R. Herrnstadt (Ames: Iowa State University Press, 1969), [67–26], 417.

8. Alcott, *Letters*, p. 69–20, 469.

9. Alcott, *Letters*, p. 470.

10. Alcott, *Letters*, p. 470.

11. Alcott, *Letters*, p. 736, 78–48.

12. See Dahlstrand, *Amos Bronson Alcott*, 343 ff.

13. One might well say that Alcott was 100 years ahead of his time. In his book *Science, Meaning, and Evolution, The Cosmology of Jacob Boehme*, trans. Rob Baker (New York: Parabola, 1991), French physicist Basarab Nicolescu argues that Böhme provides an alternate paradigm suitable for understanding modern physics in the context of post-Darwinian science. Böhmean mysticism can indeed provide a nonmaterialist cosmology for science, as Böhmean writers like Franz von Baader have pointed out. See Arthur Versluis, *Theosophia: Hidden Dimensions of Christianity* (Hudson, N.Y.: Lindisfarne, 1994).

14. See Dahlstrand, *Amos Bronson Alcott*, p. 353.

15. "Catalogue of Books," *The Dial*, 3 (April 1843): 545.

16. "Catalogue of Books," 545.

17. George Starkey, *Pyrotechny Asserted and Illustrated* (London, 1658) p. 24.

18. Starkey, *Pyrotechny*, p. 40.

19. Paracelsus, *Archidoxis* (London, 1663), p. 104.

20. Paracelsus, *Archidoxis*, appended pp. 10–11.

21. Paracelsus, *Archidoxis*, pp. 24–25.

Chapter 11

1. See Arthur Versluis, *American Transcendentalism and Asian Religions* (New York: Oxford University Press, 1993).

2. See Ivor Winters, *In Defense of Reason* (Denver: Swallow, 1943), esp. pp. 262 ff.

3. I am citing here Emerson's *Nature* (Boston: Munroe, 1836), p. 16, the first edition of the book, while checking it against the edition in Emerson, *The Collected Works of Ralph Waldo Emerson*, ed. J. Slater (Cambridge: Harvard University Press, 1971-). See also Arthur Versluis, *The Hermetic Book of Nature* (St. Paul: Grail, 1997).

4. Emerson, *Nature*, p. 35.

5. See Louis Claude de Saint-Martin, *Man: His True Nature and Ministry*, trans. E. B. Penny (London, 1864), part 1, "Nature," pp. 11ff.

6. Emerson, *Nature*, p. 43.

7. Emerson, *Nature*, pp. 32, 43, 44.

8. Emerson, *Nature*, p. 43.

9. Emerson, *Nature*, p. 45.

10. Emerson, *Nature*, p. 33.

11. An alternate quotation—from Swedenborg, whom Emerson does not name—for the source of the Transcendentalist periodical's name, *The Dial*, [1840–44].

12. Emerson, *Nature*, p. 44.

13. Emerson, *Nature*, p. 43.

14. Emerson, *Journals and Miscellaneous Notebooks*, ed. W. Gilman (Cambridge: Harvard University Press, 1960), 5.76, hereafter *JMN*.

15. *JMN*, 5.75.

16. *JMN*, 5.76.

17. See *JMN*, 8.161, quoting from Barchou de Penhoën Hilaire, *Histoire de la Philosophie Allemande depuis Leibnitz jusqu'a Hegel*, 2 vols. (Paris, 1836) 1.123, in Emerson's private library.

18. *JMN*, 8.300.

19. See for example Jacob Böhme, *De tribus principiis* (1619) in *Sämtliche Schriften*, vol. 2 (Stuttgart: Fromann, 1960), 1.§12.

20. Emerson, *Nature*, p. 77.

21. *JMN*, 5.75.

22. Emerson's inquiry here—"Whence is matter? and Whereto?"—evokes the Hermetic questions that the soul must be able to answer if it is truly illuminated: it must know whence it has come, who it really is, and where it is bound.

23. Emerson, *Nature*, p. 79.

24. See Emerson, *The Complete Works of Emerson* 12 vols., ed. Edward Emerson (1904; rprt., AMS, 1968), 1.400. In a letter to his brother William, dated 28 June 1836, Emerson wrote that "My design is to follow it with another essay, *Spirit*, and the two shall make a decent volume."

25. Stanley Vogel, *German Literary Influences on the American Transcendentalists* (New Haven: Yale University Press, 1955), p. 86.

26. Kristin Pfefferkorn, *Novalis: A Romantic's Theory of Language and Poetry* (New Haven: Yale University Press, 1988), p. 246, n. 10.

27. Henry Pochmann, *German Culture in America* (Madison: University of Wisconsin Press, 1957), p. 607, n. 418.

28. See *JMN*, 6.104; Carlyle, "Novalis," *Foreign Review* 4 (July 1829); Carlyle, *Sartor Resartus* (New York: Scribner's, 1831), book 3, ch. 6; and *JMN*, 5.119.

29. *JMN*, 6.219.

30. See also *JMN*, 6.128, 174, 202, 222, 319, each page of which contains "Novalis" quotations. The quotation on p. 222 reads: "What is Mysticism? What is it that should come to be treated mystically? Religion, Love, Nature Polity all selected things have a reference to Mysticism." From Carlyle, "Novalis," p. 22.

31. Thomas Carlyle, *Critical and Miscellaneous Essays*, 5 vols. (New York: Scribner's, 1900), 2.28.

32. Carlyle, *Critical and Miscellaneous Essays*, 2.29.

33. Carlyle, *Critical and Miscellaneous Essays*, 2.28.

34. Carlyle, *Critical and Miscellaneous Essays*, 2.30.

35. Carlyle, *Critical and Miscellaneous Essays*, 2.31.

36. See Emerson, *Nature*, pp. 87–88.

37. Emerson, *Nature*, p. 91.

38. Emerson, *Nature*, p. 88.

39. Carlyle, *Critical and Miscellaneous Essays*, 2.35.

40. Emerson, *Nature*, p. 93.

41. Arthur Versluis, trans., *Novalis, Pollen and Fragments: Selected Poetry and Prose of Novalis* (Grand Rapids, Mich.: Phanes, 1989), p. 83.

42. Versluis, *Novalis*, p. 90.

43. Emerson, *Nature*, p. 81.

44. Emerson, *Nature*, p. 121.

45. Emerson, *Nature*, p. 116.

46. Emerson, *Nature*, p. 80.

47. Emerson, *Nature*, p. 80.

48. Emerson, *Nature*, pp. 104 ff.

49. Emerson, *Nature*, p. 74.

50. Emerson, *Nature*, p. 57.

51. Carlyle, *Critical and Miscellaneous Essays*, 2.39.

52. Emerson, *Nature*, pp. 12–13.

53. Carlyle, *Critical and Miscellaneous Essays*, 2.40.

54. This accounts for some of Emerson's attraction to Novalis, as well; definitely the Emerson who wrote *Nature* found in Novalis a rare kindred spirit.

55. Carlyle, *Critical and Miscellaneous Essays*, 2.41.

56. Emerson, *Nature*, p. 56.

57. Plato suggested in his seventh letter—and here I simply accept the tradition that Plato actually wrote the letter—that true education consisted in a kind of mysterious "spark" that leapt from master to pupil, a concept closely allied to the concept of initiatory lineage found in disiplines as diverse as Hermeticism, Sufism, Kabbalism, Buddhism, and Hinduism.

58. Emerson, *Nature*, p. 56 (italics added).

59. See my *American Transcendentalism and Asian Religions* (New York: Oxford University Press, 1993), esp. pp. 51–79, on Emerson's Orientalism.

60. Versluis, *American Transcendentalism*, p. 83.

61. Emerson, *Complete Works*, 1.402.

62. See *The Hermetic Museum*, trans. Arthur Edward Waite (York Beach: Weiser, 1991), 1.73.

63. *Hermetic Museum*, 1.78.

64. Emerson, *Nature*, p. 86.

65. Emerson, *Nature*, p. 88.

66. See Elisabeth Hurth, "The Uses of a Mystic Prophet: Emerson and Boehme," *Philological Quarterly* 70, no. 2 (spring 1991): 219–36.

67. See Versluis, *Theosophia: Hidden Dimensions of Christianity* (Hudson, N.Y.: Lindisfarne, 1994); see also Versluis, *Wisdom's Children: A Christian Esoteric Tradition* (Albany: State University of New York Press, 1999).

68. Emerson, *Nature*, p. 91.

69. See for example Kenneth Burke, "I, Eye, Ay—Emerson's Early Essay 'Nature': Thoughts on the Machinery of Transcendence," in *Transcendentalism and Its Legacy*, ed. M. Simon and T. Parsons (Ann Arbor: University of Michigan Press, 1966), pp. 3–24.

70. See Emerson, *Collected Works*, 1.152.

71. Emerson, *Nature*, p. 91.

72. See *JMN*, 5.75–76.

73. Basarab Nicolescu, *Science, Meaning, and Evolution: The Cosmology of Jacob Boehme*, trans. Rob Baker (New York: Parabola, 1991).

74. See Versluis, *American Transcendentalism*, pp. 51–79.

75. Emerson, *Nature*, p. 95.

76. See, for example, Philip Sherrard, *Human Image: World Image, The Death and Resurrection of Sacred Cosmology* (London: Golgonooza Press, 1992).

77. Emerson, *Nature*, p. 90.

78. *JMN*, 7.413.

79. *JMN*, 5.481.

80. I have examined the Emerson collections in Concord and Harvard, and there is no doubt that Swedenborg's works were well represented in Emerson's personal library.

81. Emerson, *Collected Works*, 3.4.

82. Emerson, *Collected Works*, 3.10.

83. Emerson, *Collected Works*, 3.19.

84. Emerson, *Collected Works*, 3:19.

85. See Antoine Faivre, *Access to Western Esotericism* (Albany: State University of New York Press, 1994), pp. 3–35; Corbin's use of the word "imaginal" is outlined in his many books, including *Spiritual Body and Celestial Earth* as well as *Temple and Contemplation*.

86. Emerson, *Collected Works*, 3.15.

87. Emerson, *Collected Works*, 4.69.

88. Emerson, *Collected Works*, 4.72–73.

89. Emerson, *Collected Works*, 4.80–81.

90. Here I use the word "gnostic" not in the sense of the ancient Gnostics, if indeed one could speak of a single group in antiquity with that name, but simply in the esoteric sense of the word as conveying experiential spiritual knowledge beyond ratiocinative knowledge, which belongs to the separation of subject and object. Gnosis reveals the indivisibility of the knower and that which is known.

91. Emerson, *Complete Works*, 7.202.

92. Emerson, *Complete Works*, 7.202–3.

Chapter 12

1. Jeffrey Steele, editor of *The Essential Margaret Fuller*, has investigated the possible origins of Fuller's illustration, as well as Hermetic influences on her work, but the results are not yet published. For a copy of this image, see Margaret Fuller, *The Essential Margaret Fuller*, ed. Jeffrey Steele (New Brunswick, N.J.: Rutgers University Press, 1992), p. 243; see also Jeffrey Steele, "Margaret Fuller's Rhetoric of Tranformation," in the Norton Critical Edition of Fuller's *Woman in the Nineteenth Century*, ed. L. Reynolds (New York: Norton, 1998), pp. 274–93, esp. 288–92.

2. Margaret Fuller, *Memoirs of Margaret Fuller Ossoli*, ed. Ralph Waldo Emerson et al. (Boston: Phillips, 1852) 1.219.

3. Fuller, *Memoirs*, 1.220.

4. Fuller, *Memoirs*, 1.221.

5. Fuller, *Memoirs*, 1.308.

6. Fuller, *Memoirs*, 1.309–10.

7. In *Woman in the Nineteenth Century*, Fuller refers, for instance, with some familiarity to Count Zinzendorf, who was certainly influenced by various esoteric traditions and whose work exists on the boundary—if there is a boundary—between mysticism and esotericism. See Fuller, *Essential Margarent Fuller*, p. 289.

8. Fuller, *Essential Margaret Fuller*, pp. 150 ff.

9. See, for example, Paula Blanchard, *Margaret Fuller: From Transcendentalism to Revolution* (New York: Delacorte, 1978), which completely omits any mention of these esoteric elements in Fuller's life.

10. Fuller, *Essential Margaret Fuller*, p. 234.

11. Fuller, *Essential Margaret Fuller*, p. 234.

12. Fuller, *Essential Margaret Fuller*, p. 233.

13. See Margaret Fuller, *The Letters of Margaret Fuller*, ed. R. Hudspeth (Ithaca, N.Y.: Cornell University Press, 1983), 2.6; see also Ralph Waldo Emerson, *The Letters of Ralph Waldo Emerson*, ed. R. Rusk (New York: Columbia University Press, 1939–), 2.353; and Fuller, *Memoirs*, 1.308, where Emerson refers to Fuller's "ecstatic solitude" during this time of her life, around 1840, when she had experienced the low of rejection by Samuel Ward and the high of religious experience, both of which are reflected in her poetry.

14. Fuller, *Memoirs*, 1.224 ff.

15. Fuller, *Essential Margaret Fuller*, p. 247.

16. Margaret Fuller, *Woman in the Nineteenth Century*, ed. L. Reynolds. (New York: Norton, 1998), p. 5. All subsequent references are to this edition.

17. Orestes Brownson, "Miss Fuller and Reformers," *Boston Quarterly Review* 2 (1845): 249.

18. Brownson, "Miss Fuller," p. 250.

19. Fuller, *Essential Margaret Fuller*, p. 233.

20. Fuller, *Woman in the Nineteenth Century*, p. 10.

21. Fuller, *Woman in the Nineteenth Century*, p. 11.

22. On "Orbis Pictus," see Arthur Versluis, *The Hermetic Book of Nature* (St. Paul: Grail, 1997), p. 31.

23. Fuller, *Woman in the Nineteenth Century*, p. 20.

24. Fuller, *Woman in the Nineteenth Century*, pp. 40–41.

25. Fuller, *Woman in the Nineteenth Century*, p. 60.

26. Fuller, *Woman in the Nineteenth Century*, p. 60.

27. Fuller, *Woman in the Nineteenth Century*, p. 69.

28. Margaret Fuller, *The Memoirs of Margaret Fuller Ossoli*, ed. Ralph Waldo Emerson et al. (Boston: Phillips, 1852).

29. Fuller, *Woman in the Nineteenth Century*, p. 168, from *The Dial* (April 1841): 462–67.

30. Fuller, *Woman in the Nineteenth Century*, p. 169.

31. Fuller, *Woman in the Nineteenth Century*, p. 172.

32. Jeffrey Steele, editor of *The Essential Margarent Fuller* and a contributor to the Norton edition of *Woman in the Nineteenth Century*, has engaged in a close study of Fuller's occultism and its origins. See Steele, "Margaret Fuller's Rhetoric of Transformation," pp. 278–97, esp. 292–97.

Chapter 13

1. Thoreau to Harrison Blake, 6 December 1856, in Henry David Thoreau, *Familiar Letters*, ed. F. Sanborn (Boston: Houghton, 1894), p. 347.

2. Edward Carpenter, *Days With Walt Whitman* (London: George Allen, 1906), p. 43.

3. David Kuebrich, *Minor Prophecy: Walt Whitman's New American Religion* (Chicago: University of Chicago Press, 1989), p. 1.

4. Will Hayes, *Walt Whitman: Prophet of the New Era* (London: C. W. Daniel, 1921), cited in Kuebrich, *Minor Prophecy*, p. 1.

5. Kuebrich, *Minor Prophecy*, p. 2.

6. Cited by Kuebrich, *Minor Prophecy*, p. 63.

7. See Walt Whitman, *Complete Poetry and Prose of Walt Whitman*, ed. Malcolm Cowley (New York: Pellegrini, 1948), 1.19, hereafter cited as *CPP*.

8. *CPP*, 1:19.

9. *CPP*, 1.232–33.

10. *CPP*, 1.387; Walt Whitman, *Collected Writings of Walt Whitman*, ed. H. Blodgett and S. Bradley (New York: New York University Press, 1965), 1.443, hereafter cited as *CW*.

11. *CW*, 1.444.

12. *CW*, 1:444.

13. *CW*, 1.445.

14. *CW*, 1:445.

15. For more on the figure of divine Wisdom throughout European esoteric history, see Versluis, *Wisdom's Book: The Sophia Anthology* (St. Paul: Paragon House, 2000), which includes numerous writings about Sophia never before available in English.

16. *CPP*, 1.404.

17. *CPP*, 1.405.

18. *CPP*, 1.405.

19. *CPP*, 1.405.

20. *CPP*, 1.406.

21. See Wouter Hanegraaff, *New Age Religion and Western Culture: Esotericism in the Mirror of Secular Thought* (Leiden: Brill, 1996), for an extensive discussion of how esoteric currents became transformed into popular New Thought or New Age works.

22. Hanegraaff, *New Age Religion*, p. 345.

23. See Henry David Thoreau, *Letters to Various Persons* (Boston, 1865), pp. 146–48.

24. Bronson Alcott, *The Journals of Bronson Alcott*, ed. O. Shepard (Boston, 1938), pp. 293–94.

25. Alcott, *Journals*, 286–87.

26. R. M. Bucke, *Walt Whitman* (New York: Johnson, 1970), p. 201.

27. Bucke, *Walt Whitman*, p. 202.

28. *CPP*, 1.128.

29. *CPP*, 1.129.

30. *CPP*, 1.130.

31. *CPP*, 1.128–29.

32. *CPP*, 1.115.

33. *CPP*, 1.124.

34. *CPP*, 1.124.

35. See, for instance, Betsy Erkkila, ed., *Breaking Bounds: Whitman and American Cultural Studies* (New York: Oxford University Press, 1996); J. F. Buckley, *Desire, the Self, and the Social Critic: The Rise of Queer Performance within the Demise of Transcendentalism* (Selinsgrove, Pa.: Susquehanna, 1997); and Richard Dellamora, *Victorian Sexual Dissidence* (Chicago: University of Chicago Press, 1997), and *Apocalyptic Overtures: Sexual Politics and the Sense of an Ending* (New Brunswick, N.J.: Rutgers University Press, 1994). See also Tenney Nathanson, *Whitman's Presence: Body, Voice, and Writing in* Leaves of Grass (New York: New York University Press, 1992).

36. See Versluis, *The Mysteries of Love: Eros and Spirituality* (St. Paul: Grail, 1996), for an extensive discussion of all the themes mentioned here briefly. On Randolph, see John Patrick Deveney, *Paschal Beverly Randolph* (Albany: State University of New York Press, 1997); see also Randolph, *Magia sexualis: Sublimation de l'énergie sexuelle*

(St-Jean-de-Braye, France: Dangles, 1991), and, in English, Randolph, *Sexual Magic*, trans. R. North (New York: Magical Childe, 1988); regarding Naglowska, see Maria Naglowska, *Le Rite Sacré de l'Amour Magique* (Paris: O.T.O., 1932); Marc Pluquet, *La Sophiale* (Paris: O.T.O., 1981); de Naglowska, *La Lumière du Sexe* (Paris: O.T.O., 1993). De Naglowska represents a French influence of Randolph's work, which under the auspices of the magical order the O.T.O. has incorporated sexual magic into its rituals. Whether Whitman was familiar with Randolph's work is at present unknown but entirely possible inasmuch as the poet and Randolph were certainly more than once in the same cities at the same time and knew people in common, including Lincoln. What is more, sexuality is at the center of Randolph's and Whitman's work. For an extensive if somewhat odd history of sexuality and spirituality in European tradition, see Julius Evola, *The Metaphysics of Sex* (Rochester, Vt.: Inner Traditions, 1983).

37. Harold Aspiz, *Walt Whitman and the Body Beautiful* (Urbana: University of Illinois Press, 1980), pp. 148–49.

38. Walt Whitman, "Is Mesmerism True?" *New York Sunday Times*, 14 August 1842.

39. Aspiz, *Walt Whitman*, p. 158.

40. Aspiz, *Walt Whitman*, p. 165.

41. See "Walt Whitman and His Poems," in *In Re Walt Whitman*, ed. R. M. Bucke, T. Harned, and H. Traubel (Philadelphia, 1893), p. 19.

42. Andrew Jackson Davis, *The Harmonial Philosophy* (Chicago: Advanced Thought, 1919), p. 395.

43. Davis, *Harmonial Philosophy*, p. 397.

44. See Marsha Keith Schuchard, "Why Mrs. Blake Cried: Blake, Swedenborg, and the Sexual Basis of Spiritual Vision," *Esoterica: The Journal of Esoteric Studies* [http://www.esoteric.msu.edu] 2 (2000): 45–93.

45. Bucke, *Walt Whitman*, p. 27.

46. Walt Whitman, "Who was Swedenborg?" *Brooklyn Daily Times*, 15 June 1858, *The Uncollected Poetry and Prose of Walt Whitman*, 2 vols., ed. Emory Holloway (New York: P. Smith, 1932), 2.17–18.

47. *CPP*, 1.134–35.

48. *CPP*, 1.138.

49. *CPP*, 1.143.

50. *CPP*, 1.147.

51. *CPP*, 1.146.

52. Thomas Lake Harris, *Arcana of Christianity: An Unfolding of the Celestial Sense of the Divine Word* (New York: New Church, 1858–67), 1.175.

53. Harris, *Arcana of Christianity*, 1.289.

54. John Burroughs, *Whitman: A Study* (Boston: Houghton, 1902), p. 200.

55. Bucke, *Walt Whitman*, p. 185.

Chapter 14

1. Robert Weisbuch, *Emily Dickinson's Poetry* (Chicago: University of Chicago Press, 1975), p. 78.

2. See Benjamin Lease, *Emily Dickinson's Readings of Men and Books* (New York: St. Martin's, 1990); and three works by Barton Levi St. Armand: "Emily Dickinson and the Occult: The Rosicrucian Connection," *Prairie Schooner* 51 (1977/78): 345–57; "Veiled Ladies: Dickinson, Bettine, and Transcendental Mediumship," *Studies in the*

American Renaissance (1987): 1–51; and "Experienced Emblems: A Study of the Poetry of Emily Dickinson," *Prospects: An Annual Journal of American Cultural Studies* 6 (1981): 187–280. Beth Doriani discusses Dickinson's use of Protestant prophetic rhetoric in *Emily Dickinson: Daughter of Prophecy* (Amherst: University of Massachusetts Press, 1996), which is perhaps tangentially related to Dickinson's interest in esotericism, although Doriani never even alludes to such interests on Dickinson's part. In *Emily Dickinson's Gothic* (Iowa City: University of Iowa Press, 1996), Daneen Wardop surveys the Gothic influences on Dickinson's poetry.

3. Dickinson, *Emily Dickinson: Selected Letters*, ed. Thomas Johnson (Cambridge: Harvard University Press, 1971), p. 172.

4. Dickinson, *Emily Dickinson*, p. 173.

5. Sir Thomas Browne, *Selected Writings*, ed. Sir G. Keynes (London: Faber, 1968), p. 12.

6. Browne, *Selected Writings*, p. 15.

7. Browne, *Selected Writings*, p. 17.

8. Browne, *Selected Writings*, p. 21.

9. Browne, *Selected Writings*, p. 21.

10. Emily Dickinson, *The Poems of Emily Dickinson*, ed. T. Johnson (Cambridge: Harvard University Press, 1963), no. 94. Hereafter, in reference to this edition, numbers refer to the numbers of the poems, not to pagination.

11. Browne, *Selected Writings*, p. 36.

12. Browne, *Selected Writings*, p. 37.

13. Dickinson, *Poems*, 281, 282, 298.

14. Emily Dickinson, *The Letters of Emily Dickinson*, ed. Thomas Johnson (Cambridge: Harvard University Press, 1970), 3.667. Subsequent references to *Letters* are to this edition.

15. Dickinson, *Letters*, 2.647.

16. John Cody, *In Great Pain: The Inner Life of Emily Dickinson* (Cambridge: Harvard University Press, 1971), p. 291.

17. Cody, *In Great Pain*, p. 291.

18. Dickinson, *Poems*, 435.

19. Dickinson, *Poems*, 280.

20. Dickinson, *Poems*, 1039.

21. Dickinson, *Poems*, 555.

22. Dickinson, *Poems*, 1158.

23. Dickinson, *Poems*, 711; see St. Armand, "Emily Dickinson and the Occult," 345–57. St. Armand suggests that Dickinson was interested in Rosicrucianism, but I have not seen convincing evidence of this assertion. See also St. Armand's later readings of Dickinson in "Veiled Ladies," 1–51, and "Experienced Emblems, 187–280. St. Armand remains one of the only literary critics to have investigated the esoteric aspects of Dickinson's poetry; one wishes for a book-length collection of his best studies.

24. See, on Shakespeare and magic, Versluis, *Shakespeare the Magus* (St. Paul: Grail, 2001).

25. Dickinson, *Poems*, 599.

26. Dickinson, *Emily Dickinson*, pp. 207–8.

27. Higginson did write ghost stories, as is evident by his *Old Port Days* (Boston: Houghton, 1873), and he was a witness in a case of spiritualistic phenomena at Harvard. See St. Armand, "Emily Dickinson and the Occult," p. 346.

28. St. Armand, "Emily Dickinson and the Occult," p. 210.

29. Thomas Wentworth Higginson, "Emily Dickinson," *Atlantic Monthly* 68 (October 1891): 453, cited in Johnson, ed., *Selected Letters*, p. 211.

30. For a discussion Dickinson's interest in spiritualism, see Lease, *Emily Dickinson's Readings*, esp. in "Nature's Haunted House," pp. 101 ff.

31. See Howard Kerr, *Mediums and Spirit-Rappers and Roaring Radicals: Spiritualism in American Literature, 1850–1900* (Urbana: University of Illinois Press, 1972), pp. 101–102.

32. See Lease, *Emily Dickinson's Readings*, p. 102; for other examples of Higginson's involvement in spiritualism, see St. Armand, "Veiled Ladies," 5–7.

33. Higginson to editor, *Banner of Light*, 25 June 1857. Higginson goes on to remark that the spiritualist movement's philosophy is not yet of value, but perhaps will one day become significant.

34. See Wouter Hanegraaff, *New Age Religion and Western Culture: Esotericism in the Mirror of Secular Thought* (Leiden: Brill, 1996), pp. 435 ff. For more information on the history of spiritualism, see R. Laurence Moore, *In Search of White Crows: Spiritualism, Parapsychology, and American Culture* (New York: Oxford University Press, 1977); and Joscelyn Godwin, *The Theosophical Enlightenment* (Albany: State University of New York Press, 1994).

35. An excellent discussion of American spiritualism is Bret Carroll's *Spiritualism in Antebellum America* (Bloomington: Indiana University Press, 1997). Other studies in this area include Ann Braude, *Radical Spirits: Spiritualism and Women's Rights in Nineteenth-Century America* (Boston: Beacon Press, 1987); and, on English spiritualism, Alex Owen, *The Darkened Room: Women, Power, and Spiritualism in Late Victorian England* (Philadelphia: University of Pennsylvania Press, 1990). Much work still remains to be done on the European origins of spiritualism, however, and on the relationships between European esotericism and American spiritualism, which remain largely overlooked.

36. Jon Butler, "The Dark Ages of American Occultism, 1769–1848," in *The Occult in America: New Historical Perspectives*, ed. Howard Kerr and Charles Crow (Urbana: University of Illinois Press, 1963), p. 78. For the single reference to Higginson's interest in spiritualism, see Tilden Edelstein, *Strange Enthusiasm: A Life of Thomas Wentworth Higginson* (New York: Atheneum, 1970), p. 130.

Chapter 15

1. See William R. Newman, *Gehennical Fire: The Lives of George Starkey, an American Alchemist in the Scientific Revolution* (Cambridge: Harvard University Press, 1994).

2. See Versluis, *American Transcendentalism and Asian Religions* (New York: Oxford University Press, 1993).

3. On Gichtel and Pordage, see Versluis, *Wisdom's Children: A Christian Esoteric Tradition* (Albany: State University of New York Press, 1999).

4. It would be interesting to compare Dickinson's autobiographical record in her poems with the spiritual autobiographies of women like the seventeenth-century Ann Bathurst, part of whose spiritual diary is to be found in Versluis, ed., *Wisdom's Book: The Sophia Anthology* (St. Paul: Paragon House, 2000). It is obvious that Dickinson's spirituality differed from conventional Protestantism, but it has not been previously noted that her spirituality had some precedent in Protestant esotericism. I am not here suggesting that Dickinson read such works as the diaries of Bathurst, which would be

extremely unlikely, but rather that what we read in her poems occasionally parallels Christian theosophic esotericism.

5. See Kathleen Raine, *Blake and Tradition* (Princeton: Princeton University Press, 1963); Jon Mee, *Dangerous Enthusiasm: William Blake and the Culture of Radicalism in the 1790s* (Oxford: Clarendon, 1992); E. P. Thompson, *Witness against the Beast: William Blake and the Moral Law* (New York: New Press, 1993).

6. See, for instance, Desirée Hirst, *Hidden Riches: Traditional Symbolism from the Renaissance to Blake* (London: Eyre, 1964).

7. See Versluis, *Western Esotericism, Literature, and Consciousness* (forthcoming).

8. See Antoine Faivre, *The Eternal Hermes* (Grand Rapids, Mich.: Phanes, 1995).

9. *Acta Philadelphica or Monthly Memoirs of the Philadelphian Society* 1 (March 1697): 1–2.

10. Emerson, *Journals and Miscellaneous Notebooks*, ed. W. Gilman (Cambridge: Harvard University Press, 1960), 7.413.

11. See Mark Carnes, *Secret Ritual and Manhood in Victorian America* (New Haven: Yale University Press, 1989), p. 89; on esotericism in twentieth-century America, see Faivre, *Access to Western Esotericism* (Albany: State University of New York Press, 1994).

Bibliography

Acta Philadelphica or Monthly Memoirs of the Philadelphian Society. London, 1697.

Agrippa, Henry Cornelius. *Three Books of Occult Philosophy.* Trans. James Freake. London, 1651.

Albanese, Catherine. *America: Religions and Religion.* Belmont, Calif.: Wadsworth, 1981.

————. *Corresponding Motion: Transcendental Religion and the New America.* Philadelphia: Temple University Press, 1977.

————. *Nature Religion in America.* Chicago: University of Chicago Press, 1990.

————. *Sons of the Fathers: The Civil Religion of the American Revolution.* Philadelphia: Temple University Press, 1976.

————, ed. *The Spirituality of the American Transcendentalists.* Macon, Ga.: Mercer University Press, 1988.

Albertus, Frater. *Alchemist's Handbook.* York Beach, Maine: Weiser, 1974.

Alcott, Bronson. *Concord Days.* 1872. Reprt., Philadelphia: Saifer, 1962.

————. *The Journals of Bronson Alcott.* Ed. O. Shepard. 1938. Rprt., Port Washington: Kennikat, 1966.

————. *The Letters of Bronson Alcott.* Ed. R. Herrnstadt. Ames: Iowa State University Press, 1969.

————. *Table-talk.* 1877. Rprt., Philadelphia: Saifer, 1971.

————. *Tablets.* 1868. Rprt., Philadelphia: Saifer, 1969.

Alderfer, E. G. *The Ephrata Commune: An Early American Counterculture.* Pittsburgh: University of Pittsburgh Press, 1985.

Allen, Gay Wilson. *The Solitary Singer.* New York: New York University Press, 1967.

Alline, Henry. *Henry Alline: Selected Writings.* Ed. G. A. Rawlyk. New York: Paulist Press, 1987.

Anderson, James. *Constitution, Laws, Changes, Orders, Regulations . . . of the . . . Fraternity of Accepted Freemasons.* London, 1723.

Anonimus' travels throu' Europe and America, and some visions of many heavenly mansions in the house of God. . . . How he conversed with the inhabitants of the other world, and found, that their respective works had actually followed them. Ephrata, Pa., 1793; AC 152, in the Julius Sachse Collection, Historical Society of Pennsylvania.

Arndt, Karl. "George Rapp's Harmony Society." In *America's Communal Utopias*, ed. D. Pitzer. Chapel Hill, University of North Carolina Press, 1997.

Arnold, Gottfried. *Das Geheimnis der Göttlichen Sophia.* 1700. Stuttgart: Frommann, 1963.

———. *Historie und Beschreibung der Mystischen Theologie.* 1703. Stuttgart: Frommann, 1969.

Aspiz, Harold. *Walt Whitman and the Body Beautiful.* Urbana: University of Illinois Press, 1980.

Atwood, Mary Ann. *A Suggestive Inquiry into Hermetic Mystery.* London, 1850.

Aubrey, Bryan. "Influence of Jacob Boehme on the Work of William Blake." Ph.D. diss., Duke University, 1982.

Aubrey, John. *Miscellanies upon the following subjects.* London: E. Castle, 1696.

Auer, Michael. "Angels and Beasts: Gnosticism in American Literature." Ph.D. diss., University of North Carolina, Chapel Hill, 1976.

———. *Watchmen of Eternity: Blake's Debt to Jacob Boehme.* Lanham, Md.: University Press of America, 1986.

Bailey, Margaret L. *Milton and Jakob Boehme.* New York: Haskell, 1964.

Bayle, Pierre. *The Dictionary Historical and Critical of Mr. Peter Bayle.* London, 1734–38.

Das Büchlein von Sabbath. Philadelphia: Bradford, 1728.

Beissel, Conrad. *Mysterion Anomias: The Mystery of Lawlessness or, Lawless AntiChrist Discover'd & Disclosed.* Trans. M. Welfare. Philadelphia: Bradford, 1729.

Benz, Ernst. *The Mystical Sources of German Romantic Philosophy.* Allison Park, Pennsylvania: Pickwick, 1983.

———. *The Theology of Electricity.* Allison Park, Pa.: Pickwick, 1989.

Berthoff, Werner. *The Example of Melville.* Princeton: Princeton University Press, 1962.

Black, William C. *The Younger John Winthrop.* New York: Columbia University Press, 1966.

Blanchard, Paula. *Margaret Fuller: From Transcendentalism to Revolution.* New York: Delacorte, 1978.

Block, M. Beck. *The New Church in the New World: Swedenborgianism in America.* New York: Holt, 1932.

Bloodgood, Melanie. "The Gnostic Nature of the World View and Fictional Times of Herman Melville." Ph.D. diss., Oklahoma State University, 1984.

Bloom, Harold. *The American Religion.* New York: Simon and Schuster, 1992.

Boas, George. *Romanticism in America.* Baltimore: Johns Hopkins University Press, 1940.

Boehler, Eliseba. *Abgefordete Relation der Erscheinng eines entlebten Gests dem Publico ʒur Nachricht* [E. B.'s *Narrative of the visions she experienced in Virginia, her travel to Ephrata, and the following spiritual manifestations, with Beissel's concluding remarks.*] Ephrata, Pa., 1761.

Böhme, Jacob. *Aurora.* London, 1910.

———. *Christosophia.* Ephrata, Pa.: Jacob Ruth, 1811–12.

———. *Dialogues on the Supersensual Life.* New York: Ungar, 1957.

———. *Sämtliche Schriften.* 11 vols. Ed. Will-Erich Peuckert and August Faust. Stuttgart: Frommann, 1955–61.

————. *The Works of Jacob Behmen.* 4 vols. London: Richardson, 1763/81.

————. *Ein systematischer Auszug des . . . Theosophi J. Böhmens Sämmt. Schriften.* Ephrata, Pa.: Joseph Bauman, 1822–24.

————. *The Three Principles of the Divine Essence.* 1650. Chicago: Yogi, 1909.

————. *The Way to Christ.* Trans. P. Erb. New York: Paulist Press, 1978.

Bolton, James. *Treatise on the Universal Restoration.* Ephrata, 1793; AC 156, pp. 3–4, in the Cassell Collection, Historical Society of Pennsylvania.

Boyer, P., and S. Nissenbaum. *The Salem Witchcraft Papers: Verbatim Transcripts of the Legal Documents of the Salem Witchcraft Outbreak.* 3 vols. New York: Da Capo Press, 1977.

Bratcher, Meredith. "The Demiurge: A Study of the Tradition from Plato to Joyce." Ph.D. diss., Duke University, 1985.

Braude, Ann. *Radical Spirits: Spiritualism and Women's Rights in Nineteenth-Century America.* Boston: Beacon Press, 1987.

Braun, Frederick A. *Margaret Fuller and Goethe.* New York: Holt, 1910.

Brewer, Priscilla. "Emerson, Lane, and the Shakers: A Case of Converging Ideologies." *New England Quarterly* 55, no. 2 (1982): 254–75.

Britten, Emma Hardinge. *The Autobiography of Emma Hardinge Britten.* London: Heywood: 1900.

Brooke, John L. *The Refiner's Fire: The Making of Mormon Cosmology, 1644–1844.* Cambridge: Cambridge University Press, 1994.

Browne, Sir Thomas. *Selected Writings.* Ed. Sir G. Keynes. London: Faber, 1968.

Brownson, Orestes. "Miss Fuller and Reformers." *Boston Quarterly Review* 2 (1845): 249.

Bucke, R. M. *The Letters of Dr. Richard Maurice Bucke to Walt Whitman.* Detroit: Wayne State University Press, 1977.

————. *Walt Whitman.* New York: Johnson, 1970.

————, T. Harned, and H. Traubel, eds. *In Re Walt Whitman.* Philadelphia: Traubel, 1893.

Buckley, J. F. *Desire, the Self, and the Social Critic: The Rise of Queer Performace within the Demise of Transcendentalism.* Selinsgrove, Pa.: Susquehanna, 1997.

Burroughs, John. *Whitman: A Study.* Boston: Houghton, 1902.

Carlson, Larry, ed. "Bronson Alcott's Journal for 1838." *Studies in the American Renaissance* (Charlottesville, Va.: University Press of Virginia, 1994): 123–193.

Carlyle, Thomas. *Critical and Miscellaneous Essays.* 5 vols. New York: Scribner's, 1900.

————. *Sartor Resartus.* New York: Scribner's, 1831.

————. "Novalis." *Foreign Review* 4 (July 1829).

Carnes, Mark. *Secret Ritual and Manhood in Victorian America.* New Haven: Yale University Press, 1989.

Carpenter, Edward. *Days With Walt Whitman.* London: George Allen, 1906.

Carpenter, George Rice. *Walt Whitman.* New York: Macmillan, 1909.

Carroll, Bret. *Spiritualism in Antebellum America.* Bloomington: Indiana University Press, 1997.

Casaubon, Marie, ed. *A True and Faithful Relation of What Passed for Many Years between Dr. John Dee and Some Spirits.* London, 1656.

Chari, V. K. *Whitman in the Light of Vedantic Mysticism.* Lincoln: University of Nebraska Press, 1964.

Chauncy, Israel. *An Almanack of the Coelestial Motions for the Year of the Christian Aera 1663.* Cambridge, Mass., 1663.

Cheever, Samuel. *An Almanack for the Year of Our Lord 1660*. Cambridge, Mass., 1660.

Clack, Randall. "The Alchemy of Love: Hawthorne's Hermetic Allegory of the Heart." *ESQ* 41 (1995): 307–38.

———. "The Phoenix Rising: Alchemical Imagination in the Works of Edward Taylor, Edgar Allan Poe, and Nathaniel Hawthorne." Ph.D. diss., University of Connecticut, 1994.

———. "'Strange Alchemy of the Brain': Poe and Alchemy." In *A Companion to Poe Studies*, ed. Eric Carlson. Westport, Conn.: Greenwood Press, 1996.

———. "The Transformation of Soul: Edward Taylor and the Opus Alchemicum Celestial in Meditation 1:8." *Seventeenth-Century News* 50 (1992): 6–10.

"The Cloister Hospital, 1777." Ephrata, Pa.: Restored Press, 1976.

Clowes, John. *A Summary View of the Heavenly Doctrines*. Philadelphia: 1787.

———. *The True Christian Religion*. Philadelphia, 1789.

Coale, Samuel Chase. *Hawthorne and Mesmerism*. Tuscaloosa: University of Alabama Press, 1998.

Cody, John. *In Great Pain: The Inner Life of Emily Dickinson*. Cambridge: Harvard University Press, 1971.

Corbin, Henry. *Avicenna and the Visionary Recital*. Princeton: Princeton University Press.

———. *Creative Imagination in the Sûfism of Ibn 'Arabî*. Princeton: Princeton University Press, 1969.

———. *Spiritual Body and Celestial Earth, From Mazdaean Iran to Shi'ite Islam*. Princeton University Press, 1977.

———. *Temple and Contemplation*. Trans. Philip Sherrard. London: KPI, 1986.

———, ed. *Le Combat Pour l'Ame du Monde*. Paris: Berg, 1980.

Corsetti, Jean-Paul. *Histoire de l'ésotérisme et des sciences occultes*. Paris: Larousse, 1992.

Couliano, Ioan P. *The Tree of Gnosis: Gnostic Mythology from Early Christianity to Modern Nihilism*. San Francisco: Harper, 1992. Originally: *Les Gnoses dualistes d'Occident* (Paris: Plon, 1990).

Dahlstrand, Frederick C. *Amos Bronson Alcott: An Intellectual Biography*. Rutherford, N.J.: Fairleigh Dickinson University Press, 1982.

Davis, Andrew Jackson. *The Harmonial Philosophy*. Chicago: Advanced Thought, 1919.

———. *The Principles of Nature, Her Divine Revelations, and a Voice to Mankind*. London: Chapman, 1847.

Deghaye, Pierre. *La Doctrin ésotérique de Zinzendorf*. Paris: Klincksieck, 1970.

———. *La Naissance De Dieu*. Paris: Albin Michel, 1985.

Dellamora, Richard. *Apocalyptic Overtures: Sexual Politics and the Sense of an Ending*. New Brunswick, N.J.: Rutgers University Press, 1994.

———. *Victorian Sexual Dissidence*. Chicago: University of Chicago Press, 1997.

Demott, Bobby. *Freemasonry in American Culture and Society*. Lanham, Md.: University Press of America, 1986.

de Naglowska, Maria. *La Lumière du Sexe*. Paris: O.T.O., 1993.

de Puy, Harry. "Amos Bronson Alcott: Natural Resource or Consecrated Crank?" *American Transcendental Quarterly* 1 (March 1987): 55.

Deveney, John Patrick. *Paschal Beverly Randolph*. Albany: State University of New York Press, 1997.

Dexter, Franklin B., ed. *The Literary Diary of Ezra Stiles*. New York, 1901.

Dial, The. 1840–44.

Dickinson, Emily. *Emily Dickinson: Selected Letters*. Ed. Thomas Johnson. Cambridge: Harvard University Press, 1971.

———. *The Letters of Emily Dickinson*. 3 vols. Ed. Thomas Johnson. Cambridge: Harvard University Press, 1970.

———. *The Poems of Emily Dickinson*. Ed. T. Johnson. Cambridge: Harvard University Press, 1963.

Doriani, Beth. *Emily Dickinson: Daughter of Prophecy*. Amherst: University of Massachusetts Press, 1996.

Eckhartshausen, Karl. *Die Wolke über dem Heiligthum*. Philadelphia: W. Mentz, 1841.

Edelstein, Tilden. *Strange Enthusiasm: A Life of Thomas Wentworth Higginson*. New York: Atheneum, 1970.

Egyptische Geheinnisse, oder das Zigeuner-Buch gennant. . . . [Egyptian Mysteries, or The Gypsy Book]. Harrisburg, Pa.: Gustav Peters, 1844.

Elimelech, [E. Eckerling]. *Die aufehende Lilie, ist ein Theosophischer Discurs und Unpartheyisches Zeugniss zur Behauptung der Bibel und des Welt-Erloeser*. Lancaster, Pa.: Hamilton, 1815.

Emerson, Ralph Waldo. *The Collected Works of Ralph Waldo Emerson*. Ed. J. Slater. Cambridge: Harvard University Press, 1971–.

———. *Complete Works of Emerson*. 1904. Rprt., AMS, 1968.

———. *Journals and Miscellaneous Notebooks*. Ed. W. Gilman. Cambridge: Harvard University Press, 1960.

Emerson, Ralph Waldo. *The Letters of Ralph Waldo Emerson*. Ed. R. Rusk. New York: Columbia University Press, 1939–.

———. *Nature*. Boston: Munroe, 1836.

———. *Society and Solitude*. Boston: Ticknor, 1870.

Erb, Peter. *Johann Conrad Beissel and the Ephrata Community: Mystical and Historical Texts*. Lewiston, Maine: Edwin Mellen, 1985.

———. *The Pietists*. New York: Paulist Press, 1983.

———. *Pietists, Protestants, and Mysticism: The Use of Late Medieval Spiritual Texts in the Work of Gottfried Arnold*. Metuchen, N.J.: Scarecrow Press, 1989.

Erkkila, Betsy, ed. *Breaking Bounds: Whitman and American Cultural Studies*. New York: Oxford University Press, 1996.

Ernst, James. *Ephrata: A History*. Allentown: Pennsylvania German Folklore Society, 1963.

Evola, Julius. *The Metaphysics of Sex*. Rochester, Vt.: Inner Traditions, 1983.

Faivre, Antoine. *Access to Western Esotericism*. Albany: State University of New York Press, 1994.

———. "Le courant théosophique (fin XV–XX siécle): Essai de périodisation." In *Politica Hermetica* 7 (1993): 6–41. Also to be published in *Access to Esotericism*, vol. 2 (Albany: State University of New York Press).

———. *Eckhartshausen et la théosophie chrétienne*. Paris: Klincksieck, 1969.

———. "Eglise intérieure et Jérusalem céleste." In *Cahiers de l'Université St Jean de Jérusalem*. Paris: Berg, 1976.

———. *L'ésotérisme: que sais-je?* Paris: Presses Universitaires, 1992.

———. *L'ésoterisme au XVIIIème siècle en France et en Allemagne*. Paris: Seghers, 1973.

———. *The Eternal Hermes*. Grand Rapids, Mich.: Phanes, 1995.

———. *Mystiques, Theosophes et Illumines Au Siecle des Lumieres*. Hildesheim: Olms, 1976.

——————. *Philosophie de la Nature: Physique sacrée et théosophie XVIII–XIX siècle*. Paris: Albin Michel, 1996.

——————, ed. *Epochen der Naturmystik, Hermetische Tradition im wissenschaftlichen Fortshritt*. Berlin: Erich Schmidt Verlag, 1979.

——————, and J. Needleman, eds. *Modern Esoteric Spirituality*. New York: Crossroad, 1992.

Fattore, Joan Del. "John Webster's Metallographica: A Source for Alchemical Imagery in the Preparatory Meditations." *Early American Literature* 18 (1983–84): 231–41.

Fay, Bernard. *Franklin: The Apostle of Modern Times*. Boston: Little, Brown, 1930.

——————. *Revolution and Freemasonry, 1680–1800*. Boston: Little, Brown, 1935.

Flamel, Nicholas. *Exposition of The Hieroglyphicall Figures*. London 1624. New edition, ed. Laurinda Dixon. New York: Garland, 1994.

Fowden, Garth. *The Egyptian Hermes*. Cambridge: Cambridge University Press, 1987.

Franklin, Benjamin. *The Autobiography of Benjamin Franklin*. New Haven: Yale University Press, 1964.

——————. *The Writings of Benjamin Franklin*. Ed. Franklin B. Dexter. New York, 1907.

Franklin, H. Bruce. *The Wake of the Gods: Melville's Mythology*. Stanford: Stanford University Press, 1963.

Frick, Karl. *Die Erleuchteten*. Graz, Germany: Akademisches, 1973.

——————. *Licht und Finsternis*. 2 vols. Graz, Germany: Akademisches, 1978.

Fuller, Margaret. *The Essential Margaret Fuller*. Ed. Jeffrey Steele. New Brunswick, N.J.: Rutgers University Press, 1992.

——————. *The Letters of Margaret Fuller*. Ed. R. Hudspeth. Ithaca, N.Y.: Cornell University Press, 1983.

——————. *The Memoirs of Margaret Fuller Ossoli*. Ed. Ralph Waldo Emerson et al. Boston: Philips, 1852.

——————. *Woman in the Nineteenth Century*. Ed. L. Reynold. New York: Norton, 1998.

Gibbons, B. T. *Gender in Mystical and Occult Thought: Behmenism and Its Development in England*. Cambridge: Cambridge University Press, 1996.

Gichtel, Johann Georg. *Eine kurze Eröffnung und Anweisung der dryen Principien und Welten in Menschen [A Brief Opening and Demonstration of the Three Principles and Worlds in Man]*. Leipzig, 1696/1779.

——————. *Theosophia Practica*. 7 vols. Amsterdam, 1721.

Godwin, Joscelyn. *The Theosophical Enlightenment*. Albany: State University of New York Press, 1994.

——————, trans. *The Chemical Wedding*. Grand Rapids, Mich.: Phanes, 1991.

Goodman, Paul. *Towards a Christian Republic: Antimasonry and the Great Transition in New England, 1826–1836*. New York: Oxford University Press, 1988.

Gorceix, Bernard. *Flambée et agonie. Mystiques du XVIIe siécle allemand*. Paris: Editions Prèsence, 1977.

——————. *Johann Georg Gichtel: Théosophe d'Amsterdam*. Paris: L'Age D'Homme, 1975.

Greaves, James Pierrepont. *Letters and Extracts from the MS. Writings*. London: Chapman, 1845.

——————. *New Theosophic Revelations*. London: Strand, 1847.

——————. *Spiritual Culture; or Thoughts for the Consideration of Parents and Teachers*. Boston: Smith, 1841.

——————, and Christopher Walton. *Behmen, Law, and Other Mystics on the past, present and future, with regard to Creation, Written from a Knowledge of the Philosophy of Jacob Behmen*. London, 1847–48.

————. *Letters and Extracts*. 2 vols. London: Chapman, 1845.

————. *The New Nature in the Soul*. London: Chapman, 1847.

————. *Triune Life: Divine and Human*. Ed. Francis Barham. London, 1880.

Guénon, René. *L'Erreur Spirite*. 1923. Rprt., Paris: Etudes Tradionelles, 1952.

————. *Le Théosophisme, histoire d'une pseudo-religion*. 1921. Rprt., Paris: Editions Traditionelles, 1982.

Hall, David. *Worlds of Wonder, Days of Judgment: Popular Religious Belief in Early New England*. New York: Knopf, 1989.

Hanegraaff, Wouter. *New Age Religion and Western Culture: Esotericism in the Mirror of Secular Thought*. Leiden: Brill, 1996.

Harris, J. McArthur, Jr. "The Enigma of Kelpius' Cave." *Germantown Crier* 3 (summer 1983): 54–56.

Harris, Thomas Lake. *Arcana of Christianity: An Unfolding of the Celestial Sense of the Divine Word*. 2 vols. New York: New Church, 1858.

————. *The Breath of God With Man*. New York: Brotherhood, 1867.

————. *The Golden Child*. Santa Rosa, California: Fountaingrove Press, 1878.

————. *The Millennial Age: Twelve Discourses on the Spiritual and Social Aspects of the Times*. New York: New Church, 1860.

Harrison, C. G. *The Transcendental Universe*. 1893. Rprt., Hudson, New York: Lindisfarne, 1993.

Hawthorne, Nathaniel. *The Blithdale Romance*. Centenary edition text. New York: Norton, 1978.

————. *The Heart of Hawthorne's Journals*. Ed. Newton Arvin. Boston: Houghton, 1929.

————. *The Letters of Nathaniel Hawthorne*. Centenary edition. Athens: Ohio State University Press, 1965–.

————. *The Scarlet Letter*. New York: Norton, 1978.

Hayes, Will. *Walt Whitman: Prophet of the New Era*. London: C. W. Daniel, 1921.

Heilman, R. B. "Hawthorne's 'The Birthmark': Science as Religion." *South Atlantic Quarterly* 48 (1949): 575–83.

The Hermetic Museum. Trans. Arthur Edward Waite. York Beach: Weiser, 1991.

Heydon, John. *Theomagia, or, The temple of wisdome: in three parts, spiritual, celestial, and elemental: containing the occular powers of the angels of astromancy in the telesmatical sculpture of the Persians and Egyptians: the mysterious vertues of the characters of the stars . . . the knowledge of the Rosie Crucian physick, and the miraculous secrets in nature*. London: Printed by T. M. for Henry Brome, 1663–64.

Higginson, Thomas Wentworth. *Margaret Fuller Ossoli*. 1884. Rprt., New York: Haskell, 1968.

————. *Old Port Days*. Boston: Houghton, 1873.

Hilaire, Barchou de Penhoën. *Histoire de la Philosophie Allemande depuis Leibnitz jusqu'a Hegel*. 2 vols. Paris, 1836.

Hirst, Desirée. *Hidden Riches: Traditional Symbolism from the Renaissance to Blake*. London: Eyre, 1964.

Hitchcock, Ethan Allen. *Fifty Years in Camp and Field*. Ed. W. A. Croffut. New York: Knickerbocker, 1909.

————. *Remarks Upon Alchemy and the Alchemists Indicating a Method of Discovering the True Nature of Hermetic Philosophy; and Showing that the Search After the Philosopher's Stone Had Not For Its Object the Discovery of An Agent for the Transmutation of Metals. Being Also an Attempt to Rescure from Undeserved*

Opprobrium the Reputation of a Class of Extraordinary Thinkers in Past Ages. Boston: Crosby, Nichols, 1857.

————. *Swedenborg: A Hermetic Philosopher*. New York: Appleton, 1858.

Hooker, Edward. *The Triple Crown of Glory*. London, 1697.

Hughes, E. M. "The Theology of William Law and the Influence of Boehme." Ph.D. diss., London, 1952.

Hurth, Elisabeth. "The Uses of a Mystic Prophet: Emerson and Boehme." *Philological Quarterly* 70, no. 2 (spring 1991): 219–36.

Hutchinson, George. *The Ecstatic Whitman: Literary Shamanism and the Crisis of the Union*. Columbus: Ohio State University Press, 1986.

Hutin, Serge. *Les Disciples anglais de Jacob Boehme aux XVIIe et XVIIIe siécles*. Paris: Editions Denoël, 1960.

James, Henry. *The Secret of Swedenborg: Being an Elucidation of His Doctrine of the Divine Natural Humanity*. Boston: Fields, 1869.

Johnson, Melvin. *The Beginnings of Freemasonry in America*. New York: Doran, 1924.

Jonas, Hans. *The Gnostic Religion*. Boston: Beacon, 1963.

Kelpius, Johannes. *The Diarium of Magister Johannes Kelpius*. Ed. J. Sachse. Lancaster: Pennsylvania German Society, 1917.

————. *A Short, Easy, and Comprehensive Method of Prayer*. Trans. Christopher Witt. Philadelphia, 1761.

Kerr, Howard. *Mediums, and Spirit-Rappers, and Roaring Radicals: Spiritualism in American Literature, 1850–1900*. Urbana: University of Illinois Press, 1972.

Kerr, Howard, and Charles Crow, eds. *The Occult in America: New Historical Perspectives*. Urbana: University of Illinois Press, 1963.

Kittredge, George. *The Old Farmer and his Almanack*. Cambridge: Harvard University Press, 1920.

Koyré, Alexandre. *Mystiques, spirituels, alchimistes du xvi siècle allemand*. Paris: Gallimard, 1971.

————. *La Philosophie de Jacob Boehme*. Paris: J. Vrin, 1929.

Kren, Claudia. *Alchemy in Europe: A Guide to Research*. New York: Garland, 1990.

Krüger, Gustav. *Die Rosenkreuzer*. Berlin, 1932.

Kuebrich, David. *Minor Prophecy: Walt Whitman's New American Religion*. Chicago: University of Chicago Press, 1989.

LaCarriere, Jacques. *The Gnostics*. New York: Dutton, 1977.

Latham, Jackie. "Emma Martin and Sacred Socialism: The Correspondence of James Pierrepont Greaves." *History Workshop Journal* 38 (fall 1994): 215–17.

Law, William. *The Spirit of Love. Being an Appendix to the Spirit of Prayer*. London: W. Innys and J. Richardson, 1752.

————. *The Way to Divine Knowledge: being several dialogues preparatory to a new edition of the works of J. Böhme, and the right use of them*. London, 1752.

Lawson, Deodat. *Christ's Fidelity the Only Shield against Satan's Malignity*. Boston, 1692.

Leade, Jane. *Enochian Walks with God*. London: Edwards, 1694.

————. *A Fountain of Gardens: or, A Spiritual Diary of the Wonderful Experiences of a Christian Soul, under the Conduct of the Heavenly Wisdom*. 3 vols. London, 1696–1700.

————. *The Laws of Paradise*. London, 1695.

————. *The Revelation of Revelations*. London, 1683.

Lease, Benjamin. *Emily Dickinson's Readings of Men and Books*. New York: St. Martin's, 1990.

Leeds, Daniel. *The Great Mistery of Fox-Craft Discovered.* Philadelphia, 1705.

———. *News of a Trumpet Sounding in the Wilderness.* New York, 1697.

———. *The Rebuker Rebuked.* Philadelphia, 1703.

———. *The Temple of Wisdom for the Little World; in Two Parts.* Philadelphia: Bradford, 1688.

———. *A Trumpet Sounded Out of the Wilderness of America.* Philadelphia, 1699.

Lehman, Christian. Germantown and Roxborough Papers, 1742–99, MS 61–1498, D-60, HSP No. 362, in the Historical Society of Pennsylvania collection.

Levin, Harry. *The Power of Blackness: Hawthorne, Poe, Melville.* Athens: Ohio University Press, 1958.

Levine, Stuart. *Edgar Poe: Seer and Craftsman.* Deland, Fla.: Everett, 1972.

Lipson, Dorothy Ann. *Freemasonry in Federalist Connecticut, 1789–1835.* Princeton: Princeton University Press, 1977.

Ljunquist, Kent. "Prospects for the Study of Edgar Allan Poe." *Resources for American Literary Study* 21 (1995) 2:173–88.

Luedtke, Luther. *Nathaniel Hawthorne and the Romance of the Orient.* Bloomington: Indiana University Press, 1989.

McIntosh, Christopher. *The Rose Cross and the Age of Reason.* Leiden: Brill, 1992.

Marini, Stephen. *Radical Sects of Revolutionary New England.* Cambridge: Harvard University Press, 1982.

Mather, Cotton. *The Boston Ephemeris, an Almanack for the Year of the Christian Aera 1683.* Boston, 1683.

———. *Christianus per Ignum.* 1702.

Matthiessen, F. O. *American Renaissance: Art and Expression in the Age of Emerson and Whitman.* London: Oxford University Press, 1941.

Maxse, R. "The Reception of Jacob Boehme in England in the 17th and 18th Centuries." B.Litt. thesis, Brasenose College, Oxford, 1934.

Martin, Luther. "Hawthorne's Scarlet Letter: A is for Alchemy?" *American Transcendental Quarterly* 58 (1985): 31–42.

Mee, Jon. *Dangerous Enthusiasm: William Blake and the Culture of Radicalism in the 1790s.* Oxford: Clarendon, 1992.

Meikle, Jeffrey. "Hawthorne's Alembic: Alchemical Images in *The House of the Seven Gables.*" *ESQ* 26 (1980): 173–83.

Melville, Herman. "The Apple-Tree Table." *Putnam's* 7 (May 1856): 465–75.

———. *Clarel: A Poem and a Pilgrimage in The Holy Land.* In vol. 12, *The Writings of Herman Melville.* Evanston, Ill.: Northwestern University Press, 1991.

———. *The Collected Poems of Herman Melville.* Chicago: Packard, 1948.

———. *The Complete Stories.* Ed. J. Leyda. New York: 1949.

———. *The Melville Log.* Ed. J. Leyda. New York: Gordian, 1969.

———. *The Writings of Herman Melville.* 14 vols. Evanston, Ill.: Northwestern University Press, 1980–.

Merkur, Dan. *Gnosis: An Esoteric Tradition of Mystical Visions and Unions.* Albany: State University of New York Press, 1993.

Mitchell, Jonathan. "Continuation of Sermons upon the Body of Divinity," 1655–58, 8 February 1656, in Massachusetts Historical Society collection.

Moore, R. Laurence. *In Search of White Crows: Spiritualism, Parapsychology, and American Culture.* New York: Oxford University Press, 1977.

Morison, Samuel, ed. *Charles Morton's Compendium Physicae.* Colonial Society of Massachusetts Publications, no. 33. Boston, 1940.

Muses, Charles. "Dionysius Andreas Freher: An Inquiry into theWork of a Fundamental Contributor to the Philosophic Tradition of Jacob Boehme." Ph.D. diss., Columbia University, 1951.

———. *Illumination on Jakob Boehme: The Work of Dionysus Andreas Freher*. New York: King's Crown, 1951.

Myerson, Joel. "'In the Transcendental Emporium': Bronson Alcott's 'Orphic Sayings' in the *Dial*." *English Language Notes* 10 (September 1972): 31–38.

———. "William Harry Harland's 'Bronson Alcott's English Friends.'" *Resources for American Literary Study* 7 (spring 1978): 24–60.

Nag Hammadi Library. Ed. J. Robinson. New York: 1977.

Nathanson, Tenney. *Whitman's Presence: Body, Voice, and Writing in* Leaves of Grass. New York: New York University Press, 1992.

Newman, William R. *Gehennical Fire: The Lives of George Starkey, an American Alchemist in the Scientific Revolution*. Cambridge: Harvard University Press, 1994.

Nicolescu, Basarab. *Science, Meaning, and Evolution: The Cosmology of Jacob Boehme*. Trans. Rob Baker. New York: Parabola, 1991. Translated from *La Science, Le Sens, Et l'Evolution* (Paris: Editions du Felin, 1988).

Oliphant, Laurence. *Sympneumata*. Edinburgh, 1885.

Oreovicz, Cheryl. "Edward Taylor and the Alchemy of Grace." *Seventeenth-Century News* 34 (1976): 33–36.

———. "Investigating 'The America of Nature': Alchemy in Early American Poetry." In *Puritan Poets and Poetics*, ed. Peter White. University Park: Pennsylvania State University Press, 1985.

Owen, Alex. *The Darkened Room: Women, Power, and Spiritualism in Late Victorian England*. Philadelphia: University of Pennsylvania Press, 1990.

Paracelsus. *Archidoxis*. London, 1663.

Parsons, Melinda, and William Ramsey. "The Scarlet Letter and an Herbal Tradition." *ESQ* 29 (1983): 197–207.

Peabody, A. "Modern Necromancy." *North American Review* 80 (April 1855): 523–24.

Peuckert, Will-Erich. *Gabalia: Ein Versuch zur Geschichte dermagia naturalis im 16. bis 18. Jahrhundert*. Berlin: Erich Schmidt, 1967.

———. *Das Leben Jacob Böhmes*. Jena: Eugen Diederichs, 1924.

———. *Pansophie*. Berlin: Erich Schmidt, 1956.

———. *Die Rosenkreutzer. Zur Geschichte einer Reformation*. Jena, 1928.

Pfefferkorn, Kristin. *Novalis: A Romantic's Theory of Language and Poetry*. New Haven: Yale University Press, 1988.

Philalethes, Eirenaeus. *The Marrow of Alchemy*. 2 vols. London: E. Brewster, 1654/55.

———. *Ripley's Epistle*. London: G. Dawson, 1655.

———. *Ripley Reviv'd*. London: W. Cooper, 1678.

———. *Secrets Reveal'd*. London, 1669.

Pitzer, D., ed. *America's Communal Utopias*. Chapel Hill: University of North Carolina Press, 1997.

Pluquet, Marc. *La Sophiale*. Paris: O.T.O., 1981.

Pochmann, Henry. *German Culture in America*. Madison: University of Wisconsin Press, 1957.

Poe, Edgar Allan. *Complete Poems of Edgar Allan Poe*. New York: Heritage, 1943.

———. *The Complete Tales and Poems of Edgar Allan Poe*. New York: Random House, 1938.

————. *The Complete Works of Edgar Allan Poe*. 17 vols. Ed. J. Harrison. New York: Society of English and French Literature, 1902.

————. *Essays and Reviews*. New York: Library of America, 1984.

Pordage, John. *Sophia: The Graceful Eternal Virgin of Holy Wisdom, or Wonderful Spiritual Discoveries and Revelations That the Precious Wisdom Has Given to a Holy Soul*. London, ca. 1675.

————. *Theologia Mystica, or the Mystic Divinitie of the Aeternal Invisibles, viz. the Archetypous Globe*. London, 1683.

————. *A Treatise of Eternal Nature with Her Seven Eternal Forms*. London, 1681.

Price, Kenneth M. *Whitman and Tradition: The Poet in His Century*. New Haven: Yale University Press, 1990.

Quinn, Michael. *Early Mormonism and the Magic World View*. Salt Lake City: Signature Books, 1987.

Quinn, Patrick. *The French Face of Edgar Poe*. Carbondale: Southern Illinois University Press, 1957.

Raine, Kathleen. *Blake and Tradition*. Princeton: Princeton University Press, 1963.

Rajasekharaiah, T. R. *The Roots of Whitman's Grass*. Rutherford, N.J.: Fairleigh Dickinson University Press, 1970.

Randolph, Paschal Beverly. *The Ansairetic Mystery, A New Revelation Concerning Sex!* Toledo: Liberal, [1873].

————. *Eulis! The History of Love*. Toledo: Randolph, 1874.

————. *Magia sexualis: Sublimation de l'énergie sexuelle*. Trans. Maria de Naglowska. 1931; repr., St-Jean-de-Braye, France: Dangles, 1991.

————. *Sexual Magic*. Trans. R. North. New York: Magical Childe, 1988.

Ripley, George. *Compound of Alchymy*. London, 1591.

Roback, C. W. *The Mysteries of Astrology and the Wonders of magic, including A History of the Rise and Progress of Astrology and the Various Branches of Necromancy*. Boston, 1854.

Rudolph, Kurt. *Gnosis: The Nature and History of Gnosticism*. Trans. Robert McLachlan Wilson. San Francisco: Harper and Row, 1983.

Sachithanandan, V. *Whitman and Bharati: A Comparative Study*. Madras: Macmillan, 1978.

Sachs, Viola. *The Game of Creation: The Primeval Unlettered Language of Moby Dick, or, The Whale*. Paris: Editions de la Maison des Sciences de l'homme, 1982.

————. *The Myth of America*. The Hague: Mouton, 1973.

Sachse, Julius. *The German Pietists of Provincial Pennsylvania*. Philadelphia: Sachse, 1895.

————. *The German Sectarians of Pennsylvania*. Philadelphia, 1900.

————, trans. *The Diarium of Magister Johannes Kelpius*. In *The Pennsylvania-German Society, Proceedings and Addresses*, vol. 25. Lancaster, Pa., 1917.

St. Armand, Barton Levi. "Dragon and the Uroboros: Themes of Metamorphosis in 'Arthur Gordon Pym.'" *American Transcendental Quarterly* 37 (1978): 57–71.

————. "Emily Dickinson and the Occult: The Rosicrucian Connection." *Prairie Schooner* 51 (1977 / 78): 345–57.

————. "Experienced Emblems: A Study of the Poetry of Emily Dickinson." *Prospects: An Annual Journal of American Cultural Studies* 6 (1981): 187–280.

————. "Usher Unveiled: Poe and the Metaphysic of Gnosticism." *Poe Studies* 5 (1972): 1–8.

————. "Veiled Ladies: Dickinson, Bettine, and Transcendental Mediumship." *Studies in the American Renaissance* (1987): 1–51.

Saint-Martin, Louis Claude de. *Des Erreurs et de la Verité*. Edinburgh, 1775.

————. *Les Ministère de l'Homme Esprit*. Paris, 1802.

————. *Man: His True Nature and Ministry*. Trans. E. B. Penny. London, 1864.

————. *Œuvres Majeures*. Ed. R. Amadou. Hildesheim: Olms, 1973.

————. *Tableau Naturel*. Edinburgh, 1782.

————. *Theosophic Correspondence*. Trans. E. B. Penny. 1863. Theosophical Publ. House.

Schneider, Herbert. *A Prophet and a Pilgrim, Being the Incredible History of Thomas Lake Harris and Laurence Oliphant; their Sexual Mysticisms and Utopian Communities*. New York: Columbia University Press, 1942.

Schuchard, Marsha Keith. "Freemasonry, Secret Societies, and the Continuity of the Occult Traditions in English Literature." Ph.D. diss., University of Texas, Austin, 1975.

————. "Why Mrs. Blake Cried: Blake, Swedenborg, and the Sexual Basis of Spiritual Vision." *Esoterica: The Journal of Esoteric Studies* [http://www.esoteric.msu.edu] 2 (2000): 45–93.

Sherrard, Philip. *Human Image: World Image, The Death and Resurrection of Sacred Cosmology*. London: Golgonooza Press, 1992.

Simon, M., and T. Parsons, eds. *Transcendentalism and Its Legacy*. Ann Arbor: University of Michigan Press, 1966.

Smith, Hannah Whitall. *Religious Fanaticism: Extracts from the Papers of Hannah Whitall Smith*. Ed. R. Strachey. London: Faber, 1928.

Snodgrass, Adrian. "Stellar and Temporal Symbolism in Traditional Architecture." Ph.D. diss., University of Sydney, Australia, 1985.

Sorensen, Peter. "William Morgan, Freemasonry, and 'The Cask of Amontillado.'" *Poe Studies* 22 (1989): 45–47.

Starkey, George. *Liquor Alcahest*. London: W. Cademan, 1675.

————. *Natures Explication*. London: Alsop, 1657.

————. *Pyrotechny Asserted and Illustrated*. London, 1658.

Stephen, L., and S. Lee, eds. *Dictionary of National Biography*. London: Smith, 1890.

Stein, William Bysshe. *Hawthorne's Faust: A Study of the Devil Archetype*. Gainesville: University of Florida Press, 1953.

Steele, Jeffrey. "Margaret Fuller's Rhetoric of Transformation." In *Woman in the Nineteenth Century*, ed. L. Reynolds. New York: Norton, 1998.

Joseph Stellatus. *Pegasus Firmamenti sive Introductio brevis in veterum sapientum [Pegasus of the Firmament, or a Brief Introduction to the Ancient Wisdom, Once Taught in the Magia of the Egyptians and Persians and Now Lightly Called the Pansophia of the Venerable Society of the Rosy Cross*. 1618.

Stewart, Gordon, ed. *The Great Awakening in Nova Scotia*. Toronto: Champlain Society, 1982.

Stowell, Marion. *Early American Almanacs: The Colonial Weekday Bible*. New York: B. Franklin, 1976.

Strachy, Ray, ed. *Religious Fanaticism: Extracts from the Papers of Hannah Whitall Smith*. London: Faber, 1928.

Swedenborg, Emanuel. *The Economy of the Animal Kingdom*. 2 vols. 1740–41. Repr., Boston, 1843–44.

————. *The Apocalypse Revealed*. Boston, 1836.

————. *Philosophical and Minerological Works*. 3 vols. 1740–41.

————. *The True Christian Religion*. Boston, 1843.

Tafel, R., ed. *Documents Concerning Swedenborg*. London: Swedenborg Society, 1875.

Taylor, Jacob. *Almanack and Ephemeris of the Motions of the Sun and Moon*. Philadelphia: Bradford, 1746.

Taylor, William. *The Swedenborgianism of W. D. Howells*. Urbana: [n.p.], 1969.

Thompson, E. P. *Witness against the Beast: William Blake and the Moral Law*. New York: New Press, 1993.

Thompson, Lawrance. *Melville's Quarrel with God*. Princeton: Princeton University Press, 1952.

Thoreau, Henry David. *Familiar Letters*. Ed. F. Sanborn. Boston: Houghton, 1894.

————. *Letters to Various Persons*. Boston, 1865.

Thumb, Thomas. *The Monster of Monsters*. Boston, 1754.

Thune, Nils. *The Behmenists and the Philadelphians: A Contribution to the Study of English Mysticism in the 17th and 18th Centuries*. Uppsala: Almquist and Wiksells, 1948.

Tincom, H., and M. Tincom. *Historic Germantown: A Survey of the German Township*. Philadelphia: American Philosophical Society, 1955.

Toksvig, Signe. *Emanuel Swedenborg: Scientist and Mystic*. New Haven: Yale University Press, 1948.

Tomberg, Valentin. *Meditations on The Tarot*. Rockport, Mass.: Element, 1991.

Tompson, Benjamin. *A Funeral Tribute to the Honourable Dust of the Most Charitable Christian, Unbiased Politican, and unimitable Pyrotechnist John Winthrope esq.* Boston, 1676.

Trevor-Roper, Hugh. *Religion, the Reformation, and Social Change*. London: Macmillan, 1967.

Trinick, John. *The Fire-Tried Stone: An Enquiry into the Development of a Symbol*. London: Watkins, 1967.

Vargish, Thomas. "Gnostic Mythos in Moby Dick." *PMLA* (June 1966): 274–76.

Versluis, Arthur. *American Transcendentalism and Asian Religions*. New York: Oxford University Press, 1993.

————. "Bronson Alcott and Jacob Böhme." *Studies in the American Renaissance* 16 (1993): 153–59.

————. "Christian Theosophy and Ancient Gnosticism." *Studies in Spirituality* 7 (1997): 228–41.

————. *Gnosis and Literature*. St. Paul: Grail, 1996.

————. *The Hermetic Book of Nature*. St. Paul: Grail, 1997.

————. *The Mysteries of Love: Eros and Spirituality*. St. Paul: Grail, 1996.

————. *Shakespeare the Magus*. St. Paul: Grail, 2001.

————. *Theosophia: Hidden Dimensions of Christianity*. Hudson, N.Y.: Lindisfarne, 1994.

————. *Western Esotericism, Literature, and Consciousness*. Forthcoming.

————. ed. *Wisdom's Book: The Sophia Anthology*. St. Paul: Paragon House, 2000.

————. *Wisdom's Children: A Christian Esoteric Tradition*. Albany: State University of New York Press, 1999.

————, trans. *Novalis, Pollen and Fragments: Selected Poetry and Prose of Novalis*. Grand Rapids, Mich.: Phanes, 1989.

Vogel, Stanley. *German Literary Influences on the American Transcendentalists*. New Haven: Yale University Press, 1955.

Walpern, Eberhart. *Glucks-Rad oder Würfel-Buch: durch welches man nach astrologisher Art. . . . abeheilt sind, eine Antwort finden kann. . . .* Reading, Pa.: Heinrich Sage, 1820.

Wardop, Daneen. *Emily Dickinson's Gothic.* Iowa City: University of Iowa Press, 1996.

Webb, James. *The Occult Establishment.* LaSalle, Ill.: Open Court, 1976.

———. *The Occult Underground.* LaSalle, Ill.: Open Court, 1974.

Weeks, Andrew. *Boehme: An Intellectual Biography of the Seventeenth-Century Philosopher and Mystic.* Albany: State University of New York Press, 1991.

———. *Paracelsus: Speculative Theory and the Crisis of the Early Reformation.* Albany: State University of New York Press, 1997.

Weisbuch, Robert. *Emily Dickinson's Poetry.* Chicago: University of Chicago Press, 1975.

Wesley, John. *The Letters of Rev. John Wesley.* Ed. John Telford. London: Epworth, 1931.

Whitman, Walt. *The Collected Writings of Walt Whitman.* Ed. H. Blodgett and S. Bradley. New York: New York University Press, 1965.

———. *The Complete Poetry and Prose of Walt Whitman.* 2 vols. Ed. Malcolm Cowley. New York: Pellegrini, 1948.

———. "Is Mesmerism True?" *New York Sunday Times,* 14 August 1842.

———. *The Uncollected Poetry and Prose of Walt Whitman.* 2 vols. Ed. Emory Holloway (New York: P. Smith, 1932).

Wilkinson, Ronald Sterne. "The Alchemical Library of John Winthrop, Jr., 1606–1676." *Ambix* 11.1 (February 1963): 33–51.

———."The Hartlib Papers and Seventeenth-Century Chemistry." *Ambix* 15.1 (February 1968): 54–69; and 17.2 (July 1970): 85–110.

———. "New England's Last Alchemists." *Ambix* 10.3 (October 1962): 129.

———. "The Problem of the Identity of Eirenaeus Philalethes." *Ambix* 13.1 (February 1964): 24–43.

Willys, Samuel. Samuel Willys Collection, Records of Trials for Witchcraft in Connecticut, 7 August 1668, no. 7, Connecticut State Library, Hartford.

Winters, Ivor. *In Defense of Reason.* Denver: Swallow, 1943.

Wright, Nathalia. *Melville's Use of the Bible.* Durham, N.C.: Duke University Press, 1949.

Yates, Frances. *The Rosicrucian Enlightenment.* London: Routledge, 1972.

Index

Herbert, George, 128

Hermes, 10, 121, 136, 138, 173, 190

Hermetic Museum, 11, 137

Hermeticism, 4, 6, 53, 126, 135, 137, 145, 189–190

Heydon, John, 25–28

Higginson, Thomas Wentworth, 156, 172, 180

Hilaire, Auguste, Theodore, 127

Hindmarsh, Robert, 19

Hinduism, 103, 106, 128, 145, 157

Hitchcock, Ethan Allen, 61, 64–71, 82, 186

Hoar, Dorcas, 28

Hurth, Elizabeth, 139

Iamblichus, 145

I Ching, 25

Irving, Washington, 56

James, Henry, Sr., 17, 82

Jefferson, Thomas, 46, 53

Johnson, Samuel, 3, 190

Johnson, Thomas, 119

Jonas, Hans, 96–97

Jones, Sir William, 121

Jung, Carl, 160

Kabbala, 4, 16, 20, 53

Keats, John, 172

Kelly, Edward, 55

Kelpius, Johannes, 39, 45

Kerner, Justinius, 148

Kerr, Howard, 55

Khunrath, Heinrich, 121

Kuebrich, David, 158

Labadie, Jean de, 40

Lane, Charles, 147

Law, William, 46, 118, 121

Leade, Jane, 13, 16, 38, 44, 121, 189

Leach, Benjamin, 181

Lease, Benjamin, 171

Lee, Francis, 118, 189

Lee, Robert E., 71

Leeds, Daniel, 22–23, 37

Lehman, Christian, 25–28

Lewis, C. S., 11

Lincoln, Abraham, 61, 64

Ljungquist, Kent, 72

Longfellow, Samuel, 56

Luedtke, Luther, 81, 189

Lull, Ramon, 10, 66, 138

Luther, Martin, 66

magic, 4, 49

Maier, Michael, 11, 15, 30

Masonry (*see* Freemasonry)

Mather, Cotton, 28, 32, 36

Matthiessen, F. O., 6

Melville, Herman, 91–104, 187

Emerson and, 94; Gnosticism and, 95–104; Rosicrucianism and, 92; spiritualism and, 91–92

Mesmer, Friedrich, 57–58

Mesmerism, 55, 57, 65, 74–75, 87–89, 165

Milton, John, 46

Mirandola, Pico della, 6, 53

Mitchell, Jonathan, 28

Molinos, Miguel, 121

Morienus, 10

Morgan, William, 51, 78

Morton, Charles, 28, 35

Müller, Peter, 44

Mutus Liber, 11

Myerson, Joel, 105

Naglowska, Maria de, 164

necromancy, 55

Neoplatonism, 6, 53, 66, 74, 94

Nicolescu, Basarab, 140–141

Novalis (Friedrich von Hardenberg), 5, 121, 129–134, 149, 188

Noyes, John Humphrey, 61–62

Noyes, Nicholas, 36, 168

Oetinger, Friedrich Christoph, 19

orgies, 163

Oliphant, Laurence, 63

Ordo Templi Orientis, 164

Orpheus, 142

Orphism, 132

Pansophy, 15

Paracelsus, 10, 15, 31, 33, 121–122, 142, 165

Pasqually, Martinez de, 56, 181

Penny, Edward Burton, 118

Pernety, Antoine-Joseph, 56

Pfefferkorn, Kristin, 129

Philadelphian Society, 16, 38, 44, 189

Philalethes, Eirenaeus, 11, 32, 35

Pitt, William, 51

Plato, 103, 105, 113, 126, 135, 142, 164, 189

Platonism, 119

Plockhoy, Peter Cornelius, 40

Plotinus, 103, 120, 138, 142, 145

Plutarch, 142

Poe, Edgar Allan, 61, 72–80

Alcott, Emerson and, 78; Ethan Allen
Hitchcock and, 73; Hawthorne and, 76,
81; Mesmerism and, 74; Poe scholarship
and, 72; Swedenborg and, 76–77

Poiret, Pierre, 16

Polk, James, 54

Pordage, John, 13, 24, 38, 46, 118, 121, 139, 187

Pratt, F. Alcott, 121

Proclus, 105, 113, 189

Puritanism, 30, 81

Pythagoras, 126, 138, 142

Quakers, 22, 158

Quinn, Michael, 4

Rabelais, 105

Raine, Kathleen, 188

Rajasekharaiah, T. R., 157

Ramsey, Andrew Michael, 16

Randolph, Paschal Beverly, 61, 164

Rapp, Johann George, 46–47

Reynolds, David, 6

Ripley, George, 11, 33, 35, 82

Roback, C. W., 54

Rosicrucianism, 6, 14, 25–26, 30–31, 35, 39,
47–49, 91, 149, 183

Ruskin, John, 172

Sachse, Julius, 41, 42

St. Armand, Barton Levi, 171

Saint-Martin, Louis Claude de, 119, 124, 153

Satchithanandan, V., 157

Schopenhauer, Arthur, 103

Schuchard, Marsha Keith, 71, 167

secret or semi-secret societies, 14–17

sexual magic, 61

sexuality, 18, 59, 61, 161–165

Shakespeare, William, 6, 11, 64, 151

Shelley, Percy Bysshe, 5, 103

Sluyter, Petrus, 40

Smith, Hannah Whitall, 60

Sophia, 160

spiritualism, 55–57, 63, 87–88, 181–182

Starkey, George, 31, 32, 34–35, 121–122, 185

Steele, Jeffrey, 156

Stein, William Bysshe, 81

Stiles, Ezra, 36

Swedenborg, Emanuel, 17–20, 58, 65, 68–69,
76–77, 82, 141–142, 167

Tauler, Johannes, 12, 116, 120

Taylor, Edward, 36–7, 121

Taylor, Thomas, 66, 145

Taylor, Zachary, 64

Thompson, Lawrance, 96

Thoreau, Henry David, 68, 91, 125, 157

Tomberg, Valentin, 60

Tompson, Benjamin, 32

transdisciplinarity, 5

Upanishads, 3, 190

Valentinianism, 99

Valentinus, Basilius, 11

Vargish, Thomas, 95

Vaughan, Henry and Thomas, 11

Vedanta, 157, 159

Vedas, 3, 187

Versluis, Arthur, 3, 4, 12, 37, 68, 79–80, 160,
164, 172

Vogel, Stanley, 129

Voltaire, 50

Walpern, Eberhart, 54

Walton, Christopher, 118

Warren, Joseph, 51

Washington, George, 44, 50–51, 53

Weisbuch, Robert, 171

Weishaupt, Adam, 48

Wesley, John, 46

West India, 27

West Point, 73

Whitman, Walt, 157–170

Mesmerism and, 165; sexuality and,
161–165; Swedenborg and, 167–169

Willermoz, Jean-Baptiste, 56, 181

Winters, Ivor, 124

Winthrop, John, Jr., 31–33

witchcraft, 28–29, 85

Witt, Christopher, 27

Wohlfarth, Michael, 41, 42, 45

Yates, Frances, 14

Young, Edward, 46

Zimmermann, Johann Jacob, 39

Zinzendorf, Nicholas, 42

Zosimos of Panopolis, 10